THE CAMBRIDGE COMPANION TO THE TWENTIETH-CENTURY AMERICAN NOVEL AND POLITICS

Surveying the relationship between American politics and the twentieth-century novel, this volume analyzes how political movements, ideas, and events shaped the American novel. It also shows how those political phenomena were shaped in turn by long-form prose fiction. The book is made up of three major parts. Part I considers philosophical ideologies and broad political movements that were both politically and literarily significant in the United States in the twentieth century, including progressive liberalism, conservatism, socialism and communism, feminism, and Black liberation movements. Part II analyzes the evolving political valences of key popular genres and literary forms in the twentieth-century American novel, focusing on crime fiction, science fiction, postmodern metafiction, and immigrant fiction. Part III examines ten diverse politically minded novels that serve as exemplary case studies across the century. Combining detailed literary analysis with innovative political theory, this Companion provides a groundbreaking study of the politics of twentieth-century American fiction.

BRYAN M. SANTIN is Associate Professor of English at Concordia University Irvine. He is the author of *Postwar American Fiction and the Rise of Modern Conservatism: A Literary History, 1945–2008* (Cambridge University Press, 2021).

T0381630

CAMBRIDGE
UNIVERSITY PRESS

Shaftesbury Road, Cambridge CB2 8EA, United Kingdom

One Liberty Plaza, 20th Floor, New York, NY 10006, USA

477 Williamstown Road, Port Melbourne, VIC 3207, Australia

314–321, 3rd Floor, Plot 3, Splendor Forum, Jasola District Centre, New Delhi – 110025, India

103 Penang Road, #05-06/07, Visioncrest Commercial, Singapore 238467

Cambridge University Press is part of Cambridge University Press & Assessment,
a department of the University of Cambridge.

We share the University's mission to contribute to society through the pursuit of
education, learning and research at the highest international levels of excellence.

www.cambridge.org
Information on this title: www.cambridge.org/9781316516485

DOI: 10.1017/9781009030274

© Cambridge University Press & Assessment 2023

This publication is in copyright. Subject to statutory exception and to the provisions
of relevant collective licensing agreements, no reproduction of any part may take
place without the written permission of Cambridge University Press & Assessment.

First published 2023

A catalogue record for this publication is available from the British Library.

Library of Congress Cataloging-in-Publication Data
NAMES: Santin, Bryan Michael, editor.
TITLE: The Cambridge companion to the twentieth-century American novel and politics /
edited by Bryan Santin.
DESCRIPTION: Cambridge ; New York, NY : Cambridge University Press, 2023. |
Includes bibliographical references.
IDENTIFIERS: LCCN 2023013979 (print) | LCCN 2023013980 (ebook) | ISBN 9781316516485
(hardback) | ISBN 9781009015660 (paperback) | ISBN 9781009030274 (epub)
SUBJECTS: LCSH: American fiction–20th century–History and criticism. | Political fiction,
American–History and criticism. | American literature–Political aspects.
CLASSIFICATION: LCC PS374.P62 C36 2023 (print) | LCC PS374.P62 (ebook) |
DDC 813/.5093581–dc23/eng/20230503
LC record available at https://lccn.loc.gov/2023013979
LC ebook record available at https://lccn.loc.gov/2023013980

ISBN 978-1-316-51648-5 Hardback
ISBN 978-1-009-01566-0 Paperback

Cambridge University Press & Assessment has no responsibility for the persistence
or accuracy of URLs for external or third-party internet websites referred to in this
publication and does not guarantee that any content on such websites is, or will
remain, accurate or appropriate.

THE CAMBRIDGE COMPANION TO THE TWENTIETH-CENTURY AMERICAN NOVEL AND POLITICS

EDITED BY

BRYAN M. SANTIN

Concordia University Irvine

CAMBRIDGE
UNIVERSITY PRESS

For my son, Fitz

Contents

Chronology

1925   Theodore Dreiser, *An American Tragedy*
           F. Scott Fitzgerald, *The Great Gatsby*
           Anzia Yezierska, *Bread Givers*

1927   Upton Sinclair, *Oil!*

1928   Nella Larsen, *Quicksand*
           Claude McKay, *Home to Harlem*

1929   W. R. Burnett, *Little Caesar*
           Dashiell Hammett, *Red Harvest*
           Nella Larsen, *Passing*

1930   John Dos Passos, *The 42nd Parallel* (sequels *Nineteen Nineteen* [1932] and *The Big Money* [1936])
           Mike Gold, *Jews Without Money*
           Dashiell Hammett, *The Maltese Falcon*

1931   George Schuyler, *Black No More*

1932   James T. Farrell, *Young Lonigan* (sequels *The Young Manhood of Studs Lonigan* [1934] and *Judgment Day* [1935])
           Grace Lumpkin, *To Make My Bread*

1934   Henry Miller, *Tropic of Cancer*
           Nathanael West, *A Cool Million: The Dismantling of Lemuel Pitkin*

1935   Sinclair Lewis, *It Can't Happen Here*

1936   William Faulkner, *Absalom, Absalom!*
           Margaret Mitchell, *Gone with the Wind*
           John Steinbeck, *In Dubious Battle*

1937   Zora Neale Hurston, *Their Eyes Were Watching God*

1938   Dalton Trumbo, *Johnny Got His Gun*

1939   John Steinbeck, *The Grapes of Wrath*

1940   Ernest Hemingway, *For Whom the Bell Tolls*
           Richard Wright, *Native Son*

1943   Ayn Rand, *The Fountainhead*

1945   Chester Himes, *If He Hollers Let Him Go*

1946   Robert Penn Warren, *All the King's Men*

1947   Dorothy B. Hughes, *In a Lonely Place*
           Lionel Trilling, *The Middle of the Journey*

1948   Nelson Algren, *The Man with the Golden Arm*
           Norman Mailer, *The Naked and the Dead*

1949   Mary McCarthy, *The Oasis*

1951   Norman Mailer, *Barbary Shore*

1952   Ralph Ellison, *Invisible Man*

1985   Margaret Atwood (Canadian), *The Handmaid's Tale*
       Orson Scott Card, *Ender's Game*
       Cormac McCarthy, *Blood Meridian*
       Larry McMurtry, *Lonesome Dove*
1987   Toni Morrison, *Beloved*
       William T. Vollmann, *You Bright and
       Risen Angels*
       Tom Wolfe, *The Bonfire of the Vanities*
1988   Kathy Acker, *Empire of the Senseless*
       Don DeLillo, *Libra*
1990   James Ellroy, *L.A. Confidential*
       Walter Mosely, *Devil in a Blue Dress*
       Thomas Pynchon, *Vineland*
1991   Don DeLillo, *Mao II*
       Bret Easton Ellis, *American Psycho*
       Gish Jen, *Typical American*
       Norman Mailer, *Harlot's Ghost*
       Leslie Marmon Silko, *Almanac of the Dead*
1992   Dorothy Allison, *Bastard Out of Carolina*
       Cristina García, *Dreaming in Cuban*
       Neal Stephenson, *Snow Crash*
       John Updike, *Memories of the Ford Administration*
1993   Octavia E. Butler, *Parable of the Sower* (sequel *Parable of the
       Talents* [1998])
       Leslie Feinberg, *Stone Butch Blues*
       Lois Lowry, *The Giver*
1994   Julia Alverez, *In the Time of the Butterflies*
       Tim O'Brien, *In the Lake of the Woods*
1995   T. C. Boyle, *The Tortilla Curtain*
       James Ellroy, *American Tabloid*
       Tim LaHaye and Jerry B. Jenkins, *Left Behind*
       Chang-rae Lee, *Native Speaker*
1996   Joan Didion, *The Last Thing He Wanted*
       Gish Jen, *Mona in the Promised Land*
       Joe Klein, *Primary Colors*
       David Foster Wallace, *Infinite Jest*
1997   Don DeLillo, *Underworld*
       Toni Morrison, *Paradise*
       Thomas Pynchon, *Mason & Dixon*
       Philip Roth, *American Pastoral*

Introduction

Bryan M. Santin

For students and scholars of American literature, this volume is a broad resource for clear, concise, and insightful essays on the inextricable relationship between the American novel and politics in the twentieth century. In much of the existing literary scholarship, critics regularly invoke political movements, ideas, and events to illuminate their core arguments. To facilitate and enhance these kinds of critical engagement in the future, *The Cambridge Companion to the Twentieth-Century American Novel and Politics* analyzes political phenomena that have not only shaped the American novel, but have been shaped in turn by long-form prose fiction.

Essentially, this volume seeks to shed more light on a perennial question in American literary studies: What is the relationship between the twentieth-century American novel and politics? The question occurs so frequently not only because of its intrinsic complexity and thematic significance, but also because the very term "politics" is historically contingent, a protean category whose normative valences and assumed linkages to literary texts change over time. This explains why previous scholarship on the relationship between literature and politics must be understood within the sociopolitical context of its production. To take just one prominent example, Walter Rideout published his classic survey *The Radical Novel in the United States, 1900–1954* (1956) at the height of New Criticism, a formalist movement whose acolytes tended to see political literature as an impure element of aesthetic contamination. Consequently, Rideout anticipated this kind of critique by acknowledging that "the formalist critic will surely be unhappy over the very large amount of what he would call 'extrinsic' [i.e., political] material."[1] Although the hegemonic containment culture of the Cold War "did not prevent Rideout from completing and publishing his study," John Whalen-Bridge has observed,

---

[1] Walter Rideout, *The Radical Novel in the United States, 1900–1954* (Cambridge, MA: Harvard University Press, 1956), vii.

he did have to "work against the anti-political prejudice constantly to fashion his book," a defensive position that shaped how Rideout defined politics and framed its role in American fiction.[2] The point of this example is neither to celebrate nor to condemn Rideout's important book. It is merely to point out that no scholarly attempt to investigate the relationship between politics and literature will be neutral. The chapters that follow, then, intend to provoke productive debates about the politics of the twentieth-century American novel that go beyond shallow partisan categorization (e.g., progressive vs. conservative, Democrat vs. Republican, etc.) by contributing to ongoing discussions that we can see anew with two decades' worth of historical distance from the previous century. But while historical distance may usher in fresh perspectives, it does not usher in objective perspectives that hover omnisciently outside of history, granting access to some pure metaphysical definition of "politics."

That raises the obvious, fundamental question: What does this volume mean by the historically contingent term "politics," especially in relation to the twentieth-century American novel. Defined narrowly, "politics" in the twentieth-century United States is an umbrella term for a set of civic discourses and practices, referring primarily to the formal distribution of power through society at various interlocking national, state, and local levels. From this restricted perspective, statements and actions are recognizably "political" if they partake in ritualistic public acts including, but not limited to, voting, protesting, legislating, adjudicating legal disputes, campaigning for elected office, or advocating for social change. While this Cambridge Companion does not ignore the practices associated with that formal definition of politics usually associated with the specialized subgenre of the "political novel," it presupposes a more expansive vision of American political history, theory, and praxis. Defined broadly, "politics" in the present volume signifies dynamic sites of social struggle that were framed, for better or worse, by distinctly American permutations of post-Enlightenment liberalism in the twentieth century. Following Richard Hofstadter and Louis Hartz, this volume assumes that liberalism is the dominant philosophical strand in American political history. As Hofstadter famously claimed, "It has been our fate as a nation not to have ideologies, but to be one."[3] However, acknowledging that Hofstadter and Hartz were prone to oversimplification, this volume also stresses that American

[2] John Whalen-Bridge, *Political Fiction and the American Self* (Urbana: University of Illinois Press, 1998), 25.
[3] Quoted in Michael Kazin, "The Right's Unsung Prophet," *Nation* 248 (February 20, 1989), 242.

liberalism was never monolithic, as various "liberalisms" challenged one another over the course of the so-called American Century, from minimal-state liberalism to active-state liberalism.[4] In this sense, liberalism is fundamental to the politics of the American novel since specific novels can be read as affirmations of, or dissents from, the American liberal tradition. While this volume does not mean to downplay the social justice dimension of, for instance, famous feminist or antiracist activist campaigns by framing them as liberal movements, it does seek to emphasize that the forms of social justice for which American novelists have advocated are inseparable from the rhetoric (i.e., free, autonomous human agents), theoretical assumptions, and material institutions of American liberalism. From this perspective, many kinds of novels – not just classic "political novels" in which traditional political characters or settings dominate the plot – investigate and thematize the changing hopes and anxieties of free independent subjects in the United States. To put it succinctly, "politics" in this Cambridge Companion means the theoretical intersection of power, freedom, and justice – the perennial, difficult, necessary task of linking "might" to "right," or of empowering justice in a nation of putatively free citizens – within evolving historical forms of twentieth-century American liberalism.

From this dual theoretical-historical perspective, the novel form is a unique aperture from which to view political conflict and change because official power relations often intersect with personal power relations in ways that are deep, enduring, and ideologically mystifying. In the words of the political theorist Corey Robin, this "is why our political arguments – not only about the family but also the welfare state, civil rights, and much else – can be so explosive: they touch upon the most personal relations of power. It is also why it has so often fallen to our novelists to explain to us our politics."[5] So, while some of the novels featured here engage directly with unmistakable political topics and themes, many of them conceptualize American democracy as a "way of life," in the words of the political scientists Melvin L. Rogers and Jack Turner, a key insight that they attribute especially to twentieth-century African American novelists such

---

[4] For an excellent critical analysis of Hartz's theory of American liberalism, see Marc Stears, "The Liberal Tradition and the Politics of Exclusion," *Annual Review of Political Science* 10 (2007): 85–101.

[5] Corey Robin, *The Reactionary Mind: Conservatism from Edmund Burke to Sarah Palin* (Oxford: Oxford University Press, 2013 [2011]), 10.

as Ralph Ellison and Toni Morrison.[6] The upshot of this literary interrogation of American politics is a greater awareness that, "while the formal practices of democracy such as voting matter, it is a mistake to treat democracy merely as a [theoretical] form rather than a way of life that extends well beyond the voting booths."[7] If rights within America's constitutional regime are not "self-executing," Rogers and Turner conclude, then their embodied reality "depends on a set of supports – human, economic, and political – to help sustain them."[8] At its best, the novel interrogates precisely these kinds of sociopolitical supports. The novels in this volume, then, have been chosen for their propensity, as Irving Howe puts it in *Politics and the Novel* (1957), to dramatize "the literary problem of what happens to the novel when it is subjected to the pressures of politics and political ideology," particularly over the course of the twentieth century in the United States.[9]

Acknowledging that a wide swath of American novelists, working in a variety of twentieth-century literary genres, astutely dramatize American politics as a way of life, this volume assumes that it would be unhelpful to restrict its focus to the typical "political novel." In his landmark monograph *The Modern American Political Novel* (1966), Joseph Blotner defines the genre in narrow, functionalist terms as a category of novels that "deal primarily with political processes and actions," which causes him to exclude novels that focus "on the conditions out of which political action may eventually arise," such as Upton Sinclair's *The Jungle* (1906) and John Steinbeck's *The Grapes of Wrath* (1939).[10] At the same time, this volume does not assume that all twentieth-century American novels are worthy of the same kind of political analysis and attention. "We may argue that literature is inherently social," in the words of Whalen-Bridge, "but not all literature is equally political."[11] Even if one agrees with Frederic Jameson's well-known claim that, since "everything is 'in the last analysis' political," the genre of political fiction is nothing more than "a symptom and a reinforcement of the reification and privatization of contemporary life," scholars interested in the robust linkages between literature and politics are still confronted with the task of distinguishing novels that are worth their

[6] Melvin L. Rogers and Jack Turner, "Political Theorizing in Black: An Introduction," in *African American Political Thought: A Collected History*, ed. Melvin L. Rogers and Jack Turner (Chicago: University of Chicago Press, 2021), 21.

[7] Ibid., 21.   [8] Ibid.

[9] Irving Howe, *Politics and the Novel* (New York: Horizon Press, 1957), 11.

[10] Joseph Blotner, *The Modern American Political Novel* (Austin: University of Texas Press, 1966), 8.

[11] Whalen-Bridge, 4.

time – i.e., novels that they deem more politically insightful and revealing than other novels.[12] That task of discernment is neither objective nor incontestable. It does not occur from an apolitical, bird's-eye view of the literary field outside of history. A novel that may have seemed political only in a vague, cryptic sense may, in the light of history, appear more politically significant than critics would have ever guessed – e.g., Bret Easton Ellis's *American Psycho* (1991), in which a New York City investment banker who secretly tortures and mutilates women idolizes none other than Donald J. Trump. Any collection that purports to survey the relationship between the American novel and politics must justify its principles of selection within an ever-evolving political landscape, a task toward which this introduction now turns.

For this volume, the first question of methodological selection was historical periodization. Why delimit the volume's timeline to the twentieth century, especially since American novels have investigated both formal politics and political ideologies throughout the country's history? The first reason is practical. To attend adequately to the richness, depth, and sheer breadth of the various political movements, ideas, and events featured in the American novel, it was prudent to restrict the field of analysis to novels published between roughly 1900 and 2000. The second, more fundamental reason is theoretical. Unlike earlier moments in American history when republicanism dominated the public debate, a robust framework of liberalism undergirded twentieth-century American politics, different strands of which are visible in everything from the early-century Progressive movements to the midcentury "rights revolution" to late-century neoliberalism. At the dawn of the century, Progressivism was already sweeping the country, as Hofstadter has noted, in an effort to redefine liberalism and "to restore a type of economic individualism and political democracy that was widely believed to have existed earlier in America and to have been destroyed by the great corporation and the corrupt political machine."[13] But by the end of the century, in Michael Sandel's words, "the civic or formative aspect of politics [had] largely given way to the liberalism that conceives of persons as free and independent selves, unencumbered by moral or civic ties they [had] not chosen."[14] In their various explanatory accounts of how and why twentieth-century

---

[12] Frederic Jameson, *The Political Unconscious: Narrative as a Socially Symbolic Act* (Ithaca, NY: Cornell University Press, 1981), 20.

[13] Richard Hofstadter, *The Age of Reform: From Bryan to FDR* (New York: Knopf, 1955), 5.

[14] Michael Sandel, *Democracy's Discontents: America in Search of a Public Philosophy* (Cambridge, MA: Harvard University Press, 1996), 6.

American liberalism evolved, scholars have often privileged the American novel as a cultural medium not only because it occasionally influenced key ideological shifts, but also because it uniquely indexed those shifts. Thus, while any act of periodization will be arbitrary to some degree, a basic premise of this volume is that the "twentieth century" signifies a timeframe with a recognizable political-literary arc that reveals more than it obscures.

To take one of the most well-known, and still frequently cited, examples of a major intellectual utilizing the American novel to theorize the evolution of twentieth-century liberalism, let us briefly consider Richard Rorty's *Achieving Our Country: Leftist Thought in Twentieth-Century America* (1998). For Rorty, prominent American novels function like apertures through which one can understand the cultural and institutional decline of American liberalism's most progressive strands. Whereas early novels such as Sinclair's *The Jungle*, Steinbeck's *The Grapes of Wrath*, and Theodore Dreiser's *An American Tragedy* (1925) are potent social protest novels characterized by national hope and pride, later novels such as Thomas Pynchon's *Vineland* (1990), Norman Mailer's *Harlot's Ghost* (1991), and Leslie Marmon Silko's *Almanac of the Dead* (1991) are impotent and despairing political novels characterized by "national self-mockery and self-disgust."[15] In this declension narrative, the Vietnam War is the inflection point of the century since its domestic impact produced "a generation of Americans who suspected that our country was unachievable – that that war not only could never be forgiven, but had shown us to be conceived in sin, and irredeemable."[16] If the pre-1960s American novel was stimulated by pragmatic hope, then the post-1960s American novel was haunted by Gothic despair, a symptomatic dichotomy that maps (too) neatly onto an early-century, can-do reformist left and a late-century, hopeless cultural left. While Rorty's story about the relationship between the twentieth-century American novel and politics is polemically generative and, at times, illuminating, the present volume exists because Rorty's book unfortunately exemplifies the reductive interpretative tendencies that still persist in the literature. Specifically, narratives like Rorty's fail to account for the following phenomena: the complex dialectic of hope and pessimism that existed within and between political movements, which American novels, especially ones written by women and minorities, both catalyzed and registered; the undertheorized political contributions of

---

[15] Richard Rorty, *Achieving Our Country: Leftist Thought in Twentieth-Century America* (Cambridge, MA: Harvard University Press, 1998), 8.
[16] Ibid., 38.

popular literary genres beyond just canonical realist fiction and acclaimed postmodern novels; and the unique, politically astute examinations of American culture that certain novels, with the benefit of hindsight, have been recognized as providing.

To remedy these lacunae, the volume groups its twenty-four chapters into three parts: "Ideologies and Movements," "The Politics of Genre and Form," and "Case Studies." Part I considers philosophical ideologies and broad political movements that were both politically and literarily significant in the twentieth-century United States, including progressive liberalism, conservatism, neoliberalism, overlapping manifestations of socialism and communism, several waves of feminism, various sexual liberation movements, and a cluster of Black liberation movements. These political discourses were chosen for two interrelated reasons: their sustained importance in American politics over prolonged periods and the degree to which they manifested in twentieth-century American novels. This rationale throws into relief why no standalone chapter on "fascism" exists in this section, since it was largely a European movement that made inroads into both American political discourse and fictional texts in the 1930s and 1940s, but which faded from American politics as a live option later in the century, although its usage as a rhetorical pejorative persisted. These seven chapters show how novels refracted big ideas and movements, as political abstractions were bent through the prism of the novel as an embodied narrative form. Part II analyzes the evolving political valences of specific genres and forms in the twentieth-century American novel, focusing on crime fiction, science fiction, Western fiction, literary realist fiction, immigrant fiction, horror fiction, and postmodern metafiction. While a great deal of scholarship exists on the political nuances of these genres, there is no recent source that brings them together in one place and subjects them to political analysis. As perhaps the most innovative section in this volume, these seven chapters illuminate the range of genres in which political discourse manifests itself in different American novels.

Part III examines ten individual novels as exemplary case studies. Tracing the arc of the entire century, this grouping of texts features a diverse assortment of politically minded novels, from paradigmatic political fiction such as Robert Penn Warren's *All the King's Men* (1946) to watershed genre novels such as Ursula K. Le Guin's *The Left Hand of Darkness* (1969). This distinctive section assumes that readers will benefit not only from a deeper engagement with a thematically rich novel, but also from novels that dramatize political discourses that do not have their own standalone chapters – e.g., Sinclair Lewis's *It Can't Happen Here* (1935) and the speculative counter-history subgenre of American fascism; Edward Abbey's *The Monkey Wrench Gang* (1975), a post-*Silent Spring* iteration of the environmental movement; and Leslie Marmon Silko's *Ceremony* (1977) and the literary politics of Indigenous representation in the wake of the 1960s American Indian Movement. For some readers, a few conspicuous absences here may elicit confusion. Where are the famous white male "usual suspects," such as Thomas Pynchon, Don DeLillo, E. L. Doctorow, John Updike, Philip Roth, and Robert Coover? First, these important authors are by no means excluded from the volume, as their novels are treated, to varying degrees, in previous chapters. Second, this volume recognizes that a great deal of excellent political literary criticism on these novelists already exists. For any given novel, inclusion in Part III signifies not an implicit award of timeless canonical status, but rather a recognition of political insight in an ongoing disciplinary attempt to make sense of fiction and politics in the previous century. In the interest of originality and innovation, then, this section substitutes novels by those usual suspects with ones such as Charlotte Perkins Gilman's once-forgotten feminist utopian novel *Herland* (1915), James Baldwin's jeremiad against Nixonian "law and order" politics *If Beale Street Could Talk* (1974), and Octavia E. Butler's prescient critique of neoliberalism and climate change in the *Parable* series (1993, 1998).

The four opening chapters investigate the literary politics of several major political ideologies: progressive liberalism, conservatism, neoliberalism, and socialism and communism. Johannes Voelz's "Progressive Liberalism" provides a literary genealogy of twentieth-century American liberalism, showing how an early progressive form took shape that retained the utopian end of liberating individuals from arbitrary constraints but re-envisioned the state as the principle means to achieve that end. The terms "progressive" and "liberal," Voelz argues, were often tested and developed in the cultural laboratory of the literary imagination. In "Conservatism," Stephen Schryer focuses on the undertheorized relationship between the novel and American conservatism, documenting how the modern conservative movement's cultural wing adopted contradictory positions, elitism and populism, which caused them to develop a mode of counter-expertise that increasingly estranged them from mainstream literary institutions. In the next chapter, "Neoliberalism," which acts as a kind of sequel to the previous one on conservatism, Mitchum Huehls traces the story of neoliberalism from the early post-1945 fear of socialism to four overlapping historical phases: the economic (1970s), the political (1980s), the socio-cultural (late 1980s and 1990s), and the ontological (2000s). Instead of developing a strict definition of the neoliberal novel, Huehls uses this heuristic framework to model ways of grasping how different iterations of the neoliberal economy constitute contemporary American culture, particularly via the novel form. In "Socialism and Communism," Mark W. Van Wienen surveys not only the realist and naturalist literary modes typically associated with socialism and communism, but also modernist and speculative novels by authors committed to radical human liberation. Exploring the relationship between literature and socialism and communism throughout the century, Van Wienen pays special attention to Black communism in novels by Claude McKay and Richard Wright and to utopian anarcho-socialism in novels by Ursula K. Le Guin.

Part I's final three chapters examine broad political movements that existed throughout the century but peaked during the "rights revolution" of the 1960s: feminism, sexual liberation, and Black liberation. In her chapter "Feminisms," Jean Lutes documents the ways in which political feminism affected the American novel, reshaping the content, and sometimes even the form, of virtually every US novel genre by century's end. Lutes also interrogates the usefulness of the "waves" metaphor in feminist historiography, arguing that a literary perspective puts the lie to this reductive metaphor that misleadingly privileges white women at the expense of all other women. In "Sexual Liberation Movements," Guy Davidson outlines the cultural politics of sexual freedom in America, from the early legal battles over literary censorship involving Henry Miller to post-Stonewall novelistic engagements with queer liberation. On the one hand, Davidson argues, these movements were all committed to certain intersecting aims, particularly the use of literary expression to expand rights, benefits, and legal protections associated with newly legible kinds of sexual behavior. On the other hand, serious tensions existed between these movements, the most salient being the theme of radical individualism at the heart of heteronormative novels and the theme of collectivity and community at the heart of queer novels. In their co-written chapter, "Black Liberation Movements," Sheena Michele Mason and Dana A. Williams examine the African American novel as a deeply political aesthetic form that shaped an array of twentieth-century political campaigns dedicated to eliminating various forms of oppression faced by Black people because of their racialization. Like Lutes's critique of feminist "waves" in Chapter 5, Mason and Williams also question the political utility of typical frameworks of periodization in twentieth-century Black fiction, arguing that they can elide the degree to which African American novelists grappled with racism, classism, sexism, and homophobia across the century. Ultimately, they document how the African American novel, broadly conceived across many genres, did cultural work within and outside the boundaries of what scholars usually recognize as Black political movements.

In Part II, "The Politics of Genre and Form," the first three chapters take up popular genres – crime fiction, science fiction, and Western fiction – that were once associated with rigid conventions and predictable politics and deconstructs those associations by resurveying their respective genre histories. In "Crime Fiction," Andrew Pepper argues that the politics of twentieth-century crime fiction have never been straightforward or easily predictable. Even when crime novels end by reestablishing the dominant social order, they often reveal the corruption within and across the institutional domains of capital, policing, and politics. Noting that classic crime fiction was often focalized through alienated white male outsiders, Pepper also considers the politics of racial and gendered noir novels, noting how Black and female crime novelists appropriated the genre for explicitly political ends. In "Science Fiction," Jason Haslam asserts that the twentieth-century science fiction novel, with its legendary depictions of dystopias and utopias, has a rich history of engaging political questions. In the first half of the century, Haslam writes, as scientific advancements led to both spectacular progress and profound destruction, science fiction writers imaginatively interrogated the hopes and fears bound up with new forms of collective technological action, especially in relation to the postwar threat of nuclear annihilation. Toward the end of the century, as both the internet and global capitalism swept over the country, American science fiction writers shifted their focus to cyberpunk themes of postmodern decentralization and to racialized and minoritized groups within the speculative subgenres of Afrofuturism, Indigenous Futurism, and Afro-Latinx Futurism. According to Stephen J. Mexal, in the chapter "Western Fiction," the twentieth-century Western novel frequently engaged with Frederick Jackson Turner's "frontier thesis" regarding the link between the frontier and individualism, for it allegorized several of the fundamental myths of American politics, such as the cultural memory of the US Civil War and the anxieties surrounding masculine individualism during the rise of industrial – and, later, post-industrial – society. Arguing that the genre is fundamentally about the politics of individual freedom, Mexal examines Western novels stretching across the century, from Zane Grey's pulps to Cormac McCarthy's neo-Westerns, and concludes that they are meditations on the fraught history of liberalism in America.

Part II is rounded out by four chapters that examine a mix of genres and forms that have always been regarded as politically contentious: literary realism, the immigrant novel, the Gothic horror novel, and the postmodern metafictional novel. In his chapter "Literary Realist Fiction," Matthew Shipe notes that literary realism has historically been subjected to diametrically opposed political critiques. In the first half of the century, American realism was regarded as politically progressive for its ability to illuminate multiple socioeconomic class tiers. In the second half of the century, though, scholars began to see realism, despite its ability to reveal social injustice, as a conservative literary mode that was essentially complicit in bolstering existing power structures. Shipe analyzes the various political valences of realism, claiming that American realists, in their stylistic commitment to chronicling vernacular speech and everyday actions, ultimately evince a profound ambivalence toward the American project by the end of the century. In "Immigrant Fiction," Heather Hathaway contextualizes the immigrant novel in a century in which immigration was a paramount political issue. For Hathaway, the genre of immigrant fiction not only confronts the mythic promise of opportunity embedded in the "American Dream," but it does so in different ways depending on the legal-political period in which it was written – i.e., the early-century immigration boom, the restrictive period of immigration from 1924 to 1965, and the post-1965 elimination of quotas paired with the rise of multiculturalism. In the next chapter, "Gothic Horror Fiction," Kevin Corstorphine considers how American novels were placed within political categories, sometimes in binary liberal/conservative terms that proved too reductive. Just as Freud theorized that neurotic symptoms simultaneously reveal and conceal uncomfortable repressed truths, horror fiction in the American Gothic mode adumbrated the seemingly unthinkable in society, hinting at the politically unnamable in the costume of monstrosity. In its compulsive desire to allegorize shocking repressed truths, Corstorphine argues, the American Gothic horror novel has been a transgressive vehicle for discussing unpalatable political issues that persistently haunt the country. In the final chapter in this section, "Postmodern Metafiction," Rob Turner takes up a genre that has been at the center of some of the most passionate political debates in contemporary literary studies. Coalescing as a legible form in the wake of World War II, the postmodern metafictional novel has been either celebrated for its emancipatory potential or denigrated for its complicity in late capitalism. Instead of simply rehashing these debates, Turner offers a fresh interrogation of the genre's cultural politics by critiquing the implicit assumption of whiteness in those debates; he does this by linking the genre to other self-reflexive postmodern literary forms (e.g., American hip-hop) and by tracking its continued relevance into the next century.

The third and final part, "Case Studies," opens with four chapters that examine thematically rich political novels published in roughly the first half of the century. In her chapter on Charlotte Perkins Gilman's *Herland* (1915), Cynthia J. Davis interrogates the conflicted political legacy of Gilman's novel, which is an ostensible feminist utopia that at once questions "unnatural" gender hierarchies and reinforces biopolitical essentialism via its obsession with national degeneracy and social impurity. A political novel in the most explicit sense of the term, *Herland* challenges readers to imagine how and why an early feminist novelist such as Gilman combined radically progressive gender politics with reactionary eugenicist biopower. Historicizing Sinclair Lewis's *It Can't Happen Here* (1935), Christopher Vials analyzes not just the most important political novel by America's first Nobel Prize in Literature laureate, but also the founding literary tale that cautions against the rise of American fascism and that influenced later counter-histories, such as Philp K. Dick's *The Man in the High Castle* (1962) and Philip Roth's *The Plot Against America* (2004). Reading the novel in light of the dramatic post-2016 American fascism debate, Vials argues that the novel remains a valuable literary text for tracing the contours of authoritarian politics into the present, and perhaps even the future. Taking up a similar set of themes, Jonathan S. Cullick's chapter on *All the King's Men* (1946) examines Robert Penn Warren's critically acclaimed political novel, arguing that it pushes readers to gauge the best and worst dimensions of the American populist tradition. On the surface, Warren's novel explores formal political themes of corruption and demagoguery, but it also explores deeper theoretical questions about the human condition, the nature of the good society, and the tragic dilemmas of the postbellum American South. Nathaniel Mills reinterprets Ralph Ellison's monumental *Invisible Man* (1952) as a novel that thinks politics from the vital depths, instead of from the midcentury "vital center," in a quest to radically recalibrate the racial surface alignments of American society. An encyclopedic novel that emphasizes the intersections of major political ideologies in the first half of the century (e.g., the uplift reformism of Booker T. Washington, the lure of Marxism for many Black writers and intellectuals, and the cultural development of Black nationalism), *Invisible Man* eschews the cautious moderation of vital center liberalism, Mills contends, in favor of a much larger, more inclusive vision of politics born out of lived Black experiences.

The rest of Part III looks to novels published in the second half of the century that highlight salient political concerns in the wake of the tumultuous 1960s, or what the historian Daniel T. Rodgers has dubbed an American "age of fracture."[17] Claiming that *The Left Hand of Darkness* (1969) partakes of the politics of recognition, Tony Burns examines Ursula K. Le Guin's novel as a pioneering work of feminist science fiction. By radically defamiliarizing sex and gender, Burns notes, the novel not only raised profound questions about the linkages between biology, culture, and politics, but it also posed these questions in the unique idiom of Taoism during the height of second-wave feminism. In his chapter on James Baldwin's underappreciated *If Beale Street Could Talk* (1974), Douglas Field reads the novel in relation to Baldwin's claim that a criminal power resided at the heart of the American judicial system, and that its most significant manifestation was the archipelago of prisons that housed increasing numbers of Black men in the wake of Nixon's "Law and Order" campaign. Field argues that, with the benefit of hindsight, it is now clear that Baldwin anticipated the work of later historians who would shed light on the inextricable link between state oppression and institutional incarceration. In his chapter on Edward Abbey's influential environmentalist protest novel *The Monkey Wrench Gang* (1975), Christopher K. Coffman analyzes some of the central paradoxes of modern environmental thought and nature writing, such as the benefits and drawbacks of intuitive political acts of sabotage versus larger collective action. Coffman pays special attention to the elements of Abbey's thought that have proven controversial – i.e., his celebration of individual male autonomy, implicit sexism, and the conflation of wilderness appreciation with whiteness – to assess his continued relevance for environmental literature. In her evaluation of Leslie Marmon Silko's *Ceremony* (1977), Sandra M. Gustafson reads the novel as the foundational political text of the "Native American Renaissance," a term that refers to the flowering of novels by American Indian authors after N. Scott Momaday's *House Made of Dawn* (1968). Silko grounds her critique, Gustafson argues, in a decolonial politics of hope that assumes modes of cultural hybridity that embrace Indigenous knowledge along with environmentalism, feminism, and antiwar and anti-nuclear activism. In her chapter on Octavia E. Butler's *Parable* series, Claire P. Curtis surveys Butler's science fiction novels *Parable of the Sower* (1993) and *Parable of the Talents* (1998), arguing that they emerged out of a speculative engagement with Reaganism to imagine what America

---

[17] Daniel T. Rodgers, *Age of Fracture* (Cambridge, MA: Harvard University Press, 2011), 3.

could look like in the first few decades of the twenty-first century. Eerily prophetic, Butler's series is set in a post-2020s America that has been torn asunder by extreme economic inequality, climate change, political polarization, disruptive advancements in communication technology, and a reactionary Christian nationalist (Andrew Steele Jarret) who rises to the presidency vowing to "Make America great again." Claire argues, though, that this vision does not succumb to nihilistic pessimism, since Butler imagines a new kind of politics in the form of the Earthseed religion, which combines the greatest scientific achievements of the twentieth century (notably, space travel) with a hope for innovative egalitarian communities that can potentially arise out of post-apocalyptic devastation. Part III concludes with my examination of Colson Whitehead's *The Underground Railroad* (2016), a twenty-first-century novel whose literary influences read like a patchwork of twentieth-century novelists included in this volume, such as Toni Morrison, Stephen King, Ralph Ellison, Thomas Pynchon, Ursula K. Le Guin, and Octavia E. Butler. Like major novels by these authors that interrogate the ultimate meaning of "America," Whitehead's speculative neo-slave narrative evaluates the viability of the American project in the wake of previous novelistic assessments, making it an exemplary case study that reveals the enduring relationship between the twentieth-century novel and American politics.

Although the vast majority of this volume deals with twentieth-century American politics, the chapters were composed in the shadow of an array of important twenty-first-century political events and movements, most notably the 9/11 terrorist attacks, the Bush administration's post-9/11 War on Terror, the federal government's disastrous handling of Hurricane Katrina, the two-term presidency of Barack Obama, the rise and fall of the Tea Party and Occupy Wall Street movements, the Supreme Court decision to recognize same-sex marriage as a fundamental right, the disturbing increase in mass shootings across the country, the tumultuous presidency of Donald Trump in which he was impeached twice by the US House of Representatives, the rise of the Black Lives Matter and #MeToo movements, the global COVID-19 pandemic and the contentious politics surrounding vaccines, the election of Joe Biden to the presidency, the 1/6 Capitol insurrection, the ultimate fall of Afghanistan to the Taliban, and the Supreme Court's overturning of *Roe v. Wade*. My primary hope is that readers will turn to these chapters to acquire a better understanding not only of how the American novel shaped twentieth-century American politics, but also of how American politics in that century can be seen in new and deeper ways through the aperture of long-form prose fiction. But

I also hope that a robust engagement with the politics of the twentieth-century American novel can help us make sense of our political present. "To accept one's past – one's history – is not the same thing as drowning in it," James Baldwin wrote in *The Fire Next Time*, "it is learning how to use it."[18] The twentieth-century American novel is just one cultural medium that we have at our disposal to better understand American political history in the hopes of using the novel to chart a better future.

[18] James Baldwin, *The Fire Next Time* (New York: Dial Press, 1991 [1963]), 81.

PART I

Ideologies and Movements

PART I

Ideologies and Movements

CHAPTER I

Progressive Liberalism

Johannes Voelz

Shortly after having published the first two volumes of his *Main Currents in American Thought* (1927),[1] Vernon Louis Parrington wrote a letter to a correspondent in which he laid out his understanding of the term "liberal":

> I was a good deal of a Marxian, and perhaps still am, although a growing sense of the complexity of social forces makes me somewhat distrustful of the sufficiency of the Marxian formulae. You were quite shrewd ... in commenting on my use of the word liberal ... I could see no harm and some good in using the term, and warping it pretty well to the left. As a matter of fact, in my first draft I used the word radical throughout, and only on revising did I substitute the other.[2]

For Parrington, whose three-volume intellectual and literary history *Main Currents in American Thought* (1927–30) made him a founding figure of the American Studies movement, and who helped carry the intellectual tradition of the Progressive Era into the period of the New Deal, liberalism had little to do with what we now understand as "classical liberalism": a tradition of thought, based on the ideas of John Locke as well as Scottish Enlightenment thinkers and Utilitarian philosophers, that valued individual liberty, individual rights, free markets, and small government. On the contrary: For Parrington, liberalism was a term that lent itself to being "warpt pretty well to the left," that was compatible with certain elements of Marxist thought, and that could be used interchangeably with "radical."

Parrington was no outlier in using liberalism in this manner. In the United States, liberalism became a recognizable intellectual and political

---

[1] Vernon Louis Parrington, *Main Currents in American Thought: An Interpretation of American Literature from the Beginnings to 1920* (New York: Harcourt, Brace, 1927).

[2] Parrington, quoted in Alfred Kazin, *On Native Grounds: An Interpretation of Modern American Prose Literature* (New York: Reynal and Hitchcock, 1942), 159; H. Lark Hall, *V. L. Parrington: Through the Avenue of Art* (Kent: Kent State University Press, 1994), 235.

discourse only when a group of thinkers – among them the English political theorist and sociologist L. T. Hobhouse, *The New Republic*'s co-founder and first editor Herbert Croly, and philosopher and intellectual John Dewey – insisted that "old" or "classical" liberalism stood in need of renovation. In other words, the thinkers we have come to understand as constituting "classical liberalism" were not thought of as "liberal" or "liberals" until Progressives of the early twentieth century were beginning to articulate an intellectual lineage for their own political stance. Liberalism became available to them, however, only as a tradition to be revised. Ian Afflerbach, who has laid out this genealogy in detail, puts it succinctly: "[Liberalism] crucially emerged as a category of crisis, a term that intellectuals such as Dewey used to name a classical tradition untenable in modern society."[3]

Initially, thinkers associated with Progressivism seemed content with the very term "progressive." But after World War I, the Progressive movement lost political steam, and the moniker "Great Progressive" was ascribed to Herbert Hoover, of all people. So it was that in the interim between the Progressive Era and the Great Depression, erstwhile progressive radicals began to claim "liberalism" as a term of identification.

The term "progressive liberalism," however, would have seemed a mere pleonasm to this generation of thinkers, given that, in their eyes, "liberalism" was only suited for the twentieth century if indeed it coincided with the convictions and principles underlying Progressivism. The fact that "progressive liberalism" appears as a meaningful compound to twenty-first-century readers – no mere redundancy, but the designation of a special subcategory of liberalism – points back to a divergence of liberalism and leftist thought at a later point, in the early years of the Cold War, as formerly leftist liberals with pronounced anti-communist convictions strove to put themselves at a distance from a Progressive tradition they had come to feel was tainted by Stalinism. That divergence between liberalism and the left has ordered the American political landscape ever since. Indeed, particularly since the 1970s, as the new social movements increasingly extended into the humanities, most leftist thinkers – and particularly those teaching in English departments – have treated liberalism as the outright opposite of leftist or progressive thought. In this lexicon, "liberal" stands for depoliticizing individualism, laissez-faire

---

[3] Ian Afflerbach, *Making Liberalism New: American Intellectuals, Modern Literature, and the Rewriting of a Political Tradition* (Baltimore: Johns Hopkins University Press, 2021), 10.

free-marketeering, corporate capitalism, and anything else that works to sustain the status quo. "Progressive liberalism," on this view, is a curious mixture of egalitarian and reformist impulses – a radicalism manqué, as it were. At the same time, "progressive" has retained its connotation of radicalism in the American political language to this day, though what it means to be radical has changed since the 1960s.

This strange career of the word "liberalism" – from Progressivism's synonym to antonym – has underwritten not only the history of American political thought, but also that of the American novel in the twentieth century. It was in the literary imagination – from the realist and, even more crucially, the naturalist novel of the late nineteenth and early twentieth centuries to the multicultural novel of the late twentieth century – that the changing meanings of "progressive" and "liberal" were developed and tested. And, by the same token, these political categories provided a vocabulary for politically placing and adjudicating individual works and even whole genres and literary developments – efforts that became increasingly central to literary studies as the discipline became self-consciously politicized.

Given that our political category – progressive liberalism – historically leads us back to Progressivism (before it was associated with liberalism), our overview must begin with the developments of the novel during the Progressive Era. It is striking, however, how much historians and literary historians differ in periodizing the era in question. While the Progressive Era continues to mark out a relatively easily defined historical phase (roughly from the 1890s to the United States' entry into World War I in 1917) that steadily continues to generate historical scholarship, literary historians periodize the same time span through the overlapping categories of realism, naturalism, and modernism. To be sure, these latter terms have the advantage of allowing for differentiations on the level of literary aesthetics and thus help make sense of the burst of literary innovations during the forty or so years in question. On the other hand, many of the major contributors to literary naturalism had more or less direct links with the political movement of Progressivism, and they used the novel to bring to light the dismal living and working conditions of the poor – and sometimes the hardship of the middle classes facing powerful business interests and corrupt governments – in ways that literature had not known before. Indeed, many naturalists made common cause with the muckraking journalists, such as Lincoln Steffens, Ida Tarbell, and Ray Stannard Baker, who laid open the "cesspools" that turned out to hide "under every city hall and beneath every state capital," as Parrington put it in the unfinished third volume of *Main Currents*.[4] Most famously, perhaps, Upton Sinclair, whose *The Jungle* (1906) came close to obliterating any remaining difference between fiction and muckraking, gave an immediate push to reform efforts in the meatpacking industry, resulting in the Pure Food and Drug Act and the Meat Inspection Act, both signed into law in 1906.[5] Why, then, is it not common to refer to the naturalist novel as the "progressive novel"?

To find an answer, one needs to look no further than the very term "naturalism." In the worldview underlying the naturalist novel, it is forces of nature that drive social and political dynamics. In Theodore Dreiser's debut novel, *Sister Carrie* (1900), one such force takes the form of desire – for dazzling sense impressions, experiences, and, of course, money.[6] Desire, indeed, was a major preoccupation of Dreiser's: He projected his novels *The Financier* (1912) and *The Titan* (1914) to become part of his "trilogy of desire" (the final part, the unfinished *The Stoic*, appeared in 1947). *Sister Carrie* offers a study of contravening lives built on the opposite trajectories of rise and decline. While Sister Carrie makes a spectacular career in the theater, her illegitimate husband Hurstwood, who once seemed to be on his way up the social ladder, sinks into poverty, becomes a beggar, and ultimately commits suicide. As Walter Benn Michaels suggests in a classic reading of the novel, Carrie desires a career in show business, and show business in turn kindles her desire.[7] Hurstwood, on the other hand, increasingly loses his capacity for desire. Rather than dreaming of glittering stardom, he reads in the newspaper about what has already come to pass. In this novel, desire subtends the capitalist order of conspicuous consumption, leading to a world in which stars and celebrities become famous and rich (though they remain, like Carrie, deeply unhappy), while the poor end up on the street. But in the logic of Dreiser's novel, desire – and thus capitalist inequality – cannot, indeed must not, be tamed by progressive politics, since "exhausted desire and economic failure" are tied together in Dreiser's naturalist imagination.[8] Desire cannot be curbed, and doing so wouldn't help reformers achieve their goals. Society would turn into a mass of Hurstwoods.

In the work of Frank Norris, we find an even more literal emphasis on forces of nature. His Wheat trilogy, two installments of which – *The*

---

[4] Parrington, 406.   [5] Upton Sinclair, *The Jungle* (New York: Doubleday, Page & Co., 1906).
[6] Theodore Dreiser, *Sister Carrie* (New York: Doubleday, Page & Co., 1900).
[7] Walter Benn Michaels, "Sister Carrie's Popular Economy," *Critical Inquiry* 7.2 (1980): 373–90.
[8] Michaels, 385.

Octopus (1901) and *The Pit* (1903) – he managed to complete before his early death at thirty-two, was intended to capture the entire natural cycle of wheat, from its production to its consumption.[9] Planting and harvesting were the nominal topic of the first installment, the trading of wheat that of the second. These descriptions, however, are misleading, for they falsely suggest that Norris aimed at producing a massive exposé – as the muckrakers might have done – of modern agribusiness. Norris, however, aimed to define his program of literary naturalism by building a bridge back to Romantic writers such as Victor Hugo. In the literature he strove for, "everything is extraordinary, imaginative, grotesque even, with a vague note of terror quivering throughout."[10]

In *The Octopus*, the story of wheat production is turned into an epic battle between the ranchers of California's San Joaquin Valley and the railroad corporations. Norris's reformist commitments shine through in the way he details how shrewdly the corporation squeezes and dispossesses the farmers, and even kills those who try to resist its insatiable hunger for expansion. But, in classic naturalist fashion, the conflict turns out not to be political at all, because it is not driven by clashing wills of human agents, nor by social structures of power, but by forces so timeless and uncontestable that they can only be called natural. As the narrator relates in the "Conclusion":

> It was true that forces rather than men had locked horns in that struggle, but for all that the men of the Ranch and not the men of the Railroad had suffered. Into the prosperous valley, into the quiet community of farmers, that galloping monster, that terror of steel and steam had burst, shooting athwart the horizons, flinging the echo of its thunder over all the ranches of the valley, leaving blood and destruction in its path.[11]

The novel derives its moral energies from delineating how corporate capital drives proud farmers into misery, poverty, or death, but the forces at work behind this drama are so impersonal that the railroad corporation can hardly be said to be the responsible agent. Norris drives home this point by ending on a note of poetic justice: In the final scene, the railroad's agent – who to the reader is made to feel like the novel's villain – finds his

[9] Frank Norris, *The Octopus: A Story of California* (New York: Doubleday, Page & Co., 1901); Frank Norris, *The Pit* (Toronto: G. N. Morang, 1903).
[10] Frank Norris, "Zola as a Romantic Writer," in *Frank Norris: Novels & Essays*, ed. Donald Pizer (New York: Library of America, 1986), 1107.
[11] Norris, "The Octopus: A Story of California," in *Frank Norris: Novels & Essays*, 1096.

end when he is literally buried in wheat. The railroad agent finds his master in the novel's true agent.

The works of Dreiser and Norris suggest what makes the relation between Progressivism and the literary naturalism so complicated. Naturalists shared little of the optimism that mobilized Progressive reform projects. Their novels rejected the idea that social ills could be rectified through better public administration because what lay at the bottom of these ills were causes that were indeed not social but natural. Yet, reading the naturalist novel as a critique of Progressive politics would ultimately be misguided, because it provided an imaginary stage for the social struggles of, and the injustices suffered by, the downtrodden. Morally, this was a literature that called for drastic social change, even if the underlying philosophy said something else. This may explain why, as Sydney Bufkin has shown, Norris's reviewers emphasized the proximity between *The Octopus* and radical politics.[12] According to many of the reviews, "the elements of the novel that appear most reformist or even progressive rise to the surface," while the novel's deterministic emphasis on natural forces was interpreted not as the point of the novel but rather as a "generic flaw."[13]

The reform energies of the Progressive Era, its commitments to civic organizing and government regulation as a tool for social improvement, supplied a tradition on the shoulders of which the politics of the New Deal could be constructed once the USA was engulfed in the Great Depression. However, as a result of the first Red Scare following World War I and the materialist bonanza of the 1920s, the continuity was not seamless. For the 1930s version of Progressivism to gain traction, artists and intellectuals had to turn left. As Michael Denning has shown in great detail, "young plebeian artists found allies among the older generation of American modernists drawn to the Popular Front."[14] In the emerging "cultural front" – "the extraordinary flowering of arts, entertainment, and thought based on the broad social movement that came to be known as the Popular Front" – the novel played an important part, though it was hardly the dominant form of expression.[15] Many artists followed a documentary impulse, and the perhaps most celebrated novelists of the cultural front – John Steinbeck

[12] Sydney Bufkin, "Resisting Naturalism: Purpose and Literary Value in the Reception of Frank Norris's *The Octopus*," *Book History* 18 (2015): 197–234.

[13] Bufkin, 229.

[14] Michael Denning, *The Cultural Front: The Laboring of American Culture in the Twentieth Century* (London: Verso, 1996), xv.

[15] Denning, xvi.

and John Dos Passos – experimented with creating documentary effects in their fictions.

Steinbeck's *The Grapes of Wrath* (1939) clearly displays its political affiliation.[16] The characters equipped with the greatest moral authority – Tom Joad, who comes as close to being the protagonist as a collective novel will permit, and the former preacher Jim Casy, clearly designed as a Christ-figure[17] – undergo a process of political awakening that leads them to become labor organizers. That at least one of them pays for this step with his life highlights a second dimension of the novel's political self-positioning. Steinbeck critiques the anti-communist madness pervading American society, from the state and the police down to ordinary Americans, just as he also suggests that anti-communism often acts as a mere front for legitimating exploitation. "A red," explains one of the farm owners, "is any son-of-a-bitch that wants thirty cents an hour when we're payin' twenty-five." To which a farm worker replies: "I ain't no son-of-a-bitch, but if that's what a red is ... we're all reds."[18]

Formally, too, *The Grapes of Wrath* may be seen as a work aligned with New Deal liberalism: Like Dos Passos, Steinbeck aims to shift the novel's traditional, bourgeois focus on the individual toward the collective – though the collective in question is not so much the working class but rather the downtrodden common people whom Steinbeck recognizes, in populist fashion, as the foundation of American democracy (that he makes his migrant community all white is an act of imaginative displacement that makes Steinbeck pale against similar – less popular – farm labor narratives of the time, such as Carey McWilliams's non-fiction reportage *Factories in the Field* of the same year).[19] But Steinbeck holds on to the identificatory potentials that individualized characters provide – which may be one of the reasons for the novel's extraordinary popular success. To this end, Steinbeck deftly employs two narrative strategies. He limits the collective to the unit of the Joad family (and the families they team up with) – a unit small enough to feature fully individualized characters, including their most intimate relationships. And, more intriguingly, he intersperses the main plot of the Joads' migration from Oklahoma to California with shorter chapters in which the experiences of his protagonists are echoed or anticipated by unnamed characters who stand in for the larger collective.

---

[16] John Steinbeck, *The Grapes of Wrath* (New York: Modern Library, 1939).
[17] For a reading of the novel's pronounced scriptural resonances, see Katerina Koci, *The Land Without Promise: The Roots and Afterlife of One Biblical Allusion* (London: Bloomsbury/T&T Clark, 2021).
[18] Steinbeck, 407.   [19] See Denning, 267.

If, in these interchapters, Steinbeck ventures into the didactic, it is a didacticism that remains grounded in particularized experiences, fleshed out in the main narrative. As a result, Steinbeck not only interlaces the individual and the collective but also offers, within the confines of an emotionally gripping story, a vernacular education in socialist theory that dispenses with theoretical language altogether.

At the same time, however, *The Grapes of Wrath* does not always fit easily with the state-centered politics of the New Deal. The novel's only moment of utopian hope emerges when the Joad family arrives at the Weedpatch Camp, a migrant camp set up by the federal government. Although the New Deal was intent on enabling collective action rather than simply providing for citizens in need, Steinbeck takes this idea so far that the empowering state seems to anticipate its own withering. The camp's chief attraction lies in allowing the community of migrants to self-govern. Its members come and go, but as long as they're there, their sub-state practices of self-rule fill them with dignity, joy, safety, and relative material comfort. In effect, Steinbeck equips the New Deal state with an anti-statist heart.[20]

In Steinbeck's populist imagination, the poor form a community that holds out the promise for a better America: "I'm learnin' one thing good," the Joad family's matriarch (the family's secret power center) proclaims at one point. "Learnin' it all a time, ever' day. If you're in trouble or hurt or need – go to poor people. They're the only ones that'll help – the only ones."[21] Steinbeck's use of the vernacular underlines the authenticity of the dispossessed – they are the poor as much as the people – and he charges their poverty with special moral authority, in effect reinterpreting destitution as a state adverse to material corruption. Knowing that they rely on each other's help, his impoverished migrants develop forms of solidarity that come closest to the fulfillment of the nation's political and moral ideals.

In this regard, *The Grapes of Wrath* differs sharply from John Dos Passos's *USA* trilogy, published separately between 1930 and 1936 and as an omnibus edition with an additional, much-quoted, preface in 1937. In the final sentence of that preface, Dos Passos writes, "But mostly USA is the speech of the people."[22] Yet that speech is not Steinbeck's vernacular of

---

[20] For a reading that emphasizes the continuity of Steinbeck's Great Depression novels and FDR's New Deal, see William James Connor, "Steinbeck's Phalanx Theory: Reflections on His Great Depression Novels and FDR's New Deal," *Steinbeck Review* 17.2 (2020): 214–29.

[21] Steinbeck, 513–14.   [22] John Dos Passos, *USA* (New York: Library of America, 1996), 3.

the downtrodden. It is a language infiltrated by social tendencies of standardization and leveling that received a major push from the emerging profession of public relations.

The rise of PR is itself only a symptom, however. The larger trend is there even before the profession develops, in the very early pages of the first volume, *The 42nd Parallel*. Here, Dos Passos introduces the reader to Mac, the first of the trilogy's twelve principal characters, by relating experiences from his early childhood. Following the early death of Mac's mother, his father and Uncle Tim move the family to Chicago in order to flee from unpaid debts. Uncle Tim tries to assuage Mac's father's bad conscience, resorting over and over to the same clichéd phrase: "it's the fault of poverty, and poverty's the fault of the system."[23]

Already at this early point, we encounter the complex stance Dos Passos takes toward the standardizing effects that characterize his USA. On the one hand, America suffers from a plague of the unauthentic. People cannot help but reproduce the endlessly repeated word and thought patterns that increasingly characterize modern America. (This tendency gets much more dramatic once these patterns are peddled by the likes of J. W. Moorehouse – the books' secret protagonist, modeled after Ivy Lee, the inventor of public relations – who rises to be a PR mogul of sorts.) But if such an implicit critique puts Dos Passos in communion with the critical theorists of the Frankfurt School, he supplements it with the ironic twist that Mac's uncle – as disingenuous as he may be in uttering the phrase – is nonetheless spot on: it is indeed "the fault of the system." "Wrong life cannot be lived rightly,"[24] Dos Passos seems to suggest (anticipating Adorno's famous adage from *Minima Moralia*), but importantly, to Dos Passos, that doesn't devalue the truisms of the left.

Indeed, Dos Passos's trilogy finds its point of political identification with the left – workers, strikers, political organizers, public speakers – and, even more crucially, it rues an America that the left pursued but failed to bring to fruition. The trilogy can thus be read as a testament to the labor movement: The first of its portraits is reserved for Eugene Debs (Dos Passos turns him into a mythical legend); each of the three volumes begins with an extended narrative of a working-class character; and, at the trilogy's emotional high point, toward the end of the third volume – *The Big Money* – Dos Passos turns Sacco and Vanzetti into martyrs.

Yet, on the whole, Dos Passos's trilogy features what literary critic T. K. Whipple, in a review for *The Nation*, called "midway people in somewhat

---

[23] Ibid., 21.   [24] Theodor W. Adorno, *Minima Moralia* (London: Verso, 2005), 39.

ambiguous positions – intellectuals, decorators, advertising men."[25]
Indeed, they are "midway" regarding their social position: The majority
of them, at some point in their careers, belong to the middle class, and
nearly all of them end up in one or another branch of the white-collar
profession of "word slinging." But they are "midway" also in a more radical
sense. Dos Passos doesn't design them as the well-rounded characters
known from the realist novel. They are devised to remain flat: They hardly
ever reflect and reminisce; they don't wrangle with ideas; and, most
importantly, their lives do not form a narrative arch. Precisely because
they do not amount to individuality, these main characters – and not the
famous personages to whom Dos Passos pays tribute in his series of
portraits spread throughout the three volumes – become *USA*'s representative men and women. The idea of the collective novel here finds its most
radical instantiation: Not only does Dos Passos spread out the readers'
attention to twelve characters and a whole host of minor ones, but he
additionally de-individualizes them. The result is as ambiguous as the
architecture of modernist housing projects: Is this the world as envisaged
by socialist egalitarianism, or is it an instance of capitalist mass culture?

Reviewing *USA* for *Partisan Review* in 1938, Lionel Trilling prophesied
that "no writer, I think, will go to school to Dos Passos."[26] Trilling was
wrong, though it took a decade for this to become obvious. Writers as
different as Norman Mailer and Mary McCarthy would come to invoke
Dos Passos's trilogy as their literary model. Doing so, they made a gesture
of reaching back to 1930s radicalism at a point in time when New Deal
liberalism had been supplanted by Cold War liberalism. By this point, the
political landscape had drastically changed, and so had the meaning of
liberalism. Many of those who had become radicalized during the 1930s
had in the meantime experienced their "Kronstadt" moment and turned
anti-communist.[27] Trilling, in his review of *USA*, phrases it in a manner
characteristic for the disillusioned leftists. Though he praises Dos Passos's
trilogy, he does so only after having made it clear that Dos Passos
"embodies ... the cultural tradition of the intellectual Left,"[28] the key
problem of which is that "among liberals" – notice again the treatment of
"left" and "liberal" as interchangeable – "the idea of social determination,

[25] T. K. Whipple, "Dos Passos and the USA," in *John Dos Passos: The Critical Heritage*, ed. Barry
Maine (London: Routledge, 2005), 151–4, here 152.
[26] Lionel Trilling, "The America of John Dos Passos," in *John Dos Passos: The Critical Heritage*, 157.
[27] "Kronstadt" as a metonymy of disillusionment refers to the Soviet leadership's violent suppression
of the rebellion in the naval fortress Kronstadt in 1921.
[28] Trilling, 157.

on no good ground, appears tacitly to exclude the moral concern."[29] For Trilling, always keen on defending what he calls "moral realism," judging *USA* therefore depends on the novel's focus on individuals and the moral dilemmas and uncertainties they face. He believes to have detected such an orientation in *USA* and regards it as its saving grace, despite the fact that Dos Passos was a liberal of the now outmoded kind.

What is now called "Cold War liberalism" – but what at the time was not always understood to be "liberal" at all, given the term's established association with Progressive radicalism – provided an ideological framework subtending the aesthetic doctrines of the quickly spreading creative writing programs.[30] Arguably, it also injected a shot of creativity into the American novel. Ralph Ellison's *Invisible Man* (1952) and Saul Bellow's *The Adventures of Augie March* (1953) are only two of the now canonical novels that came to give aesthetic form to the revised form of liberalism (one might also consider the early works of James Baldwin, Bernard Malamud, and Philip Roth, among many others). Both Ellison and Bellow themselves had fostered leftist ties in their early careers, and both joined in the conversion from New Deal liberalism to Cold War liberalism. In their respective masterworks, this becomes apparent in the ways in which they center on individual heroes on a quest for identity. Bellow weaves his novel around a picaro whose life path spirals outward from the narrow confines of his Jewish Chicago neighborhood into ever greater cosmopolitan orbits. In characteristic Cold War liberal fashion, critics praised him for having "universalized the marginal," as Louis Menand puts it.[31] In Ellison's narrative, the intractability of racism pervading American society makes the trajectory from the particularity of the individual to the universal more difficult, but in his much debated final sentence – "Who knows but that, on the lower frequencies, I speak for you?"[32] – he nonetheless gestures in this direction by building an imaginary bridge to a potentially unlimited readership that included the members of the Cold War liberal establishment, in whose publications he published.[33]

---

[29] Ibid., 161.

[30] See Mark McGurl, *The Program Era: Postwar Fiction and the Rise of Creative Writing* (Cambridge, MA: Harvard University Press, 2009).

[31] Louis Menand, "Young Saul: The Subject of Bellow's Fiction," *The New Yorker*, May 11, 2015, 71–7, here 76.

[32] Ralph Ellison, *Invisible Man* (New York: Vintage, 1995), 581.

[33] For an extended reading of Ellison and Bellow, see my essay "The Liberal Imagination Revisited: Saul Bellow, Ralph Ellison, and the Crisis of Democracy," in *The Oxford Handbook of*

However, among the younger generation of American writers, the turn away from 1930s liberalism also brought forth dissenters. At their forefront was Norman Mailer, who, already in 1948, at the age of twenty-five, invoked *USA* in his debut novel *The Naked and the Dead* by borrowing the format of short biographies for its "Time Machine" sections.[34] The novel focuses on one platoon during World War II, and thus has a much smaller cast than Dos Passos's epic collective. Indeed, it is closer to Steinbeck's Joad family, or – a more precise comparison still – the *Pequod* crew in Melville's *Moby-Dick*. Yet Mailer averred that it was Dos Passos, not Melville, who guided him in writing his novel: "Dos Passos gave me the strongest, simplest, most direct idea about what it is to write a great American novel."[35] By 1962, his alliance with Dos Passos's brand of radicalism led him to reject the term liberalism altogether, a sure sign that by now liberalism was associated with the likes of Trilling: "I don't care if people call me a radical, a rebel, a red, a revolutionary, an outsider, an outlaw, a Bolshevik, an anarchist, a nihilist, or even a left conservative, but please don't ever call me a liberal."[36] Liberalism and the left had parted ways, and it is only at this point that the phrase "progressive liberalism" begins to make sense.

Somewhat less obviously, but ultimately more interestingly, Mary McCarthy also leaned on Dos Passos in writing her 1963 bestseller *The Group*.[37] Looking back in 1984, she singled out *USA* as the formative work for both her political and literary maturation: "Like a Japanese paper flower dropped into a glass of water, it all unfolded, magically, from Dos Passos."[38] While it was Dos Passos's role as pallbearer of America's socialist potential that initially drew the young McCarthy to him, by the time she wrote *The Group*, it was Dos Passos's critique of standardization – the aspect of *USA* that in fact made Dos Passos a kindred spirit of Cold War liberals – that seems to have inspired her most. Her novel centers on the life trajectories of eight young women, mostly from the upper classes of the East, who, at the novel's outset, in 1933, have just graduated from Vassar College. They have been trained to become good Progressives, yet, as the

Twentieth-Century American Literature, ed. Leslie Bow and Russ Castronovo (New York: Oxford University Press, 2022), 337–55.

[34] Norman Mailer, *The Naked and the Dead* (New York: Rinehart & Company, 1948).

[35] J. Michael Lennon, ed., *Conversations with Norman Mailer* (Jackson: University of Mississippi Press, 1988), 189.

[36] Norman Mailer, "Letter to the Editor," quoted in Afflerbach, 3.

[37] Mary McCarthy, *The Group* (New York: Harcourt, Brace, 1963).

[38] Mary McCarthy, "The Lasting Power of the Political Novel," *The New York Times*, January 1, 1984, Section 7, 1.

novel tracks them through the 1930s, their ambitions for the most part falter in both the political and – much more central to the characters' preoccupation – personal dimensions. McCarthy's novel thus registers a cultural and political shift from New Deal liberalism (pointing back to which is the novel's overt theme and less overt sign of political allegiance) to 1960s progressive liberalism. The question most pressing for her characters is not the class struggle or the government's reform agenda but rather the aspiration to female self-realization. Much in line with the counterculture to come – whose politics and aesthetic sensibilities she otherwise did not share – radical politics becomes reconceptualized as emancipatory politics.

For McCarthy, what stands in the way to attaining that goal is a cultural conformism that plays out, much like in *USA*, on the level of language. With the exception of the first and the last, each of the chapters centers on one of the eight young women, turning each one into the focalizer and rendering her perspective in free, indirect discourse. As McCarthy explained at a public reading, her intent was not to give the reader access to the private minds of her characters, but, on the contrary, to show that every thought her characters entertained "was on the point of being turned into gossip."[39] Groupthink and group-talk blend into one another, "as if each of these girls no longer had a private life."[40] McCarthy settles how to understand the ambiguity between socialist egalitarianism and PR-driven standardization that had characterized *USA*. In revisiting New Deal liberalism, she ends up singling out concerns with the mass-culture characteristic of Cold War liberalism and ties that characteristic to a program of self-realization that would come to preoccupy the next generation of progressive liberals.

As can be intimated here only by way of a short coda, the generation of progressive liberals that came to shape American cultural politics in the aftermath of the student movement and the rise of the so-called new social movements took its cue from the broadened understanding of radicalism that McCarthy, Mailer, and like-minded writers had been driving toward. To put it somewhat crudely, progressive liberals of the late twentieth century turned away from a class-based politics toward the politicization of identity. And although identity was now conceptualized as a category pertaining to collectives, it also continued to be moored to the problem of

---

[39] Mary McCarthy, interview with introduction by Dwight Macdonald, *The Paris Review*, podcast audio, 1963, https://soundcloud.com/user-243983744/mary-mccarthy-at-the-92nd-street-y,00:15:34–00:17:04.
[40] Ibid.

individual self-realization. With ethnic and multicultural fiction finally getting its due attention as a result of the canon debates, the novel yet again played a crucial role in fleshing out how to imagine this new variant of liberalism.

Toni Morrison's *Beloved* (1987), which earned her the Pulitzer Prize in 1988 and ultimately the Nobel Prize in 1993, brings these developments together in condensed fashion.[41] Morrison makes the case for a politics of memory that calls on Americans to finally work through their past of slavery in order to address the racism persisting through the 1980s. The psychoanalytic term "working through" is crucial here, for the difficult and painful learning process exemplified by the novel's protagonist, Sethe – a runaway slave who killed her little daughter in order to keep her from being snatched back into slavery by slave catchers and who, in the course of the novel, needs to come to terms with her guilt – follows a therapeutic script. In the end, Sethe is made to realize by her companion, Paul D, "You your best thing, Sethe. You are."[42] Sounding not unlike a therapist, Paul D drives home the point that, as much as progressives of the recent past set themselves apart from liberalism by emphasizing the importance of the collective and the community, in the end politics must aim to allow individuals to overcome trauma and repair their violated sense of self. To be sure, Morrison equips the community with at least as much hope as Steinbeck does in *The Grapes of Wrath*: It is the African American community of the novel's Cincinnati suburb that collectively chases away Beloved, the life-sucking ghost of the past. But Morrison's communitarianism remains individualist at heart. While it promises to overcome the individualist legacy of Cold War liberalism, it does so by subscribing to identity politics and the politics of memory. Although these are framed as anti-liberal, collectivist forms of politicization, in the end they tend to consolidate the triumph of the therapeutic and ultimately concern the chances of individual survival and flourishing. With exceptional clarity, Morrison's *Beloved* reveals how deeply indebted contemporary Progressivism remains to liberalism – not only to that of the New Deal, but to Cold War liberalism as well.

---

[41] Toni Morrison, *Beloved* (New York: Alfred A. Knopf, 1987).
[42] Toni Morrison, *Beloved* (London: Vintage, 1997), 273.

CHAPTER 2

Conservatism

Stephen Schryer[*]

In *The Liberal Imagination* (1950), Lionel Trilling asserts, "[I]n the United States today, liberalism is not only the dominant but even the sole intellectual tradition."[1] Most historians of American conservatism cite this passage as evidence of liberals' overweening confidence after World War II. In Kevin Mattson's terms, Trilling helped establish the "historical myth" that conservatism expresses itself in popular prejudices rather than ideas.[2] Since the 1990s, historians have worked hard to undo this myth, to uncover the centrality of conservatism within twentieth- and twenty-first-century politics and culture.[3] Literary critics, in contrast, have doubled down on Trilling's relegation of conservatism to the far margins of American intellectual life. For Trilling, liberalism's dominance was something to be bemoaned rather than celebrated; it signified the calcification of the liberal tradition. He sought to revive that tradition by challenging it with literature that he considered essentially conservative. "[I]t is in general true," he argued, "that the modern European literature to which we can have an active, reciprocal relationship, which is the right relationship to have, has been written by men who are indifferent to, even hostile to, the tradition of democratic liberalism as we know it."[4] Since the 1960s, in contrast, critics have tended to align literature with the attitudes of the

[*] The research for this chapter was funded by the Social Sciences and Humanities Research Council (SSHRC).
[1] Lionel Trilling, *The Liberal Imagination: Essays on Literature and Society* (New York: New York Review Books, 2008 [1950]), xv.
[2] Kevin Mattson, *Rebels, All!: A Short History of the Conservative Mind in Postwar America* (New Brunswick, NJ: Rutgers University Press, 2008), 14.
[3] In "The Problem of American Conservatism," *American Historical Review* 99 (1994): 409–29, Alan Brinkley argues that historians had neglected American conservatism. By the early 2000s, historians were working to overcome this neglect, publishing pathbreaking books such as Lisa McGirr's *Suburban Warriors: The Origins of the New American Right* (Rutgers, NJ: Princeton University Press, 2001) and Rick Perlstein's *Before the Storm: Barry Goldwater and the Unmaking of the American Consensus* (New York: Hill and Wang, 2001).
[4] Trilling, 301.

political left. In Michael Kimmage's terms, "the world of conservatives . . . acquired great power at the political center in the years after 1968, without generating much of a literary culture." This failure derives, he claims, from "the anti-utopian cast of the conservative mind. The literary imaginative thrives on the left, where utopia has long been at home."[5] Only recently have critics such as Christopher Douglas and Bryan Santin begun to challenge this equation of leftism and the literary imagination and take seriously conservatism's literary impact.[6]

The essay that follows sketches the history of intellectual conservatism in twentieth- and twenty-first-century America, focusing on the conservative renaissance of the 1950s. I argue that midcentury conservatives, in their war against an intelligentsia that they, like Trilling, perceived as dominated by liberal voices, evolved a model of counter-expertise that continues to inform right-wing intellectual practice today. This model was influenced by midcentury disciplinary conflicts between literature and the social sciences, with conservatives affirming a literary model of truth against the rationalism of social scientific discourse. From the 1950s to the 1960s, this conservative model of counter-expertise attracted a significant minority of writers and critics. *National Review*, the most influential journal of the intellectual right, featured a robust book review section that featured essays by writers including Hugh Kenner, Joan Didion, Garry Wills, and Guy Davenport, all of whom were or would soon become notable critics, fiction writers, and literary journalists. However, the conservative critique of the liberal intelligentsia was in the process of turning into a critique of expertise as such; this critique pushed many of these writers away from the magazine and helped fashion the version of the left/right divide that defines American politics today.

When Trilling claimed that "nowadays there are no conservative or reactionary ideas in general circulation," he overlooked a host of conservative intellectuals who made their mark in the 1930s and 1940s.[7] Foremost among these in the field of humane letters were the Southern Agrarians, a community of poets, critics, and historians centered at Vanderbilt University in Tennessee. Their 1930 manifesto, *I'll Take My*

---

[5] Michael Kimmage, "The Plight of Conservative Literature," in *A New Literary History of America*, ed. Greil Marcus and Werner Sollors (Cambridge, MA: Harvard University Press, 2009), 948.

[6] Christopher Douglas, *If God Meant to Interfere: American Literature and the Rise of the Christian Right* (Ithaca, NY: Cornell University Press, 2016); Bryan Santin, *Postwar American Fiction and the Rise of Modern Conservatism: A Literary History, 1945–2008* (Cambridge: Cambridge University Press, 2021).

[7] Trilling, xv.

Stand, offered a defense of the South's culture and agricultural economy that would influence generations of Southern intellectuals. Their leading figure, John Crowe Ransom, also developed a formalist theory of literary criticism that would be institutionalized in the 1940s and 1950s as the New Criticism. Trilling's own discipline, in other words, was in the midst of a conservative upsurge that would push literary studies to the right of most humanities disciplines until the mid-1960s.[8] The Great Depression also saw the emergence of two of the founding figures of contemporary libertarianism: Ayn Rand and Albert Jay Nock. Both wrote in response to the New Deal, depicting it as a proto-totalitarian regime that would reallocate privately owned wealth into the hands of federal bureaucrats. By the 1940s, émigré economists from the Austrian School, such as Friedrich Hayek and Ludwig von Mises, were challenging the dominant Keynesian paradigm, reviving classical liberalism and laying the foundations for the rise of neoliberal economic reforms in the 1970s and 1980s. By 1950, when Trilling published *The Liberal Imagination*, an American conservative intellectual renaissance was just around the corner. The key texts of this renaissance – William F. Buckley, Jr.'s *God and Man at Yale* (1951), Whittaker Chambers's *Witness* (1952), and Russell Kirk's *The Conservative Mind* (1952) – would all gain national attention in the next two years.

American conservatism in the early 1950s, however, was a fractured entity, marked by fundamental disagreements between right-wing intellectuals, who were divided into three camps: traditionalists, libertarians, and anti-communists. Traditionalists such as Russell Kirk were followers of Edmund Burke; they sought to temper the rationalism and individualism of the West, instead underscoring the importance of tradition, community, and faith. Many traditionalists, such as the Southern Agrarians, were hostile to industrialism and ambivalent toward free-market capitalism, yearning for a return to a Jeffersonian America made up of independent landowners. Libertarians, in contrast, were pro-business and promoted absolute individual liberty (especially in economic matters). Some libertarians, like Ayn Rand, were atheists, for whom collectivism was the culmination of the Christian tradition. Anti-communists, many of them former communists such as Whittaker Chambers and James Burnham, were primarily concerned with the danger posed by the Soviet Union's imperial ambitions.

---

[8] The field of literary studies was also shaped by Irving Babbitt and Paul Elmer More's New Humanism, an essentially conservative movement influenced by Matthew Arnold and Edmund Burke.

William F. Buckley, Jr. was the central figure who welded together these three camps. His first book, *God and Man at Yale*, drew themes from traditionalists, libertarians, and anti-communists (not always, as we shall see, in a logically coherent fashion). He envisaged *National Review*, which he founded with James Burnham, Willi Schlamm, and others in 1955, as a magazine that would bring together every kind of conservative. By the 1960s, the magazine was promoting a theory called fusionism that sought to broker the differences between traditionalists and libertarians. At the same time, the magazine expelled trends and people who threatened the conservative movement's fractious harmony and public respectability. Buckley excommunicated Ayn Rand for her atheism, arranging for Chambers to write a scathing review of *Atlas Shrugged* (1957). In 1961, the magazine distanced itself from the John Birch Society, which was promoting a paranoid version of anti-communism that most Americans found too extreme. In the 1970s and 1980s, the magazine sought to integrate new groups of conservatives: the Christian New Right and the neoconservatives. This unification of conservative intellectuals helped *National Review* achieve a remarkable degree of influence on the Republican Party. In the early 1960s, the magazine rallied behind Senator Barry Goldwater, shaping his policies and playing a key role in his nomination as the 1964 Republican presidential candidate. Presidents Nixon and Reagan regularly consulted with Buckley; the Reagan administration, in particular, marked the apex of *National Review*'s ambition to influence public policy.

To effect this intellectual synthesis, Buckley drew attention to the shared enemies of traditionalists, libertarians, and anti-communists: communists and liberals. Domestically, by 1955, the latter were the more pressing threat, and Buckley cast *National Review* as a magazine that would challenge liberals and the institutions they controlled. Employing an inverted historical determinism popularized by former Trotskyites like James Burnham, Buckley insisted that ideas and the elites that make them are the driving forces of history. As such, he emphasized the university's centrality to American politics. At America's colleges, Buckley wrote in the "Publisher's Statement" for the magazine's first issue, "a number of energetic social innovators, plugging their grand designs, succeeded over the years in capturing the liberal intellectual imagination. And since ideas rule the world, the ideologues, having won over the intellectual class, simply walked in and started to run things."[9] *National Review* would challenge this liberal intellectual dominance, which extended beyond the academy

---

[9] William F. Buckley, Jr., "Publisher's Statement," *National Review* 1.1 (1955): 5.

into the media and government. Against the "Social Engineers, who seek to adjust mankind to conform with scientific utopias," conservatives would stand on the side of the "disciples of Truth, who defend the organic moral order."[10]

In their opposition to the liberal intelligentsia, *National Review* conservatives adopted a contradictory position, at once elitist and populist. Postwar conservatives viewed themselves, in Jay Alfred Nock's terms, as members of "the Remnant," an elite subset of the intelligentsia who resist their civilization's decline.[11] Conservatives, Buckley writes, are on "the side of excellence," against "the conformity of intellectual cliques which, in education as well as the arts, are out to impose upon the nation their modish fads and fallacies."[12] This elitism led conservatives to embrace a Trillingesque conception of liberal ideology. In *The Liberal Imagination*, Trilling argues that, during the New Deal administration, the liberal tradition fell prey to its "organizational impulse." Ideas that can be filtered through "agencies, and bureaus, and technicians" tend to be "ideas of a certain kind and of a certain simplicity: they give up something of their largeness and modulation and complexity."[13] Faced with an American intellectual class that had grown complacent and predictable, Trilling sought to recall that class to its lost sense of "contingency and possibility" by confronting managerial liberalism with an essentially conservative literary tradition.[14] In figuring literature in this way, Trilling shaped midcentury debates about the relative importance of literature and the social sciences within the American intelligentsia and, more broadly, within the welfare state.[15] He juxtaposed the fluidity and complexity of literature against the rationalistic rigidity of the social sciences, which he believed had captured and degraded the imagination of America's educated middle classes. *National Review* conservatives, similarly, viewed literature as the right's greatest asset in its war with liberalism. As Bryan Santin argues, they "identified the 'great' works of Western literature in general, and American literature in particular, as *de facto* conservative in their depth, complexity and tragic profundity."[16]

---

[10] Ibid., 6.
[11] Jay Alfred Nock, *Memoirs of a Superfluous Man* (New York: Harper & Brothers, 1943).
[12] Buckley, "Publisher's Statement," 6.   [13] Trilling, xx.   [14] Ibid., xxi.
[15] For more on Trilling's impact on midcentury debates about the relative importance of literary studies and the social sciences, see Stephen Schryer, *Fantasies of the New Class: Ideologies of Professionalism in Post-World War II American Fiction* (New York: Columbia University Press, 2011), 1–27.
[16] Santin, 5.

At the same time, conservatives also embraced political populism, speaking on behalf of the American masses, whom they viewed as essentially conservative. This populism was central to the work of political scientist Willmoore Kendall, Buckley's mentor at Yale University. Kendall argued that "the survival of societies depended on the existence of a 'public orthodoxy' to which the members adhered and to which the majority would brook no exceptions."[17] This majoritarianism was central to conservatives' anti-communism, shaping their response to Senator Joseph McCarthy, whom Buckley viewed as the voice of public orthodoxy at odds with the liberal elite. More broadly, Kendall's majoritarianism informed conservatives' sense of alienation from an intellectual class to which they belonged by virtue of their education. Whittaker Chambers voiced this sense of alienation in *Witness*, his memoir of his experiences as a Soviet spy. New Dealer Alger Hiss's trial for committing perjury, Chambers writes, revealed "the jagged fissure ... between the plain men and women of the nation and those who affected to act, think and speak for them."[18] In Chambers's account, America's intellectuals are the deracinated inheritors of the Enlightenment; everyday Americans, in contrast, still hold on to the Christian faith that is essential to America's struggle against international communism. Chambers, although educated at Columbia University alongside Trilling, saw himself as one with the plain folk. As Chambers delivered his testimony against Hiss, he spoke on behalf of "my people, humble people, strong in common sense, in common goodness, in common forgiveness, because all felt bowed together under the common weight of life."[19]

Conservatives thus positioned themselves above and below a dominant liberal intelligentsia; they sought to challenge that elite with wisdom that was embedded within a literary tradition that liberals could not understand and within common folkways that liberals condescended to and ignored. The paradoxes of this divided positioning are especially evident in Buckley's *God and Man at Yale*, the Rosetta Stone of the postwar conservative movement. As Nathan Robinson observes, the book invented "the whole 'colleges are being ruined by relativists' genre," which would flourish in the 1980s and 1990s with texts including Allan Bloom's *The Closing of the American Mind* (1987) and Dinesh D'Souza's *Illiberal Education*

---

[17] John B. Judis, *William F. Buckley, Jr.: Patron Saint of the Conservatives* (New York: Simon & Schuster, 1988), 29.
[18] Whittaker Chambers, *Witness* (Washington, DC: Regnery History, 2014 [1952]), 701.
[19] Ibid., 702.

(1991).[20] Buckley takes the reader on a tour of his alma mater's course calendar, demonstrating that the majority of Yale faculty "seek to subvert religion and individualism."[21] This subversion takes place under the cover of an official doctrine of academic freedom; faculty imagine that they are fashioning a "free and open contest" in which "truth will be victorious and error defeated over the long run."[22] Buckley objects to this doctrine on two grounds. First, it is relativist, locating truth in the give and take of academic exchange. Echoing traditionalists like Kirk, Buckley argues that "conservatism is the tacit acknowledgment that all that is finally important in human experience is behind us."[23] Second, the doctrine of academic freedom doesn't correspond to liberal practice in the classroom; it acts as a cover for liberal indoctrination. Every university, Buckley insists, subscribes to an orthodoxy; the problem with Yale faculty is that they are disseminating the wrong one: liberal ideas instead of conservative ones. Buckley calls for Yale's president to discipline the faculty, firing the liberals before they succeed in creating a generation of atheist collectivists.

God and Man at Yale prefigures the synthesis of traditionalism, libertarianism, and anti-communism that would be central to *National Review*; it champions Christianity and free-market capitalism, without acknowledging any contradiction between the two. It also weaves together conservatism's elitist and populist impulses. On one level, Buckley indicts Yale faculty for their vulgar scientism, for their trust in short-term methodological processes for generating truth. For liberals, "method is king – because things are 'real' only in proportion as they are discoverable by the scientific method."[24] He instead appeals to the longer test of tradition and history, recalling faculty to an older, humanistic model of scholarship that preserves and disseminates received wisdom. On another level, Buckley accuses faculty of arrogantly ignoring the prejudices of the community they serve. He argues that it is not the faculty but the president and trustees who should decide the orthodoxy that governs pedagogy at Yale. These figures represent the institution's customers: the parents who pay to send their children to Yale and the alumni who were taught there and expect the institution to reflect their values. Buckley thus gives Kendall's

[20] Nathan Robinson, "How to Be a Respectable Public Intellectual," *Current Affairs*, September 10, 2020, www.currentaffairs.org/2020/09/how-to-be-a-respectable-public-intellectual
[21] William F. Buckley, Jr., *God and Man at Yale: The Superstitions of "Academic Freedom"* (Chicago: Henry Regnery, 1951), xiii.
[22] Ibid., 143.
[23] William F. Buckley, Jr., *Up from Liberalism* (New York: Stein and Day, 1984 [1959]), 182.
[24] Ibid., 144.

majoritarianism a curiously economic, libertarian twist. "Every citizen in a free economy," he argues, "no matter the wares that he plies, must defer to the sovereignty of the consumer."[25] Academic liberalism is a case of an intellectual minority forcing its products on an unwilling public. In insisting on conservative orthodoxy, "the educational overseer – the father who sends his son to school, or the trustee who directs the policy of the school" – is not violating academic freedom. Rather, he is "asserting his own freedom," just as he does when buying shoes or planning a new factory.[26] Buckley at one and the same time grounds his two pedagogical principles (Christianity and individualism) in the long test of tradition and the short test of consumer satisfaction. He argues that academic disciplines should become closed to their institutional outsides (they should disseminate received truths, gleaned from the classics) and radically open to them (pedagogy should be determined by parents' and trustees' cultural mores).

God and Man at Yale develops an alternative conception of expertise: a pseudo-expertise cultivated on the margins of the academy that is not subject to the same procedures of verification as disciplinary knowledge. Unlike liberal pedagogy, conservative teaching will be rooted in eternal verities. Unlike liberal teachers, conservatives will not pretend that they are engaged in a disinterested pursuit of the truth. Conservatives will own their prejudices, presenting them as a cultural inheritance that students must appreciate and defend. This anti-institutional, outsider pose has proven remarkably durable for conservatives. Writing in 2003, Ann Coulter assails liberal intellectuals using a rhetoric virtually identical to Buckley's in the 1950s: "They have the media, the universities, the textbooks. We have ourselves."[27] In launching *National Review*, Buckley and his fellow editors were self-conscious that they were waging war on an interlocking set of epistemic communities that they considered hostile to conservatives. An epistemic community, in Peter Haas's terms, is "a network of professionals with recognized expertise and competence in a particular domain." In order to function, these communities must be made up of individuals with "shared notions of validity – that is, intersubjective, internally defined criteria for weighing and validating knowledge."[28] As Jonathan Rauch observes, these communities together determine what counts as reality; they fashion a "constitution of knowledge" with "its

---

[25] Buckley, *God and Man at Yale*, 185.   [26] Ibid., 184.
[27] Ann Coulter, *Treason: Liberal Treachery from the Cold War to the War on Terrorism* (New York: Crown Forum, 2003), 17.
[28] Peter M. Haas, "Introduction: Epistemic Communities and International Policy Coordination," *International Organization* 46.1 (1992): 1–35, here 3.

own equivalents of checks and balances (peer review and replication), separation of powers (specialization), governing institutions (scientific societies and professional bodies), voting (citations and confirmations), and civic virtues (submit your beliefs for checking if you want to be taken seriously)."[29] In attacking not just the specific ideas tested by epistemic communities, but the very process of testing as such, *National Review* conservatives helped usher in a new epistemic reality: a fragmented one, in which truth is decided by power struggles between competing groups. In spite of their allergy to relativism – or, rather, because they conceived of truth achieved through methodological testing as relativistic – movement conservatives introduced postmodern relativism to American politics. In Kevin Mattson's terms, they "raised questions about unified or objective interpretations of reality and pioneered an intellectual style we now label postmodernism – a worldview that embraces multiple viewpoints versus overarching claims to absolute truths."[30]

Conservatives' strategies for responding to this changed epistemic reality were both compelling and ultimately repellant for many of the literary intellectuals who wrote for *National Review* in the 1950s and 1960s. From the very beginning, the magazine laid claim to one prominent novelist: John Dos Passos, who had migrated from the fellow-traveling left to the anti-communist right between the 1930s and 1950s. The magazine also attracted a cohort of young writers near the beginning of their careers: modernist critic Hugh Kenner, best known for his magisterial study *The Pound Era* (1971); novelist and literary journalist Joan Didion, arguably the most famous *National Review* alumnus; historian and journalist Garry Wills, best known for *Nixon Agonistes* (1970); and modernist critic and fiction writer Guy Davenport, who would reinvent the short story in collections such as *Tatlin!* (1974) and *Da Vinci's Bicycle* (1979). These writers perceived *National Review* as a venue for literary criticism that challenged the liberal dogmas that governed the academy and publishing industry. "NR is the kulchural New Frontier," Kenner wrote to Davenport

---

[29] Jonathan Rauch, "The Constitution of Knowledge," *National Affairs* 45 (2018), www.nationalaffairs.com/publications/detail/the-constitution-of-knowledge

[30] Mattson, 63. Mattson argues that postmodern conservatism culminates in contemporary Christian conservative arguments for Intelligent Design, which proponents present as an alternative paradigm that should be offered to students. Christopher Douglas also remarks on this congruence: "Intelligent Design – and its historical and theological ancestor, creation science – are postmodern forms of science comprehensible in the terms developed by Jean-François Lyotard" (208).

in 1961.[31] In his role as the magazine's poetry editor, Kenner published work by modernist writers including Ezra Pound, Louis Zukofsky, William Carlos Williams, and Robert Creeley, sometimes to the bewilderment of the magazine's readers.[32] Book reviews editor Frank Meyer did not, for the most part, censor his writers. As Jeffrey Hart remarks, Meyer wanted to turn "*National Review* into a place for young writers to appear," and he accomplished this by "welcoming a great variety of talents," including "writers with whom he might disagree."[33] As a result, the book reviews section exhibited an exceptional catholicity of opinion; Joan Didion, for instance, favorably reviewed Norman Mailer, whom *National Review* had previously criticized as America's most notorious literary radical.[34]

This literary circle, however, did not last long. Didion stopped writing for *National Review* in 1965. Wills broke with conservatism in the late 1960s due to his growing sympathy with Civil Rights activists and Vietnam War protestors. Davenport stopped contributing regularly in 1973. Only Kenner continued to publish in the magazine throughout the late 1970s and 1980s, and even his contributions tapered off after a 1969 conflict with Meyer and Hart. The writers who replaced this first cohort in the 1970s, like the novelist and self-styled Christian pornographer D. Keith Mano, were often lesser-known figures who never achieved the national and international reputation of their predecessors. Many, like David Brudnoy, Joseph Sobran, and Terry Teachout, made their mark as conservative editorialists or Republican speechwriters.[35] By the 1970s, *National Review* alumni were commenting on the magazine's literary decline. "NR grows utterly unreadable," Kenner complained to Davenport in 1970. "I did well to leap off when I did."[36] This flight of writers from *National Review* reflected a more general trend in American letters. After 1970, the political center of the literary field shifted decisively to the left. The American right still claimed some writers, such as

[31] Guy Davenport and Hugh Kenner, *Questioning Minds: The Letters of Guy Davenport and Hugh Kenner*, ed. Edward M. Burns (Berkeley: Counterpoint, 2018), 31.
[32] For more on Hugh Kenner's association with *National Review*, see Stephen Schryer, "Conservative Circuits: Hugh Kenner, Modernism, and *National Review*," *Modernism/modernity* 26.3 (2019): 505–20.
[33] Jeffrey Hart, *The Making of the American Conservative Mind: National Review and Its Times* (Wilmington, DE: ISI Books, 2014), 233.
[34] Joan Didion, "A Social Eye," *National Review* 17.16 (1965): 329–30.
[35] There were exceptions to this downward trend in the literary prestige of *National Review*'s contributors. Poet Donald Hall, historical novelist Thomas Mallon, and literary biographer Jeffrey Meyers all contributed to the magazine in the 1970s and 1980s.
[36] Davenport and Kenner, 1316.

Saul Bellow, Tom Wolfe, and Mark Helprin; however, the majority of novelists and poets identified as liberals or leftists. As the New Critics and their students grew older and began to retire from the academy, the same could be said for literary critics. Conservative critics allied with *National Review* continued to lay claim to the literary tradition, chastising English professors for abandoning the canon during the culture wars of the 1980s and 1990s. However, they no longer saw their ideals reflected in contemporary American literature.

Santin discusses some of the reasons for this leftward shift of the political field, arguing that it was a response to the conservatives' abandonment of their earlier veneration of literary complexity. Conservatives, he writes, "found it increasingly difficult to position themselves simultaneously as the disinterested champions of complex, morally ambivalent literature *and* as the populist defenders of aggrieved white innocence, laissez-faire capitalism, and aggressive American nationalism."[37] The magazine's synthesis of elitism and populism came under increasing strain. Many key members of *National Review*'s literary coterie became aware of this unraveling after the Goldwater campaign. Most of the magazine's writers supported Goldwater; Kenner and Wills wrote essays endorsing his candidacy, and Didion later reflected that she "voted, ardently, for Barry Goldwater."[38] However, all three writers glossed over Goldwater's populism, instead trying to recast him as an elitist figure in their own mold. Kenner predicted that a Goldwater win would rewire the academic "communications network," activating "standby circuits" occupied by conservative thinkers.[39] Other conservatives offered similar assessments of the senator: "Goldwater," Russell Kirk wrote to Buckley, "is the only politician of note who has real respect for ideas and people with ideas."[40] Within a few years, however, the anti-intellectual trend of the conservative movement became evident to Kenner, Didion, and Wills; to varying degrees, they expressed dismay at the populist rhetoric that Ronald Reagan, Goldwater's political heir, used to win the governorship of California. As a professor in the University of California system, Kenner gained a vivid glimpse into the real-world impact of Buckley's demand in *God and Man at Yale* that pedagogy be subordinated to the market. Kenner chafed

---

[37] Santin, 7.   [38] Joan Didion, *Political Fictions* (New York: Vintage, 2001), 7.
[39] Hugh Kenner, "A View of a Goldwater Administration from the Academy," *National Review* 16.28 (1964): 597–9, here 597.
[40] Russell Kirk, *Imaginative Conservatism: The Letters of Russell Kirk*, ed. James E. Person, Jr. (Lexington: University Press of Kentucky, 2018), 99.

especially at Reagan's insistence that the state of California "has no business 'subsidizing intellectual curiosity.'"[41]

Garry Wills's defection from the conservative movement is especially telling, since it was a direct response to conservatives' twinned elitism/ populism on the subject of Black Civil Rights. The conservative anti-Civil Rights argument of the late 1950s and early 1960s hinged on an elitist defense of what Buckley called the "claims of civilization." The white Southern community, Buckley argued, "is entitled to take such measures as are necessary to prevail, politically and culturally ... because, for the time being, it is the advanced race."[42] This elitist position informed Garry Wills's review of James Baldwin's *The Fire Next Time* (1963), one of the decade's most searching explorations of Civil Rights politics. Wills chastised liberals' adulatory response to the book, claiming that they failed to take seriously Baldwin's apocalyptic indictment of Western civilization. Baldwin's message is that everything that "our religion, our civilization, our country stand for" is "an elaborate lie, a lie whose sole and original function is to fortify privilege."[43] Acknowledging the existence of racial injustice, Wills nevertheless argues that the American, Christian civilization offers white and Black Americans the best framework for working out their differences. Wills spelled out the political implications of this position in his subsequent endorsement of Goldwater, arguing that the senator, who voted against the 1964 Civil Rights Act, was the presidential candidate best capable of resolving the nation's racial conflicts. If elected president, Wills enthuses, Goldwater would lend his "pervasive influence to voluntary programs" aimed at promoting integration "in the heart." At the same time, he would enforce the nation's laws, establishing a clear framework within which racial conflict could play out without destroying society. Against those who would tear down American civilization, Goldwater "leads a new kind of 'rebellion' from within meant to *man* the walls with new confidence."[44] Wills cast Goldwater's candidacy as analogous to his critique of Baldwin; Wills and Goldwater were defending the claims of civilization against its anarchic challengers.

[41] Hugh Kenner, "A Nervous View of Ronald Reagan," *National Review* 20.18 (1968): 444–6, here 444. For more on Kenner and Didion's responses to Goldwater and Reagan, see Stephen Schryer, "Writers for Goldwater," *Post45* 4 (2020), https://post45.org/2020/01/writers-for-goldwater/

[42] William F. Buckley, Jr., "Why the South Must Prevail," *National Review* 4.7 (1957): 149. Buckley did not sign this essay but later admitted that he was its author. See Nicholas Buccola, *The Fire Is Upon Us: James Baldwin, William F. Buckley, Jr., and the Debate over Race in America* (Princeton, NJ: Princeton University Press, 2019), 96.

[43] Garry Wills, "What Color Is God?," *National Review* 14.20 (1963): 408–17, here 416.

[44] Garry Wills, "Who Will Overcome?," *National Review* 16.38 (1964): 819–20.

This critique of Baldwin and assessment of Goldwater downplayed the other side of the conservative response to Civil Rights: conservatives' willingness to excuse or defend vigilante terror tactics. Writing about white mob attacks on Freedom Riders in 1961, Buckley described the violence as a "spastic response" by a people whose "way of life" had been threatened.[45] In his Goldwater essay, Wills similarly uses a grotesque metaphor that trivializes racial violence; he writes of Black and white Americans whom, "like the little boys in a strange playground, we must fight before we become friends."[46] This erasure of white terror increasingly troubled Wills, eroding his traditionalism. In the fall of 1967, Wills traveled the country, speaking to Civil Rights activists, police officers, and manufacturers of riot gear. The result was *The Second Civil War*, his first mature work of literary journalism and the book that convinced Buckley that Wills "had 'gone over to the militants.'"[47] Wills rejects his earlier assumption that there is a singular, color-blind American civilization, insisting that "I am white, that 'we' are white, that 'our' country is."[48] He instead echoes Baldwin's assertion that the American tradition is built on white privilege and arrives at an even more pessimistic conclusion about how to expunge it. Baldwin ends *The Fire Next Time* with a plea for love, understood as a mutual commitment by white and Blacks to challenge each other's delusions. Wills, in contrast, spends much of *The Second Civil War* exploring the efforts of arms' manufacturers to develop nonlethal crowd control techniques such as pepper spray. His hope is that riot violence can be pacified to the extent that Black protestors survive their confrontations with white police. Otherwise, he fears that America will massacre its racial minorities and, in the process, render its national legacy indefensible.

For Wills, as for Kenner and Didion, the post-Goldwater era exposed contradictions that had always been latent in movement conservatism's brand of anti-intellectual intellectualism. Conservatives' attempt to position themselves as dissident outsiders on the margins of the intelligentsia at first appealed to these writers; in Pierre Bourdieu's terms, it offered them a risky but potentially lucrative strategy for achieving distinction in the literary field. Ultimately, however, the magazine's attempt to promote conservative forms of counter-expertise threatened their existence as literary intellectuals. Wills recognized this threat when he began writing for

[45] William F. Buckley, Jr., "Let Us Try, at Least, to Understand," *National Review* 10.21 (1961): 338.
[46] Wills, "Who Will Overcome?," 818.
[47] Garry Wills, *Confessions of a Conservative* (New York: Doubleday, 1979), 76.
[48] Garry Wills, *The Second Civil War: Arming for Armageddon* (New York: Signet, 1968), 12.

Esquire and had to refashion himself as a literary journalist. *National Review*, he later commented, was the "wrong place for learning how to be a journalist." The magazine "lived on little nutriment of fact," instead fashioning its contributors into "ideologues."[49] Only by leaving the magazine could Wills test his traditionalist certitudes against the uncomfortable facts of American experience. More broadly, literary intellectuals' flight from conservatism was a symptom of the postwar consolidation of a new class: a professional and managerial elite, defined by its possession of cultural capital, and increasingly associated with urban centers. Much of what we today identify as left-wing thinking is, for better or for worse, the ideology of this class. Writers' rejection of an emerging right that questioned the value of expertise was an act of self-preservation.

---

[49] Wills, *Confessions of a Conservative*, 13.

CHAPTER 3

Neoliberalism

Mitchum Huehls

Depending on how you conceive the economy and its relationship to culture, "the neoliberal novel" names either no, some, or all contemporary novels. If you think, for example, that "neoliberalism" is an apt name for the dominant economic order that has reigned in the United States since the Nixon Shock of 1971, and if you think that cultural production largely mediates contemporaneous economic conditions, then it's appropriate to describe all novels published in the United States since the 1970s as neoliberal novels. Of course, such an approach renders the concept virtually meaningless and neglects the variety and variability of the novel over the past half-century. It also fails to account for: the fact that neoliberalism is not just an economic phenomenon but is also, depending on which theorists one subscribes to, a political ideology, a mode of governance, a rationality, a social order, and/or a way of being; the fact that the cultural mediation of material economic conditions is, as Raymond Williams taught, an ongoing, disjointed, uneven, and frequently circular affair; and the fact that there are other features and facets of the contemporary economy – globalization, technology, finance, inequality, debt, and precarity – that are related to neoliberalism but are not necessarily isomorphic to it. In other words, it's complicated.

Consequently, my goal here is not to develop a stable definition of the neoliberal novel that will in turn allow us to determine which novels are neoliberal and which are not. Because those kinds of determinations depend on your understanding of neoliberalism and its mediation of culture, that definitional approach yields only idiosyncratic frameworks that appeal to some but seem wrongheaded to others. Walter Benn Michaels, for example, defines the neoliberal novel as any novel that "make[s] the central problems of American society a matter of identity instead of a matter of money."[1] By this definition, key neoliberal novels

---

[1] Walter Benn Michaels, "Model Minorities and the Minority Model – the Neoliberal Novel," in *The Cambridge History of the American Novel* (Cambridge: Cambridge University Press, 2011), 1023.

would include Gayl Jones's *Corregidora* (1975), Alice Walker's *The Color Purple* (1982), Toni Morrison's *Beloved* (1987), Chang-rae Lee's *Native Speaker* (1995), Colson Whitehead's *The Intuitionist* (1999), Michael Chabon's *Yiddish Policeman's Union* (2007), Chimamanda Adichie's *Americana* (2013), and Yaa Gyasi's *Homegoing* (2016). This might seem counterintuitive – neoliberal novels are those texts that aren't in any way about neoliberalism – but for Michaels that's precisely the point. These novels are paradigmatically neoliberal because their emphasis on cultural difference obscures the more pressing problem of economic inequality. Consequently, these texts work on behalf of neoliberal capital, effectively facilitating and normalizing gross economic inequality by not talking about it.

Michaels's provocative take on the neoliberal novel, however, seems perfectly wrongheaded to Jeffrey Williams, who suggests that what Michaels calls a neoliberal novel should in fact be called a "diversity" or "multicultural" novel and that "neoliberal" novel should instead name those texts that "depict the inside of plutocracy, or the consequences of plutocratic policies," by "focus[ing] on class and the force of political economy."[2] Williams's representational approach (neoliberal novels are those novels that represent the neoliberal economy and its participants) leads him to divide the category into those texts that "put the CEO class center stage" and those that focus "instead on the white-collar workers who carry out the global work of the super-rich." The former camp would include Tom Wolfe's *Bonfire of the Vanities* (1987), Brett Easton Ellis's *American Psycho* (1991), Don DeLillo's *Cosmopolis* (2003), Teddy Wayne's *Kapitoil* (2010), and Christina Alger's *The Darlings* (2012). The latter group includes Benjamin Kunkel's *Indecision* (2005), Ed Park's *Personal Days* (2008), David Foster Wallace's *The Pale King* (2011), Colson Whitehead's *Zone One* (2011), Dave Eggers's *A Hologram for the King* (2012), Nathaniel Rich's *Odds Against Tomorrow* (2013), Ling Ma's *Severance* (2018), and Emily Leichter's *Temporary* (2020). To these two categories I would add a third: novels that aren't necessarily about CEOs or white-collar workers but that nevertheless explicitly situate the neoliberal economy as a constitutive force in contemporary life. Here, for example, I'm thinking of David Foster Wallace's *Infinite Jest* (1996), Karen Yamashita's *Tropic of Orange* (1997), Jonathan Franzen's *The Corrections* (2001) and *Freedom* (2010), Jess Walter's *The Financial Lives*

---

[2] Jeffrey Williams "The Plutocratic Imagination," *Dissent* (Winter 2013).

of the Poets (2009), Rachel Kushner's *The Flamethrowers* (2013), and Ben Lerner's *10:04* (2014) and *The Topeka School* (2019).

In lieu of these definitional accounts, I recommend a more heuristic approach that asks not which novels are neoliberal and why, but rather how the concept of neoliberalism, in all its multifarious variety, can help us think about the contemporary US novel. Scholarship more in line with this approach includes those studies that use neoliberalism as a conceptual tool to examine key formal and generic developments in the contemporary novel. Williams gestures in this direction, for instance, when he distinguishes the neoliberal novel from earlier examples of politically engaged fiction by noting a conspicuous shift "from moral allegory to a resigned realism." Although they prefer the term "capitalist realism" to "neoliberal novel," Alison Shonkwiler and Leigh Claire La Berge pursue this line of thought when they contend that capitalism's increasingly totalized grasp on everyday life and culture explains contemporary fiction's pivot toward more realist literary modes at the expense of postmodern experimentation.[3] For Andy Hoberek, that totalization also helps us understand the contemporary novel's renewed commitment to genre fiction (e.g., Cormac McCarthy's Westerns, Gillian Flynn's suspense thrillers, Kim Stanley Robinson's science fiction, McCarthy's, Whitehead's, and Emily St. John Mandel's post-apocalyptic fiction, and Junot Diaz's, Jonathan Lethem's, and Michael Chabon's embrace of comics). Despite its pre-scripted conventions, the *unrealities* of genre fiction provide authors with a conceptual terrain not entirely absorbed into capitalist realism. In their attempt to think otherwise, Hoberek contends, many authors make themselves at home among the fixities and formulas of genre.[4] Neoliberalism's concepts, ideologies, and values have also been foregrounded to explicate other formal trends in contemporary fiction. Rachel Greenwald Smith, for example, observes a shift from earlier twentieth-century novels that "pit the autonomous individual against a monolithic society" toward more recent works that "are increasingly concerned with communities and groups." Far from offering a collective vision hostile to neoliberal individualism, however, Smith argues that this new form of characterization values "connection with others" only as a means for the ultimate "growth and

---

[3] Alison Shonkwiler and Leigh Claire La Berge, *Reading Capitalist Realism* (Iowa City: University of Iowa Press, 2014), 15.

[4] Andrew Hoberek, "Cormac McCarthy and the Aesthetics of Exhaustion," *American Literary History* 23.3 (2011): 483–99.

enrichment of the self."[5] Similarly, Stephanie Lambert uses the cultural logics of neoliberalism to critique the formal aesthetics associated with the post–Cold War rise of the New Sincerity, a literary movement typically associated with David Foster Wallace, Jonathan Franzen, and Dave Eggers.[6] And Arne De Boever uses the neoliberal commodification of subjectivity as a critical lens for understanding the recent proliferation of autofiction from authors such as Chris Kraus, Sheila Heti, Ben Lerner, Teju Cole, Maggie Nelson, Valeria Luiselli, and Ocean Vuong.[7]

Before laying out my own heuristic approach, some historical context and clarity on the what, when, where, how, and why of neoliberalism should prove helpful.[8] Neoliberalism's foundational concepts grow out of a profound post–World War II fear of socialism and the perceived threat it posed to Western liberal democracy. In 1947, to confront that threat, F. A. Hayek, a British-Austrian economist, founded the Mont Pelerin Society, a collection of European and US economists, philosophers, and historians committed to promoting market-driven economics while battling the spread of social welfare programs, labor unions, and other collectivizing forces that were anathema to the classical liberal tradition. Although the values of these early neoliberals are thoroughly anti-statist, neoliberals have historically embraced state regulation and intervention when deployed in the service of the market. Their foundational commitments are to individualism, liberty, and market rationality, and if the state can promote those values by, say, bailing out the banking industry, then neoliberals view such state action as perfectly aligned with their broader goals.

But how did these theoretical ideas, developed among midcentury European and American intellectuals, become lived economic and social reality for so many global citizens by the beginning of the twenty-first century? For starters, the Mont Pelerin intellectuals populated university economics departments (Stanford, Princeton, Brown, and most notably Chicago were all hotbeds of neoliberal economic thought), think tanks (the Institute of Economic Affairs, the Reason Foundation, the American

---

[5] Rachel Greenwald Smith, *Affect and American Literature in the Age of Neoliberalism* (Cambridge: Cambridge University Press, 2015), 41–2.

[6] Stephanie Lambert, "'The Real Dark Side, Baby': New Sincerity and Neoliberal Aesthetics in David Foster Wallace and Jennifer Egan," *Critique: Studies in Contemporary Fiction* 61.4 (2020): 1–18.

[7] Arne De Boever, "What Is 'the' Neoliberal Novel? Neoliberalism, Finance, Biopolitics," in *New Approaches to the Twenty-First-Century Anglophone Novel*, ed. Sibylle Baumbach and Birgit Neumann (Cham: Palgrave, 2019), 157–74.

[8] Neoliberalism is a global phenomenon, emerging in different ways and for different reasons in various parts of the world. However, because this collection treats US literature, the ensuing narrative focuses primarily on the economic, political, and social history of the United States.

Enterprise Institute, the Cato Institute, the Mises Institute, and the Heritage Foundation all have Mont Pelerin pedigrees or connections), journalism (Henry Hazlitt and William Buckley, Jr. were both Mont Pelerin members), and the government (in the United States, for example, Arthur Burnes served on President Eisenhower's Council of Economic Advisers, was Counselor to President Nixon, and chaired the Federal Reserve from 1970 to 1978; George Schultz served as Nixon's Labor Secretary, Office of Budget Management Director, and Treasury Secretary, and was later named Reagan's Secretary of State; and Alan Greenspan, a close acolyte and friend of Ayn Rand, served on President Ford's Council of Economic Advisers and chaired the Federal Reserve from 1987 to 2006 – and all were members of the Mont Pelerin Society).

Men with ideas in positions of institutional authority still require material justification for deploying those ideas as policy, and that material justification is precisely what the economic crises of the 1970s provided. With the postwar economic boom fading and inflation running high, Nixon signed the Economic Stabilization Act of 1970, a remarkably non-neoliberal set of reforms granting the government control over wages, interest rates, and the price of consumer goods. In 1971, to further combat inflation and curtail speculative currency manipulation, Nixon withdrew the United States from the postwar Bretton Woods monetary agreement that had governed international currency exchange for more than two decades. That agreement had established the gold-backed dollar as the international reserve currency, but the so-called Nixon Shock in August 1971 cancelled the dollar's gold convertibility, creating the freely floating currency rates we still have today. At the time, detethering the dollar from gold was understood as a regulatory action, accompanied as it was with increased price and wage controls and a ten percent import tariff. (Just six months earlier, the *New York Times* reported that Nixon had declared himself "a Keynesian in economics."[9]) The effect, however, was quite the opposite, as floating currency rates opened the door to international finance and the globalization of capital, which in turn accelerated dein-dustrialization and economic inequality in the United States and abroad.[10] In 1974, when Nixon's Keynesian price controls expired, the country had just lived through the 1973 oil crisis and was at the nadir of an economic recession marked by stagflation (high unemployment combined with

[9] "Nixon Reportedly Says He Is Now a Keynesian," *New York Times*, January 7, 1971, 19.
[10] See Youn Ki and Yongwoo Jeung, "Ideas, Interests, and the Transition to a Floating Exchange System," *Journal of Policy History* 32.2 (2020): 151–82.

inflation). In line with the ultimately deregulatory Nixon Shock that shifted capital control from the state to global corporations and financial institutions, economic recovery under Presidents Ford (1974–6) and Carter (1976–80) embraced the deregulatory market-based solutions promulgated by neoliberal intellectuals. The deregulation of major US industries initiated under Ford and Carter was pursued with even more vigor in the Reaganite 1980s and continued apace in the 1990s with the Telecommunications Act of 1996 and the Financial Services Modernization Act of 1999 (the deregulatory move that made the 2007–8 financial crisis possible). Beginning in 1979, when Carter appointed Paul Volcker to chair the Federal Reserve, these deregulatory policies were accompanied by anti-Keynesian monetary policies that promoted capital accumulation at the expense of labor and employment. The neoliberal monetarism that Volcker instituted at the Federal Reserve would endure until Alan Greenspan retired as Fed chairman in 2006.

In the introduction to *Neoliberalism and Contemporary Literary Culture*, Rachel Greenwald Smith and I describe the realization of neoliberal thought via deregulatory and monetarist economic policy as the "economic phase" of neoliberalism. In an effort to appreciate the varied valences and modalities of neoliberalism, and to provide a heuristic framework for thinking about the relationship between neoliberalism and literature, we identify three other phases: the political, sociocultural, and ontological. Although there is a historical component to these phases, with different facets and features of neoliberalism gaining prominence at different moments in time, we do not intend them to describe a strictly linear, teleological narrative. Instead, these four phases are mutually imbricated and constantly informing each other even as they crystallize and become more dominant at distinct historical moments.[11]

Thus, the economic phase schematized above always intersects with politics, but neoliberalism's distinctly conservative political valence grows much more pronounced under Ronald Reagan in the 1980s. Think, for instance, of the tax-cutting Economics Recovery Tax Act of 1981, dubbed "Reaganomics," a "supply-side," "trickle-down" economic model that ends

---

[11] We probably should have explained this better in "Four Phases of Neoliberalism and Literature," *Neoliberalism and Contemporary Literary Culture*, ed. Mitchum Huehls and Rachel Greenwald Smith (Baltimore: Johns Hopkins University Press, 2017). Although we wanted to capture an overlapping phase relation that is both historical and simultaneous, our critics have taken issue with what they read as an overly teleological model. See, for example, Bruce Robbins, "Everything Is Not Neoliberalism," *American Literary History* 31.4 (2019): 840–9; Sharae Deckard and Stephen Shapiro, *World Literature, Neoliberalism, and the Culture of Discontent* (Cham: Palgrave, 2019).

up codified as Republican Party doctrine for decades. The Republican Party platform of 1980 explicitly grounds its political vision in "a bold program of tax rate reductions, spending restraints, and regulatory reforms," but, before Reagan, the alignment between economics and politics wasn't so clear.[12] Nixon was a Keynesian; Carter a champion of deregulation and privatization. Free-market economics, in other words, weren't always linked with conservative politics the way they have been since Reagan (Donald Trump notwithstanding).[13] That link was further reinforced through the Reagan administration's anti-communism and Christian morality (James Dobson started Focus on the Family in 1977 and Jerry Falwell cofounded the Moral Majority in 1979). Neoliberal Reaganomics, in other words, was just one key component of a politically conservative, anti-statist worldview that championed individuality, liberty, and so-called family values as a bulwark against the amoral Soviets. Reagan, in effect, deployed neoliberalism not just as economic policy but as political ideology.

After the West won the Cold War, neoliberalism maintained its political-ideological function, but, no longer threatened by communism, it need not be deployed so overtly. Instead of neoliberalism defining *our* way of life, always under threat from the Soviets, it gradually became the only way of life – life itself. This is what Francis Fukuyama meant, of course, when he suggested in 1989 that "worldwide ideological struggle . . . [would] be replaced by economic calculation, the endless solving of technical problems, environmental concerns, and the satisfaction of sophisticated consumer demands,"[14] and it's what Smith and I have in mind when we talk about neoliberalism's sociocultural phase. Wendy Brown's influential definition of neoliberalism as a "rationality" that "disseminates the *model of the market* to all domains and activities – even where money is not at issue" also provides an apt characterization of this particular function of neoliberalism.[15] Here we find not just the rampant commercialization and commodification of everyday social and cultural formations, but also the subjection of governmental policies and goals

---

[12] "Republican Party Platform of 1980," adopted July 15, 1980. Available at The American Presidency Project, www.presidency.ucsb.edu/documents/republican-party-platform-1980

[13] See Johanna Bockman, *Markets in the Name of Socialism: The Left-Wing Origins of Neoliberalism* (Stanford: Stanford University Press, 2011).

[14] Francis Fukuyama, "The End of History?," in *Globalization and the Challenges of a New Century: A Reader*, ed. Patrick O'Meara et al. (Bloomington: Indiana University Press, 2000), 178.

[15] Wendy Brown, *Undoing the Demos: Neoliberalism's Stealth Revolution* (New York: Zone Books, 2015), 31.

(e.g., providing welfare services, reducing carbon emissions, reforming healthcare, curtailing drug abuse) to both the political ideology of individual responsibility and the bottom-line logic of economic rationality. This move is most pronounced in Bill Clinton's fiscally conservative "third way" policies and programs, which co-opted the free-market neoliberalism of Reagan Republicans, establishing it as the commonsense approach to governance for both the left and the right, as the tenures of both George H. W. Bush and Barack Obama showed.[16] In this way, neoliberal thought saturates both the mainstream right and left, enhancing the sense that it's increasingly difficult to find political, social, or cultural space outside it.

Finally, the idea that neoliberalism registers ontologically – in addition to its economic, political, and sociocultural registers – is intended to capture a certain intensification of that saturation. Neoliberalism isn't just an ideology, logic, discourse, or rationality that shapes the way we think and talk about the world; it's also a mode of being in the world that informs our affects, actions, and relations. For me, the rise of digital technology and social media is key for understanding the ontological function of neoliberalism. When Michel Foucault dubs the neoliberal subject *homo economicus*, his species thinking gestures in an ontological direction, but his concept is usually deployed to describe an entrepreneurial subject who views her life choices through the lens of economic rationality. I would argue, however, that neoliberalism's ontological effects supersede rational entrepreneurial calculation and instead, through the profit-driven algorithms of corporate social media technologies, become the basis for the feelings, desires, drives, and affections that define who we are and how we relate to others.[17] This idea is controversial because it seems to decenter neoliberalism's economic foundations, diverting our attention from the profound material immiseration neoliberalism has wreaked around the globe. But this four-phase heuristic model doesn't view these many facets of neoliberalism as mutually exclusive. Neoliberalism's technologically facilitated ontological influence doesn't mean that it stops being an economic, political, and sociocultural phenomenon as well. The point in identifying the various forms that neoliberalism takes isn't to provide the final, definitional word on neoliberalism

---

[16] See Nancy Fraser, "The End of Progressive Neoliberalism," *Dissent*, January 2, 2017, www
.dissentmagazine.org/online_articles/progressive-neoliberalism-reactionary-populism-nancy-fraser

[17] Although there is plenty of disagreement about how to interpret Foucault's work on neoliberalism,
I use his thinking to support this ontological conceptualization. For a greater elaboration, see
Mitchum Huehls, "A World Without Norms," *On Culture* 7 (Summer 2019), www.on-culture
.org/journal/issue-7/world-without-norms/

but rather to complicate it in a way that makes neoliberalism a heuristically useful concept for making sense of our contemporary world.

As I suggested above, one part of our world that it can help us think through is the contemporary literary field. To be sure, neoliberalism is not the only relevant conceptual lens, and it doesn't purport to explain everything that's happening in contemporary US literature, but it does provide a useful interpretive framework for drawing meaningful distinctions among a diverse body of novels that engage neoliberalism in various ways. In what follows I use this four-phase heuristic model of neoliberalism to briefly discuss three novels – Wolfe's *Bonfire of the Vanities*, Dana Spiotta's *Eat the Document* (2006), and Jennifer Egan's *A Visit from the Goon Squad* (2010) – that might all be understood as neoliberal novels, albeit in different ways and for different reasons.

When it comes to US fiction, the distinction between neoliberalism's economic and political phases doesn't register in a particularly pronounced way. Rather, the economic and the political are always already wrapped up together in early examples of the neoliberal novel, which, lagging a good decade behind the neoliberal economic changes of the 1970s, doesn't emerge until the 1980s. That's in large part because, with the exception of Thomas Pynchon's *Gravity's Rainbow* (1973), which locates the origins of corporate power in the post–World War II reorganization of the global order, and William Gaddis's *JR* (1975), which satirically anticipates the financialization of the US economy, the most influential and widely read US fiction from the 1970s was busy processing the sociocultural upheavals of the 1960s, not the economic shifts of the 1970s. By the 1980s, however, texts such as Jay McInerney's *Bright Lights, Big City* (1984), Wolfe's *Bonfire*, and Ellis's *American Psycho* bring corporate greed and consumerist materialism to the fore as readers encounter yuppies and rapacious Wall Street investors who have replaced the titans of industry as the nation's economic elite. (We might read William Gibson's *Neuromancer* [1984] as a dystopian, cyberpunk version of this narrative and Don DeLillo's *White Noise* [1985] as a Midwestern, middle-class take on the same set of concerns.) All these novels integrate their economic critiques of neoliberalism with intersecting political concerns. In *Neuromancer* and *White Noise*, for example, neoliberal consumerism and corporatism go hand in hand with anti-communist Cold War politics. In *Bright Lights*, it's the apparent apoliticality of the emerging yuppie class, and in *American Psycho* it's the personal-responsibility politics connected to homelessness and welfare.

I find *Bonfire* most interesting, however, because its downtown/uptown plot – split between Sherman McCoy, the "master of the universe" bonds

trader who manufactures wealth out of Manhattan's thin air, and Reverend
Bacon, the Harlem race leader who leverages political power out of
manufactured outrage – highlights the intersection between neoliberal
economics and racial politics. After McCoy and his socialite girlfriend hit
a young Black man, Henry Lamb, with their car while trying to flee the
Bronx's disorientating streets, they assume that they can return to their
Upper East Side fortress and act like nothing happened. Of course, they're
wrong, and as Reverend Bacon – along with a politically cynical district
attorney, his careerist assistant, and a tabloid journalist – begins to investigate the hit and run, Wolfe implicitly asks how we should understand the
relationship between McCoy's WASPy economic success and the marginalized minority populations in Harlem and the Bronx. The easy answer
would conceive that relationship as one of direct victimization. The rich
move through the world with privileged impunity while young Black men
lay injured in the street. That reading isn't entirely correct, however, as the
novel ends with McCoy handcuffed in court, arraigned for vehicular
manslaughter. But he's only there because it's the most expedient political
solution that reinforces the interests of a neoliberal order reinforced by the
police, the courts, the media, the financial industry, and even racial justice
politics. Neoliberalism, not justice, is being served.

   It's easy to understand how the legal system keeps the world safe for the
free flow of neoliberal capital and how the media, particularly the tabloid
newspaper industry, is forced to pursue profit over truth. But what is racial
justice politics doing on this list of institutions that succumb to the
neoliberal status quo? Wolfe makes the connection clear when he uses
the same economic language to describe McCoy's bonds trading as he does
to describe Reverend Bacon's Black political work. When McCoy's daughter asks him about his work as a bonds trader, he wants to explain how he
provides financing to build useful things like roads and hospitals, but
unable to point to any actual roads or hospitals that he's built, his wife
intervenes, encouraging their daughter to "imagine that a bond is a slice of
cake, and you didn't bake the cake, but every time you hand somebody a
slice of the cake a tiny little bit comes off, like a little crumb, and you can
keep that … If you pass around enough slices of cake, then pretty soon
you have enough crumbs to make a *gigantic* cake."[18] Similarly, when two
white men representing the Episcopal Diocese of New York ask Reverend
Bacon to account for the $350,000 that the diocese has invested to fund a
Harlem daycare center that Bacon never actually built, Bacon explains that

---

[18] Tom Wolfe, *The Bonfire of the Vanities* (New York: Picador, 1987), 236.

the diocese is naïve to imagine that their money will be used to build anything as tangible as a daycare center. Instead, Bacon explains, they are investing in "steam control" – that is, they are effectively paying Bacon to control the "*righteous* steam building up in the souls" of Harlem's Black residents, a steam that is "ready to blow" unless a race leader like Bacon is given the power, and the financing, to modulate and manipulate it. This investment in "the souls of the people," Bacon asserts, is "the capitalism of the future."[19]

Bacon's racial justice project nominally serves the people, but it more directly lines his pockets while protecting the interests of those white institutions willing to pay the price. Or, demonstrating the inextricability of neoliberalism's economic and political functions, Bacon's racial justice politics are ultimately deployed in the service of maintaining the neoliberal status quo. Crucially, as Lisa Duggan explains, there is no single form of racial politics that most closely aligns with neoliberal values. Instead,

> to facilitate the flow of money up the economic hierarchy, neoliberal politicians have constructed complex and shifting alliances, issue by issue and location by location – always in contexts shaped by the meanings and effects of race ... These alliances are not simply opportunistic, and the issues not merely epiphenomenal or secondary to the underlying reality of the more solid and real economic goals, but rather, the economic goals have been (must be) formulated in terms of the range of political and cultural meanings that shape the social body in a particular time and place.[20]

Given the mutual imbrication of the economic and the political, as Duggan describes it, it's no surprise that early neoliberal novels such as *Bonfire*, which aim to capture the economic zeitgeist of the 1980s, so frequently embed their vision of neoliberal economics in a broader analysis of neoliberalism's intrusion into and influence over the contemporary political terrain as well.

Maintaining Wolfe's interest in the mutually reinforcing relationship between neoliberal economics and politics, Dana Spiotta's *Eat the Document* layers in a heightened attention to neoliberalism's cultural effects, consistently framing the possibility of revolutionary politics (against Vietnam in the 1970s and against neoliberal capital in the 1990s) as an aesthetic matter of cultural form. In the 1970s, for example, the novel's protagonists, Mary and Bobby, debate the proper form of

---

[19] Ibid., 155.
[20] Lisa Duggan, *The Twilight of Equality? Neoliberalism, Cultural Politics, and the Attack on Democracy* (Boston, MA: Beacon, 2003), xvi.

revolutionary protest against the corporation that produces napalm. Mary
wants "tangible, unequivocal action"; she wants to plant bombs.[21] The
men who make napalm think nothing of the humanity of their victims, so
why should she think about theirs? But Bobby isn't so sure. Instead, he
makes protest films that function as "polemical propaganda pieces." For
Mary, however, Bobby's films show the complexities and complications of
reality in a way that doesn't prompt outrage and action. For example, one
film shows Bobby confronting the inventor of napalm with the famous image
of a naked Vietnamese girl running down a street, skin searing. Bobby's
camera zooms in on the man's "weary, defeated face" for several minutes
before turning its attention to the quotidian artifacts of his home: "the wreath
surrounding the door knocker. The woven welcome mat ... Some garden
gloves." Mary condemns Bobby for allowing the man's "humanity" to come
through in the film, and she insists that the film, far from revealing the
complexities of human existence, is mere "sentimentality."[22]

   Similar aesthetic debates continue to rend the revolutionary left in the
1990s. After the bombing, Bobby changes his name to Nash and opens a
bookstore in Seattle. He uses the bookstore to host an array of protest
groups, but, echoing Mary's critiques from more than two decades earlier,
a young revolutionary named Miranda has grown disillusioned, concluding that Nash's "groups [have] no intention of executing" any of their
ideas. Their "actions [are] the discussion and planning of actions."[23] Nash,
however, draws on the language of cultural performance to justify his
projects. "We do an action for the action itself. Our act is the end, the
point," he explains to his acolytes. At one meeting, for example, Nash
proposes that a large group of them, dressed in business attire, converge in
the center of a new downtown shopping district to perform "a kind of Busby
Berkeley synchronized dance" of "sheer whimsy." Instead of challenging,
shaming, or educating the public, as Miranda advocates, the goal according
to Nash is to "entertain them ... amuse them, intrigue them." Nash wants
to produce a "formal disruption" that will allow audience and dancers, for
one shimmering moment, to feel like they don't "have AOL Time Warner
or Viacom tattooed on [their] asses."[24] Temporarily embodying the world
they want to inhabit – a world of whimsical street dancing – Nash believes
that their performance can achieve true significance.

   As a later conversation between Miranda and her boyfriend Josh reveals,
Spiotta thinks about culture's formal-aesthetic response to neoliberalism's

---

[21] Dana Spiotta, *Eat the Document* (New York: Scribner, 2006), 188.   [22] Ibid., 225–8.
[23] Ibid., 130, 134.   [24] Ibid., 144.

cultural dominance as a question of (re)contextualization. Debating the right way to think about a Subcomandante Marcos shower curtain they come across while shopping at Suburban Guerilla, Josh argues that such recontextualization – a recontextualization made possible by neoliberal capitalism's ability to commodify anything, including a revolutionary such as Marcos who has devoted his life to defeating neoliberalism – is "subversive. Even liberating."[25] Like Nash's desire to relocate a Busby Berkeley dance number to downtown Seattle, Josh argues that things gain political value when placed in different contexts. For Miranda, however, such recontextualization can only ever be depoliticizing. "A confused context is the essence of alienation," she insists.[26]

Such formal considerations bear directly on Spiotta's own literary project. Her recourse to historical fiction recontextualizes the 1990s in the 1970s, and vice versa, formally disrupting the present and insisting that present reality isn't the only reality. And yet, unable to stabilize the meaning and value of its formally disruptive recontextualizations (depending on whom you ask, Bobby's films are either political or sentimental, Nash's dance number is either provocative or ridiculous, the shower curtain is either democratizing or exploitative), the novel can't guarantee the effectiveness of its recontextualizing methods. To be sure, Spiotta's work marks a crucial departure from the presentist social realism of Wolfe's *Bonfire*, a departure that we can understand via neoliberalism's perceived encroachment into the literary-cultural sphere. Wolfe has confidence in the novel's capacity for sociopolitical critique and never entertains the possibility that his work might be easily captured by the neoliberalism he critiques.[27] Spiotta, however, remains keenly aware of that possibility and consequently produces a novel that explores whether and how cultural production under neoliberalism can function critically. Her work thus provides an important diagnosis of a turn-of-the-century moment when the neoliberal novel can't control the context of its production and consumption. Desperate to be revolutionary but unable to determine how, *Eat the Document* straddles the line between critique and capitulation, ultimately offering a compromised aesthetic[28] that musters an equally compromised critical force.

Jennifer Egan's *A Visit from the Goon Squad* doesn't even bother to straddle that line and instead assumes the inevitability of capitulation.

---

[25] Ibid., 261.   [26] Ibid., 258.
[27] See Tom Wolfe, "Stalking the Billion Footed Beast," *Harper's* (November 1989): 45–56.
[28] See Rachel Greenwald Smith, "Six Propositions on Compromise Aesthetics," *The Account*, Fall 2014, https://theaccountmagazine.com/article/six-propositions-on-compromise-aesthetics

A young woman and her therapist, for example, are "writing a story whose end had already been determined"; a punk rocker becomes a corporate music executive and facilitates the "aesthetic holocaust" against which he used to rebel; characters on a safari experience only generic emotions that are overdetermined by the social structures in which they are embedded; thousands attend a concert in the park because a sub rosa marketing technology has tricked them into thinking that they're freely choosing to do so.[29] For Egan, the triumph of corporate, for-profit, digital technologies represents not just the neoliberalization of culture via the digitalization of music, movies, and the arts, but also the neoliberalization of being itself via social media's digitalization of human feeling, agency, and action. Everyone in *Goon Squad* becomes the hollow, complicit, sold-out subject of neoliberalism that they never wanted to be but can't help becoming.

As the novel's famous PowerPoint chapter demonstrates, Egan extends neoliberalism's ontological effects to the text itself, reducing narrative to slide-show visualizations that echo what Lulu, the woman responsible for digitally marketing the concert in the park, describes as the "pure language" of technology: "*if thr r children, thr mst b a fUtr, rt?*"[30] In fact, the novel suggests, children don't necessarily guarantee the future when art, language, and being itself have been captured by neoliberalism's for-profit technologies. Instead of combating this situation, however, *Goon Squad* leans into it, accepts its inevitability, and tries to deploy neoliberalism's ontological forms to different, more productive ends. It's easy to think of this as selling out, but, as Lulu explains to Alex, a reluctant participant in her marketing scheme, that's an antiquated way to think about things. Charging Alex with an "atavistic purism" that "implies the existence of an ethically perfect state, which ... doesn't exist and never existed," Lulu suggests instead that if the world has always already sold out, then Alex should move past his "ethical ambivalence" and see what he can make from his new reality.[31] Notably, the entirely contrived and for-profit concert produces rapturous joy for the audience. Should that joy be dismissed because of the neoliberal means by which it was achieved? Should the compelling narrative that Egan constructs out of PowerPoint slides be dismissed because of its total capitulation to reductive visual technologies? Do our feelings and actions remain meaningful even when generated by digital algorithms that serve the bottom-line interests of neoliberal corporations?

---

[29] Jennifer Egan, *A Visit from the Goon Squad* (New York: Anchor Books, 2010), 6, 23, 64, 329.
[30] Ibid., 331.   [31] Ibid., 319.

Goon Squad doesn't answer these questions, but it does ask and explore them, and, in doing so, it signals its engagement not only with neoliberalism's profound cultural effects, but with its ontological effects as well. Or to flip that around, understanding neoliberalism to be a complicated phenomenon that touches economics, politics, culture, and ontology in various ways and to various degrees helps us make sense of both the content and form of *Goon Squad* and other neoliberal novels like *Bonfire* and *Eat the Document*. The heuristic model detailed here, in fact, helps us think about each of these texts as a neoliberal novel while also appreciating key distinctions across the texts, which, when taken together, provide a fuller picture of neoliberalism's implications for contemporary literature. The interaction of neoliberalism's economic and political valences, for example, explains the function of Black racial justice politics in *Bonfire*; its co-optation of the cultural sphere provides a productive lens for reading Spiotta's meditations on the ambivalent political valences of aesthetic form in *Eat the Document*; and its influence over states and conditions of ontological being clearly informs *Goon Squad*'s analysis of digital technology's effects on our ability to be human. The different facets of neoliberalism that these texts explore also explain the distinct formal positions each novel takes relative to its object of inquiry, from Wolfe's socially realist critique to Spiotta's critical equivocation and Egan's post-critical search for productive forms within the neoliberal matrix. To be clear, this isn't a story of decreasing critical options in the face of increasing neoliberal totalization. Rather, it's a story about different formal-critical approaches that emerge in response to a multifarious neoliberal project that foregrounds different features and facets at different times and under different circumstances. Admittedly, that's a lot of difference to contend with, but it's worth it for the overall thicker understanding of neoliberalism and the neoliberal novel that it affords.

CHAPTER 4

Socialism and Communism

Mark W. Van Wienen

Introducing *Proletarian Literature in the United States* in 1935, Joseph Freeman demanded that American writers take sides in the class struggle; indeed, writers already *had* taken sides, if only unconsciously:

> The Communist says frankly: art, an instrument in the class struggle, must be developed by the proletariat as one of its weapons. The fascist, with equal frankness, says: art must serve the aims of the capitalist state. The liberal, speaking for the middle class which vacillates between monopoly capital and the proletariat, between fascism and communism, poses as the "impartial" arbiter in this, as in all other social disputes.[1]

Freeman, together with the editors of *Proletarian Literature*, offered an influential as well as suggestive approach for the study of socialist novelists in the United States. Their focus on the Communist Party, centered on the Depression – the volume included only communist-affiliated writers from the previous five years – has been adopted by numerous subsequent studies.[2] Such predispositions do have some basis, for, as Alan Wald observes, the Party catalyzed "a cultural movement engaging hundreds of writers, and influencing thousands more, over several decades."[3] Equally significant is the moment of decision narrated by Freeman as a political choice between communism, fascism, and capitalism, which is central to the political novel as conceived by socialist writers, typically narrativized as a political conversion experience of a key character or characters from an individualistic to a collective consciousness.

---

[1] Granville Hicks, et al., eds., *Proletarian Literature in the United States: An Anthology* (New York: International Publishers, 1935), 9.
[2] A sample of scholars taking this approach is in Janet Galligani Casey, ed., *The Novel and the American Left: Critical Essays on Depression-Era Fiction* (Iowa City: University of Iowa Press, 2004).
[3] Alan M. Wald, *Exiles from a Future Time: The Forging of the Mid-Twentieth-Century Literary Left* (Chapel Hill: University of North Carolina Press, 2002), 4.

Yet Wald's remark also suggests that a broader canvas is needed, and his career canvassing the literary left dramatically demonstrates that communist-affiliated novelists continued to publish through the 1940s and 1950s. Before the 1930s, too – in fact, stretching back into the nineteenth century – an extended tradition of socialist writing developed in which fiction was prominent.[4] This work often was yoked with particular political groups, but after 1901 it came to revolve around the Socialist Party of America, just as in the 1930s the Communist Party dominated the cultural sphere. In short, Freeman's attention to the interrelationship of a specific socialist political party with radical writers – alternately catalyzing, supporting, and challenging them – is entirely germane to the topic of the novel and politics, but his communist focus must be broadened, his 1930s scope extended in both directions. To provide an overview of socialist writing in the twentieth century, we must also push beyond the realist and naturalistic modes dominating socialist and communist fiction, including some modernist experimentation as well as speculative fiction, both utopian and dystopian. And we must reckon, too, with texts that challenge the collectivist and confidently progressive trajectory of the bulk of novels affiliated with the major socialist parties, even while their authors seek to remain true to the goal of radical human liberation professed by these parties.

A history of novelists' engagement with explicitly socialist politics may properly be said to begin with Nathaniel Hawthorne's *The Blithedale Romance* (1852). There is some irony here, for Hawthorne's satirical account of the egalitarian community at Brook Farm, Massachusetts, was meant to ridicule such experiments out of existence, and yet without this account there would be little record at all in American literary history of the widespread movement to found utopian communities in the United States, most frequently upon models provided by the Frenchman Charles Fourier or the Welsh industrialist Charles Owen. In fact, Transcendentalists, including Ralph Waldo Emerson, Bronson Alcott, Margaret Fuller, and Henry David Thoreau, were far more supportive of such communities.[5] Yet their short lifespans largely validated the criticism of Hawthorne – and, for that matter, Karl Marx – that local alternatives to capitalism could not be sustained when surrounded by a market economy.

---

[4] Mark W. Van Wienen, *American Socialist Triptych: The Literary-Political Work of Charlotte Perkins Gilman, Upton Sinclair, and W. E. B. Du Bois* (Ann Arbor: University of Michigan Press, 2012), especially 3–6.
[5] See Richard Francis, *Transcendental Utopias: Individual and Community at Brook Farm, Fruitlands, and Walden* (Ithaca, NY: Cornell University Press, 1997).

A second key nineteenth-century antecedent to later socialist fiction, Edward Bellamy's *Looking Backward: 2000–1887* (1888), addressed the problem of scale forthrightly, insisting that revolutionary transformation must take place on the level of the nation – hence the name "Nationalism" taken by the political movement rapidly spawned by the novel. At the same time – contrary to the Marxist philosophy of class struggle – Bellamy continued to believe, like the communitarian socialists, that revolutionary transformation could be achieved by peaceful means. Bellamy projects that the rapid advances of business monopolies might result in "the final consolidation of the entire capital of the nation" before the end of the nineteenth century, little more than a decade away when he was writing.[6] Bellamy's vision of a highly regimented but meritocratic and generous socioeconomic system was a sensation. Readers not only bought hundreds of thousands of copies of the book but assiduously studied it in organized reading groups, "Nationalist Clubs," which exerted an influence upon the leading grassroots reform movement of the era, sending delegates to the founding convention of the People's Party, or the Populists, in 1892.[7]

The enthusiasm surrounding Nationalism also fueled a burst of productivity in the writing of socialist and socialistic utopian fiction. A listing of just a few of the titles indicates the variety and specificity of the connections: *The Birth of Freedom: A Socialist Novel* (1890); *The People's Program: The Twentieth Century Is Theirs* (1892); *'96: A Romance of Utopia, Presenting a Solution to the Labor Problem, a New God and a New Religion* (1894); *In Brighter Climes, Or Life in Socioland* (1895); *President John Smith: The Story of a Peaceful Revolution* (1897); *Hilda's Home: A Story of Woman's Emancipation* (1899); *The World a Department Store* (1900).[8] Meanwhile, the leading realist, William Dean Howells, was an early adherent of Bellamy's Nationalist movement and presently turned his hand to socialist utopian fiction as well, publishing *A Traveler from Altruria* in 1894 and *Through the Eye of the Needle* in 1907.

It was always possible for readers to object to their schemes not only on practical but also on ideological grounds. Some readers of *Looking Backward*, for instance, found that Bellamy's scheme for labor organization (the "industrial army," he often called it) offered little relief from the

---

[6] Edward Bellamy, *Looking Backward: 2000–1887*, ed. Cecelia Tichi (New York: Penguin, 1982), 65.

[7] For the radical potential of populism, see Michael Kazin, *The Populist Persuasion: An American History* (New York: Basic Books, 1995).

[8] See the bibliography in Susan M. Matarese, *American Foreign Policy and the Utopian Imagination* (Amherst: University of Massachusetts Press, 2001).

alienation of labor.[9] Such problems led other socialist writers to adopt the opposite approach to speculative fiction – the dystopian subgenre. In 1890, for example, sensationalist fiction writer and Populist organizer Ignatius Donnelly wrote *Caesar's Column*, in which the twentieth century is portrayed as a nightmare world of oligarchic domination, apparently to mobilize Americans to vote the Populist ticket before it was too late. Written from a perspective further left, Jack London's *The Iron Heel* (1907) foresees hundreds of years of revolution and violence before the dawning of a new, cooperative socialist society. Here, the contrast with Bellamy reflects differences among American socialists: the non-Marxian socialist Bellamy foreseeing some one hundred years of cooperative social harmony by the year 2000; the Marxist London anticipating an additional two hundred years of repression, struggle, and bloodshed.

By 1900, the wave of socialist utopian fiction wave had crested, but some radical writers would continue to work the speculative genre, particularly by demonstrating its potential to critique the existing system as well as to present more egalitarian alternatives. In retrospect, the most important of these works was Charlotte Perkins Gilman's *Herland*, which depicts an all-female community whose socialist elements include collective ownership of land and production, strictly equal distribution of good and services, and communal child-raising. As Cynthia J. Davis notes in Chapter 15 of this volume, Gilman belonged to the generation of socialists schooled by Bellamy and antipathetic to class struggle. Gilman's socialism is highlighted further when her other two utopian novels (also mentioned by Davis) are considered. All three initially appeared in *The Forerunner*, the journal Gilman published and wrote entirely herself between 1909 and 1916. Like Bellamy's *Looking Backward*, the first of Gilman's utopian fictions, *Moving the Mountain* (1911), projects a much better social order in the United States just one generation into the future, catalyzed by a new religion, oriented to a re-conception of labor that is intrinsically socialist.[10] But *Moving the Mountain* foregrounds not only socialist utopianism but also – quite unwittingly – dystopianism. Bellamy's *Looking Backward* had opened the door to authoritarianism; Gilman's *Herland* would suggest that asocial members of society might be persuaded not to reproduce; but *Moving the Mountain* takes a no-holds-barred approach, as Gilman's

---

[9] Daniel Borus, "Introduction," in Edward Bellamy, *Looking Backward: 2000–1887* (Boston, MA: Bedford, 1995), 15, 22–7.

[10] Charlotte Perkins Gilman, *Utopian Novels*, ed. Minna Doskow (Madison, NJ: Fairleigh Dickinson University Press, 1999), 88.

utopian eugenicists explain that to achieve rapid social improvement they "killed many hopeless degenerates, insane, idiots, and real perverts, after trying our best powers of cure" and that "[c]ertain classes of criminals and perverts were rendered incapable of reproducing their kind."[11]

Gilman's *With Her in Ourland* (1915), the sequel to *Herland*, is both less offensive and more insightful. Much of its technique is in fact realist, as it follows the world travels of Van, the protagonist of both novels, and Ellador, his Herlander wife, as they reconnoiter the male-as-well-as-female world outside Herland, beginning with a sharp encounter with the Great War in Europe. Yet a utopian measuring stick is employed at key moments in Gilman's narrative to critique the ways in which class and gender and (in spite of Gilman's well-known prejudices) racial and national inequalities reinforce one another. Encountering the United States last, Ellador critiques both US imperialism – as displayed in the Hawaiian islands – and US political economy that permits private monopolies to parasitize the social body: "your oil-suckers and coal-suckers, water-suckers, and wood-suckers, railroad suckers and farm suckers."[12] If, to some degree, *With Her in Ourland* hints at the power of the realist novel – well established by other socialist writers as their genre of choice by the mid-1910s – the utopian/realist interplay offered by the *Herland/Ourland* duology also suggests the value of a definite philosophical perspective.

The kinship between socialism as it emerged in the United States after 1900 and fictional realism seems straightforward enough. Communitarian and nationalist socialisms were "utopian," hence suited to fiction in that genre. Marxian socialism, which provided the theoretical basis for the Socialist Party of America, founded in 1901, was "scientific." Hence, as Walter Rideout, an early and important literary historian of the "Radical Novel," observes: "[R]ealism and Socialism were mutually implicit; one was the best way to 'tell the truth' in literature as the other was the only way to tell it in politics."[13]

Undeniably, Upton Sinclair's *The Jungle* (1906) gained impact by the power of realistic fictional representation, which called upon readers with little acquaintance either with Chicago's packinghouse district or with Lithuanian immigrants to experience the conditions of a single family of such immigrants working for the meatpacking moguls. Its claim to fame – that its depiction of food contamination in Chicago's slaughterhouses

[11] Ibid., 136, 86.   [12] Ibid., 210.
[13] Walter B. Rideout, *The Radical Novel in the United States, 1900–1954: Some Interrelations of Literature and Society* (New York: Columbia University Press, 1992 [1956]), 23.

catalyzed passage of the federal Pure Food and Drug Act of 1906 – also received a boost generally from the progressive climate cultivated by muckraking journalism.[14] But to his muckraking realistic depiction Sinclair added another, overtly political element: the scene of conversion to socialism. *The Jungle* insists that the social problems experienced by Jurgis Rudkus and his family could be solved only by a fundamental socialist transformation of society – and, consequently, Jurgis must also experience a fundamental conversion of his mindset, which takes place when he stumbles into a socialist meeting where, guided by a particularly charismatic speaker, he suddenly finds "unfolding of vistas before him, a breaking of the ground beneath him, an upheaving, a stirring, a trembling," and "[feels] himself suddenly a mere man no longer – there were powers within him undreamed of."[15]

The religious character of this effusion is central to its impact, even as it marks the phenomenon as distinctively American, drawing from American religious evangelicalism. It is also indebted to the strength of the social gospel movement among liberal protestants in the Progressive Era, which offered not only ethical but literary models. As Gregory S. Jackson points out, a nineteenth-century "homiletic" tradition in religious fiction employed a central character's confrontation with harsh social reality to propel that character – and readers – "from personal introspection to social intervention, transforming the individually focused conversion experience into a communal awakening toward social salvation and a more public, pragmatic ethic of participation."[16] The formula as exemplified in *The Jungle*, which substituted a secular conversion to socialism for the Christian "awakening toward social salvation," proved both incredibly flexible and durable, as can be shown from examples ranging from the early days of the Socialist Party right through the rise and fall of the Communist Party in the USA.

As was the case in many of Upton Sinclair's novels, Ernest Poole's *The Harbor* (1915) centers on a well-born protagonist, a college-educated journalist who covers a strike of dockyard workers led by anarcho-syndicalist leaders, events unmistakably paralleling successful labor organizing carried out by the Industrial Workers of the World (IWW) among longshoremen. The IWW, or Wobblies, had been founded in 1905 and

[14] Ibid., 19–20, 47.
[15] Upton Sinclair, *The Jungle: An Authoritative Text, Context and Backgrounds, Criticism*, ed. Clare Virginia Eby (New York: W. W. Norton, 2003), 291–2.
[16] Gregory S. Jackson, "'What Would Jesus Do?': Practical Christianity, Social Gospel Realism, and the Homiletic Novel," *PMLA* 121.3 (2006): 641–61, here 653.

affiliated with the Socialist Party until 1912, when they were expelled for
their support for industrial sabotage.[17] At first skeptical about the IWW's
radicalism, Poole's protagonist, William, is won over by the IWW's ability
to unite workers across boundaries of ethnicity, race, gender, nationality,
and language. He begins to work for the socialist movement; he converts
when, as with Jurgis, his own personality becomes immersed within a
collective labor identity: "[W]e were members of the whole and took on its
huge personality . . . Slowly I began to feel what It wanted, what It hated,
how It planned and how It acted. And this to me was a miracle, the one
great miracle of the strike."[18] *The Harbor* thus not only brings into fiction
the work of the most radical wing of the socialist movement before
1920 but also offers an early example of the strike as a central plot element;
here, as often in later communist fiction, it is the catalyst behind the lead
character's conversion.

Upton Sinclair's fiction included several variants on the conversion
narrative. *Jimmie Higgins* (1920), set in World War I, starts with a rank-
and-file socialist who is enlisted in the US army and sent to Russia to
oppose the Bolsheviks, whereupon he experiences an epiphany about the
class injustice of this mission, acts to support the Russian Revolution, and
is tortured into insanity by the army, thus achieving a kind of socialist
martyrdom. In *Oil!* (1926), the heir to an oil fortune, Bunny, is also
converted to the revolutionary movement in part through the inspiration
of the Bolsheviks: He becomes a "Millionaire Red" when a comrade's
reports on the success of the revolution in Russia "transvaluated all values
[so that] things that had been wicked became suddenly heroic, while
things that had been respectable became suddenly dull."[19] In *Boston*
(1928), Sinclair's account of the trial and execution of Sacco and
Vanzetti, the radicalization of social elites is again featured, but, as with
Jimmie Higgins, the working-class characters become martyrs, and the
agency of the masses around the world is galvanized by the Italian
anarchists: "Black men, brown men, yellow men – men of a hundred
nations and a thousand tribes – the prisoners of starvation, the wretched of
the earth – experienced a thrill of awe. It was the mystic process of blood-
sacrifice, by which through the ages salvation has been brought to
mankind!"[20]

[17] Daniel Bell, *Marxian Socialism in the United States* (Cornell University Press, 1996 [1952]), 75–7.
[18] Ernest Poole, *The Harbor* (New York: Macmillan, 1915), 321.
[19] Upton Sinclair, *Oil!* (New York: Albert and Charles Boni, 1926), 268.
[20] Upton Sinclair, *Boston* (New York: Albert and Charles Boni, 1928), 754.

While Upton Sinclair ultimately spurned the Communist Party despite championing the Bolshevik-led Third International with which it was aligned,[21] other fiction writers who did join the new party demonstrated the ready adaptability of the socialist conversion plot. For instance, in *Jews Without Money* (1930), Michael Gold's autobiographical *bildungsroman* set on Manhattan's Lower East Side, Gold shows that the socialist conversion could be expressed through Messianic Judaism as well as revivalist Christianity: "O workers' Revolution, you brought hope to me, a lonely, suicidal boy. You are the true Messiah. You will destroy the East Side when you come, and build there a garden for the human spirit."[22] As an editor, Gold was a central catalyst in the literary production that blossomed with the emergence of the Communist Party, serving as the editor of the Party-aligned *New Masses* from 1928 to 1930, then continuing on its editorial board until 1934.[23] Indeed, Walter Rideout documents a surge in the publication of communist-inspired fiction that Gold helped to orchestrate – some seventy novels published in the 1930s, fifty already by 1935.[24]

These novels were much more likely to feature a strike than the earlier novels associated with the Socialist Party, but the communist-led strike and communist conversion were often closely intertwined, and other carryovers from the religious formulations of earlier work are also evident. In Grace Lumpkin's *To Make My Bread* (1932), one of six novels written about the textile strike of 1929 in Gastonia, North Carolina, the climactic moment occurs when a walkout orchestrated by communist organizers is crushed by armed force, with one of the strike leaders, Bonnie Kirkland, shot down by deputies while speaking at a union meeting. Like Sacco and Vanzetti in Sinclair's *Boston*, Bonnie becomes a martyr for labor, her life and death symbolic of a struggle greater than the life of any one individual and an inspiration for others to join in that struggle: "what she had begun was not ended with her: and never would be until what she had dreamed about had become a fact."[25] Her loss helps to complete the conversion of her brother, who joins secret meetings staged by communist organizers to introduce radicalized workers to the Party.

The language and symbols of religion were also particularly apt as applied to Party appeals to African Americans. Antiracism was fundamental to the Communist Party's strategy in the United States, and Christian

[21] See Bell, 122–33; Rideout, 305.
[22] Michael Gold, *Jews Without Money* (New York: Liveright, 1930), 309. [23] Wald, *Exiles*, 39.
[24] Rideout, 171.
[25] Grace Lumpkin, *To Make My Bread* (Urbana: University of Illinois Press, 1995 [1932]), 384.

pastors were key leaders in Black communities, both North and South. The twin importance of mobilizing Black clergy and forging interracial alliances is evident in Richard Wright's "Fire and Cloud," the last of four novellas collected in the 1938 version of his first book, *Uncle Tom's Children*. At the narrative's center is the Reverend Taylor, the religious and social leader of a Black community in a small Southern town during the Depression, who is in communication not only with the leading white citizens but also, clandestinely, with communists who are seeking to organize an interracial demonstration for the equitable distribution of relief funds. He experiences his epiphany, deciding to side with the communists, when he is brutalized by white hoodlums acting on the direction of white community leaders. Taylor enjoins his parishioners: "We gotta get together ... Gawds done spoke! Gawds done sent His sign. Now its fer us t ack [act]."[26] The novella closes with another typical gesture, the immersion of individual identity in collective purpose: When the white mayor appeals to Taylor as the traditional pacifier of the Black community, Taylor refuses to stand apart from the crowd, and a "baptism of clean joy swept over Taylor" when white and Black protesters join in drowning out the mayor's voice.[27]

Alexander Saxton's complex, multigenerational *The Great Midland* (1948) adapts the essential conversion formula despite explicitly rejecting the religious vocabulary of other radical novels. The classic tension between individual interests and collective responsibility is played out between and within the novel's central characters, the married couple Stephanie and Dave Spaas. Both are loyal Communist Party members working in Chicago, but Stephanie resists the demands of Party work as intrusive to their marriage and to her career as a scientist. Late in the novel, Stephanie retreats by herself to northern Michigan to think things over, waiting for some kind of revelation, but the narrator reports instead:

> She had heard no angels singing in the trees of Ludington, and so returned as she had come. For she had known the decision from the beginning; she found it rooted inside her as irrevocably as the conflict itself. One with a crippled foot did not appeal to angels; but learned to walk in the one way possible: by walking.[28]

---

[26] Richard Wright, *Richard Wright Reader*, ed. Ellen Wright and Michel Fabre (New York: Harper and Row, 1978), 343.

[27] Ibid., 345.

[28] Alexander Saxton, *The Great Midland* (Urbana: University of Illinois Press, 1997), 338–9.

Saxton rejects the usual theatrics of soul-shattering revelation, yet this *is* a turning point, functioning just as other scenes of socialist conversion do in priming the characters to do whatever is required to carry on revolutionary work. The novel ends with the couple still married, still loyal communists, but working apart: Stephanie in war industry research, Dave as a merchant seaman serving on Atlantic convoys. Among other interesting aspects of the novel is the way in which it captures the period when the circumstances of World War II succeeded in recasting ideological foes as wartime allies.

Of course, the ideological fissure reopened with new fury when the war ended and the Cold War began, and yet the essence of the conversion plot remained even as its political context dramatically shifted. Joseph Bonosky's *Burning Valley* (1953) infuses another religious dimension into the formula, depicting the Catholic religious culture of Eastern European steelworkers in Pennsylvania and casting a priest from that community, Benedict Bulmanis, as a central character. In a scene that manages to supply much of the *strum-und-drang* of the usual conversion scene through naturalistic devices – with Benedict's longtime parish church undergoing demolition around him, a bitter strike led by communist agitators collapsing, and a tremendous thunderstorm brewing that will destroy the steelworkers' suburban slum, Hunky Hollow – Benedict chooses to renounce fidelity to the institutionalized church in favor of a wider calling to social service: "I wish to remain poor, I wish only to serve my people."[29] The redirection of Benedict's calling is symbolically profound, as his final act is to visit an imprisoned communist labor leader, although its minimalism also bespeaks communist marginalization in the 1950s. Coincidentally, Bonosky's novel, like *The Jungle*, depicts Lithuanian immigrant workers, yet how far removed from the triumphant election-day scene that concludes Sinclair's novel is the incident that concludes *Burning Valley*: a lone priest delivering a few oranges to a communist agitator in prison.

In sum, we can say that realist and naturalistic novels featuring a character's or characters' conversion experience served as the "red thread" connecting many radical novels produced over some six decades in support of the socialist or communist parties. Yet, as Alan Wald has taken the lead in showing, the novel of socialist conversion accounted for only a fraction of the literary output of radical writers. Alternatives may suggest the diverse forms of socialist commitment; they may indicate fluctuations in the fortunes of the socialist movement or variations in the party line; or

---

[29] Joseph Bonosky, *Burning Valley* (Urbana: University of Illinois Press, 1998), 264.

they may offer critique, whether directly or obliquely, of mainstream socialist activism and philosophy. This section considers a sample of these variations.

Theresa S. Malkiel's *Diary of a Shirtwaist Striker* (1911) in fact offers several such variations. The first unconventional element is that it *begins* with a strike. *Diary* offers a day-by-day account of the November 1909– February 1910 walkout of workers in the New York garment trades, mostly Jewish and Italian women: the "Uprising of the Twenty Thousand." A second unconventional element is that it ends with a labor *victory* – very unusual indeed in American socialist fiction, and somewhat at odds with the messier real-life outcome, in which employers settled with strikers by raising pay but refused union recognition.[30] The author of *Diary* was herself a Jewish-American immigrant; Malkiel had also been a garment worker and was a longtime member of the Socialist Party, especially promoting immigrants' and women's issues.[31] Although the novel charts the increasing radicalization of its narrator, Mary, and of her fiancé, Jim, the couple stop short of joining the Party: "[A]fter the many weeks of strike this has almost settled Jim and me – we're about ready to join the great army of comrades."[32] The novel's departures from the standard socialist formulae have two important dimensions. First, in making the narrator less pivotal, the novel's protagonist becomes more genuinely collective: the many working women, some men, and a few non-working-class women allies, who combine to win the strike. Second, the story emphasizes women as leaders and men as obstacles to women's independence, for Jim at first opposes Mary's union activities and her father does so throughout the novel. In the 1910s, not only socialist women writers outside the Party, such as Gilman, but card-carrying socialists like Malkiel emphasized the centrality of gender equality to class struggle.

Another anomalous contribution to radical fiction is Claude McKay's *Home to Harlem* (1928). McKay was a member of the Communist Party in the 1920s, an enthusiastic visitor to the Soviet Union, and a member of the editorial board of the communist-affiliated *New Masses*.[33] Broadly political

---

[30] Laura Hapke, "Revolution: Imagining a Counternarrative," in *American Literature in Transition: 1910–1920*, ed. Mark W. Van Wienen (New York: Cambridge University Press, 2018), 165–6.

[31] Theresa S. Malkiel, *Diary of a Shirtwaist Striker*, ed. Françoise Bach (Ithaca, NY: Cornell University Press, 1990 [1910]), 51–60.

[32] Ibid., 209.

[33] For Claude McKay's travel in and impressions of the USSR, see his articles entitled "Soviet Russia and the Negro," *The Crisis* 27.2 (1923): 61–3; 27.3 (1924): 114–18.

on issues of economic justice and racial inequality – whether portraying the hard-scrabble lives of Black Harlemites or the regimentation of Black labor in the railroad industry – *Home* offers only glancing views of socialist politics. Ray, one of the novel's two principal characters, condemns the recent world war and commends the Bolshevik Revolution, but McKay's narrator suggests that "Ray was not prophetic-minded enough to define the total evil that the one had wrought nor the ultimate splendor of the other."[34] And this is scarcely all there is of socialism in the novel. The party line on McKay's kind of realistic depiction of Black life – sans a more openly political dimension – was to affirm its essentially proletarian character but suggest the need, ultimately, for a more disciplined Marxist orientation. In a *New Masses* review of *Banjo* (1929), McKay's sequel to *Home*, Michael Gold praises McKay's depiction of "Negro workers and migratories with the truthfulness and intimate sympathy of a proletarian writer" but faults his work for "let[ting] his Negro patriotism swell too huge."[35]

Other Black novelists closely connected with the communist movement similarly resisted political direction from the Party. Richard Wright turned from the pro-communist polemic of "Fire and Cloud" to a more complex approach in his first full-length novel, *Native Son* (1940). Wright's protagonist, Bigger Thomas, does find his strongest supporters among the communists, especially his lawyer, Max, who explicates Bigger's killings as a natural response to a racist, capitalist environment. Yet, in the end, Bigger rejects both his mother's spiritual panaceas and Max's exculpatory explanations, embracing his murderous acts as moments of agency and self-definition. There is a kind of epiphany here, certainly, but a sharp alternative to conversion to Party allegiance. An equally somber view of Black proletarian culture and self-definition may be found in a roughly contemporary novel by another communist-affiliated Black writer, William Attaway's *Blood on the Forge* (1941), which portrays Black and white workers in the steel industry. Attaway was a Party member not only in the 1930s but through subsequent decades.[36] *Blood on the Forge*, however, includes no socialist characters at all; its climax features one of the novel's three main Black characters participating in strike-breaking

---

[34] Claude McKay, *Home to Harlem* (Boston, MA: Northeastern University Press, 1987 [1928]), 225–6.

[35] Michael Gold, "Drunk with Sunlight" [review of *Banjo* by Claude McKay], *New Masses* 5.2 (1929): 17, *Marxists Internet Archive*, online.

[36] Alan Wald, *Trinity of Passion: The Literary Left and the Antifascist Crusade* (Chapel Hill: University of North Carolina Press, 2007), 65.

violence, and its denouement traces the retreat from the steel mills to Pittsburgh's Black ghetto by the other two main characters. The novel's implicit communism may lie in its depicting a strike from 1919, before antiracist communists were on the scene, and yet the novel's turn to Black social connections and folk culture seems to share in the "Negro patriotism" that Gold found suspect in McKay's fiction and that Bigger's defiance also declares.

Even as the most prominent Black novelists affiliated with the Party came to express ambivalence toward its leadership, another important trend in communist fiction was afoot: proletarian novels by white authors that made African American characters central. The most ambitious is John Sanford's *The People from Heaven* (1943), which deploys modernist techniques of multiple points of view in order to explore, simultaneously, the race prejudices of an Adirondack Mountains community, European Americans' dispossession of the Original Nations, and the early history of Black enslavement in New York. While presenting a multiplicity of perspectives – introducing forty-six different narrators in the opening chapter alone – the novel's one Black character, the mysterious and evocatively named America Smith, is both the catalyst of the book's action and the person who resolves its central conflict. When America shoots down the community's leading citizen and principal malefactor, Sanford offers a compelling presentation of violence as a necessary tool for labor self-defense.

Another race novel by a white author, Alfred Maund's *The Big Boxcar* (1957), daringly expands its Black cast; indeed, it reverses Sanford's proportion, so that all of the major characters are Black except for one white man, an escaped convict whose pursuers are likely to jeopardize the safety of the Black hoboes – five men, one woman – who have been thrown together traveling in an empty boxcar on a slow-moving freight train. Maund's novel, too, features multiple narrators, with each boxcar rider taking a turn to tell the story of why they are on the run from various mishaps, petty crimes, and threats of racist violence. Both novels carry a certain risk of stereotyping, with Sanford's America being too wholly a race symbol instead of a flesh-and-blood character and Maund's lumpenproletariat embodying multiple negative racialized types. Yet the resolution of *The Big Boxcar* turns on precisely this issue, as the Black characters exploit white stereotypes. As with Sanford, the lone Black woman is the most creative and decisive character: Maund's Marie pretends to copulate trackside with one of the men, Sam, to distract the police and give the others the opportunity to escape. Elsewhere in the novel, there are alliances between progressive whites and Blacks, and when the police deliberate what to do about Marie and Sam, apprehended in flagrante, a sympathetic white railroad yardman interposes, preventing them from being arrested. As Sam reflects, "a white man who doesn't like to see Negroes beat and killed can stop a good bit of it, and do it easy."[37] In balancing Black and white agency, Maund offers a novel that not only reflects the best impulses of the Communist Party's interracial politics but anticipates a renewal of antiracist activism, in which white progressives would follow Black leaders, in the decades to come.

The return of progressive activism in the 1960s – the "New Left" – along with its expressions in fiction, I will leave to other essays in this volume to canvass in detail. But there have also been post-1960 novels that show the endurance of socialist concepts that can be traced directly to the earlier era of left-wing activism, and in closing I will touch on a few of these later novels, which include a continuation of the realist tradition and a remarkable return to speculative fiction.

Most notable as a continuation of realism – but with no conversion experience – is Tillie Olsen's *Yonnodio* (1974). The novel was drafted in the 1930s but did not appear until 1974, part of a feminist project of recovering neglected or previously unpublished texts in which Olsen herself was a leading agent.[38] Olsen had joined the Communist Party in 1931 and remained active through the McCarthy period. Although Olsen's larger plan for the novel included a strike that might have aligned the finished work more closely with standard communist expectations,[39] the book as published in 1974 departs rather widely from them, not only for the unrelenting squalor of working-class life depicted but also for its focus on the double burden carried by proletarian women. In the final episodes of this "unfinished" novel, workers in an Omaha slaughterhouse on an excruciatingly hot day are able to slow the pace when working together, hinting at a proletarian solidarity celebrated in 1930s leftist fiction. But, in a parallel scene, Anna, the mother of the family upon whom the narrative centers, "works on alone," canning fruit in a similarly sweltering kitchen and trying to comfort her children.[40] The heterodox

---

[37] Alfred Maund, *The Big Boxcar* (Cambridge, MA: Riverside Press, 1957), 174.

[38] Corrina K. Lee, "Documents of Proletarian Fiction: Tillie Olsen's Yonnondio: From the Thirties," *Journal of Modern Literature* 36.4 (2013): 114.

[39] Tillie Olsen, *Yonnondio: From the Thirties* (New York: Delta, 1994 [1974]), 135.

[40] Tillie Olsen, *Yonnondio: From the Thirties* (Lincoln: University of Nebraska Press, 2004 [1974]), 184.

implication is plain: Men gain by class solidarity; women are left stirring the pot and minding the kids.

A publication by another notable feminist writer in 1974 marks a revival of speculative fiction as a mode for conscious exploration of socialist ideas. While Ursula K. Le Guin's *The Left Hand of Darkness* (1969), discussed in Chapter 19 in this volume, is hailed for its exploration of gender roles and sexual identity, *The Dispossessed* (1974) offers a utopian/dystopian comparison of dramatically different socioeconomic systems: an imaginary anarcho-syndicalist colony on a habitable moon orbiting an earth riven by an ideological Cold War and dominated by an enormously wealthy capitalist nation. The novel is evenly divided between an exploration of anarchic Anarres and its opposite, the "archic" Urras, and in many ways it is a throwback to *both* the utopian and dystopian modes. In spite of this novelty, Le Guin's dystopic depiction of the leading capitalist nation on Urras works much as Jack London's *The Iron Heel* does, exaggerating the lineaments of the United States only just enough to make her satirical points and, at the same time, render the target of that satire unmistakably clear. Meanwhile, in Anarres, Le Guin offers a credible rendering of a society in which the radical freedom of every individual is the first principle, and the second is voluntarily given mutual aid. As such, it marks a return to both the nineteenth-century roots of American socialism in the communitarian experiments and to the most radical of socialist options after 1900, the anarcho-syndicalism of the IWW and the anarchism of Sacco and Vanzetti.

Le Guin's speculative fiction is especially fruitful because, even in a highly schematic form such as *The Dispossessed*, her dystopian worlds are not altogether abysmal and her utopian worlds fall well short of perfection. This flexibility in the application of utopian and dystopian modes has been exploited to great effect by the contemporary science fiction novelist Kim Stanley Robinson. In the "California Trilogy" that marked the beginning of his career, Robinson depicted plausible near-future (mid-twenty-first-century) realities for the United States through the locale of Orange County, California, including a post-nuclear-apocalypse survivor community (*The Wild Shore*, 1984); a nation addicted to consumerist fantasies and utterly dominated by the military-industrial complex (*The Gold Coast*, 1988); and a country that has embraced ecologically sound and socialist principles through a peaceful, legislatively orchestrated revolution (*Pacific Edge*, 1990).[41] These are but the first three of twenty-two books of

---

[41] All three recently have been republished in a single collection: Kim Stanley Robinson, *Three Californias* (New York: Tor Essentials, 2020).

speculative fiction written by Robinson, to date, with the "Mars Trilogy" (1992, 1993, 1996), which largely builds out further the vision of *Pacific Edge*, being the most renowned.

The speculative fictions of Le Guin and Robinson reflect both departures and continuity from the socialist and communist proletarian novels of the earlier twentieth century. Neither author pledges fealty to any particular political organization, nor have they founded any. Their renunciation of the realist novel in favor of postmodernist refractions of the here and now not only speak to changes in the art of novel-writing but are also a far cry from the practical, on-the-ground organizational work that the proletarian novel preached and many of its producers practiced. Their conviction that individual expression must be – and can be – reconciled with an egalitarian common good may be a necessary corrective to the religious self-abnegation of the socialist conversion plot. Yet they convey indirectly a commitment to social equality that was, after all, the central point of the conversion narrative, and Le Guin's vision of voluntary mutual aid and Robinson's of peaceful revolutionary transformation likewise take pages from the social democratic fiction that appeared several decades earlier and lasted for many decades.

CHAPTER 5

Feminisms

Jean Lutes

Novelists have always been preoccupied by the idiosyncratic ways that individual lives register societal imperatives and structural change. It's not surprising, then, that the slogan "the personal is political" – coined by the women's movement of the 1960s and 1970s – reverberates through the history of the American novel. When feminists insisted that all personal experiences, no matter how private, were rooted in the economic and legal realities that disempowered women, they articulated a capacious vision that encompassed eighteenth-century seduction novels, nineteenth-century sentimental novels, and twentieth-century postmodern novels. But feminist politics after 1900 did far more than simply put a new spin on the novel's longstanding commitment to chronicling intimacies large and small. Twentieth-century feminist activism and thought spread with an urgency and ambition not seen before. Advocates for women achieved mass recognition, unsettling long-held convictions and upsetting the status quo in ways unimaginable in previous centuries. Resistance to gender-based oppression existed long before the twentieth century, of course. Indigenous women sought protection from sexual predation by European colonizers; seventeenth-century enslaved women devised ways to avoid rape, pregnancy, and separation from their families; and white women, discouraged from voicing their political views in the early republic, turned mothering into a political act. In the early nineteenth century, the anti-slavery movement fostered a bold campaign for women's rights. But women remained, for the most part, legally, socially, and economically subordinate. In 1900, women couldn't vote, serve as jurors, become lawyers, keep their jobs during pregnancy, or apply for a loan without their husband's or father's signature.

As the twentieth century unfolded, restrictions on women and girls lifted. Feminists fought for changes in private and public spaces, the home and the workplace, dinner tables and ball parks, bedrooms and classrooms, courtrooms and medical offices. Shifting social norms, new legal protections, and medical advances paved the way for an unprecedented expansion in women's roles. In 1920, women were granted the right to vote. By the century's end, women were legally entitled to no-fault divorce, abortion, and birth control regardless of marital status. They made up nearly half of the paid labor force.[1] They outnumbered male students on college campuses. They could serve in the military, and they could sue if they were discriminated against or sexually harassed. Lesbians had become publicly recognizable, and many had nurtured a vital women's culture that included bookstores and music festivals. At times, feminist political actions ran aground or lost their way – as in 1971, when both the House and Senate passed comprehensive childcare legislation and President Nixon promptly vetoed the measure. After the Equal Rights Amendment (ERA) passed Congress easily with bipartisan support in 1972, Phyllis Schlafly and other opponents kept it from becoming law, successfully derailing its ratification by the states. Still, many of the developments Schlafly warned about – women in combat, shifting gender roles within traditional marriages, same-sex marriages, and unisex bathrooms – happened anyway.

No novel genre escaped these changes or failed to register them, from finely observed realist fiction to bold modernist experiments, from crime fiction page-turners to fragmented postmodern narratives. Feminist politics reshaped the content, and sometimes the form, of the novel. Twentieth-century American novelists narrated multiple feminisms, triumphant and defeated, jubilant and anguished, razor-focused and utterly lost. Only in a few specific historical moments – the fight against Jim Crow laws, the suffrage campaign, and the women's liberation movement of the 1960s and 1970s – did activists make novels central to their political projects. For the most part, feminist thought percolated in fiction in less overt ways. Not all the novels discussed here were written by authors who called themselves feminists, but all of them reckoned with the disempowerment of women and girls in ways that acknowledged and inspired feminist work. Because the best stories are rarely simple, novelists were often drawn to failures and setbacks, documenting the psychic and material damage caused by patriarchal systems along with the costs and challenges of the quest for gender equality. Seeking self-determination, finding meaningful work, surviving sexual and domestic violence, maintaining communities, and

---

[1] Bureau of Labor Statistics, US Department of Labor, "Women in the Labor Force: A Databook," February 2004, Report 973, www.bls.gov/opub/reports/womens-databook/archive/womenlaborforce_2004.pdf

acknowledging the full range of women's sexuality – including lesbian desire – are all pervasive themes. Explorations of biopolitics – the state's power to shape life and to discipline the human body – recur throughout the century, beginning with Pauline E. Hopkins's *Contending Forces: A Romance Illustrative of Life North and South* (1900), written during a time of pervasive, brutal violence against African Americans. Like many women of color, Hopkins advocated women's empowerment as part of a broader racial justice agenda. Through a multigenerational plot that revised the conventions of sentimental melodrama, Hopkins redefined virtuous Black womanhood and called for federal intervention to stop lynching, compensate victims, and provide financial reparation to the heirs of enslaved people. She also used interracial romance to illustrate the absurdity of the racial boundaries that Jim Crow laws enforced.[2] *Contending Forces* depicts racial injustice and gendered violence as deeply intertwined, a theme common among Hopkins's nineteenth-century predecessors and one that would be further explored by her many twentieth-century successors, including Ann Petry, Gloria Naylor, Alice Walker, and Toni Morrison.

Dramatic as the twentieth-century expansion of US women's opportunities was, progress was never universal and was often challenged. Women's overall safety, wealth, and authority didn't improve nearly as much as their opportunities did. As early as the 1920s, advertisers were appropriating feminist goals to their own ends, adopting the rhetoric of female empowerment to sell products, a practice that continues to flourish.[3] American culture absorbed feminism, taking women's calls for emancipation into account without fundamentally transforming basic power structures. The decade after women got the right to vote, advocates seeking to restrict white men's sexual privilege scored a major victory by reforming statutory rape laws. But the legal changes had minimal practical impact in the treatment and prosecution of rape cases, since women and girls were still seen as culpable for sex crimes.[4] In 2000, men still outnumbered women, by significant margins, in elected offices and corporate

---

[2] See, among others, Laura Korobkin, "Imagining State and Federal Law in Pauline E. Hopkins's *Contending Forces*," *Legacy: Journal of American Women Writers* 28.1 (2011): 1–23; Siobhan Somerville, "Inverting the Tragic Mulatta Tradition: Race and Homosexuality in Pauline E. Hopkins' Fiction," in *Queering the Color Lines: Race and the Invention of Homosexuality in American Culture* (Durham, NC: Duke University Press, 2000), 77–110.

[3] Nancy F. Cott, *The Grounding of Modern Feminism* (New Haven, CT: Yale University Press, 1987), 174.

[4] See Estelle B. Freedman, *Redefining Rape: Sexual Violence in the Era of Suffrage and Segregation* (Cambridge, MA: Harvard University Press, 2013), 139–48.

boardrooms, and women's earnings were lower than men's for full-time employees across all broad occupation categories.[5] As more women entered the paid workforce, the unequal distribution of caregiving and household labor produced what sociologist Arlie Hochschild called the "second shift" for working women.[6] By 2000, two-thirds of mothers with children under six worked for wages, but affordable daycare remained nonexistent.[7] Inequities persisted outside the world of work and caregiving, too. Even after a federal law was passed in 1972 that required schools to give women and girls equal chances to play sports, resources for women's athletic programs lagged well behind those for men.[8]

Throughout the century, feminist political gains inspired significant backlash. After the Supreme Court's decision in Roe v. Wade legalized abortion in 1973, abortion opponents sprang into action, and by the 1990s they succeeded in limiting women's access to abortion through incremental restrictions imposed by individual states. Even in the giddy 1970s, as creative acts of rebellion sprouted across the nation, supporters of the patriarchy abounded. The bestselling non-fiction book of 1974 was Marabel Morgan's advice guide *The Total Woman*, which instructed wives to submit to their husbands and, infamously, suggested that they meet their hard-working husbands at the door at the end of the day draped only in Saran wrap. Opponents of gender equality weren't the only obstacle, either. Feminist organizing often fractured from within, as proclamations of universal sisterhood failed to overcome differences of race and class. Before the twentieth century even began, women of color were explaining why they couldn't be expected to identify *only* as women, as if all women belonged in a single category.[9] But their message often went unheeded, particularly in the most widely circulated versions of feminist thought.

Ever since activists in the 1960s began calling themselves "second-wave" feminists, both scholars and the general public have described American

[5] Bureau of Labor Statistics, US Department of Labor, "Gender Pay Gap Largest in Sales, Lowest in Farm Occupations," *Economics Daily*, January 24, 2000, www.bls.gov/opub/ted/2000/jan/wk4/art01.htm

[6] See Arlie Hochschild and Anne Machung, *The Second Shift: Working Families and the Revolution at Home* (New York: Viking Books, 1989).

[7] See Ruth Rosen, *The World Split Open: How the Modern Women's Movement Changed America* (New York: Viking, 2000), 360.

[8] For more details on the women's movement from the 1960s forward, see ibid.

[9] See, among others, Anna Julia Cooper, "The Intellectual Progress of the Colored Woman of the United States since the Emancipation Proclamation: A Response to Fannie Barrier Williams," in *The Voice of Anna Julia Cooper*, ed. Charles Lemert and Esme Bahn (Lanham, MD: Rowman & Littlefield, 1998).

feminism in terms of waves.[10] The "first wave," the story goes, began with abolitionists and women's rights advocates in the 1840s and concluded some eight decades later, with US women finally achieving the right to vote through the Nineteenth Amendment in 1920. Progress then subsided until a powerful "second wave" of feminism crashed through American politics in the 1960s and 1970s, bringing with it an explosion of feminist print culture, the first federal laws against sex discrimination, the legalization of first-trimester abortion, widespread access to birth-control pills, the proliferation of consciousness-raising groups encouraging women to analyze their lives and assert their own needs, and the establishment of women's studies as a recognized discipline in academic institutions. A "third wave" built momentum in the 1990s, fueled by concerns about reproductive rights and workplace harassment and discrimination, as well as frustration over white feminists' failure to listen to women of color and to take action against racial oppression. When third-wave feminists embraced intersectionality – the idea that people are defined not only by gender but also by race, ethnicity, class, and other identity markers such as religion, ability, age, and sexual orientation – they elevated an idea with a long history, particularly in texts by women of color.[11] Advocates in each successive wave have, in turn, criticized their foremothers and proclaimed themselves to be more inclusive, more global, more progressive, more innovative.[12] In the 1990s, trans activists overturned the biologically determined gender binary that had structured feminist political organizing from its inception and often excluded trans men and women.[13] Because waves keep coming, they have been used as a shorthand for the ebb and flow of feminist activism that has unsettled basic assumptions about love, work, sexuality, intimacy, family, morality, and identity.

---

[10] For one of many critiques of the wave metaphor, see Kimberly Springer, "Third Wave Black Feminism?," *Signs* 27.4 (2002): 1059–82. For more history, see Elizabeth Evans and Prudence Chamberlain, "Critical Waves: Exploring Feminist Identity, Discourse, and Praxis in Western Feminism," *Social Movement Studies* 14.4 (2015): 396–409; Nancy A. Hewitt, "Feminist Frequencies: Regenerating the Wave Metaphor," *Feminist Studies* 38.3 (2012): 658–80.

[11] In addition to Cooper, cited above, see, among many others, Harriet Jacobs, *Incidents in the Life of a Slave Girl* (London: Penguin Classics, 2000); Frances Ellen Watkins Harper, "We Are All Bound Up Together," Eleventh National Women's Rights Convention, New York City, 1866, www .blackpast.org/african-american-history/speeches-african-american-history/1866-frances-ellen-watkins-harper-we-are-all-bound-together/

[12] Hewitt, 663–4.

[13] See Abram J. Lewis, "'Free Our Siblings, Free Ourselves:' Historicizing Trans Activism in the US, 1952–1992," *The American Historian* (May 2019), www.oah.org/tah/issues/2019/may/free-our-siblings-free-ourselves-historicizing-trans-activism-in-the-u.s-1952-1992/

But the wave metaphor, appealing as it may be, does not explain the many ways in which American novelists chronicled, resisted, inspired, and did feminist work. The 1970s, a high point of the second wave, saw a burst of important feminist novels, as varied as Toni Morrison's brilliant indictment of racist beauty culture, *The Bluest Eye* (1970); Rita Mae Brown's lesbian coming-of-age story *Rubyfruit Jungle* (1973); and Erica Jong's *Fear of Flying* (1973), which invented the term "the zipless fuck" for a passionate, uncomplicated sexual encounter and left unresolved the challenge of reconciling heterosexual desire with rage at patriarchal oppression. But as we chart the path of US feminisms – and, yes, the term should be plural – through twentieth-century fiction, we find feminist ideas shaping novels in every decade, sometimes especially during the quieter moments between the waves. More importantly, the wave model is misleading because it pays too much attention to the experiences of privileged white women at the expense of all other women. At no point in US history were all feminists white, and from the first decade of the twentieth century women's advocates said that they wanted to unite women across race and class. Yet even in the early 1970s, when radical socialist feminists sought earnestly, against great odds, to build cross-racial coalitions to enact change, few women of color shared in the joy and optimism white feminists found in the work.[14] It was always true that privileged white women found it easier to pursue gender equality with singular purpose, as if other forms of oppression were less important. For Indigenous women, for instance, decolonization, not feminism, was often their primary concern. The wave model misrepresents the intensely fraught politics of gender by ignoring how much racial privilege and racial oppression shaped feminist activism. Even worse from the standpoint of literary history, when we hold onto the wave model, we risk sidelining the achievements of some of the most aesthetically daring feminist novelists of the twentieth century – including Nella Larsen, Zora Neale Hurston, Ann Petry, Sandra Cisneros, Edwidge Danticat, Louise Erdrich, and Ana Castillo – all of whom represented gender as just one of several defining elements in their characters' lives.

Many Black feminists have observed that accounts of first- and second-wave feminism tend to highlight white feminist organizing and ignore the lived experiences of women of color. As Kimberly Springer wryly notes, acknowledging African American women makes "the wave, shall we say, a

---

[14] Winifred Breines, *The Trouble between Us: An Uneasy History of White and Black Women in the Feminist Movement* (Oxford: Oxford University Press, 2006), 14–19.

much bigger swell."[15] The wave model oversimplifies the fierce, vibrant feminist movements that burst forth, clashed, and subsided in the twentieth century, leaving both frustrated aspirations and lasting changes in their wake. It also minimizes the fractious trajectory of racial justice among women's rights advocates, who emerged from the abolitionist movement but split, notoriously, after the Civil War, when Congress proved more willing to give Black men the vote (via the Fifteenth Amendment, passed in 1870) than white women. When white feminists such as Elizabeth Cady Stanton declared that white women deserved the vote more than Black men, they enshrined white supremacism in the mainstream feminist movement and betrayed their high-minded calls for universal rights. Most damagingly, they wrongly suggested that the specific concerns of white middle-class women defined *the* women's politics of their era. The winking title of Marjorie Shuler's epistolary suffrage novel *For Rent – One Pedestal* (1917) applied only to women with class privilege; women who were never put on that pedestal in the first place had other, more pressing problems. The white supremacist version of feminism – the one that elevated white middle-class experiences over those of working-class, Indigenous, Black, Latina, and Asian women – attracted the most media attention throughout the twentieth century, whether it was 1916 and thousands of women holding suffrage banners were staring down Democratic Party convention delegates in St. Louis, Missouri, or the 1980s, when the editors of *Ms.*, the first mass-market feminist magazine, avoided putting Black women on the cover for fear of lowering newsstand sales.[16]

The overrepresentation of middle-class whiteness obscured the contributions of women of color and discouraged them from identifying with mainstream feminism. But that wasn't the sole reason feminist activism went only so far toward achieving justice for women who lacked racial and class privilege. The women's liberation movement was indebted to the political tradition of American liberalism – namely, the idea that free, self-directed individuals make up the foundation of civil society and have individual rights that warrant special protection by the state. This vision of independent selfhood, heady as it was, originated in a gendered division

---

[15] Springer, 1062.
[16] Mary Chapman, *Making Noise, Making News: Suffrage Print Culture and US Modernism* (Oxford: Oxford University Press, 2014), 55; Abigail Pogrebin, "How Do You Spell Ms.," *New York*, October 28, 2011, https://nymag.com/news/features/ms-magazine-2011-11/. For more on the intertwined resurgence of the Black and white feminist movements in the late 1960s and early 1970s, see Breines.

of labor, with a family unit where the father was responsible for women and children.[17] It worked best for middle-class white feminists who could afford to pay for college, childcare, domestic workers, and reproductive healthcare, among other things. Overall, it was an insufficient foundation for gender equality, given that so few women lived "free" from domestic and family responsibilities, and given that the consequences for defying conventions were so much harsher for women than for men. Edith Wharton gestures toward this problem early in the century in *The House of Mirth* (1905), when the struggling society heroine is entranced – but ultimately betrayed – by her erstwhile lover's masculinist ideal of a "Republic of the Spirit" where material concerns and societal expectations no longer matter. Radical socialist feminists of the 1970s, among others, pushed hard for structural changes to fight inequities and acknowledge human interdependency, but the major transformations they hoped for did not arrive.

This account of feminist politics and the novel is organized not by waves but by broad feminist themes and trajectories. Opening with a collaborative suffrage novel, it then considers how realist and modernist novels imagined women's quests for self-determination in the early decades of the century, the rise of domestic critiques at midcentury, and how novelists registered the evolution of two highly charged political issues: sexual and racial violence and abortion. It concludes with a brief discussion of transnational feminism in the 1990s.

Feminist activists have often forged collaborative projects, eschewing top-down, single-leader organizational models. The most influential suffrage novel, which featured collaboration and deliberation in both its form and content, followed this cooperative path. In 1917, as part of a massive and ultimately successful campaign that would make New York the only East Coast state to grant women full suffrage before the passage of the Nineteenth Amendment, suffragists used *The Sturdy Oak*, a collectively authored novel, as a successful publicity stunt. The Woman Suffrage Party in New York, with the help of author and editor Elizabeth Garver Jordan, enlisted fourteen popular writers – nine women and five men from various regions of the US, with a range of political affiliations – to contribute one chapter each to *The Sturdy Oak*, based on a scenario drafted by author Mary Austin. The composite novel was serialized in *Collier's Weekly* and then published as a book in the weeks before the

---

[17] See, among others, Wendy Brown, *States of Injury: Power and Freedom in Late Modernity* (Princeton, NJ: Princeton University Press, 1995).

November 1917 referendum on women's suffrage in New York state. As it narrates the ingenious, sustained efforts of suffragists in an upstate New York town to convert a white, anti-suffrage male political candidate to their cause, *The Sturdy Oak* celebrates consensus-building, unconventional gender roles, and a renewed democracy's triumph over corruption.[18] Its innovative use of multiple authors notwithstanding, *The Sturdy Oak* joined an established tradition of reform novels featuring political dialogues. In the last decade of the nineteenth century, for instance, African American abolitionist and suffragist Frances Ellen Watkins Harper anticipated the emphasis on conversation in *Iola Leroy* (1892), her intricately plotted account of inheritance, political affiliation, and an enslaved woman's quest for justice. In *Contending Forces*, Hopkins also makes conversation a key theme, using sewing-group discussions to call attention to Black women's political consciousness.

In the early decades of the century, feminist realist and modernist novels frequently depicted the suffocating contradictions of patriarchal ideology, which treated women as objects of sexual desire and property to be defended while denying women's own sexual desires and agency. Willa Cather's *O Pioneers!* (1913) recounts an epic tale of Alexandra Bergson, a young Swedish immigrant whose vision transforms the struggling Nebraska farm she inherits from her father. As the exclamatory title suggests, Cather celebrates the glorious fertility Alexandra nurtures. But Cather also undermines her own pastoral treatment of the prairie by acknowledging some of the damage wrought by patriarchy and settler colonialism. She makes apparent Alexandra's isolation and sexual repression, and she concludes the novel with the violent consequences of Alexandra's brother's affair with a beautiful bohemian woman unhappily married to a possessive husband. Told with more urban grit than epic sweep, Anzia Yezierska's *Bread Givers* (1925) details a young Jewish immigrant's lonely fight to escape poverty and her father, an Orthodox rabbi who exploits his daughters for personal gain, on the Lower East Side of Manhattan. Yezierska's protagonist and narrator, Sara Smolinsky, passionately resists the expectation that she marry and subordinate herself to a husband. Yet she never escapes her father, even after she educates herself and marries a man of her own choice. Nella Larsen, writing in spare, sensory prose, took readers even more deeply into a female psyche tortured by oppressive ideas that have been internalized. The devastating

---

[18] For an illuminating reading of *The Sturdy Oak* as a model of deliberative democracy, see Chapman, 154–73.

narrative arc of Larsen's *Quicksand* (1928) dramatizes the consequences of American culture's racist hyper-sexualization of Black women. The white supremacist myth that Black men posed a constant sexual threat to white women, which was used to justify a rising tide of lethal white mob violence against African Americans in the late nineteenth and early twentieth centuries, also constructed Black women as always consenting to sex. The reality that most white violence against African Americans was designed to perpetuate social and economic subordination was obscured by this damaging lie, which carried the vicious legacy of slavery and its institutionalized rape of enslaved women forward into the twentieth century. Larsen's mixed-race heroine, an educated woman fearful that her sexual desires confirm white stereotypes about Black savagery, flees the racist USA for Denmark, only to find herself treated as an exotic sexual object. When she finally finds release by marrying a Black preacher, she slips into a nightmare of endless domestic labor and childbearing, sinking into the quicksand of the title. In the lyrical *Their Eyes Were Watching God* (1937), Zora Neale Hurston crafts a more hopeful vision, adapting Black folklore and oral traditions to show the evolution of her heroine, Janie Crawford, through three marriages and multiple vibrant communities. Hurston showcases Janie's wit, courage, sexual joy, and longing for adventure as she navigates the male-dominated culture that tries to control her. Yet Janie cannot shake off patriarchal oppression entirely; the novel's most controversial scenes portray intimate partner violence in an otherwise happy marriage.

Along with the post–World War II economic boom came a crackdown on dissent. Women who had entered the workforce during the war were told that it was their patriotic duty to give up their jobs to men and return home. The 1950s idealization of the white middle-class housewife eager to spend money on commodities and services soon inspired a subversive confessional genre that would prove foundational for the women's liberation movement. Novels such as Alix Kates Shulman's *Memoirs of an Ex-Prom Queen* (1972), Dorothy Bryant's *Ella Price's Journal* (1972), Sheila Ballantyne's *Norma Jean the Termite Queen* (1975), and Marilyn French's *The Women's Room* (1977) came to be known as housewife fiction.[19] With verve, wit, and intensely personal first-person narratives, housewife fiction defied the glorification of domesticity. It refused to dismiss the mundane activities of daily living as unworthy of mention and it often included

---

[19] See Imelda Whelehan, *The Feminist Bestseller: From* Sex and the Single Girl *to* Sex and the City (London: Palgrave Macmillan, 2005), especially 63–72; Lisa Maria Hogeland, *Feminism and Its Fictions* (Philadelphia: University of Pennsylvania Press, 1998).

candid references to unsatisfying sex and unwanted pregnancies. The genre was a logical outgrowth of the boom of consciousness-raising, the practice of women meeting in small groups to reflect on their lives. It included formal innovations, too, such as nonlinear plots, narrative fragments, surreal sequences, montages, and aestheticized recastings of household items like grocery lists and cleaning products.[20] A formally adventurous novel that anticipated the genre by nearly two decades is Gwendolyn Brooks's elliptical *Maud Martha* (1953). Composed of thirty-four chapters of verse, *Maud Martha* recounts the girlhood, courtship, marriage, and motherhood of its title character, a Black woman whose rich interior life reveals how deeply constraining she finds conventional domestic life. At its most transformative, housewife fiction exposed fault lines in patriarchal systems; broke taboos about menstruation, sexuality, and pregnancy; and manifested in stark terms the strangling confinement of domestic norms for women.

Many authors credited the feminist movement with inspiring them to write, among them novelist Dorothy Allison, who wrote, in the foreword to a twenty-first-century edition of French's international bestseller *The Women's Room*: "Young women of the new millennium have no idea of the passionate sense of connection and purpose all us 'women's libbers' knew. Read *The Women's Room* for a bit of that revolutionary intoxication."[21] Allison gestures toward the collective thrill felt by the radical feminists who banded together to create change. Housewife novels, however, did not manifest the broad range of women's experiences. They featured hetero-sexual women and were written largely by white middle-class women. Occasionally, authors drew on white supremacist tropes to make their case against women's oppression, shoring up the very racial divisions that many feminists said they wanted to dismantle. In Anne Richardson Roiphe's satiric *Up the Sandbox!* (1970), a young, college-educated mother rails against the routine drudgery of domestic labor by ironically claiming sisterhood with an Indigenous woman from the distant past.[22] Using an ethnic and sexual slur for Native women, Roiphe's heroine erases

---

[20] See Megan Behrent, "Suburban Captivity Narratives: Feminism, Domesticity, and the Liberation of the American Housewife," *JNT: Journal of Narrative Theory* 49.2 (2019): 247–86; Rachele Dini, "'The House Was a Garbage Dump': Waste, Mess, and Aesthetic Reclamation in 1960s and 1970s 'Mad Housewife' Fiction," *Textual Practice* 34.3 (2020): 479–505.

[21] Dorothy Allison, "Foreword," in Marilyn French, *The Women's Room* (New York: Penguin, 2009), xiv.

[22] "Despite computers and digit telephone numbers, nuclear fission, my life hardly differs from that of an Indian Squaw settled in a tepee on the same Manhattan land centuries ago. Pick, clean, prepare, throw out, dig a hole, bury the waste – she was my sister." Ann Richardson Roiphe, *Up the Sandbox!* (New York: Simon & Schuster, 1970), 18.

contemporary Native women and invokes a presumably less-evolved fore-
bear to illustrate the absurdity of her own repetitive labor in the modern
world. Indigenous feminist writers countered these portrayals. Beginning
with her first novel, *Love Medicine* (1984), Louise Erdrich, a member of
the Turtle Mountain Band of Chippewa Indians, reimagined Native
womanhood in empowering ways, integrating racial and ethnic mythologies in her storytelling to celebrate Native women and men's survival and
humanity. Its origins as a protest genre notwithstanding, housewife fiction – defined as it was by private property, since the "wife" belonged to
the "house" – promised a limited societal transformation. For Erdrich and
her Indigenous sisters, the genre could only be yet another extension of
settler colonialism, a practice that displaces Indigenous populations and
asserts ongoing state sovereignty and control over their lands. The Native
writers' goal was not so much to refuse restrictive gender norms, but rather
to imagine Indigenous self-determination.[23]

Violence against women – threatened and actual – recurs in feminist
novels. Writers often contested the misunderstanding of rape as erotically
fulfilling for women, a notion widely circulated in hugely popular narratives including Margaret Mitchell's *Gone with the Wind* (1936) and Grace
Metalious's *Peyton Place* (1956). This distortion – which brought together
several contradictory and wrongheaded assumptions about women's
sexuality – made it difficult for survivors to come forward and for perpe-
trators to be prosecuted. As the century progressed, novelists became more
explicit in their depictions of women's sexual pleasure, their rejections of
the idea that female sexual desire could be unlocked only by male aggres-
sion, and their indictments of domestic violence and sexual assault. Early
in the century, Hopkins's *Contending Forces* showed a rape survivor's
triumph over humiliation and disinheritance, while Wharton's *The
House of Mirth* included a chilling but subtle scene of a protagonist barely
escaping assault.[24] By the late twentieth century, a whole host of novels
represented the trauma of rape and incest survivors and illustrated the
many ways in which sexual violence was used to control women and girls,
among them Toni Morrison's *Beloved* (1987), which became one of the
most highly regarded novels in American literary history. Strikingly, these

---

[23] See Mark Rifkin, "Feeling, Memory, and Peoplehood in Contemporary Native Women's Poetry,"
in *Gender in American Literature and Culture*, ed. Jean M. Lutes and Jennifer Travis (Cambridge:
Cambridge University Press, 2021), 332–49.

[24] Catherine Keyser, "US Women Writers, Sexual Violence, and Narrative Resistance," in *Gender in
American Literature and Culture*, ed. Jean M. Lutes and Jennifer Travis (Cambridge: Cambridge
University Press, 2021), 160–72.

novels also mark women's erotic desire as a source of power and incorporate the poetic force of vernacular speech to give voice to experiences and to people who have been systematically silenced.[25] Alice Walker's novel *The Color Purple* (1982) relates, in a series of extraordinary letters, the uneducated Celie's survival of incest and spousal abuse. At the same time, the novel celebrates the sexual joy Celie finds with another woman. In *Bastard Out of Carolina* (1992), a groundbreaking novel that refuses to desexualize Bone, the illegitimate, poor white child and abuse survivor who narrates the story, Dorothy Allison hints at Bone's lesbianism and makes a savior out of Bone's lesbian aunt Raylene, who teaches Bone to resist the message that women must be selfless wives who accept their husbands no matter what. In the warm, often funny *Memory Mambo* (1996), Achy Obejas writes in the voice of Juani, a twenty-five-year-old Cuban-born American lesbian on a search for self-understanding and self-forgiveness in the wake of domestic violence and in the midst of her own political awakening. A nonlinear narrative obsessed with the process of remembering, *Memory Mambo* dramatizes the complexity of sexual desire, reckons with the consequences of exile, and shows that home is no haven from predators. The many other novels that address sexual violence include Maxine Hong Kingston's *The Woman Warrior* (1976), Marilyn French's *The Women's Room* (1977), Sandra Cisneros's *The House on Mango Street* (1983), Bharati Mukherjee's *Jasmine* (1989), Jane Smiley's *A Thousand Acres* (1992), and Patricia Chao's *Monkey King* (1996).

Ann Petry's evocative bestseller *The Street* (1946) was a midcentury standout in this rich tradition of critique. A critical and popular success that combined realist and Gothic conventions, it quickly sold more than 1.5 million copies. *The Street* is set in Harlem in the 1940s, where Petry's protagonist, the beautiful, smart, isolated Lutie Johnson, struggles to raise her son alone. Despite Lutie's determination and work ethic, she cannot escape male oppression, and the novel ends in violence and tragedy. Although Lutie is subjected to violence by both white and Black men, Petry shows that racial oppression is central to her downfall. Lutie's deep preoccupation with sexual propriety – a reaction against the oversexualization of Black women – fails to protect her from sexual predators and contributes to her failure to thrive.[26] In her depiction of Lutie's

---

[25] Audre Lorde, "Uses of the Erotic: The Erotic as Power," in *Sister Outsider: Essays and Speeches* (Berkeley, CA: Crossing Press, 2007).

[26] See Evie Shockley, "Buried Alive: Gothic Homelessness, Black Women's Sexuality, and (Living) Death in Ann Petry's *The Street*," *African American Review* 40.3 (2006): 439–60, especially 444.

neighborhood as an environment that prohibits flourishing, Petry antici-pated the principles of the reproductive justice movement, launched in the 1990s by women of color who argued that the pro-choice rhetoric of the abortion debate failed to take into account the broader societal circum-stances that constrain women's choices. Instead of focusing on an individ-ual woman's right to choose, reproductive justice advocates insist on the human right to maintain bodily autonomy, to choose to have children or not to have children, and to parent children in safe, sustainable communities.[27]

Reproductive healthcare for women has always been a feminist flash-point for exposing fundamental injustices based on class, race, and gender. Abortion was criminalized in the late nineteenth century, thanks to an avowedly anti-feminist campaign by the newly formed American Medical Association.[28] In the early twentieth century, eugenics proponents sought to use birth control and abortion to limit reproduction by immigrants and people of color, while urging white, middle-class women to have more babies. From the 1940s until the early 1970s, restrictions on abortion increased while demands for abortion intensified. Historical records show, unsurprisingly, that white women who could afford abortions were most likely to get them.[29] After the Supreme Court ruled in Roe v. Wade in 1973 that the right to abortion was a fundamental liberty protected by the constitution, abortion became legal but remained highly contested.

Novelists engaged abortion politics from multiple angles, usually with attention to economic costs and class status. Some writers dramatized abortion as an absolute evil, as F. Scott Fitzgerald did in *The Beautiful and the Damned* (1922), when a young wife's barely-spoken-of (possible) abortion sends a profligate, hard-partying couple's marriage into a down-ward spiral. In contrast, feminist novelists focused more on how women negotiated biological imperatives, material circumstances, and systematic disempowerment. Many described unwanted pregnancies in coming-of-age narratives with female protagonists. In *Summer* (1917), Edith Wharton crafted a troubling portrait of Charity Royall, a smart, poor, ambitious,

---

[27] See Loretta J. Ross, Lynn Roberts, Erika Derkas, Whitney Peoples, and Pamela Bridgewater Toure, eds., *Radical Reproductive Justice: Foundations, Theory, Practice, Critique* (New York: Feminist Press of the City University of New York, 2017); Sistersong, "Reproductive Justice," www.sistersong.net/reproductive-justice

[28] Leslie J. Reagan, *When Abortion Was a Crime: Women, Medicine, and the Law in the United States, 1867–1973* (Berkeley: University of California Press, 1997), 10–14.

[29] Karen Weingarten, *Abortion in the American Imagination: Before Life and Choice, 1880–1940* (New Brunswick, NJ: Rutgers University Press, 2014), 140.

and fiercely proud young woman whose small-town sexual awakening ends in an unintended pregnancy. After visiting a profiteering abortionist's office and searching unsuccessfully for other options, Charity (named to remind her to be grateful, we are told) submits to marriage with her guardian, a middle-aged, alcoholic widower who adopted her years before, when his wife was still alive. In *Weeds* (1923), Edith Summers Kelley recounts the physical and spiritual suffocation of Judith, a poor tobacco-farm wife in rural Kentucky who, convinced she won't survive her third pregnancy in three years, tries unsuccessfully to induce a miscarriage with a knitting needle. *Weeds* sold poorly but was revived in the early 1970s as a feminist achievement. Eventually a graphic chapter describing the brutally difficult birth of Judith's first child was restored; Kelley's first publisher had refused to include it. In Agnes Smedley's radical-leftist *Daughter of the Earth* (1929), the protagonist's two abortions make manifest the disempowerment of women in the market economy.[30] The pregnant, sixteen-year-old Dewey Dell's failed quest to get an abortion is central to the plot of William Faulkner's *As I Lay Dying* (1930), which uses a collective of voices to tell the story of the impoverished Bundren family's journey to bury their mother. In a series of interior monologues that represent individual characters' flow of thoughts, Faulkner fore-grounds Dewey Dell's anguish, dread and determination, as well as her vulnerability to a corrupt, patriarchal system that exploits her.

Fictional treatments of abortion became more graphic, and more point-edly critical, as frustration with the ban on abortion mounted. The year before abortion was legalized, two novels intervened in especially strong terms. Shulman dramatized the hypocrisy and painful consequences of medical authorities' position by including a graphic at-home abortion scene in *Memoirs of an Ex-Prom Queen*, a sardonic send-up of beauty culture and heterosexual courtship and marriage. Bryant concluded her tale of the political awakening of a working-class suburban wife, *Ella Price's Journal*, with Ella waiting to terminate her pregnancy on Christmas Day. Through Ella's sweeping rejection of domesticity and motherhood, Bryant posed abortion as a condition of rebirth for her protagonist. After abortion was legalized, even more novels referenced the procedure, most often stressing moral ambiguity and emotional ambivalence. In *Meridian* (1976), Alice Walker tells of a young Black Civil Rights activist who, pregnant after unrewarding sex with her inattentive lover, gets an abortion, a choice for which she seeks self-forgiveness throughout the novel.

[30] Ibid., 97.

The anxiety caused by the anti-feminist resurgence of the 1980s is vividly manifested in Margaret Atwood's dystopic *The Handmaid's Tale* (1985), which imagines a future US where political chaos and a fertility crisis have allowed Christian fundamentalists to enslave women and enforce brutal, Old Testament-inspired punishments on dissenters. Framing the narrative as an anthropological find in a far-distant future, Atwood introduces the story as an ancient fragment of a first-person manuscript written by a "Handmaid," a fertile woman who was required to have sex and bear children on behalf of the theocratic state.

The transnational dimensions of feminist practice in the US grew in the late twentieth century, spurred by postcolonial theory, globalization, and activists seeking to avoid complicity with imperialist, capitalist nation-states dominated by men. Feminist novels shifted as well, with nuanced accounts of border crossing and the complexities of gender equality across cultural contexts, among them Edwidge Danticat's *Breath, Eyes, Memory* (1994), which examines the repercussions of individual and state forms of violence in Haiti and the US through a young immigrant's eyes; Julia Alvarez's *In the Time of Butterflies* (1994), which tells a multivocal fictionalized account of the lives of the Mirabal sisters, who were killed for their resistance to the dictatorship of Rafael Trujillo in the Dominican Republic; and Ruth Ozeki's *My Year of Meats* (1998), a narrative meditation on fertility, globalization, and the meat industry that tracks the crossed paths of a Japanese American documentary maker and a Japanese housewife struggling to escape her overbearing husband. As the century closed, in other words, novelists were insisting that there was more feminist work to be done than ever. The early decades of the twenty-first century would certainly bear that out.

CHAPTER 6

Sexual Liberation Movements

Guy Davidson

Reflecting on the immediate postwar moment in *Advertisements for Myself* (1959), a compendium of essays and short fictions, Norman Mailer wrote:

> There was a frontier for my generation of novelists. Coming out of the orgy of the war, our sense of sex and family was torn in two. The past did not exist for us. We had to write our way out into the unspoken territories of sex – there was so much there, it was new, and our talent depended on going into the borderland.[1]

Mailer's statement elaborates the excitement of novelists about new possibilities of sexual representation that had been made possible by the war and its aftermath, which set in place the coordinates for what came to be known as the "sexual revolution." The war saw massive mobilization, with millions of men and many women joining the military, as well as millions of civilians moving to another county or state for war jobs. Living and working alongside others different from themselves in terms of background and outlook, many Americans were subjected to a kind of involuntary cosmopolitanism. The situation was compounded in the early Cold War period, despite its reputation (in many ways deserved) for airless conformism and political repression. Prosperity, increased social mobility, and enhanced communication networks enabled the significant expansion of civil society. To an unprecedented extent, ethnic and racial minorities began to count in political discussion and cultural representation. Concomitantly, the popularization of social scientific knowledge encouraged the uptake of a degree of cultural relativism across significant swathes of the population; and this cultural relativism was matched by a significant degree of moral relativism with regard to sexual behavior, promulgated by the discourse of psychiatry, then entering the zenith of its prestige – although psychiatry continued to pathologize homosexuality. The mobilizations of the war had enhanced

---

[1] Norman Mailer, *Advertisements for Myself* (Cambridge, MA: Harvard University Press, 1992), 476.

opportunities for heterosexual contact outside of marriage, as well as for the self-actualization and community-building of homosexuals. These changed behaviors and patterns of association only increased after the war, and by the second half of the 1960s, a simultaneously cultural and political sexual revolution was spectacularly in swing. To an important degree, the 1960s moment of the revolution marked shifts in representation rather than behavior, with the relaxation of censorship and self-censorship across the gamut of media ushering in unprecedented levels of explicitness in the representation and discussion of sex. Yet notions of sexual freedom were also important to the political projects of the counterculture and broad sections of the New Left, which opposed monogamy and sexual hypocrisy as part of their radical critique of American social structures.[2]

If Mailer's 1959 statement indicated a new openness about sex, it also anticipated the divisions that marked the sexual revolution and that played out in the fiction associated with it. Invoking the political myth of the frontier, Mailer's investment in heroic masculinist individualism could hardly be less obvious; although, if his metaphor is unsubtle, it's also something of a palimpsest, suggesting, along with its appeal to America's history of westward colonization, both the long-established metaphor of the land as woman's body and Freud's comment about the "dark continent" of the unconscious. Mailer's phallocentrism and heteronormativity here, which were also elaborated in his fiction, indicate the general tendency of the sexual revolution, which was dominated by the interests and attitudes of straight men. His invocation of the frontier of sex is revealing in its very stridency, bringing into relief the similar, if more muted and occasionally less self-serious, attitudes of other straight male authors of sexually daring works, most notably John Updike and Philip Roth, authors respectively of *Couples* (1968) and *Portnoy's Complaint* (1969), both works of breakthrough frankness. Straight men have never needed a movement

[2] This paragraph draws on Beth Bailey, *Sex in the Heartland* (Cambridge, MA: Harvard University Press, 2002); John D'Emilio and Estelle B. Freedman, *Intimate Matters: A History of Sexuality in America*, 3rd edition (Chicago: University of Chicago Press, 2012); Matthew Frye Jacobson, *Roots Too: White Ethnic Revival in Post-Civil Rights America* (Cambridge, MA: Harvard University Press, 2008), 151–3. For an analysis of statistical data, primarily of "illegitimate" births from the 1940s and 1950s, which establishes that a "revolution" in significant areas of sexual behavior preceded the 1960s, see Alan Petingy, *The Permissive Society: America, 1941–1965* (Cambridge: Cambridge University Press, 2009), 100–33. For an argument that the 1960s sexual revolution was largely a revolution in media representation rather than behavior, see, Eric Schaefer, "Introduction: Sex Seen: 1968 and Rise of 'Public' Sex," in *Sex Scene: Media and the Sexual Revolution*, ed. Eric Schaefer (Durham, NC: Duke University Press, 2014), 1–22. For discussion of the political dimensions of the sexual revolution, see David Allyn, *Make Love, Not War: The Sexual Revolution: An Unfettered History* (New York: Routledge, 2001).

to organize around, and novels centering straight male sexuality in the decades after the war played into the tradition of white American masculine individualism – albeit complicated by a new literary attention to ethnic difference, of which Roth is a famous exemplar. But if Mailer, in his 1959 statement, not too implicitly reserved the task of exploring and conquering the "unspoken territories" of sex for straight men, novels showing the impress of feminism and the gay, lesbian, and trans liberation movements in the following decades complicated his picture. Novels interacting with these movements were necessarily engaged by collectivity and community in ways absent from the straight male novel. If these novels eschew the mythic cadences of a Mailer, however, they echo his characteristically American emphasis on personal freedom. In this chapter, I highlight the tensions and connections between individualism and collectivism in some key novels and literary movements that responded to and helped shape the postwar discourse of sexual freedom, attending first to battles over literary censorship and then to novelistic engagements with queer liberation.[3]

Freedoms to Read and Write

Mailer's statement in *Advertisements for Myself* about the terra incognita of sex introduces "The Time of Her Time," a mildly sexually explicit excerpt from a then in-progress novel that was never finished. Vaingloriously, Mailer inserts his uncompleted novel into a storied panoply of banned novels, predicting that, "by present standards of publishing practice, it will be, if I can do it, an unpublishable work ... I do not have the confidence that you will see it in its completed form, except as an outlaw of the underground, like *Tropic of Cancer, Ulysses,* or *Les Cent-Vingt Journées de Sodome.*"[4] Mailer's metaphor of the frontier of sexual representation that

---

[3] Space does not permit exploration of the second-wave feminist novel, whose narratives typically combined sexual and political awakening, as in Erica Jong's blockbuster *Fear of Flying* (1977); for a discussion, see Meryl Altman, "Beyond Trashiness: The Sexual Language of 1970s Feminist Fiction," *Journal of International Women's Studies* 4.2 (2003): 7–19. Feminist ideology was also compellingly combined with gay and lesbian liberation politics in a series of 1970s science fiction novels imagining post-capitalist futures in which sexual and gender hierarchies are abolished, including Ursula Le Guin's *The Dispossessed* (1974), Joanna Russ's *The Female Man* (1975), Samuel Delany's *Trouble on Triton* (1976), and Marge Piercy's *Woman on the Edge of Time* (1976); on these novels, see Tom Moylan, *Demand the Impossible: Science Fiction and the Utopian Imagination* (London: Methuen, 1986).

[4] Mailer, 477.

opened up after the war suggests a sudden change, but there was still significant print media censorship of obscenity at midcentury. Acclaimed for its gritty depiction of military experience, Mailer's debut novel, *The Naked and the Dead* (1948), nevertheless famously had its "fucks" changed to "fugs." Yet the same year that *Advertisements* was published saw the battle against print censorship gain sudden momentum. In 1959, the ban on D. H. Lawrence's *Lady Chatterley's Lover* was lifted, initiating a series of successful legal challenges to obscenity rulings against literary works throughout the 1960s. These were spearheaded by the avowedly countercultural publisher Grove Press and largely hinged on the defense that the books concerned had literary "merit."

Mailer's description of the exploration of the dark continent of sex simultaneously invoked a boundary-pushing of literary form: "The past did not exist for us ... [O]ur talent depended on going into the border-land." His prediction, or hope, that his never finished book would join other "outlaw[s] of the underground" speaks not only to the 1950s climate of censorship but also to the emergent construction of a modernist counter-canon, in which sexual explicitness intersected with literary inno-vation. Beginning with books with elite credentials (the work of Sade, *Madame Bovary, Ulysses*), this tradition, as developed in the US by writers such as Henry Miller, William S. Burroughs, John Rechy, and Hubert Selby, Jr., is characterized by democratic aspirations. Loren Glass usefully names this development "vulgar modernism" to indicate both "its vernacular aspirations and ... its erotic preoccupations."[5]

The original exponent of vulgar modernism, Miller was also a louche father figure for sexually frank writers of a more middlebrow stripe, including Philip Roth and Erica Jong. From a working-class New York background, Miller transplanted in 1930 to Paris, where, beginning with *Tropic of Cancer* (1934), he wrote works whose explicitness rendered them at first unpublishable in his native country. Instead, Miller's books were published mainly by the Paris-based English-language Obelisk Press, which specialized in publishing books banned or likely to be banned in anglophone jurisdictions. Obelisk publications were often smuggled into the US, and the transportation of many of Miller's books by GIs returning from the war and their subsequent circulation established him as a widely read writer by the dawn of the 1960s, giving Grove the impetus to wage a

---

[5] Loren Glass, *Counterculture Colophon: Grove Press the* Evergreen Review, *and the Incorporation of the Avant-Garde* (Stanford, CA: Stanford University Press, 2013), 123.

censorship battle over *Cancer* from 1961 to 1964.[6] Outside the courtroom, Grove conducted a publicity campaign on behalf of the book that, in the spirit of the emerging New Left, emphasized the expansion of democracy. In 1962, in its magazine *Evergreen Review*, it published a "Statement in Support of the Freedom to Read" based on the pronouncement of the judge in one of the *Tropic* trials: "[A]s a corollary to the freedom of speech and the press, there is also a freedom to read."[7] Signed by a long list of luminaries, including James Baldwin, Saul Bellow, Hugh Hefner, Carson McCullers, Marianne Moore, and Lionel Trilling, the statement argued that "the issue is not whether *Tropic of Cancer* is a masterpiece of American literature" but rather "the right of a free people to decide for itself what it may or may not read."[8] The statement and the surrounding campaign helped shift the argument about literary obscenity from one about merit to one that positioned reading as one of the individual freedoms central to America's self-conception.

If the campaign to publish him was organized around readerly freedom, Miller's own literary project was spurred by a radical commitment to a freedom to write that undermined the very idea of the "masterpiece" (although he would be ironically taken up as a literary master in the rush of academic enthusiasm for vulgar modernism that followed Grove's successful legal challenge). Miller's work was explicitly anti-novelistic, anti-literary, and anti-aesthetic. In the opening pages of *Cancer*, he announces: "This is not a book. This is libel, slander, defamation of character. This is not a book, in the ordinary sense of the word. No, this is a prolonged insult, a gob of spit in the face of Art, a kick in the pants to God, Man, Destiny, Time, Love, Beauty . . . what you will."[9] Miller's one-man assault on art, literature, and civilizational values was realized in a scatological, autobiographical narrative that obsesses over scenes of sexual intercourse, bluntly rendered in a profane vocabulary of "fucks," "cunts," "pricks," and "cocks." *Tropic* provided the model for the rest of his novelistic output, which constitutes a massive work (two trilogies' worth) of what Elisabeth Ladenson calls "autography."[10] *Tropic* – and Miller's work generally – is scatological not only because of its sexual preoccupation but also because of the pervasion of its diegesis by grime, squalor, and,

---

[6] Ibid., 112. Miller's less explicit works were published in the US by New Directions.
[7] Quoted in ibid., 114.   [8] Quoted in ibid., 114.
[9] Henry Miller, *Tropic of Cancer* (London: Calder and Boyars, 1963), 2.
[10] Elisabeth Ladenson, *Dirt for Art's Sake: Books on Trial from* Madame Bovary *to* Lolita (Ithaca, NY: Cornell University Press), 165. Miller's two trilogies comprise *Tropic of Cancer, Black Spring* (1936), and *Tropic of Capricorn* (1939); and *Sexus* (1949), *Plexus* (1953), and *Nexus* (1960).

above all, shit.[11] Miller's unsparing rendition across his trilogies of a hand-to-mouth life in Paris and New York has affinities with the "underground man" narratives established by Fyodor Dostoevsky and continued in the work of Louis-Ferdinand Céline (both acknowledged influences on Miller). But Miller's stylistic and affective exuberance offsets the resentment and nihilism associated with the figure of the underground man; that exuberance also arguably complicates the misogyny for which Miller was famously attacked by Kate Millett in her germinal feminist work *Sexual Politics* (1970).[12]

Miller's commitment to autography entailed the demolition of the barriers between art and life; he described the spirit of *Cancer* in a letter as "first person, uncensored, formless – fuck everything!"[13] Elsewhere, he wrote of the novel, "I used my own name throughout. I didn't write a piece of fiction: I wrote an autobiographical document, a *human* book."[14] Rejecting the shaping form of art, Miller's novels stand athwart modernism, with its dedication to aesthetic novelty. As Ladenson and Glass have shown, his project is clearly indebted to modernist innovations: It takes up the model of "seemingly endless autography" bequeathed by Proust; and its devotion to the unmitigatedly personal is dialectically related to the modernist doctrine of impersonality.[15] Paradoxically, Miller's "fuck everything" stance, which aims to do away with literary values, enables an advancement of literary form. Anticipating Mailer's metaphor of the terra incognita of sexually frank literature, Jack Kahane, the owner of Obelisk, wrote that, when he first read Miller, he was "exalted by the triumphant sensation of all explorers who have at last fallen upon the object of their years of search."[16] It was Miller's representation of the unrepresentable that was important here; as Miller wrote in *Cancer*: "there is only one thing which interests me vitally now, and that is the recording of all that which is omitted in books."[17]

Although Miller was important for many other writers interested in representing the unrepresentable, the other most lastingly influential vulgar modernist, William S. Burroughs, had little time for him (the feeling was mutual). There are significant historical and aesthetic affinities between the two writers, however. Burroughs's *Naked Lunch* (1959) was, like *Cancer*, subject to a (partly concurrent) landmark censorship battle. After the publication of excerpts in little magazines in the US ran into

[11] Ladenson, 173.   [12] See ibid., 159.   [13] Quoted in ibid., 250, n.9.
[14] Quoted in ibid., 167.   [15] Ibid., 166; Glass, 112.   [16] Quoted in Ladenson, 171.
[17] Miller, *Tropic of Cancer*, 11.

difficulties with the authorities, the novel was first published in Paris by Olympia Press (a rebrand of Obelisk) in advance of the US legal challenge, again mounted by Grove; the 1966 ruling in favor of the book marked the effective end of literary censorship. Burroughs's novel, like Miller's, combined obscenity and a lack of plot, and Burroughs, like Miller, opposed his project to conventional novelistic form: "THIS IS NOT A NOVEL," he wrote, emphatically, in a letter to one of his editors.[18] *Lunch*'s lack of a clear intentional structure, one of the key evidences of artistic merit, meant that Grove's legal team was faced with the challenge, as one early scholarly appraisal put it, to "prove to the court's satisfaction that *Naked Lunch* is a book."[19]

Burroughs pushed the combination of obscenity and formlessness in still more transgressive directions than Miller. While Miller's work cleaved to autobiographical and naturalist protocols, *Lunch* is freewheeling and surrealistic, a series of loosely connected nightmarish-comic vignettes. The novel begins in a more or less realistically rendered version of New York's junkie underworld, but the scene soon shifts to the Interzone, a hallucinatory landscape pervaded by political paranoia, in which fantastical scenarios of addiction, sadism, and encounters with bad-trip monsters play out. The most notorious episode is an intensely profane and explicit description of the erotic hangings and cannibalistic consumption of teenage boys. Politically alert, if nihilistic, Burroughs's novel seemed to other members of the literary vanguard such as Mailer and Allen Ginsberg (both of whom gave expert testimony in support of the book) to indicate the "triumph" of the vulgar modernist vision, in which the "subversive energies of literary modernism" were translated "into the political and sexual realm."[20]

Burroughs's queerness – and the queerness of much of his writing about sex – is interesting to consider in this respect. The politics for which Burroughs – and Miller – were claimed involved the pushing aside of hypocrisies that the emerging New Left and counterculture saw as distorting authentic sexual expression, rather than rallying around any particular sexual identity. In the 1960s struggle for the freedom to read, male homosexuality took on a transgressive cachet, evidenced not only in the acclaim given to *Lunch*, but also in the cultic appreciation of Jean Genet,

[18] William S. Burroughs, "Letter to Irving Rosenthal [1960]," in William S. Burroughs, *Naked Lunch: The Restored Text*, ed. James Grauerholz and Barry Miles (London: Penguin, 2015), 249.
[19] Frank McConnell, "William Burroughs and the Literature of Addiction," *Massachusetts Review* 8.4 (1967): 668; quoted in Glass, 118.
[20] Glass, 120.

whose novelistic renditions of a Parisian criminal homosexual underworld were also published by Grove. Burroughs and the other Beats idolized Genet; like him, they celebrated male homosexuality as a form of social outlawry. But if Genet's underworld had an edgy glamor, Burroughs and the Beats were repelled by the American gay subculture. In this, the Beats resembled many other midcentury commentators on homosexuality, who, even when they were sympathetic to homosexual self-expression, phobically associated the subculture with effeminacy. Invested in a defiantly masculine notion of queerness, Burroughs was one of the most vociferously effeminophobic of midcentury writers, once writing in a letter, for instance, that "[a]ll complete swish fairies should be killed."[21] Catharine Stimpson has argued that the Beats' frank representation of homosexuality helped create the conditions for gay liberation;[22] yet their hostility to homosexual collectivity also put them at odds with the gay liberationist impulse, which was necessarily based on a sense of shared identity. The literary representation of ideas of gay and lesbian liberation was instead played out in a less aesthetically transgressive, more conventionally realist tradition that began immediately after the war.

Literature and Liberation

The circumstances of World War II both affirmed homosexual identity and strengthened the stigmatization and surveillance to which homosexuals were subjected. During the war, the armed services for the first time sought to identify homosexual enlistees and to exclude them from their ranks. Yet military service and mass mobilization on the home front also greatly increased opportunities for those already interested in same-sex sexuality or awakened people to that possibility. Subsequently, demobilization helped consolidate a sense of homosexuals as an oppressed minority deserving of rights. On the one hand, many returning homosexual service personnel settled in major cities, with the consequent enlargement and revitalization of those cities' subcultures deepening a sense of gay community. On the other, thousands of gay and lesbian veterans received undesirable discharges from the military for homosexuality and were thus shut out from the benefits afforded by the 1944 GI Bill, as well as frequently

---

[21] William S. Burroughs, *The Letters of William S. Burroughs: 1945–1959*, ed. Oliver Harris (Harmondsworth: Penguin, 1994), 119.

[22] Catharine R. Stimpson, "The Beat Generation and the Trials of Homosexual Liberation," *Salmagundi* 58–9 (1983): 373–92.

discriminated against by employers, colleges, and other institutions. This unfair treatment precipitated the foundation of the homophile rights groups, beginning with the Mattachine Society in 1950.[23]

Responding to and exemplifying the new gay visibility, a wave of middlebrow novels dealing with the agony of the homosexual individual appeared in the immediate postwar moment, including Charles Jackson's *The Fall of Valor* (1946), Gore Vidal's *The City and the Pillar* (1948), and Loren Wahl's *The Invisible Glass* (1950). Usually dealing with the experience of gay serving officers or veterans, these novels' investigations of homosexuality were almost exclusively concentrated on men. Elsewhere I have discussed this group of novels under the heading "homosexual problem novels," because of their affinities with other so-called social problem novels of the era dealing with the difficulties of ethnic and racial minorities, usually Jews and African Americans.[24] Yet the homosexual novels are beset by an ambivalence that is not evident – or certainly not so pervasively evident – in literature dealing with the African American or Jewish experience. Inflected by the deep stigmatization of homosexuality, they elaborate an uneasy mix of assertion and aversion with regard to queer identity.

Aversion is visited on the homosexual problem novel protagonist himself, whose experience characteristically involves much shame and suffering and who is either killed off at the end or left tragically resigned to the unhappiness of homosexuality. But the novels are fundamentally pleas for sympathy for the gay individual's plight; it is in representations of the effeminate and effeminizing subculture that aversiveness is concentrated. The subculture is a destructive threat to the protagonist, whom the novels depict as masculine-presenting but somewhat compromised in his gender identity by his sexual orientation. In James Barr's *Quatrefoil* (1950), a late entry in this series, the protagonist, Philip, is prepared by his wise lover Tim for the experiment of living as a socially assimilated homosexual. Involvement in the gay world, Tim advises, is a "slide" into "degeneracy."[25] The novel ends on an ambiguously positive note; while Tim is killed off, Philip survives an attempted suicide by drowning and emerges from the water to symbolically "slowly [climb] the hill."[26] Breaking off

---

[23] This paragraph draws on Allan Bérubé, *Coming out under Fire: The History of Gay Men and Women in World War Two* (New York: Free Press, 1990).

[24] Guy Davidson, "The Queerness of World War II: Problems and Possibilities," in *The Cambridge History of Queer American Literature*, ed. Benjamin Kahan (Cambridge: Cambridge University Press, forthcoming).

[25] James Barr, *Quatrefoil* (Boston: Alyson, 1982), 350.   [26] Ibid., 373.

before Philip can rejoin society, *Quatrefoil* suggests the difficulty in the early Cold War moment of imagining an asserted yet integrated gay identity. Yet in the face of this difficulty, Philip's final "climb" also suggests the determination that would sustain gay people as they wrestled with both internalized and externally manifested homophobia in the decades to come. Midcentury fiction concerned with homosexuality was unconnected to the political project of homophile groups, which had small memberships and little impact until the 1960s. But gay novels of this period often engage speculatively and yearningly with ideas and images of emancipation. This is not to suggest that there was anything inevitable about liberation, but rather that fiction's negotiation of homosexuality continually invoked it as a possibility, however hedged about with doubt and aversion.

James Baldwin's *Another Country* (1962) provides a suggestive example. A major literary figure and commentator on American racism from the 1950s until his death in 1987, Baldwin always insisted on the life-enhancing role of human connection across barriers of race, gender, and sexual orientation. For Baldwin, sexual love was one of the universal experiences that connect people, and the genders of those involved was (supposedly) irrelevant. Yet Baldwin's universalism is complicated by his tendency in his fiction to describe homosexual love in particular in elevated, quasi-religious terms. *Another Country*, Baldwin's most ambitious novel, uses the turbulent romantic lives of a multiracial cast of aspiring artists in Greenwich Village to elaborate a critique, in Baldwin's words, of "the spiritual state of our country."[27] Baldwin reverses the pathologizing schema of midcentury American sexual categorization, depicting heterosexuality rather than homosexuality as unrelentingly unhappy. The main gay character, Eric, is the least psychically troubled of the characters, and he actively resists the pathologization of his sexuality – what the novel calls "the definitions, the hideously mechanical jargon of the age." "It was up to him," Baldwin tells us, "to find out who he was, and it was his necessity to do this, so far as the witch doctors of the time were concerned, alone."[28] In his defiance, Eric presages or parallels liberationist discourse. He claims, like the homophile or gay activists of the 1960s, the right to forge his own "definitions" and "standards" in opposition to those promulgated by the accepted authorities ("witch doctors"). However, for Eric,

---

[27] Quoted in David Leeming, *James Baldwin: A Biography* (New York: Henry Holt, 1995), 201.
[28] James Baldwin, *Another Country* (London: Michael Joseph, 1963), 206.

unlike those activists, alternative definitions have no collective context. His self-affirmation and self-definition are things he must do "alone."

In this novel and elsewhere, Baldwin rejected gay politics and the gay subculture, which, like the earlier problem novelists, he depicted as a soul-destroying underworld. Instead, he idealized homosexuality in its manifestations in the individual and in the couple. The presentation of gay coupledom is quite self-consciously utopian in *Another Country*: We first meet Eric in an Edenic south-of-France setting with his lover Yves (Eve). Yet Baldwin also inadvertently suggests the potentially liberatory dimension of gay collectivity. Although he paints the subculture in damningly lurid hues, the notionally strictly personal liberation embodied in Eric is informed by and refers back to it. A passage describes Eric's use of the subcultural institution of public sex and his encounters with an "army of lonely men."[29] Eric laments their loneliness and wishes, "[I]f only someone, somewhere, loved them enough to caress them ... in the light, with joy!"[30] While Baldwin's image of homosexual caresses "in the light, with joy" most obviously instances his quasi-religious conviction in the sanctifying, shame-defying power of love, the invocation of illuminated openness also anticipates the central metaphor of gay and lesbian liberation: coming out of the closet.

The moment of liberation is conventionally dated to the 1969 Stonewall Inn riots in New York City, in which gay men, lesbians, and transgendered people fought back against police harassment. This famous event was preceded by steadily building political agitation for gay rights in the second half of the 1960s; increasing openness about homosexuality and the gay world in literature, cinema, and even television also helped pave the way for the liberation moment. The new discourse of gay and lesbian liberation, like second-wave feminism, also engaged dialectically with the New Left, drawing on its energies and ideas, while seeking to correct its sexism and heterosexism. At the same time, gay liberation continued the efforts of the less radical homophile groups, drawing on the older political project of civil rights in an effort to amend legal inequities regarding consenting sexual behavior and workplace discrimination.

The mood of pride established by liberation was evident in the 1970s in newly vibrant manifestations of gay culture – for instance, in expanded, highly commercialized gay male "ghettoes." However, there was something of a lag between the advent of liberation and the emergence of an "out" gay literature, with a niche market for gay literary writing not

---

[29] Ibid., 204.   [30] Ibid., 205.

emerging until 1978. This was the year in which Andrew Holleran's *Dancer from the Dance*, Larry Kramer's *Faggots*, and Edmund White's *Nocturnes for the King of Naples* were published. All written by New York-based white men, and all published by major houses, these works were the first literary novels to respond to and represent the new gay ghetto and the new, unapologetic homosexuality. (This is not to say that they were unambiguously celebratory; indeed, Kramer's depiction of the New York gay world was savagely satirical, and consequently controversial among gay critics and readers.) White's autofiction trilogy *A Boy's Own Story* (1982), *The Beautiful Room Is Empty* (1988), and *The Farewell Symphony* (1997) traces the changes between pre-liberation and post-liberation periods, moving from a provincial Midwestern childhood and adolescence in the 1940s and 1950s, through adventures in bohemian and gay settings in Michigan and Chicago, to adult life in New York's gay world in the 1960s, 1970s, and 1980s. The trilogy is a magisterial realization of the capacities of the bildungsroman to present what Mikhail Bakhtin, in his account of the genre, called "an image of *man growing* in *national-historical time*," although it disrupts Bakhtin's assumptions of masculine, heterosexual representativeness in its focus on the specificities of gay identity and gay culture.[31] Lennard Davis has provocatively proposed that the realist novel's "reliance on the biographical mode" means that it "must oppose the individual to the collective."[32] Yet in the gay, lesbian, and queer fiction of the post-1970 period, for which the bildungsroman has proved an enduring choice, the collective movement of liberation always informs the account of the individual life, although the relations between individuality and collectivity play out in contrasting ways across different novels.

Rita Mae Brown's *Rubyfruit Jungle* (1973), the most famous postwar lesbian bildungsroman, sought, like other lesbian novels of the early liberation period, to displace negative stereotypes of lesbianism; unlike those other novels, largely produced by independent feminist presses, Brown's book was a "crossover" success. Recounting the relentlessly

[31] M. M. Bakhtin, "The Bildungsroman and Its Significance in the History of Realism (Toward a Historical Typology of the Novel)," in *Speech Genres and Other Late Essays*, trans. Vern W. McGee, ed. Caryl Emerson and Michael Holquist (Austin: University of Texas Press, 1986), 25. As an elaboration of both personal and sociopolitical development, the modern bildungsroman also figures developments in capitalism; see Jed Esty, *Unseasonable Youth: Modernism, Colonialism, and the Fiction of Development* (Oxford: Oxford University Press, 2012). I discuss the interrelations of the bildungsroman form, liberation, and consumer capitalism in White's trilogy in Guy Davidson, *Queer Commodities: Contemporary US Fiction, Consumer Capitalism, and Gay and Lesbian Subcultures* (New York: Palgrave Macmillan, 2012).

[32] Lennard J. Davis, *Resisting Novels: Ideology and Fiction* (London: Methuen, 1987), 119.

successful trajectory of its talented, beautiful, and sexually confident heroine Molly Bolt, from a working-class Florida childhood to the beginnings
of a filmmaking career in New York, the novel reads as liberationist wish
fulfilment. As in *Another Country*, though this time to ostensibly humor-
ous effect, it is heterosexuality rather than homosexuality that is patholo-
gized, with a straight couple with whom Molly becomes sexually involved
unable to find fulfilment outside of complex role-playing fantasies. Tiring
of these shenanigans, Molly moves on to a relationship with their adult
daughter, who "hadn't one sexual quirk in her mind . . . She was there, all
there with no hang-ups, no stories to tell, just herself. And I was just
me."[33] "This is reverse discourse with a vengeance," Jonathan Dollimore
observes of the novel, referring to Foucault's discussion of how homosexual politics repurposes the pathologizing categorization of homosexuality
to argue for its authenticity and legitimacy.[34] Yet *Jungle*'s investment in
authenticity also entails a rejection of subcultural forms, in a fresh manifestation of the tension between affirmative gay identity and collective gay life.
Like many 1970s lesbian feminists, Molly rejects butch-femme bar culture as
an expression of inauthentic "roles," not that different from the role-playing
of the hapless straight couple. Molly is given to butch-phobic disparagement
of the "truck drivers" who patronize New York's bars: "What's the point of
being a lesbian if a woman is going to look and act like an imitation man?"
she exclaims.[35] In spite of the novel's imbrication with the collective lesbian
politics of its time, Molly's insistence on being "just me" strongly recalls
American myths of self-betterment: In a rare moment of reflexive irony,
Molly is chided by one of her lovers as "Horatio Alger."[36]

A more nuanced account of the interrelations between individual,
subculture, and liberation is provided by another bildungsroman, Leslie
Feinberg's landmark *Stone Butch Blues* (1993). The novel has been proposed as marking the beginning of the contemporary transgender novel in
America, although its relation to trans experience and to the ideology of
trans liberation – still emerging at the time of its publication – is complex.[37] Closely based on Feinberg's own experience, the novel follows the

[33] Rita Mae Brown, *Rubyfruit Jungle* (New York: Bantam, 1977), 210.
[34] Jonathan Dollimore, *Sexual Dissidence: Augustine to Wilde, Freud to Foucault* (Oxford: Clarendon
Press, 1991), 53; Michel Foucault, *The History of Sexuality. Vol. 1: An Introduction*, trans. Robert
Hurley (Harmondsworth: Penguin, 1990), 101.
[35] Brown, 147.   [36] Ibid., 173.
[37] Feinberg's pamphlet *Transgender Liberation: A Movement Whose Time Has Come* (1992) was
instrumental in repurposing the medical term *transgender* as a badge of political identity; *Stone
Butch Blues* does not use the term, however. For a useful summary of the contested status of *Stone
Butch Blues* in lesbian and trans scholarship and an insightful reading of the novel, see Roshaya

life of Jess Goldberg, a gender-non-conforming individual from a working-class Jewish family, in Buffalo in the 1960s and 1970s and later in New York City. Jess lives first as a stone butch lesbian (a masculine-presenting woman whose eroticism is focused on satisfying her partner rather than her own pleasure). She later undergoes hormonal and surgical transition into life as a trans man, then finally moves into a more "complicated" identity, giving up her daily injections of testosterone to live as a queerly gendered "he-she" individual.[38]

Feinberg identified as a revolutionary communist, and the book entwines a story of coming to political consciousness with its story of gender transformation through the verbal leitmotif of "change." The political and cultural transformations of the 1960s palpably inform the narrative. While the struggle for civil rights goes on, a high-school teacher expresses her disappointment at Jess's economically motivated decision not to go to college by telling her, "I wanted to help you change the world" (45). Later, the America of 1968 is described as "exploding with change" (124), while "the birth of gay pride" in the succeeding years is described as bringing about a world "changing so fast. I wondered if this was the revolution" (135). Jess excludes provincial, working-class Buffalo from these excitements ("we only dreamed at night" [124]), but her involvement in union politics at the factory where she works and in the Buffalo lesbian bar community are the determinants of her own revolutionary consciousness. The novel is unsparing in its depictions of the brutal enforcement of gender and sexual norms, including several scenes of rapes and violence visited on Jess and her friends by police and other straight men. But oppression is offset by the compensations of communitarian life in Buffalo's bar world and later in the multiplex world of queer New York in the 1970s and 1980s. The novel ends with Jess researching and planning to write about the history of non-gender-conforming individuals, with the intention of helping to shape a sense of transgender community.

Simultaneously, the novel stresses the importance of individual fulfilment. Jess's teacher tells her that "what it takes to change the world" is "to figure out what you really believe in and then find other people who feel the same way. The only thing you have to do alone is to decide what's important to you" (46). Late in the novel, as she decides to stop taking

Rodness, "Hard Road Ahead: Stone's Queer Agency in *Stone Butch Blues*," *Criticism* 62.4 (2020): 547–71.

[38] Leslie Feinberg, *Stone Butch Blues* (Ithaca, NY: Firebrand, 1993), 254. Subsequent page references are cited parenthetically in the text.

hormones, Jess states: "When I sat alone and asked what it was I really wanted, the answer was *change*" – a statement that refers simultaneously to her commitment to a more equitable society and to her felt need to rework her gender identity in a way that lines up with her psychic being. She continues: "I was still steering my own course through uncharted waters, relying on constellations that were not fixed ... I was the only expert on living my own life, the only person I could turn to for answers" (224). Recalling again Mailer's metaphor of the unexplored territory of sexuality, though in a context that stresses the importance of collective politics, Feinberg's passage – and her book overall – indicates the continuing value of the novel form for an accounting of the social and individual effects of sexual liberation.

CHAPTER 7

Black Liberation Movements

Sheena Michele Mason and Dana A. Williams

Since its emergence as a discrete field of study, African American literature has been organized, mainly, by periods – literature of slavery and freedom, literature of Reconstruction, literature of the New Negro Movement or the Harlem Renaissance, and so on. Most of the literature canonized as endemic to the field has participated in some way in Black Americans' quest for equal citizenship. Far more than responsive, this literature has imagined a better world, experimented with form, and reflected the artistic and cultural sophistication of Black people. Novelists grappled with racism, classism, sexism, and homophobia with a complexity that is often smoothed out by periodization and canonization. The African American novel worked within and outside of the limits of what we have come to recognize as movements. Still, thinking about the twentieth-century African American novel in the context of liberation movements helps us organize our thinking about the ways in which writers used long fiction to explore the social, political, ideological, and historical realities that informed the time period in which they were writing.

We define "Black Liberation Movements" as loosely organized, sustained campaigns of like-minded people committed to eliminating the various forms of oppression Black people experience as a direct result of their racialization. While the word "movements" gives the illusion that there are stops and starts to collective efforts to dismantle systemic oppressions, the reality is that movements tend to be far more fluid than scholarship might suggest. Another challenge is the fact that movements are often fortified in the public imagination after a seemingly spontaneous event that warrants external recognition. The intellectual and political labor that predates the demarcating moment is devalued at best and unnoticed at worst. To avoid the silences that lie dormant when this happens, we have organized this chapter in terms of loose "movements" and hearty "interregnums" to avoid the marginalization and exclusion that adherence to historical movements might otherwise demand. We try to show the nuance and complexities of novelists who use the novel form to articulate, as Larry Neal has dubbed it, "visions of a liberated future."[1]

Post-Reconstruction: 1900–1910

The successes and failings of the Reconstruction era are all reflected in the novels written by Black authors in the United States between 1900 and 1910. As economic and social mobility expanded among Black people at the turn of the century, the number of lynchings increased, as did the emergence of Jim Crow laws to discourage Black people's political power, which had grown significantly during Reconstruction. The novel's function was like that of other genres: to offer a favorable view of Black people, which would then translate into material benefits – increased upward mobility, integration into society as an equal, and the elimination of racialized violence against Black people. Novelists in the first decade of the century experimented with form and content. Some tried their hand at drafting blueprints for the future. Some explored economic and social class differences as a way of showing the many faces of Black life. Others imagined times past to reckon with present and future realities.

As one of the few authors whose work was met with commercial success, Paul Laurence Dunbar was perhaps best known as a poet. But he also wrote essays, short stories, a play, and the lyrics for *In Dahomey* (1903), the first all-African American musical on Broadway. As a novelist, Dunbar's most successful book is *The Sport of the Gods* (1902),[2] which follows the Hamilton family and their move to the urban North after Berry Hamilton, the family patriarch, has been wrongly imprisoned. When city life disrupts the family's good values and they fare no better in New York than they did back home, they must concede that northern cities do not provide an escape from racial oppression and discrimination. A year before publishing *The Sport of the Gods*, Dunbar published *The Fanatics* (1901),[3] a novel about white families in Ohio in conflict at the start of the Civil War because of each other's respective sympathies for the North and the South. Both novels reflected literature at the turn of the century, so much of which was concerned with white responses to Black/white relations after slavery and with critiquing the urban North as less racist than the South.

---

[1] Larry Neal, *Visions of Liberated Future: Black Arts Movement Writings* (New York: Thunder's Mouth Press, 1989).
[2] Paul Laurence Dunbar, *The Sport of the Gods* (New York: Dodd, Mead and Company, 1902).
[3] Paul Laurence Dunbar, *The Fanatics* (Scotts Valley, CA: CreateSpace Independent Publishing Platform, 2017).

As Dunbar makes clear in *Sport of the Gods*, the urban North was not less racist, only differently so. Black families, even when they left the South, struggled to do well in a country determined to treat them as second-class citizens, the Thirteenth and Fourteenth Amendments notwithstanding.

Charles Chesnutt published three novels in the early twentieth century: *The House behind the Cedars* (1900), *The Marrow of Tradition* (1901), and *The Colonel's Dream* (1905).[4] Chesnutt's signature use of melodramatic subplots and his exploration of integration and desegregation occur in each novel. *The House behind the Cedars* was one of the first to portray an "interracial" romance and was considered scandalous even though it was well received. John Warwick and Rena Walden – brother and sister – leave their hometown of Patesville, North Carolina, to pursue greater economic opportunities in South Carolina available to them as racialized white people. The novel is one within the "passing" tradition, a dominant theme of early African American novels. In *The Marrow of Tradition*, Chesnutt gives a fictional account of the Wilmington massacre of 1898. The novel's exploration of the violence of white supremacy makes explicit Black resistance to racialized oppression. While the novel was not well received in the South, it did provide a historical representation of the movement in Black communities determined to maintain the voting rights they had won during Reconstruction. *The Colonel's Dream* continues the author's portrayal of the violence inspired by racism in North Carolina after the Civil War. Each of Chesnutt's novels provides a fictional account of the historical conditions that would then lead to the Great Migration and the Harlem Renaissance after 1910.

Sutton E. Griggs was another writer who portrayed the violent impact and acts of racism in his three novels *Overshadowed* (1901), *The Hindered Hand: or, The Reign of the Repressionist* (1905), and *Pointing the Way* (1908).[5] Critics interpret Griggs alternately as an integrationist or as a militant separatist, which makes clear the range of themes and ideologies at play in his novels. One dichotomy that threads through the sometimes reductive reception of many African American novels from this period is how scholars label writers such as Griggs, Chesnutt, and Dunbar. Often, the writers and their novels are read through the lens of integrationism,

---

[4] Charles Chesnutt, *The House behind Cedars* (Boston, MA: Houghton, Mifflin and Company, 1900); *The Marrow of Tradition* (Boston, MA: Houghton, Mifflin and Company, 1901); *The Colonel's Dream* (Scotts Valley, CA: CreateSpace, 2018).

[5] Sutton E. Griggs, *Overshadowed* (Singapore: Mint Editions, 2021); *The Hindered Hand: or, The Reign of the Repressionist* (Scotts Valley, CA: CreateSpace, 2018); *Pointing the Way* (London: Orion, 1908).

assimilationism, or separatism regarding race and nationalism. Yet, many authors' philosophies of race and culture and their corresponding approach to Black citizenship changed within texts and between texts. Between 1900 and 1910, African American writers explored – and often disagreed about – the radically different ways of unifying Black and white people, healing the wounds of enslavement, and reconciling feelings of betrayal and the need to forgive brought on by the Civil War. The one thing the novelists had in common was a shared desire for the violence of racism to cease.

The Harlem Renaissance: 1910–1937

If social and political equality proved difficult to obtain for African Americans in the twentieth century, cultural and artistic production did not. While Black people fled the South and its violence and headed to northern, western, and Midwestern states in search of more liberty, the Harlem Renaissance emerged as a creative arts movement, which involved visual, literary, and performance arts excellence unmatched in any other period. Although the renaissance exceeded the boundaries of the New York borough, the movement coalesced after a dinner in March 1924 at the Harlem Civic Club held to honor and recognize Jessie Redmon Fauset and her debut novel *There Is Confusion* (1924). When Alain Locke, considered one of the movement's architects, edited an anthology of fiction, poetry, and essays as *The New Negro: An Interpretation* (1925), art emerged as an agreed-upon collective response to Black people's freedom dreams all over the country.

Like their contemporaries, Harlem Renaissance novelists saw themselves as distinct from America's "Old Negro," who assumed that embracing "white" refinement and Victorian morals would win them equal rights. This "New Negro" stood boldly in American Blackness and in the rich history and culture of Africa. Novelists used long fiction to explore questions and themes central to the movement: What is Black art? What is the role of the Black artist? What was the surest path to equal rights available to all of America's first-class citizens? In addition to *There Is Confusion*, Fauset published *Plum Bun* (1928), *The Chinaberry Tree* (1931), and *Comedy, American Style* (1933). The novels entered contemporary conversations about the Black middle class, about mixed-race ancestry and colorism among Black people, and about the politics of respectability in Black life and culture. Wallace Thurman's *The Blacker the Berry: A Novel of Negro Life* (1929) echoed the conversations about color, while his *Infants of the Spring* (1932) offered a satirical exploration of the movement and the pretentions of some of the creative artists he thought were overrated. George Schuyler's *Black No More* (1931) combined satire and colorism themes to argue for the instability of race and against the ways in which race functions as a commodity in America. In the novel, a Black scientist can transform Black people's skin color, features, and hair to those of white people. While white people obsessed over racial purity, Black people argued for racial solidarity – with both groups arguing against the race-changing techniques. Even babies could be whitened shortly after their birth. When it becomes clear that the process makes formerly Black people whiter than "pure" white people, a new makeup line is created to darken people's skin to affirm that true whiteness. The newly white people are, at that point, almost as dark as Black people. Schuyler's point is that racial prejudice is based squarely on racialization and the lie of racial superiority.

Writers such as Jean Toomer experimented with form and genre during the Renaissance. After the publication of *Cane* (1923), Toomer was credited by others as having written the first "Negro novel" of the New Negro Movement, an accolade he readily rejected for two reasons. His novel was not the first novel of the period, and he outright rejected race ideology and racialization. He tried to see and write himself and his literature outside of the bounds racism created to contain him and other writers. As a reflection of his resistance to flattened-out understandings of race and of his experimentation with form, *Cane* is a series of vignettes that alternate between narrative prose, poetry, and play-like passages of dialogue. In terms of genre, *Cane* has been classified as everything from a composite novel and a short story cycle to a single-authored cross-genre anthology. As a novel, it is a classic example of modernism that would inspire future writers.

Like Toomer, James Weldon Johnson experimented with form. Johnson had some success on Broadway as a songwriter, and he had been United States consul to Puerto Cabello, Venezuela, and to Nicaragua during the Theodore Roosevelt administration. Although first published as an autobiography in 1912, Johnson's *The Autobiography of an Ex-Colored Man* is in fact a fictionalized account of a bi-racial man who decides to pass for white after experiencing racial discrimination when he goes south to college. The book was later published in 1927 as a novel and continued the trend of examining the theme of passing in novels during the period. Nella Larsen's tellingly named novel *Passing* (1929) joins this conversation, while her first novel, *Quicksand* (1928), troubles the idea

that Black people can educate and behave themselves into white acceptance. Claude McKay's *Home to Harlem* (1928) makes this fallacy clear in
its portrayal of the raunchiness and exoticism that animated the cultural
and artistic scene during the movement. His second novel, *Banjo* (1929),
reveals racial discrimination as an international issue in its portrayal of the
racist ways in which the French treated Black African seamen in Marseilles,
while his third novel, *Banana Bottom* (1933), traces the protagonist's
search for cultural identity in a white society.

W. E. B. Du Bois, a sociologist by training, tried his hand at fiction with
his novels *The Quest of the Silver Fleece: A Novel* (1911) and *Dark Princess:
A Romance* (1928).[6] In *The Quest of the Silver Fleece*, Du Bois does what he
later calls an "economic study"[7] in a fictional post-Reconstruction town
and county in Alabama, where two protagonists, a man and a woman,
build an economic community that gives its citizens a way to overcome
racism. Paradoxically, the silver fleece of the title refers to cotton, a
valuable crop Du Bois felt would help rural communities become economically stable and self-sufficient. In *Dark Princess*, Du Bois explores
transnationalism and transnational solidarity in the continued fight against
racism. Matthew Townes, the protagonist, exiles himself to Germany to
escape dreams deferred in America. For the first time, Townes transcends
the black and white framework caused by racialization in the United States
to have a more clear-eyed understanding of what racism is. Du Bois's
earliest novels give readers insight into what would become increasingly a
Pan-Africanist and separatist inclination.

The broader public and participants in the Harlem Renaissance mostly
agreed or otherwise felt compelled to create literature that reflected their
version of the reality of Black life. Zora Neale Hurston's *Their Eyes Were
Watching God* (1937); George Wylie Henderson's *Ollie Miss* (1935);
Walter White's *The Fire in the Flint* (1924), *Flight* (1926), *Black
Thunder* (1936), and *Drums at Dusk* (1939); Langston Hughes's *Not
Without Laughter* (1930); Countee Cullen's *One Way to Heaven* (1932);
Rudolph Fisher's *The Walls of Jericho* (1928); John Edward Bruce's *The
Awakening of Hezekiah Jones: A Story Dealing with Some of the Problems
Affecting the Political Rewards Due the Negro* (1916); and Zara Wright's
Black and White Tangled Threads and *Kenneth* (both 1920) – these were
just a few novels that subverted the traditions of American literature just as

---

[6] William Edward Burghardt Du Bois, *The Quest of the Silver Fleece: A Novel* (Scotts Valley, CA:
CreateSpace, 2014); *Dark Princess, A Romance* (San Diego: Harcourt Brace, 1928).
[7] Du Bois, *Quest*, 269.

they rejected racist ideas about racialized Black people. These writers blurred the boundaries between fact and fiction, history and present, logical and ludicrous, religious and blasphemous, and dialectical and consensus – all to present a diverse body of literature large enough to capture the fullest possible range of varied Black experiences.

Interregnum: 1937–1954

Although scholars have not formally organized the years after the Harlem Renaissance and before the Civil Rights and Black Arts movements, this interregnum period was critical to the development of the African American literary tradition as one distinct from but in conversation with American literature. Literature between 1937 and 1954 was largely inspired by people's experiences during World War II and the beginning of the Cold War, by their response to communism, and by their resistance to Jim Crow. With few exceptions, Jim Crow laws were enforced until 1965, especially throughout most of the South. Unequal upward economic mobility all over the country continued to impact Black people negatively, until the end of the Great Depression when the second wave of the Great Migration created opportunities for those who dared to cast their lot in industrial towns less tied to an agrarian economy.

Novelists such as Waters Turpin, Richard Wright, Ann Petry, Frank Yerby, Willard Motley, Dorothy West, James Baldwin, Ralph Ellison, and Gwendolyn Brooks remained deeply interested in grappling with the realities of life in America. With few exceptions, Yerby notable among them, these writers continued to experiment with form and to create literature that reflected the spirit of protest. Their determination to imagine a better world and their engagement with each other's work, especially through coalitions like the National Negro Congress, increasingly illustrated the complexity of the literature they created and this literature's connection to and continuation of civil rights efforts and broadly conceived liberation movements – at home and abroad.

Published in 1940, Richard Wright's *Native Son* tells the story of Bigger Thomas, whose first name is crafted intentionally to sound close to the racist slur directed at him and his community. Over the course of the novel, we learn how Bigger, a poor twenty-year-old Black man living in Chicago's South Side in the 1930s, was predestined to criminalization and subsequently incarcerated. Bigger has no choice but to live up to America's racist expectations of him, the Old Negro minstrel ways of being that continued to be imposed on African Americans. The novel's impact was undeniable (and continues to be so), but critics were apt to point out the ways in which Wright's development of Bigger depicted a stereotype, not a real character, a failure his critics thought detracted from his message: America's racism creates the very type of person it proclaims to despise.

Petry's *The Street*, published in 1946, became the first novel written by an African American woman to sell over a million copies.[8] Set in Harlem during World War II, the novel follows Lutie Johnson, a single mother, who is regularly confronted with racism, sexism, and classism as she pursues upward economic and social mobility for herself and her son. Lutie's palpable powerlessness results in her murdering Boots after he sexually assaults her. Petry critiques the myth of the American Dream through her literature in ways strikingly like Wright's novels. Yerby's *The Foxes of Harrow* (1946) broke records to become the first book by an African American author to sell over a million copies, predating Petry. But his novels, which upheld the romance genre's most notable conventions while avoiding the vicious racist images of African Americans, were more popular than literary. As a result, his work was never canonized or critically engaged, especially since he was writing during the protest period without offering substantive critique of the very injustices most Black writers were protesting.

Ellison's *Invisible Man* (1952) was another first – his was the first book by an African American writer to win a National Book Award for Fiction.[9] *Invisible Man* explored race ideology, racism, Black respectability, folk culture, migration, and political philosophies. Ellison pursued each of these themes in fresh and varied ways that came together in an exemplary text, in terms of craft, that also maintained distinct cultural resonances. The story of a metaphorically invisible man who remains unnamed throughout the book enables an enriched exploration of the complexity of Black life and culture and helps move the novel beyond protest as theme, even as it traffics in the politics of protest.

Published in 1953 and set in Harlem, Baldwin's *Go Tell It on the Mountain* (1953) highlights the role of the Pentecostal church in the lives of some African Americans and how the church often collides with, exacerbates, or alleviates the harsh reality of racism.[10] Baldwin experiments with a nonlinear structure and a shifting narrative voice to explore religion, class, race ideology, sexuality, and gender in ways that garnered positive

---

[8] Ann Petry, *The Street* (Boston, MA: Mariner Books, 2020).
[9] Ralph Ellison, *Invisible Man* (New York: Vintage Books, 1995).
[10] James Baldwin, *Go Tell It on the Mountain* (New York: Knopf Doubleday, 2013).

attention. Baldwin's first novel was published right before what would become the next major political and artistic movement in twentieth-century America: the Civil Rights Movement and the subsequent Black Arts Movement.

The connecting thread between novelists writing in 1900 and those working between 1937 and 1954 remained, in large part, a desire to self-define and achieve liberation, which many people identified as being recognized as first-class citizens. From decade to decade, twentieth-century authors honored those who came before them and tried their hand at future-making, creating art that would influence the subsequent material impact of racism and other hierarchies.

Civil Rights Movement: 1954–1968

Consistent with earlier literary and artistic movements, the Civil Rights Movement (1954–68) produced writers who often doubled as activists and activists who saw themselves as writers in the struggle against different forms of dehumanization and for their human rights. Dr. Martin Luther King, Jr., Malcolm X, James Baldwin, Amiri Baraka, Chester Himes, Lorraine Hansberry, Adrienne Kennedy, Gwendolyn Brooks, and many other writers contributed to the causes of the Civil Rights Movement and to the types of literature created between 1954 and 1968 and beyond. Novelists during this period emphasized, used, and theorized performance and their efforts through art to reproduce and recreate Blackness outside of the strictures of racism, sexism, heteronormativity, religious dogma, and so on, what it meant to be racialized and variously human and American, and what would be dubbed the Black Aesthetic. There was a steady rise of "Black consciousness" and unity that primed the field for what would follow: the Black Arts Movement. Through form and content, authors emphasized the interconnection and value of aesthetics, politics, and social critique.

Many novelists experimented with aesthetics, politics, and critique, such that, even when efforts were made to pin down the portrayal and meaning of national, gendered, sexual, racial, and class identities, the result was a sustained and profound questioning of these identities by both readers and writers. The simultaneous challenging and creation of identities is often clouded by periodization and canonization. Studying these authors enables us to examine the historical, political, and sociocultural contexts that enrich our understanding of African American literature, the Civil Rights Movement, prior and subsequent movements, and ourselves. Additionally,

Chester Himes, James Baldwin, Willard Motley, and Richard Wright (*Savage Holiday* [1954], *The Long Dream* [1958], and *Lawd Today!* [1963]) also help us consider the ways in which authors generate dialogic and discursive discourses that help us understand identity as a production that many people still see differently.

Himes published the *Harlem Detective* series of nine novels featuring Grave Digger Jones and Coffin Ed Johnson, two NYPD detectives and antiheroes who predate their contemporary equivalents like Detective Stabler (*Law & Order SVU* and *Organized Crime*), Erik Killmonger (*Black Panther*), or Venom (*Venom*). Scholars generally categorize the novels as hard-boiled fiction, as the books share some conventional features of crime and detective fiction, but they also breach those generic boundaries – which is interesting since the very nature of hard-boiled fiction is transgressive. In *A Rage in Harlem* (1957) – originally and alternatively titled *For Love of Imabelle* – *The Real Cool Killers* (1959), *The Crazy Kill* (1959), *The Big Gold Dream* (1959), *All Shot Up* (1960), *The Heat's On* (1966), and *Cotton Comes to Harlem* (1965), Himes uses dark humor to give comedic effect to otherwise tragic circumstances.[11] Common themes of Himes's novels include racism, political corruption, sex, and culture (food and jazz, for example). In 1958, Himes won France's Grand Prix de Littérature Policière, the most prestigious award for crime and detective fiction in France. Between the award and the film adaptations, Himes's prolific career and far-reaching impact reflect the universal appeal of art that sprang up during and from the Civil Rights Movement.

Baldwin's *Giovanni's Room* (1956) and *Another Country* (1962) defied racist and heteronormative expectations.[12] In *Giovanni's Room*, David, the protagonist, is a blonde American man who lives in Paris, France, and whose racial identity remains central and yet invisible because racelessness and whiteness in literature often go hand in hand. David's racialization, though absent, is central in its very absence, a strategy other writers have used in different literary periods and in different political movements to highlight the effects of racialization and the interconnectedness of racialization and the impact of racism. Further, David struggles to accept his queerness, as it pertains to his gender expression and sexuality, resulting in

---

[11] Chester Himes, *Cotton Comes to Harlem* (New York: Vintage, 1988); *A Rage in Harlem* (New York: Vintage, 1989); *The Heat's On* (New York: Vintage, 1988); *The Real Cool Killers* (New York: Vintage, 1988).

[12] James Baldwin, *Giovanni's Room* (New York: Library of America, 1998); *Another Country* (New York: Library of America, 1998).

an unhappy ending to a novel rife with internal and external rejection. *Another Country* was banned in many states because of Baldwin's use of sexuality and racialization to critique American norms. Set primarily during the 1950s in Greenwich Village and Harlem, New York, Baldwin again explored themes still considered taboo at the time of the book's release, including – but not limited to – bisexuality, infidelity, interracial couples, internalized oppression, nationalism (including Black nationalism), and heteronormativity. Baldwin's frequent liminality has given his work a requisite sense of timeliness and timelessness.

Published in 1958, *Let No Man Write My Epitaph*,[13] Motley's third novel, which continues where *Knock on Any Door* (1947) ends, illustrates Motley's consistent strategy for transcending racial and racist expectations and limitations often placed on African American writers. The novel features Nick Romano, Jr., an Italian American protagonist who tries to overcome the legacy of impoverishment and addiction he inherited. Motley's use of the conventions of naturalism to convey Romano's family story led to the novel's successful reception and adaptation into the 1960 film, starring jazz singer Ella Fitzgerald and directed by Philip Leacock. Critics accused Motley of avoiding issues related to racism by featuring characters who were white; he infamously replied by saying that his race was human. Published posthumously in 1966, *Let Noon Be Fair* is set in a fictional Mexican community of Las Casas. In the sense that the novel calls for a "Black Aesthetic" and simultaneous attempts to reconcile Americanness and racism, it serves an additional function of blurring the lines between the Civil Rights Movement and the Black Arts Movement, both of which were determined to transgress boundaries often perceived to be fixed but that were vibrantly and necessarily fluid.

Black Arts Movement: 1968–1980

The Black Arts Movement's overlap with the end of the Civil Rights Movement was inevitable even if unintentional. If the Civil Rights Movement called for an immediate end to social and political second-class citizenship, the Black Arts Movement demanded African Americans' cultural liberation from the hegemony of whiteness. While Larry Neal was the first person to dub it the "Black Arts Movement" (BAM) and to use the term "the Black Aesthetic" regularly, writers and critics such as Amiri

[13] Willard Motley, *Let No Man Write My Epitaph* (New York: Random House, 1958).

Baraka, Addison Gayle, and Hoyt Fuller were also central to its aesthetic articulation. Just as progenitors of BAM questioned the success and effectiveness of preceding literary periods, they also understood the variability of the movement in which they participated. A key difference, however, was that theirs was an intentional, self-defining movement, not one that was coalesced retrospectively through a critical lens. Neal especially was apt to note that BAM had no fixed ideologies or tenets, only a commitment to raise anew questions about what constituted Black writing and the ways it could reflect Black culture.

Connected to and operating in tandem with the Black Power Movement, BAM novelists crafted and coined a Black Aesthetic (or aesthetics) that highlighted a unique idiom that sprang out of an initially violent contact and history of the Middle Passage and chattel slavery. Although the perspectives and approaches were varied, their shared aim was to stop justifying or presenting Blackness to white Americans and to offer instead a cultural aesthetic that centered on positive affirmation and agency, culture, nuance, and urgency that served as a weapon against unjust strictures. Black publishers, including Dudley Randall's Broadside Press, Haki Madhubuti's Third World Press, Amiri Baraka's Jihad Press, Naomi Long Madgett's Lotus Press, and Drum and Spear Publishing, along with Black-owned magazines, created the climate necessary to execute the self-determination the movement espoused.

Although not all of them would self-identify as BAM writers, authors who published noteworthy novels during the period included Baraka (*The System of Dante's Hell*, 1965), William Melvin Kelley (*Dunfords Travels Everywheres*, 1970), John Oliver Killens (*The Cotillion; or, One Good Bull Is Half the Herd*, 1971), Clarence Major (*All-Night Visitors*, 1969; *No*, 1973; *Reflex and Bone Structure*, 1975; *Emergency Exit*, 1979), Claude Brown (*Manchild in the Promised Land*, 1965), Sarah E. Wright (*This Child's Gonna Live*, 1969), John A. Williams (*The Man Who Cried I Am*, 1967), Ernest J. Gaines (*Catherine Carmier*, 1964; *Of Love and Dust*, 1967; *The Autobiography of Miss Jane Pittman*, 1971), and Piri Thomas (*Down These Mean Streets*, 1967). Two factors are critical to note in any conversation about BAM novels: First, the period was dominated by poetry and drama. The urgency of the movement made these genres preferable because they could be quickly written, printed, distributed, read, and performed. Second, and relatedly, novelists did not always see a place for themselves in the movement. While they may have shared BAM's cultural motivations and its interest in writing about and for Black people, novelists were less sure about the way in which a critical segment of

BAM enthusiasts seemed less concerned with the craft of long fiction than with the art/politics/culture continuum.

Rosa Guy, a Trinidad-born American writer, along with Killens, formed a workshop that was to become the Harlem Writers Guild. Founded in 1950, the mission of the Guild was to develop and aid the publication of works by Black writers. African nations' independence movements also inspired Guild members to consider the ways in which Africa and her cultural traditions might inform the future of Africans/African Americans now permanently located in the US and across the diaspora. Participants included John Henrik Clarke, Audre Lorde, Maya Angelou, Alice Childress, Ossie Davis, Ruby Dee, and Douglas Turner Ward. The Guild was credited with aiding more than half of all successful African American writers between 1950 and 1971, including its founders. Guy wrote a trilogy of novels for young readers that garnered much success: *The Friends* (1973), *Ruby* (1976), and *Edith Jackson* (1978). The novels feature young girls who come of age in trying circumstances. In the process, the characters learn about relationships with family, friends, and themselves. These books earned Guy *The New York Times* Outstanding Book of the Year citation, the Coretta Scott King Award, and the American Library Association's Best Book for Young Adults Award.

Like Guy, Childress, though known primarily as a playwright, also wrote novels for young readers. In *A Hero Ain't Nothin' but a Sandwich* (1973),[14] we hear the life story of thirteen-year-old Benjie. Reminiscent of Motley's Nick Romano, Jr., Benjie lives in an underserved neighborhood and succumbs to heroin addiction, though he vows to quit. The novel earned Childress the Coretta Scott King Award and an award from the American Library Association. Like some of Baldwin's work, *A Hero Ain't Nothin' but a Sandwich* was banned from a New York City school district and became the subject of a US Supreme Court case (1982). Published in 1979, Childress's second novel, *A Short Walk*, explores interracial and economic class relations, migration, domestic violence, the politics of separationists and integrationists, and the process of coming of age for people and a nation.[15] The tenor of Guy's and Childress's work might not readily connect with how critics have tried to shape and narrate the Black Arts Movement or the Black Aesthetic but it does highlight the seeming discontinuity between periodization and canonization and the complexity of how we categorize literature in real time.

[14] Alice Childress, *A Hero Ain't Nothin' but a Sandwich* (London: Puffin, 2000).
[15] Alice Childress, *A Short Walk* (New York: Putnam, 1979).

Conclusion: 1980 and Beyond

A distinct achievement of the Black Arts Movement was its role as a springboard for the emergence of Black Studies programs across the country. While the formalized study of Black literature, life, and culture helped ensure the widespread adoption of more inclusive and expanded curricula, the move into the university was also attended by a move away from BAM's community orientation in some ways. As Black Studies programs grew nationwide, so did presumptions about what works should be included in the literary canon. With a growing Black reading audience, made possible by the volume of writing and the prevalence of Black publishing outlets, mainstream publishers also became more acutely aware of how lucrative Black literature could be. These same publishers began to greatly influence the types of books published. The novel, the least dominant genre of BAM, re-emerged as the signature genre of African American literature, and Black women novelists were at the fore of this shift.

Toni Morrison, a recipient of the Pulitzer Prize and Nobel Prize in Literature, contributed her own novels to this period, and she also helped other writers publish theirs – among them Gayl Jones (*Corregidora*, 1975; *Eva's Man*, 1976), Leon Forrest (*There Is a Tree More Ancient than Eden*, 1973; *The Bloodworth Orphans*, 1977; *Two Wings to Veil My Face*, 1984), Toni Cade Bambara (*The Salt Eaters*, 1980), Wesley Brown (*Tragic Magic*, 1978), and Henry Dumas (*Jonoah and the Green Stone*, 1976). Morrison is easily the most canonized and acclaimed novelist of the period and, perhaps, among the most challenging to readers. From her first novel, *The Bluest Eye* (1970), to *Paradise* (1997), which she published near the end of the twentieth century, Morrison's novels survey the past to identify usable elements to survive the contemporary moment.[16] Her determination, not unlike that of BAM writers, to ignore the white gaze and to center Black culture won the day, while at the same time creating space for other Black women writers, like Alice Walker, Gloria Naylor, Sherley Anne Williams, Ntozake Shange, J. California Cooper, Terry McMillan, Tina McElroy Ansa, Breena Clarke, Marita Golden, and Thulani Davis. These women's novels stretched the limits of what was typically considered "literary," but there was no disputing that they increased the Black reading audience exponentially.

---

[16] Toni Morrison, *The Bluest Eye* (New York: Knopf Doubleday, 2007).

Ishmael Reed joins Morrison as a literary novelist who confounds categorization as a writer both within and outside of the Black Arts Movement, though Reed, unlike Morrison, certainly did see his early work as a part of the movement. Arguably, his best-known work, *Mumbo Jumbo* (1972), depicts the nefarious effects of racialization and what happens when the cultural products of one racialized group are another's mumbo jumbo and kryptonite. Reed incorporates and interweaves various languages, traditions, media (including poetry, portraits, and paintings), religions, histories, real and magical elements, and fictional and non-fictional characters and organizations, including Harlem Renaissance writers James Weldon Johnson, Claude McKay, W. E. B. Du Bois, Countee Cullen, and Wallace Thurman. The novel transgresses many stylistic conventions and borrows from film, scholarly texts, the visual arts, theology, mythology, folklore, oral traditions, and more. Some scholars have labeled the novel Afrofuturist, a reclamation of history, and a critique and presentation of both Black and Western forms and conventions.

By the end of the decade, Reed's experimental novels keep good company with writers whose careers begin near the end of the twentieth century and continue in the twenty-first. Writers such as Trey Ellis, Percival Everett, Paul Beatty, Jake Lamar, and Nathaniel Mackey, among others, account for a renewed interest in the literary marketplace in novels by Black male writers, following an extended period of success among Black women writers. The categorization of Black writers along gender lines, however, has severe limitations that are better addressed by the subgenres Valerie Babb articulates in *A History of the African American Novel*:[17] the neo-slave narrative, the detective novel, the speculative novel, African American pulp, the Black graphic novel, novels adapted for the screen, and novels of the diaspora. At every turn toward freedom, an aspiration that persisted historically and one that is still not a completely realized achievement, writers used the full range of forms to reflect and inspire shared visions of a liberated future.

---

[17] Valerie Babb, *A History of the African American Novel* (Cambridge: Cambridge University Press, 2017).

PART II

The Politics of Genre and Form

CHAPTER 8

Crime Fiction

Andrew Pepper

In Dashiell Hammett's 1929 novel *Red Harvest*, a bootlegger called Pete the Finn tells a motley assortment of gangsters, police, and businessmen that the tit-for-tat violence unleashed by the Continental Op in order to regain control of Personville is 'no good for business';[1] this sentiment is echoed and complicated in Hammett's follow-up novel, *The Maltese Falcon*, where Sam Spade tells Brigid O'Shaughnessy that 'when one of your organization gets killed it's bad business to let the killer get away with it'.[2] In both instances, the term 'business' is used to speak about a mode of social and economic organization tied to the logic of capital accumulation: for example, where 'good' or 'bad' business depends on smoothing out the impediments to what David Harvey calls 'continuity in the flow of the circulation of capital', whereby '[c]apital is not a thing but a process in which money is perpetually sent in search of more money'.[3] Business may also be a euphemism for crime, even if it 'should be transacted in a business-like manner',[4] as Hammett's Casper Gutman puts it, with self-evident irony. In other words, the violence that undergirds the business of business is both essential to its operation and something that needs to be covered up as 'just' crime. In both cases, Hammett draws our attention to the role that the hard-boiled crime novel plays in exposing and, conversely, smoothing out the ill effects of capitalism, and in drawing attention to the joins between crime, business, and law, while at the same time leaving these relations largely untouched because to do otherwise would be 'no good for business'. Meanwhile, the imperative to expose violent wrongdoing (because it would be 'bad business' not to) speaks to a wafer-thin

[1] Dashiell Hammett, *The Four Great Novels: Red Harvest, The Dain Curse, The Maltese Falcon, The Glass Key* (London: Picador, 1982), 136.
[2] Dashiell Hammett, *The Maltese Falcon* (New York: Vintage Crime/Black Lizard, 1992), 214.
[3] David Harvey, *The Enigma of Capital* (London: Profile, 2011), 40, 41.
[4] Hammett, *The Maltese Falcon*, 195.

ethical code where it is only the appearance of sanction and punishment that matters, rather than more substantive claims to rightness and justice.

Even in these brief examples, one can see some of the complications that abound when considering the political orientations and allegiances of Hammett's crime novels. Business and crime are shown to be synonymous, and both are seen to pollute and degrade the society that produces them. As such, there is a strong trace of leftist critique in these works. Yet the novels demonstrate little appetite for unstitching the threads linking crime, business, law, and politics. At the start of *Red Harvest*, the otherwise nameless Continental Op arrives in the western US town of Personville after a vicious labour dispute between striking miners and the mine owner, Elihu Willsson, has been settled in Willsson's favour. But following his use of hired gunmen to break the strike, Willsson loses control of the city to the gunmen who 'took the city for their spoils'[5] and who proceed to fight against one another: they represent proto-capitalists fighting against monopoly interests and the forces of the state, albeit on disadvantaged terms.[6] The Op is tasked with 'investigating crime and corruption in Personville', which he does by 'stirring things up' and setting the gunmen against one another so that '[e]verybody's killing everybody'.[7] In the end, the Op hands the city back to Willsson, 'all nice and clean and ready to go to the dogs again'.[8] The vanquished miners, supported by the Industrial Workers of the World (IWW), play no part in the narrative; the workers are only mute figures glimpsed in the pool bars and drinking joints, rather than proletarians agitating for social change. And while Willsson, who 'owned Personville, heart, soul, skin and guts',[9] comes across as weak and vacillating, the novel ultimately and reluctantly backs him over the gunmen, and in doing so reveals the interpenetration of the forces of the state and capital. Meanwhile, the Op – who would seem, initially at least, to embody the kind of muscular, unco-opted individualism synonymous with what we might call a fantasy of right-wing vigilantism (e.g. the strongman capable of exposing and punishing moral and hence social permissiveness) – is gradually drawn into the networks of power and authority linking capital and the state. In the process, he finds that his capacity to intervene effectively in the poisoning of the town is radically curtailed. If there is a politics at work in Hammett's novel, it functions

---

[5] Hammett, *The Four Great Novels*, 12.
[6] See Andrew Pepper, *Unwilling Executioner: Crime Fiction and the State* (Oxford: Oxford University Press, 2016), 151.
[7] Hammett, *The Four Great Novels*, 60, 80, 130.   [8] Ibid., 181.   [9] Ibid., 12.

through ambivalence rather than propagandizing and didacticism, showing how the Op is gradually made complicit in the crimes he is tasked with clearing up.

In his study of the political and philosophical orientations of US hard-boiled crime fiction, *Gumshoe America*, Sean McCann uncovers the tensions and contradictions at play in hard-boiled US crime fiction's efforts to map and interrogate the genre's traditional preoccupation with liberalism alongside the ruptures and complications caused by 'the rise of organized capitalism and the evident failures of the unfettered market to deliver a just society'.[10] If this move constitutes part of this genre's emerging political critique, it is bound up with and complicated by the doomed efforts of writers such as Hammett and Raymond Chandler, and also Jim Thompson, Charles Willeford, and Chester Himes, to reinvigorate the public domain and 'to assert public values over private desires', in turn echoing 'the rhetoric that ran through the contemporaneous development of New Deal liberalism':

> The various methods they chose to pursue or to depict that effort mirrored particular strains of New Deal thinking, and the frustrations they inevitably encountered in their pursuit of a utopian, democratic culture dramatized the conflicts and contradictions that would dog New Deal liberalism as it evolved from the 1930s through the 1950s and beyond.[11]

McCann traces these complications and this scepticism from Hammett's vision of public contamination and negation (in which 'reformism leads to no reform and populism summons no people') and Chandler's depiction of 'the exploitation and erasure of that popular spirit' through to the despairing post–World War II critiques of Willeford and Thompson, writers who 'took advantage of the postwar consumer market to envision a unified literary public' but who 'depicted the dissolution of that common people and the consequent disappearance of the popular artist'.[12]

Thompson's *Pop. 1280* (1964) is a particularly good example of this despairing vision, not least because it dramatizes the emptying out of democracy and the political processes that underpin mass democracy, and hence of the values and logic that underpin civic responsibility and a reinvigorated public sphere. In the novel, Nick Corey, high sheriff of Potts County, is waging an election campaign against a vigorous and well-thought-of rival, but rather than representing the people and breathing

---

[10] Sean McCann, *Gumshoe America: Hard-Boiled Crime Fiction and the Rise and Fall of New Deal Liberalism* (Durham, NC and London: Duke University Press, 2000), 6.
[11] Ibid., 5.   [12] Ibid., 80, 36.

life into the political process, Corey cheats, lies, and murders his way to victory, his good-ol'-boy charm (barely) concealing a personality with no inner life and no capacity for self-generated thought. Here, then, Corey's greed, sexual promiscuity, and racism speak both to a kind of nihilistic anti-existence – what happens when 'you're already dead inside, and all you'll do is spread the stink and the terror, the weepin' and the wailin', the torture, the starvation, the shame of your deadness'[13] – and more specifically to a world despoiled by relentless privileging of private desires over public virtue, self-interest over communitarian need, rich over poor, and violence over law. The nightmare terminus of this process is Corey's 'success' as a law enforcer and elected official, but this success, as he makes clear in a rare moment of self-insight, is dependent on his willingness, as popular representative and sheriff, to act as a kind of absurd grim reaper for entrenched wealth and privilege. 'By rights,' he says towards the end of the novel, 'I should be rompin' on the high an' mighty, the folks that really run this country. But I ain't allowed to touch them, so I've got to make up for it by being twice as hard on the white trash an' Negroes.'[14]

McCann has valuable insights into the complications and contradictions that ensue when the liberal underpinnings of the crime novel come unstuck in the face of massive social upheaval, but he overreads the genre's liberal sympathies to begin with. In doing so, he is too quick to characterize the hard-boiled crime novel as distinctive from earlier generic types: for example, the classic detective story, which operates according to a more schematic and reassuring logic whereby 'society can return to its ordinary workings … once the threat of criminal inference is removed'.[15] In Unwilling Executioner, I try to 'delineate the richness and complexity of a long tradition of crime writing in which crime, and indeed policing, is rooted in the social and economic conditions of its time'. As such, the constitutive tension of much crime writing – between accommodations that must be made 'towards the articulation of law and the reinstitution of order' and 'a refusal to turn a blind eye to institutional failure and corruption'[16] – is just as visible in earlier examples of crime fiction as in the US hard-boiled novels of the 1930s and 1940s. In this sense, the politics of crime fiction in general and of American crime fiction in particular – 'neither inherently conservative nor radical',[17] to quote Lee Horsley – can be found in this structuring tension, with the fraught,

---

[13] Jim Thompson, Pop. 1280 (London: Orion, 2006), 170.   [14] Ibid., 177.   [15] McCann, 9.
[16] Pepper, Unwilling Executioner, 2.
[17] Lee Horsley, Twentieth-Century Crime Fiction (Oxford: Oxford University Press, 2005), 158.

agonized, ambivalent positions taken up by *Red Harvest* an example of this irreconcilability.

Much has been made of Hammett's leftist politics, especially in light of his post-writing biography: he joined the Communist Party of America in the mid-1930s and was briefly imprisoned in 1951 for refusing to provide information about the Civil Rights Congress's bail fund. Precisely because of this, Horsley notes, 'there has been a marked critical tendency to read back into his novels – *Red Harvest* especially – a Marxist political agenda'.[18] Zumoff, too, warns against this 'tendency to read Hammett backwards', concluding that 'Hammett's early stories do not lend themselves to a coherent political reading, much less a radical one'.[19] The point is well taken, and, as McCann argues, there are elements of Hammett's fiction – and also of Carroll John Daly's Race Williams novels – that fit with a white, populist, nativist agenda[20]: distrust of outsiders, especially foreigners, a desire to purify or cleanse society of its social ills, faith in the capacity of unco-opted individuals to make the necessary interventions, and suspicion regarding the motives of social and political elites. And yet in works such as *The Maltese Falcon*, there is also a highly sophisticated critique of the ills of free-market capitalism, with its wildly fluctuating markets and where commodities, such as the statuette in the novel, are worth up to a hundred thousand dollars one day and nothing the next.[21] In his study of the long history of the US hard-boiled novel, *Hard-Boiled Sentimentality*, Leonard Cassuto argues that the invention of trust in *The Maltese Falcon* moves 'a family metaphor into the world of business'.[22] Hence Brigid's exhortation, uttered three times in a single page, that Spade 'trust' her is interpreted by Cassuto as comment on the move to designate monopolies as trusts in the late nineteenth and early twentieth centuries and to use 'the idea of trust in the public sphere' to try to smooth over the sharper edges associated with monopoly capitalism.[23] Cassuto uses the fact that '[t]rust and sympathy between and among people proves almost impossible in the novel'[24] as evidence of Hammett's vaguely leftist critique

[18] Ibid., 166.
[19] J. A. Zumoff, 'Politics and the 1920s Writings of Dashiell Hammett', *American Studies* 52.1 (2012): 77–98, here 78.
[20] McCann argues that 'hard-boiled fiction and nativist fantasy competed on the same ground during the twenties'. McCann, 41.
[21] See Andrew Pepper, 'Dashiell Hammett's The Maltese Falcon as World Literature: Global Circuits of Translation, Money and Exchange', *Modern Fiction Studies* 66.4 (2020): 702–23.
[22] Leonard Cassuto, *Hard-Boiled Sentimentality: The Secret History of American Crime Stories* (New York: Columbia University Press, 2008), 52.
[23] Ibid., 52.   [24] Ibid., 47.

of what transpires when 'business relationships govern family relations and other intimate ties': namely, 'a world of self-interested individuals cut loose from family ties and obligations, who have abandoned sympathy to chase the dollar'.[25] For Cassuto, this move, in which sympathy is abandoned or made impossible in the hard-boiled crime novel, is part of a more complicated logic whereby even the negation of sympathy is taken as evidence of its centrality to the shaping of American crime fiction and of the close links between hard-boiled and sentimental or domestic fictions.

Racial and Gendered Noir

There are self-evident problems associated with reducing American crime fiction as a broad category to the works of a handful of white, male practitioners, mostly associated with the hard-boiled 'school'. This approach ignores the fact that contemporaries of Hammett and Chandler were producing notable works in other subgenres (e.g. the American Golden Age mysteries of Ellery Queen and S. S. Van Dine or the Gothic noirs of Cornell Woolrich and John Dickson Carr), and it runs the risk of overlooking the contributions of female and Black crime writers more generally. Cassuto's move to explore the close links between domestic and hard-boiled fiction is welcome in this respect, in that it collapses the gendered distinction between public and private and shows how both spheres – and, indeed, both genres – constantly bleed into one another. Other notable critical interventions include Chris Breu's work on hard-boiled masculinities, the title of his 2005 book, and on racial and gendered noir. Breu argues for 'hard-boiled masculinity' as 'cultural fantasy' – a 'prophylactic toughness organized around the rigorous suppression of affect' and shored up by punishing 'gendered, sexual and racial others',[26] in order to project competence and authority in the face of enormous social and economic transformation. But insofar as 'hard-boiled masculinity was surreptitiously modelled on an understanding of Black masculinity as vitally and violently primitive',[27] Breu shows us how the complex interplay between projection and negation at work in these texts was appropriated and transformed by Black and female 'noir' writers such as Chester Himes and Dorothy B. Hughes for explicitly political ends.

---

[25] Ibid., 52.
[26] Christopher Breu, *Hard-Boiled Masculinities* (Minneapolis and London: University of Minnesota Press, 2005), 1.
[27] Ibid., 2.

In order to more fully understand the politicizations at work in novels such as Himes's *If He Hollers Let Him Go* (1945) and Hughes's *In a Lonely Place* (1947), we need to better understand the role played by affect – or, to be more precise, negative affect – in the wider genre. For, as Breu argues, while crime fiction and hard-boiled detective fiction are 'about mastering affects (as well as mastery as an affect)' – even if this mastery, as in *The Maltese Falcon*, is 'proven to be more about the toughness and endurance of the protagonist rather than any restoration of justice' – noir is 'predicated on the inability of the protagonist to master the affects dramatised by the narrative'.[28] To put this another way, noir is intimately related to hard-boiled crime fiction, featuring many of the same formal and narrative characteristics, but while the trajectory of the hard-boiled crime story is towards some kind of reaffirmation of character and law, noir emphasizes 'negative affects' such as fear, rage, sickness, dread, and ultimately failure and even death. In the case of Himes's *If He Hollers Let Him Go*, the staging of negative affect takes the form of a complex rearticulation of the kind of Black primitivism and violence that Breu associates with an affirmation and repudiation of hard-boiled masculinity more generally.

Bob Jones is a crew leader at the Atlas shipyard in Long Beach, California, struggling to overcome the everyday racism directed at him and at the other Black workers at the shipyard and 'to be accepted as a man – without ambition, without distinction, either of race, creed, or colour; just a simple Joe walking down an American street'.[29] Rather than stage this struggle in ultimately redemptive terms, Himes places Jones's rational understanding of the predicament of Black workers, who are set against and made subordinate to their white counterparts to keep the union weak, in tension with the negative affects of rage, fear, dread, and sickness that this racism produces and which Jones internalizes, although often without self-awareness of this fact. When Jones confronts or is confronted by Madge Perkins, a white, female co-worker transplanted from the Jim Crow South – 'thirty and well sexed, rife but not quite rotten'– their conjoined response is likened to grotesque pantomime. Here, the roles allotted to them ('she was a naked virgin and I was King Kong'[30]) speak to or about the long history of demeaning racist stereotypes circulating in the white, popular imaginary. Rather than allowing Jones's rational side to win out, Himes doubles down on these negative affects,

---

[28] Christopher Breu, 'Affect', in *The Routledge Companion to Crime Fiction*, ed. J. Allan, J. Gulddal, S. King, and A. Pepper (London and New York: Routledge, 2020), 244.
[29] Chester Himes, *If He Hollers Let Him Go* (London: Pluto Press, 1986), 153.   [30] Ibid., 19.

especially after Perkins reports Jones to his supervisor. He is stripped of his leadership role and loses his draft status in the process – at which point he decides (though it is hardly a conscious act) to inhabit the most demeaning of all white-derived stereotypes of Black masculinity: 'I felt castrated, snake-bellied, and cur-doggish ... Cheap, dirty, low ... What I ought to do is rape her.'[31] As in Richard Wright's *Native Son* (1940), Himes takes this most degrading of stereotypes and turns it against the culture that has produced it as a kind of politicized 'fuck you'. But it is a protest – if it *is* a protest – that goes nowhere and yields nothing. Not only does Jones not follow through with this notion, but, in the larger schema of the novel and the racially determined universe that Jones belongs to, he needs to be punished for being unable to master the negative affects that to a greater or lesser degree consume him. Falsely accused of rape by Perkins, he is fast-tracked by a white judge into the US army.

Himes's *If He Hollers Let Him Go* is a complex response to the reaffirmation of white masculinity in the period immediately following the end of World War II and social and workplace gains made by women and African Americans during the war. Hughes's *In a Lonely Place*, first published in 1947, swims in similar waters, with its forensic examination of war veteran Dix Steele's disintegrating psyche as the reader discovers his complicity in the strangling of a number of working women in West Los Angeles. Hughes tells the story from Steele's perspective using the third-person limited mode, but rather than aligning us with his worldview and thereby humanizing him, this mode gradually exposes his misogyny and that of the wider culture, without explicitly and gratuitously detailing the violent acts themselves (which remain hidden from our view). As such, Lisa Maria Hogeland argues that Hughes's novel is feminist, both for its refusal to show the misogynistic violence it identifies and condemns, and because it reconfigures the trope of the femme fatale so that the threat posed to Steele's autonomy does not originate from a vampiric sexuality but rather from the sleuthing abilities of two women, Sylvia Nicolai and Laurel Gray, who ferret out his guilt.[32] However, along with the proble-matization of progressive politics one finds in Hammett, for example, this feminist critique, as Breu notes, is 'complicated by the way the novel engages the negativity of noir to undertake its political work, a political

---

[31] Ibid., 126.
[32] Quoted in Christopher Breu, 'Radical Noir: Negativity, Misogyny, and the Critique of Privatization in Dorothy B. Hughes's *In a Lonely Place*', *Modern Fiction Studies* 55.2 (2009): 199–215, here 202.

work that is aimed at the twin forms of privatization that characterized the postwar era' – namely, the push to return women to the domestic or private sphere and the 'violent encroachment of the state into the policing of public life'.[33] In the novel, Steele is partly aware of Sylvia's scepticism – the fact that '[y]ou didn't fool Sylvia. She burrowed under words, under the way of a face and a smile for the actuality'[34] – but he is blind to Laurel's suspicions and is instead 'burned up with the radiant promise of the future'.[35] The fact that Steele does not take the threat posed by the two women seriously speaks to the wider societal misogyny the novel seeks to expose: instead, he is fixated on the efforts of the police and his wartime buddy, Brub Nicolai – Sylvia's husband – a police detective who seems resolutely unaware of Steele's culpability throughout. The detective work undertaken by Sylvia and Laurel moves uneasily from private to public sphere when their honeytrap results in Steele's arrest by the police, but Hughes's point would seem to be that the police's ignorance regarding the violence facing women on a daily basis is testament to a wider misogyny operating in the public sphere.

Ride the Pink Horse

In order to inveigle his way into Brub Nicolai's good books and gain insight into the failing police investigation, Dix Steele claims to be writing a detective novel. When asked about his influences – 'Who are you stealing from, Chandler or Hammett or Gardner?' – Steele replies, 'Little of each ... With a touch of Queen and Carr.'[36] In a neat, self-reflexive touch, Hughes slyly places herself and her writing in this pantheon while inferring obvious points of departure: Steele is no Chandleresque knight nor even a Hammettian everyman (despite the fact that Humphrey Bogart played the role of Steele in the 1950 movie version, as well as playing Sam Spade and Philip Marlowe). And yet in an irony she may not have foreseen, while Chandler's and Hammett's reputations have steadily risen in the years following their deaths, Hughes's work remains little known and little appreciated. This is particularly the case with her 1946 novel *Ride the Pink Horse*, which, despite this lack of recognition, marks a radical point of departure and high moment in the politicization of American crime fiction. At first glance, this novel would seem to be an essentially

---

[33] Breu, 'Radical Noir', 202.
[34] Dorothy Hughes, *In a Lonely Place* (London: Penguin, 2010), 86.   [35] Ibid., 127.
[36] Ibid., 40.

derivative tale of politics and crime cut from the same cloth as Hammett's *The Glass Key*. Sailor, a fixer for ex-Chicago senator Willis Douglass, known as the Sen, follows his boss to a nameless New Mexico 'hick town' a few miles outside of Albuquerque.[37] Sailor has participated, at the Sen's behest, in the murder of the Sen's wife, so that his boss can secure a large insurance pay-out. Sailor has been promised $1,500 but is paid only $500 and hence follows the Sen to the border, where his boss has gone with wealthy friends as tourists to escape Chicago and take part in a 234-year-old fiesta, which plays out over the three days of the novel. The Sen and Sailor are joined by McIntyre, head of Chicago's homicide bureau, who tries to convince Sailor to turn on his boss. For his part, Sailor is seeking to cajole and blackmail the Sen into paying him what he is owed: initially $1,000 and later $5,000. As such, *Ride the Pink Horse* would appear to be a competent but not especially original variation on the hard-boiled formula: Sailor's individualism and his desire to cut his ties with the political corruption represented by the Sen set against his complicity in the Sen's murky affairs. As for offering us insight into the politics of the form, Hughes's novel would seem to tell us little that we do not know already. Chicago has been a watchword for criminal and political corruption since the days of Al Capone.

But *Ride the Pink Horse* is not set in Chicago, and nor is it really about Chicago, even though the ostensible crime – the murder of the Sen's wife – has taken place there. Rather, the novel takes place on the US–Mexico border, a liminal space that is neither American nor Mexican and where the violent conquest first by the Spanish of territory belonging to the Native American population and later by the United States is written into the performance of the fiesta and indeed into the novel as its foundational crime:

> Fiesta. The time of celebration, of release from gloom, from the spectre of evil. But the celebration was evil; the feast was rooted in blood, in the Spanish conquering of the Indian. It was a memory of death and destruction. Now we are one, Pancho said. A memory of peace but before peace death and destruction. Indian, Spaniard, Gringo; the outsider, the paler face.[38]

Hence, the territory that the Sailor enters at the start is not akin to Hammett's Personville, despite the ostensibly related western US locations. While Hammett's city, modelled on Bute, Montana – 'an ugly

---

[37] Dorothy Hughes, *Ride the Pink Horse* (Edinburgh: Canongate, 2002), 3.   [38] Ibid., 24.

city . . . set in an ugly notch between two ugly mountains that had been all dirtied up by mining'[39] – bears no trace of the territorial and genocidal conquest of the continent's Indigenous peoples, *Ride the Pink Horse* explicitly names the violence underpinning this endeavour, which is kept alive and also ameliorated by the rituals and spectacle of the fiesta: the memory of death and destruction endures but the rituals of celebration are also a reminder that 'now we are one'. As such, the fiesta is not merely a backdrop, neutral or otherwise, for the unfolding drama of the Sailor–Sen–Mac crime story; it is also brought to bear on the identity of the hard-boiled protagonist and, in doing so, on the longstanding associations between the hard-boiled crime novel and US national identity.

The Continental Op's arrival in Personville at the start of *Red Harvest* is immediately evocative of the gunslinger, and, as Cynthia Hamilton argues, the Western and hard-boiled forms are intimately connected in the ways in which they chronicle and also subvert some of the foundational mythologies of US national identity.[40] For McCann, these myths include the way in which a 'commitment to radical individualism and moral neutrality' – both features of the mythic gunslinger of western lore – 'could issue in extreme violence',[41] a move that would be made in revisionist Westerns such as John Ford's *The Searchers* (1956) and later Clint Eastwood's *Unforgiven* (1992). When he first shows up in the 'hick' border town, Sailor tries to use a strategy and language tied to, and derived from, the hard-boiled worldview, one that 'was defined as the civilized opposite of the primitive forms of male identity ostensibly occupied by African-Americans and other racialized groups'.[42] Thus, the bus company employee who pulls 'baggage out of the compartment' only to dump it clumsily on the ground is described as 'a greaser, a spic' who 'needed his face shoved in', while the townspeople are written off as a racially ill-defined mass: 'They all spic but they might have been Indian as well.'[43] Much has been written about the racial identity of the hard-boiled protagonist and whether or to what extent the stereotyping and 'othering' at work here – and at the start of Chandler's *Farewell, My Lovely* (1940), for example – shore up and/or inadvertently expose the authority and

---

[39] Hammett, *The Four Great Novels*, 7.
[40] Cynthia S. Hamilton, *Western and Hard-Boiled Fiction in America: From High Noon to Midnight* (Basingstoke: Palgrave Macmillan, 2014). Porter argues that the 'private eye with his gun derives . . . from a tradition that is at least as old as the United States'. Dennis Porter, *The Pursuit of Crime: Art and Ideology in Detective Fiction* (New Haven, CT: Yale University Press, 1981), 171.
[41] McCann, 78.   [42] Breu, *Hard-Boiled Masculinities*, 2.   [43] Hughes, *Ride the Pink Horse*, 3, 5.

legitimacy of the white, male detective.[44] We can never be sure whether the casual racism – or rather, the general indifference – directed towards racialized groups in novels by Hammett and Chandler is symptomatic, consciously or otherwise, of a racist ideology. By contrast, in *Ride the Pink Horse*, Hughes sets herself the task of unravelling the racist assumptions that Sailor brings to the early parts of the novel and, in doing so, severing the affective attachment between whiteness, territoriality, and national belonging.

The hard-boiled protagonist should be able to master affects, in Breu's terms, and bring these to some kind of order, as Sam Spade manages to do in *The Maltese Falcon*, where his refusal to 'play the sap' constitutes a rejection of emotion or sentiment in favour of a rigid commitment to procedure and protocol: 'When a man's partner is killed, he's supposed to do something about it.'[45] By contrast, the affects that assail Sailor in Hughes's novel – tied to the sounds, sights, and smells of the fiesta – are not ones he is able to decode: 'skyrockets flaring into the sky, firecrackers exploding';[46] 'the crowd . . . laughing, talking too loud, as if for a moment they realized the bestiality they'd conjured . . . People were moving and their feet kicked dust to add to the fumes of the smoke';[47] the 'wild and cruel song' of the mariachi 'baring their teeth, pounding their knuckles on the gourd-like guitars';[48] a 'current of excitement' and 'a million pinpoints of light'.[49] Sailor experiences these sensations 'as a kaleidoscope'[50] – an affective overload that coalesces in the papier-mâché figure of Zozobra, 'a giant grotesquerie' and 'personification of evil'[51] that needs to be ritually slaughtered in order to bring peace and harmony to the townspeople. Sailor wants to dismiss the spectacle as a 'charade',[52] but in short staccato sentences Hughes conveys his unease and entrapment: 'He saw and he was suddenly frightened. He wanted to get away. He couldn't get away. Even as Zozobra couldn't get away. He was hemmed in by the crowd.'[53] Rather than being able to master this barrage of affects, Sailor is undone by them, a state that is intensified by his interactions with the locals and by the complex claims of territory and belonging. The town may be 'American'[54] in one sense, by dint of its location on one side of the US–Mexico border, but among the descendants of the Indigenous populations and Spanish

[44] McCann, for example, argues that while Marlowe 'may be more sensitive than the racist police at negotiating an urban terrain to which they are effectively blind', *Farewell, My Lovely* still 'reeks of racial prejudice'. McCann, 161, 162.
[45] Hammett, *The Maltese Falcon*, 213.   [46] Hughes, *Ride the Pink Horse*, 19.   [47] Ibid., 19.
[48] Ibid., 24.   [49] Ibid., 17.   [50] Ibid., 22.   [51] Ibid., 18.   [52] Ibid., 19.   [53] Ibid., 19.
[54] Ibid., 23.

invaders, recast in the contemporary timeframe of the novel as Indians and Mexicans, it is Sailor who is 'foreign' and who is made to feel – affectively – the unease of not belonging: 'The panic of loneliness; of himself the stranger although he himself was unchanged, the creeping loss of identity.'[55] This affect is compounded on meeting Pila, a fourteen-year-old Indigenous girl, whereupon what we might call a 'liberal politics of recognition' – which, as Xine Yao argues, is typically tied to the gaze of the colonizer (and, of course, the detective) – is reversed and its assumptions of power complicated.[56] 'His first reaction was to turn away, not to recognize her. But he could not. She was there. She existed. He was the one without existence.'[57]

In the crime plot, Sailor's goals and actions are straightforward – to secure the money he is owed, to exact his revenge on the Sen, and to do this without being apprehended by Mac. But the hard-boiled persona he brings to these tasks, which requires a rigorous suppression of affect, is the very thing that needs to be abandoned in order for Sailor to make any progress in the novel's second or alternate plot: that of the fiesta and how to make sense of the complex problem of territory, identity, and belonging. Here, the small kindness Sailor shows Pila, paying for her to ride the pink horse on 'Tio Vivo' – a small merry-go-round operated by 'Pancho', who comes from Apache and Spanish stock – is reciprocated by Pancho, who puts Sailor up when he can't find a hotel room and arranges for the '*abuelita*' (little grandmother) to treat the stab wound he receives at the hands of an assassin dispatched by the Sen. But Sailor's growing awareness of the affective possibilities of non-hierarchical recognition and hospitality ('When I got in here I thought they were all just a bunch of dirty spics . . . But you take Pancho now'[58]) runs up against what it takes to deal with the Sen. In the novel's climactic passage, Sailor shoots the Sen after the Sen has tried to shoot him; he shoots McIntyre after Mac has tried to apprehend him; and Hughes finishes the novel with Sailor running blindly 'into open country . . . plunging into the wastes of endless land and sky', with Mac's refrain 'You can't get away' going through his head.[59] This is not an escape to the frontier, with its meretricious promises of rebirth, but the point at which the two plots collapse in on one another: Sailor's failure to master the affects in the Sen–Mac plot, resulting in failure and death; and his

---

[55] Ibid., 57.
[56] See Xine Yao, *Disaffected: The Cultural Politics of Unfeeling in Nineteenth-Century America* (Durham, NC and London: Duke University Press, 2021).
[57] Ibid., 117.   [58] Ibid., 222.   [59] Ibid., 248.

flight into 'open country', which, as the other plot has shown us, is not open at all and is where the original sin or crime of US nation-building, the slaughter of the Indigenous population, has seeped into the land itself. In the end, it is Sailor's failure to see and comprehend this in the latter plot ('A piece of land couldn't trap a man. Even if it spread on and on like eternity ... He wasn't trapped. He was getting out'[60]) that leads to his entrapment in the former.

Conclusion

The parallel tracks of Hughes's novel set the more progressive or hopeful aspects produced by Sailor's partial recognition of his own complicity and xenophobia, and the hospitality he extends to Pancho and is extended to him, against his determination to squeeze money from the Sen and eventually his failure and death. These in turn speak to the larger tension that I have tried to map out in this chapter and where we can locate the ambivalent politics of much American crime fiction: between, on the one hand, the desire for community and for a workable notion of the public, and, on the other hand, the incorporation of this notion of the public by private enterprise and the allure of greed, profit, and gain. If the subsumption of the former by the latter, for critics such as McCann and Breu, is one of the features of the development of American crime fiction in the twentieth century (and something we can see in *Ride the Pink Horse*), the genre's commitment to ambivalence or holding open the potential or possibility of seemingly contradictory positions would continue to characterize its politics. Certainly, one can find exemplary crime novels of the era that pursue a clear leftist politics – Ira Wolfert's *Tucker's People* (1943), for example, offers a sharply critical take on 'the endemic gangsterism of corporate organization'.[61] Similarly, Mickey Spillane's Mike Hammer novels took Hammett's sceptical, ambivalent, hard-boiled loner and turned him into an avenging, anti-communist crusader. But the politics of most American crime fiction, neither exclusively left nor right, would be most easily discerned in the complex positions and counter-positions taken up and developed in stories about individual action and organizational complicity and where the related domains of law, crime, and business are brought into an uneasy conflagration. Such complexity would allow

[60] Ibid., 224.
[61] Alan Filreis, 'Introduction', in Ira Wolfert, *Tucker's People* (Urbana and Chicago: University of Illinois Press, 1997), xvi.

readers of James Ellroy's 'Los Angeles Quartet' – a series of crime novels about LA in the 1940s and 1950s written in the 1980s and 1990s – to simultaneously identify Ellroy as a right-wing fascist railing against social permissiveness and the polluting effects of Black people, homosexuals, and women and a left-wing rabble-rouser shining a light on organizational corruption and unearthing the hidden links between capital, policing, and the political process. And, to a lesser or greater degree, both positions could be said to be true, emphasizing once again the genre's structuring tension.

CHAPTER 9

Science Fiction

Jason Haslam

Neal Stephenson's science fiction (SF) novel *Anathem* (2008) is set in a monastery whose inhabitants are denied access to the technological developments of the outside world. To this extent, it can be read as an inversion of a classic novel that, in many ways, signaled the end of SF's so-called Golden Age,[1] Walter M. Miller's *Canticle for Leibowitz* (1959), in which monks protect scientific knowledge after the world is devastated by nuclear war. Beyond the general similarity in setting, the two novels, and the periods in which they were written, are at first glance radically dissimilar. Miller's piece is a product of Cold War dread and the fear of nuclear annihilation; *Canticle* offers a dystopian response to the prewar technological fetishism of Golden Age SF and the postwar optimism of economic booms and a burgeoning youth culture. Stephenson's novel, conversely, seems as disconnected from its post-9/11 political world as its monks are separated from the world outside their enclaves. Focused more on scientific and philosophical debates regarding whether the human mind functions as a quantum computer, the novel works primarily as a meditation on the ontological nature of knowledge.[2]

This narrow pairing of two novels by white men is not intended to present a trajectory of SF's engagement with politics – far from it. It can, however, be used to frame a central problem that haunts political SF: the disconnect between its spectacular escapism and its political imaginings. That the genre has a long history of addressing political matters is clear on any quick overview, and the connection between SF and utopian literature all but ensures that SF is an inherently political form. This fact has been variously addressed by critics and authors of the genre, with several

---

[1] Adam Roberts writes that, for fans, the "Golden Age" mostly refers to "stories published in the late 1930s and 1940s." Adam Roberts, *Science Fiction*, 2nd edition (New York: Routledge, 2006), 56, 60.
[2] Neal Stephenson, *Anathem* (New York: Harper, 2008); Walter M. Miller, Jr., *A Canticle for Leibowitz* (New York: Bantam, 1997 [1959]).

volumes dedicated specifically to the relationship.[3] Combining utopian elements and world-building – following Darko Suvin, a strategy of "cognitive estrangement," wherein SF's invented worlds are radically different from the material world of their publication and yet simultaneously logically extrapolated from it – SF could appear to be a fundamentally comparative, if not allegorical, form destined to be read as social and political commentary on the author's or reader's own reality.[4]

And yet, as British SF author China Miéville has written, the inherent kernel of non-realism and fantasy in SF – Suvin's "novum" – cannot so easily claim to be logically extrapolative: "A lot of science fiction that pretends it is about scientific rigor is actually predicated on ... a kind of caste or class model that is, in a way, the Enlightenment's betrayal of itself, since it says: do not ask questions because we have an expert here who will understand this stuff for us."[5] Likewise, the oft-touted "sense of wonder" of SF's nova, bordering on a transcendent sublime, would seem to pull SF toward a naïvely Romantic form of disconnection. The identification of this problem for SF's political claims predates Miéville – indeed, it predates the twentieth century and the interwar creation of the genre per se. For instance, Engels argued that the immaterial element of socialist utopianism denies it the ability to truly engage the world politically or scientifically.[6] Framed in more philosophical terms, the ontological division between the real and the intellectual fantasies of utopianism – and the (technological) utopianism of much SF – is not so easily bridged. This gap then renders the politics of SF into, at best, mere entertainment, or at worst a form of political pretense.[7] Fredric Jameson tries to tackle this division by invoking Ernst Bloch's formulation of the "utopian impulse," which, at its most basic, can both inspire change and lead one back to the material conditions one needs or wants to change, for what may become good or ill. Using Ridley Scott's *Alien* as his own allegory for this process, Jameson posits an

[3] See, e.g., Julia Weldes, ed., *To Seek Out New Worlds: Science Fiction and World Politics* (New York: Palgrave Macmillan, 2003); Donald M. Hassler and Clyde Wilcox, eds., *New Boundaries in Political Science Fiction* (Columbia: University of South Carolina Press, 2008); Patrick Parrinder, *Learning from Other Worlds: Estrangement, Cognition, and the Politics of Science Fiction and Utopia* (Liverpool: Liverpool University Press, 2000).

[4] Darko Suvin, *Metamorphoses of Science Fiction* (New Haven, CT: Yale University Press, 1979).

[5] China Miéville, "Gothic Politics: A Discussion with China Miéville," *Gothic Studies* 10.1 (2008): 63–4.

[6] Frederick Engels, *Socialism: Utopian and Scientific*, trans. Edward Aveling (1892), available at www.marxists.org/archive/marx/works/1880/soc-utop

[7] On eutopia, dystopia, and related terms, see Lyman Tower Sargent, "The Three Faces of Utopianism Revisited," *Utopian Studies* 5.1 (1994): 1–37.

ongoing dialectic, in which utopian and SF world-building serves not as synthesis, but as symptom of larger material, political analyses.[8]

With these quandaries as a background, both Miller and Stephenson can be read as theorizing the relationship between politically inflected SF and political life: Like the "ivory towers" of their monasteries, SF can be read as a rarified form that reflects (and reflects upon) political reality from a distance, a distance that simultaneously enables and disables actual political action based on its speculations. SF writer and critic Samuel R. Delany refers to this moment in SF, which could also be seen as the "sense of wonder," as "that gravitically neutral space (free-fall) where imagination streaks between worlds," where "worlds" can be figured as a reigning symbolic order. But some readers, he argues – and, one could add, some texts – "cannot get free of the gravitic orientation" or the mundane of the status quo.[9] The distancing created by the spectacle of SF can thus render its allegories amorphous, subject to such wide and often contradictory political interpretations that the form, as Engels would argue, can risk its political interventions becoming stale entertainments.

And yet, in treating the future as a site of discursive debate, SF reminds us that history – or any historical narrative – is also such a site, and that the ground of political action is always the same unstable ground of interpretation itself, leaving reality – scientific or otherwise – open to collective reformation. The (un)realisms of SF rearticulate Jacques Rancière's definition of "aesthetic acts" of representation, which serve "as configurations of experience that create new modes of sense perception and induce novel forms of political subjectivity."[10] SF demonstrates – sometimes wittingly, sometimes not – how imaginative cultural responses to the material conditions of various institutions (scientific, technological, political) can both reinforce and challenge the foundational ideologies that prop them up.

That historical-theoretical introduction needs to be contextualized for the focus of the current volume. SF is, in some ways, the central genre of the "American century." Taking its modern form and being named during the pulp period of the interwar years, developing its political awareness through the Cold War and globalism, SF and twentieth-century American

---

[8] Fredric Jameson, *Archaeologies of the Future: The Desire Called Utopia and Other Science Fictions* (London: Verso, 2005), 13–14.

[9] Samuel R. Delany, *The American Shore: Meditations of a Tale of Science Fiction by Thomas M. Disch – "Angouleme"* (Middletown, CT: Wesleyan University Press, 2014 [1978]), 160.

[10] Jacques Rancière, *The Politics of Aesthetics: The Distribution of the Sensible*, trans. Gabriel Rockhill (New York: Continuum, 2004), 9.

and global politics grew alongside each other and, as Julia Weldes argues, influenced each other in mutually reenforcing – and mutually critical – ways.[11] Often focused on the rapid development of technologies and their dangers, American SF novels have highlighted how the twentieth century is characterized by truly global crises and possibilities, from the mass migrations and various exploitations of them in the early twentieth century, to the Cold War and the direct threat of global nuclear destruction, to giving voice to those denied rights and silenced both in the earlier SF canon and in the larger body politic, and finally to the climate emergency. This chapter offers not a comprehensive overview, but instead stresses moments in time, to misquote Roy Batty (Rutger Hauer) in *Blade Runner* (1982), Scott's adaptation of Philip K. Dick's *Do Androids Dream of Electric Sheep?* (1968). Distancing these moments from real, twentieth-century SF novels may risk making specific political moments seem fantastic, but they can simultaneously enable new forms of global and communal visions that are (increasingly) necessary for political action. The remainder of this chapter therefore discusses how various forms of SF have explored some of the central elements of twentieth-century politics. In doing so, it also points to the many other structures of SF that have been somewhat hidden behind the genre's public-facing, very *ivory* towers.

Enter the Twentieth Century: Early Pulps and the Alien Other

In the introduction to the first issue of *Amazing Stories* (1926), editor Hugo Gernsback defines the scope of the new genre, "scientifiction," even as he explicitly connects it to earlier work:

> There is the usual fiction magazine, the love story and the sex-appeal type of magazine, the adventure type, and so on, but a magazine of "Scientifiction" is a pioneer in its field in America ... Two hundred years ago, stories of this kind were not possible. Science, through its various branches of mechanics, electricity, astronomy, etc., enters so intimately into all our lives today, and we are so much immersed in this science, that we have become rather prone to take new inventions and discoveries for granted ... For the best of these modern writers of scientifiction have the knack of imparting knowledge, and even inspiration, without once making us aware that we are being taught. And not only that! Poe, Verne, Wells, Bellamy, and many others have proved themselves real prophets.[12]

---

[11] See Julia Weldes, "Popular Culture, Science Fiction, and World Politics," in Weldes, 1–27.
[12] Hugo Gernsback, "A New Sort of Magazine," *Amazing Stories* 1.1 (1926): 3.

Eschewing love, sex, and adventure for a supposedly more "scientific" form of literature, Gernsback solidifies what many readers and critics of SF would come to see as its most accepted form (and formulas). Present in this description are what Suvin would frame as the two primary generic components of SF: the "novum," or new technology (be it scientific, social, political, or so on), which, in the world of the text, radically reshapes the "entire mode of living"; and the notion of "cognitive estrangement," where those new modes of living are so different from the author's or reader's own that they create a sense of estrangement, but one that is "cognitive" because the novum, for Suvin as for Gernsback, is logically extrapolated from existing knowledge. But Gernsback also makes another move here: He explicitly connects this new form to every facet of modern life, and, implicitly, to politics through his invocation of Edward Bellamy, whose utopia, *Looking Backward 2000–1887* (1888), would spawn nationalist and populist movements, and eventually political parties.[13]

The works that populated Gernsback's and later pulp magazines continued to weave together these trajectories, often in distinctly pernicious ways. One of the most influential figures to come out of *Amazing Stories* was the character who would later be known as Buck Rogers, initially named William in Philip Francis Nowlan's 1928 serialized novella *Armageddon 2419 A.D.* and its 1929 sequel *The Airlords of Han.* Becoming a mass-media icon (from the novels, to one of the first serialized comic strips, to radio, film, and television), "Buck Rogers" was synonymous for much of the twentieth century with "science fiction" itself. And yet this iconic figure also shows how the destructive elements of utopianism can be perpetuated by SF. Nowlan's novels are firmly entrenched in, and influential examples of, the "yellow peril" tradition of twentieth-century US literature. Sleeping for centuries through massive social change (as did Bellamy's protagonist), Rogers awakens to an America invaded and controlled by China. Echoing the fears of the 1924 anti-Asian Immigration Act,[14] Nowlan's first Rogers tale depicts a white American population forced to "return" to the land in an effort to resist a racialized other who, in the sequel, are revealed to be aliens in the extraterrestrial, and not just national and ethnic, sense.

---

[13] On Bellamy's ties to nationalist and populist movements, see Alex MacDonald, introduction to *Looking Backward 2000–1887* (Peterborough: Broadview, 2003), 17–28.

[14] On the 1924 Immigration Act, see Lee A. Makela, "The Immigration Act of 1924," in *Asian American Politics: Law, Participation, and Policy,* ed. Don T. Nakanishi and James S. Lai (Oxford: Rowman & Littlefield, 2003), 51–79.

As the return to the land and a connection to a "homeland" would indicate, Nowlan's character is fully steeped in the nascent ideologies of fascism. Nor is this connection between fascism and pulp SF unique: Aaron Santesso has argued that, while much academic SF criticism focuses on the "progressive" bona fides of the genre, its utopian underpinnings and functions of estrangement are equally elements of authoritarian political philosophy. Certain repeated tropes in SF (from a "worship of masculinity" to "a celebration of a 'pure' race or group over a 'decadent' one," to "a fascination with technology as an indicator of historical progress or corruption"), Santesso argues, bring with them at least the trace of oppressive politics, even among authors who would consider themselves anything but fascist.[15] Certainly, after World War II, there was a distinct move away from technological fetishism and assumptions of power, but the earlier tropes and the political forms they echo never fully went away. Similarly, but beyond the specifics of twentieth-century fascism, the narratives of exploration and alien others present in the pulps also continue to reproduce ideologies of settler colonialism, as outlined by John Rieder in his foundational work.[16]

Moving away from the professional pulps, however, proves enlightening as to how the form can be used politically in other ways, even in these early years. Three telling examples come from early African American SF. First, Pauline Hopkins's *Of One Blood*, originally serialized in *The Colored American Magazine* (1902–3), which Hopkins edited, explores mesmerism and early psychology, as well as African-centric anthropological theories.[17] Tied to the latter, Hopkins creates an African utopia, Telassar, technologically advanced and free from European influence, over half a century before Marvel Comics would create Wakanda and a century before that city came to the silver screen in the Afrofuturist *Black Panther* (2018). A few decades later, W. E. B. Du Bois's story "The Comet" (1920) and George Schuyler's novel *Black No More* (1931) likewise both offer a political trajectory directly opposed to Nowlan's racist and isolationist allegory.[18] In his novel, Schuyler presents a world in which science can

[15] Aaron Santesso, "Fascism and Science Fiction," *Science Fiction Studies* 41.1 (2014): 145; also see Andrew Pilsch, "Self-Help Supermen: The Politics of Fan Utopias in World War II-Era Science Fiction," *Science Fiction Studies*, 41.3 (2014): 524–42.

[16] John Rieder, *Colonialism and the Emergence of Science Fiction* (Middletown, CT: Wesleyan University Press, 2008).

[17] Pauline Hopkins, *Of One Blood* (New York: Washington Square Press, 2004).

[18] George Schuyler, *Black No More: Being an Account of the Strange and Wonderful Workings of Science in the Land of the Free, A. D. 1933–1940* (Boston, MA: Northeastern University Press, 1989 [1931]); W. E. B. Du Bois, "The Comet," in *Darkwater: Voices from Within the Veil* (New York:

turn Black skin white; in the process, he satirizes everyone and everything, from the skin-lightening industry of the period, to the Klan, and even to Du Bois himself. Racism ends up reproducing itself by the end of the novel, however, because, as Schuyler highlights, anti-Black racism is a rhizomatic form of social violence fully entangled with and inseparable from American capitalism. Similarly, Du Bois, in his short story "The Comet," presents a post-apocalyptic New York City where the only survivors of a cataclysm caused by the titular comet are a Black man and a white woman. Having to fight through their socially conditioned perceptions of race, especially as informed by racist sexual politics, the two eventually seem poised to recognize their common humanity, only to have this utopian moment interrupted as white people from outside the city arrive and again enforce racist social expectations. That these two antiracist (if differently politically oriented) texts don't ultimately imagine a world beyond racism highlights what Nowlan and some other pulp authors exploit: Even in the future-oriented worlds of political SF novels, it is easier to imagine the end of America than it is to imagine the end of racism.

Cold War Modernity and the Alien Within

I obviously echo the statement, commonly ascribed to Fredric Jameson, that "it is easier to imagine the end of the world than it is to imagine the end of capitalism."[19] This analysis – now almost a truism – takes on specific resonance in the SF novels of the 1950s and 1960s, especially those that deal with the Cold War and what seemed like an immanent nuclear apocalypse.[20] The novels written during the height of the period's paranoia again fall between the poles of allegorical othering that entrenches existing political visions, at one end, and, at the other, attempts to present more nuanced, if still somewhat cynical, visions of a future decimated by the bomb and political Manicheanism. A well-known example of the first is Jack Finney's oft-adapted and referenced *The Body Snatchers* (1955).[21] Even there, though, the slipperiness of SF's estranging distance can lead to

---

Washington Square Press, 2004), 195–209. Both works appear in Sheree R. Thomas's foundational anthology, discussed below. Sheree R. Thomas, *Dark Matter: A Century of Speculative Fiction from the African Diaspora* (New York: Warner Aspect, 2000).

[19] Mark Fisher notes that this line has been attributed to both Jameson and Slavoj Žižek, in *Capitalist Realism: Is There No Alternative?* (Winchester: O Books, 2009), 2.

[20] For a touchstone on the topic, see David Seed, *American Science Fiction and the Cold War* (Chicago: Fitzroy Dearborn, 1999). Also see, e.g., Cyndy Hendershot, *Paranoia, the Bomb, and 1950s Science-Fiction Films* (Bowling Green, OH: Bowling Green State University Popular Press, 1999).

[21] Jack Finney, *The Body Snatchers* (New York: Scribner, 1989 [1955]).

other evaluations: While it is easily read as a classic "red scare" novel that employs a collectivist alien threat taking over the minds and bodies of more individualist (American) humans, still it – and its adaptations – can also be read somewhat against the temporal grain as critiques of burgeoning postwar American suburbanism.

Likewise, Dianne Newell and Victoria Lamont resituate Cold War narratives within a much longer American tradition developed out of settler colonialism and Manifest Destiny, arguing that post–World War II nuclear tales regularly reproduce a "frontier mythology" in which "the post-atomic frontier is represented as the modern version of American civilization's ongoing cyclical encounter with savagery."[22] This settler-colonial mentality replicates the Western's othering of Indigenous peoples, while the post-apocalyptic setting repositions the genocidal violence lying at the foundation of US "civilization." Newell and Lamont, however, analyze the ways in which such a blunt reformation of Manifest Destiny is, on occasion, disrupted by women SF authors of the period. Judith Merril's *Shadow on the Hearth* (1950), as these critics point out, is a rare "domestic" portrayal of the effects of nuclear war, but they argue that it still reproduces the othering logic of military SF. At the end of the novel, Newell and Lamont suggest, "The juxtaposition of the husband's arrival with the end of the war symbolically links the restoration of the normal, nuclear family with the military victory, making Gladys's rugged domesticity as symbolically important a weapon as the remote-controlled missiles that have subdued the enemy." However, they note, such a blunt ending may be more connected to the troping demands of SF publishing than to Merril's intent, since "this ending was inserted by the publishers; in her original, the husband is killed near their home."[23]

Such inklings of more subversive articulations of Cold War paranoia can point to the other end of the political spectrum I referenced, with works that undermine such forms of othering. To return to this chapter's opening, in both *A Canticle for Leibowitz*, by Miller, and Ray Bradbury's *Fahrenheit 451* (1953), nuclear Armageddon and McCarthyism are combatted through a preservation of information. Meanwhile, Philip K. Dick's novels present worlds driven to mass apathy, on the one hand, and mass paranoia driven by mass media and political theatre, on the other. No one seems to be in control of their own lives or of society's future(s), even as Dick's own politics

---

[22] Dianne Newell and Victoria Lamont, "Rugged Domesticity: Frontier Mythology in Post-Armageddon Science Fiction by Women," *Science Fiction Studies* 32.3 (2005): 423–4.
[23] Ibid., 428.

confuse the critique being offered.[24] *Canticle*, especially, warns that knowledge and technology pursued *sans* ethics, and used for the purposes of a
paranoid politics, can lead to a return of imperial and genocidal ideologies.
In the world of Miller's novel, the preservation of pre-apocalyptic learning
by a group of monks is separated from its historical and hermeneutic
context, allowing it to be appropriated by technological fetishists, in an echo
of earlier pulp SF. The belletristic and the bellicose may seem oppositional,
Miller suggests, but they can also be inextricably imbricated.

Such complex SF visions of Cold War institutions and their distorted
cultural reflections are best articulated in meditations on the discursive
formation of the "enemy," and especially the "enemy within," both a
material reality and a cultural bogeyman exploited by McCarthy and,
running in parallel, the House Committee on Un-American Activities.
SF's focus on the alien other can highlight elements of the othering process
itself. Two works can stand in for a number of others: Richard Matheson's
vampire *cum* zombie post-apocalypse in *I Am Legend* (1954) and Delany's
linguistic theory as space opera *Babel-17* (1966). Matheson plays with
limited perspective to reimagine the protagonist as monstrous other, about
whom the new vampire society will tell their own tales of terror. Delany's
novel, written a decade after Matheson's, takes this inversion and renders it
more directly political for the Vietnam age. Building on theories of
linguistic relativity as well as early computer programming, Delany reimagines language itself as the technological novum, with the language Babel-
17 being created by the alien Invaders to train a human as a perfect spy and
assassin. A language lacking the concept and structures of the first person,
Babel-17 renders its speakers as simply objects in a world of objects, while
its exacting descriptive capacity makes them able to understand their
surroundings perfectly and instantaneously. At the end of the novel,
however, the poet protagonist, Rydra Wong, decodes the language and
defuses the spy through a Lacanian love plot, awakening him to the inner
lives of others and to his own sense of self. In so doing, she discovers that
the Invaders' word, in Babel-17, for the "good guy" Alliance translates to
"one-who-has-invaded."[25] Like Matheson's novel, the lines between self
and other, enemy and friend, are shown instead to be inseparable in a play
of difference.

---

[24] Dick's paranoid vision of the world led, famously, to him writing to the FBI about the Marxist
influence on SF criticism in the 1970s. See Robert M. Philmus, "The Two Faces of Philip K. Dick
(Les Deux Visages de Philip K. Dick)," *Science Fiction Studies* 18.1 (1991): 91–103.

[25] Samuel R. Delany, *Babel-17* (New York: Vintage, 2001 [1966]), 215.

While remaining a fairly standard space opera, Delany's novel participates in some later SF trends by offering explicitly experimental elements: The most visible element of this experimentation is pages with two columns of text representing Wong's ability to think in both English and Babel-17 simultaneously, but equally challenging to some SF traditions was the incorporation of linguistic and psychological theory, not to mention having an Asian woman protagonist and queer polyamorous piloting partnerships.

I return to the importance of Delany's work in general below, but I mention these linguistic, political, and genre-aware elements here because earlier works – not regularly included in SF anthologies – also participate in an even more explicit experimentation that challenges SF's pulp assumptions. One can point to the grotesqueries of William S. Burroughs, of course, but even more notable is Ralph Ellison's *Invisible Man* (1952). As Lisa Yaszek argues, Ellison "strategically deploys the language of science fiction to emphasize the alienation of black subjects from ... whitewashed futures," noting his use of such descriptors as "robots" and "mechanical man" to highlight such alienation.[26] Beyond this, Yaszek argues, the novel refuses any future – communist or capitalist, utopian or dystopian – in which an enforced racist alienation continues: All such futures fail to offer one in which the protagonist can flourish on his own terms. By the waning days of the pulps, then, works were already on the rise that relied on but simultaneously, and self-reflexively, critiqued the reactionary politics of certain SF tropes.

The New Wave: Feminist SF and the Personal as Political

It is thus a mistake to see SF as only a vehicle for reproducing dominant political ideologies and the various forms of othering woven into them – although it is an equal mistake to err on the other side and imagine SF as only progressive in its political outlook. Many works mix the two together; utopias can simultaneously be dystopias, after all, as the white supremacy of Charlotte Perkins Gilman's feminist utopian novel *Herland* (1915) makes clear.[27]

---

[26] Lisa Yaszek, "An Afrofuturist Reading of Ralph Ellison's *Invisible Man*," *Rethinking History* 9.2/3 (2005): 305.

[27] On the imbrication of *Herland*'s feminism and white supremacy, see, e.g., Lynne Evans, "'You See, Children Were the – the *Raison d'Être*': The Reproductive Futurism of Charlotte Perkins Gilman's *Herland*," *Canadian Review of American Studies* 44.2 (2014): 302–19.

But the period from the early 1960s through to the 1970s (and arguably beyond) became a flashpoint for discussions of SF and politics, with the advent of the so-called New Wave. Primary among the American creators associated with this loosely connected group are the previously mentioned Delany and Merril, but also such luminaries as Ursula K. Le Guin and Joanna Russ, and other critically understudied figures, including Pamela K. Zoline and Roger Zelazny. Framed by J. G. Ballard as a shift from "Outer Space to Inner Space,"[28] the New Wave is associated with a transition from the technophilia of the pulps to a focus on the psychological, social, and human sciences. As Helen Merrick argues, the "trend" toward using political and social issues as a text's "novum" "can be traced back at least to the 1940s, but it was certainly consolidated and intensified by the impact of the New Wave and the 'mainstream' *avant garde*, feminist, and ecological movements."[29] Of course, neither women nor feminism had ever been separate from SF in any real way, but the visibility, centrality, and recognition of these authors and works saw a distinct increase in this period.

Two works can again serve as imperfect reflections here: Le Guin's *The Left Hand of Darkness* (1969) and Russ's *The Female Man* (1975). Both create worlds in which gender operates differently than in the hierarchized patriarchal binaries of the time. Le Guin's better-known novel invents a world whose inhabitants exist in a largely sexually undifferentiated and "gender neutral" space; the novel thus challenges overly determinative patriarchal and heteronormative hierarchies (although it has been critiqued for Le Guin's initial decision to use "he/him" pronouns as "neutral" descriptors for the non-binary characters). *The Female Man*, more than *The Left Hand of Darkness*, meditates on the role of SF speculation itself in feminist history and politics. The novel follows the interactions of different incarnations of the same woman, named Joanna, Janet, Jeannine, and Jael. Through these characters, Russ traces the development of feminist politics from an alternative, patriarchal America that did not experience World War II and is stuck in an endless Depression; to a world much like Russ's own; to a female separatist utopia, Whileaway (echoing that of Gilman's *Herland*); to a society where women and men are at war. This series of worlds is thus not a linear "future history" but a series of possible realities.

---

[28] J. G. Ballard, "Which Way to Inner Space?," *New Worlds Science Fiction* 40.118 (1962): 2–3, 116–18.
[29] Helen Merrick, "Fiction, 1964–1979," in *The Routledge Companion to Science Fiction*, ed. Mark Bould, Adam Roberts, and Sherryl Vint (New York: Routledge, 2009), 110.

The Female Man, as Susan Ayres, quoting Judith Butler, has written, positions gender and gendered semiotics as a space of contestation, "sug-gest[ing] that women can 'speak their way out of their gender,'" engaging in a form of what Hélène Cixous coined *"écriture féminine"* in the same year Russ's novel was published. "In the beginning are our differences," Cixous writes, noting that "[t]he woman arriving over and over again does not stand still; she's everywhere, she exchanges, she is the desire-that-gives."[30] This poetic formation could serve as a description of Russ's work, insofar as Russ's multiple, interacting women's worlds modify the power structures that are reliant on and fully entangled with gender binaries (in so doing, however, the novel strays into a trans-exclusionary politics that Russ would later recant).[31]

Indeed, forms of *écriture féminine* repeat throughout New Wave femi-nist SF. Perhaps the best and most ambitious example is Suzette Haden Elgin's *Native Tongue* (1984). Published the year before Canadian author Margaret Atwood's better-known *The Handmaid's Tale*, Elgin's novel also imagines a future where women have been stripped of fundamental human rights in a patriarchal dystopia. In a post-alien-contact world, families of linguists become a de facto ruling class (linguistics being the primary skill necessary for interplanetary diplomacy and trade), while women of all classes are stripped of voting and most other rights. Connecting to theories of linguistic relativism, just as Delany's *Babel-17* did, Elgin's novel shows women developing their own language, Láadan, which begins to allow them to control men and effectively serves as a form of self-defense and as a possible end to violence. This linguistic goal was more than a plot device for Elgin; a linguist herself, she invented Láadan to serve women and help to reduce the harms of patriarchal violence.[32] Work connected to and developing out of the New Wave articulated other such experiments, included Delany's *Trouble on Triton* (1976), which expands this utopian

---

[30] Hélène Cixous, "The Laugh of the Medusa," trans. Keith Cohen and Paula Cohen, *Signs* 1.4 (1976): 893.

[31] Susan Ayres, "The 'Straight Mind' in Russ's *The Female Man*," *Science Fiction Studies* 22.1 (1995): 32. In an interview Delany conducted with Russ in 2006, an audience member asked Russ if her views of transwomen had changed, to which Russ replied, "Oh yes, oh yes, it's almost as if my life has arranged itself to disabuse me of one prejudice after another. And all of these have gone because none of them were real, really." "The Legendary Joanna Russ," interview by Samuel R. Delany, transcribed by Lettie Press, in *The WisCon Chronicles*, vol. 1, ed. L. Timmel Duchamp (Seattle: Aqueduct Press, 2007), 162.

[32] See Karen Bruce, "A Woman-Made Language: Suzette Haden Elgin's Láadan and the *Native Tongue* Trilogy as Thought Experiment in Feminist Linguistics," *Extrapolation* 49.1 (2008): 44–69.

thinking into an "ambiguous heterotopia" that presents a series of societal developments from a patriarchal Earth, to a matriarchal Mars, to various moon societies – the last exemplified by Triton, where gender and sexuality are acknowledged as spectrums and society is founded on a fundamental respect for and non-hierarchization of difference.

Cyberpunk: Anti-Capitalist Street or Digital Buck Rogers

The New Wave's explicitly political, often feminist visions have been connected to its move away from so-called hard sciences, an implicitly gendered metaphor in this context, and one that Nicola Nixon exploits in her analysis of the return to technology (albeit digital tech) in 1980s SF, and specifically in cyberpunk.[33] Often identified with William Gibson's *Neuromancer* (1984), cyberpunk, as its name implies, combines digital technology with what Dick Hebdige has called punk rock's *bricolage*, or its ability to use the codes of the dominant culture against itself.[34] In his essay "Rocket Radio" (1989), Gibson characterizes this political aesthetic using a phrase he had earlier used in fiction: "the street finds its own uses for things." These are uses, he continues, that

> manufacturers never imagined. The microcassette recorder, originally intended for on-the-jump executive dictation, becomes the revolutionary medium of *magnitizdat*, allowing the covert spread of suppressed political speeches in Poland and China. The beeper and the cellular telephone become tools in an increasingly competitive market in illicit drugs. Other technological artifacts unexpectedly become means of communication, either through opportunity or necessity.[35]

Decidedly anti-utopian, cyberpunk is not about the development of revolution in the service of ideals, which arguably characterizes many of the categories of SF discussed above. Instead, it was a disruptive form, one that aimed to exploit cracks in the burgeoning global economic system that, far from ushering in a "global village" of possibilities, was in fact investing political and cultural power in multinational corporate entities. The global – and anti-global – perspective of such cyberpunk authors as Gibson, Stephenson, and others prefigures contemporary concerns around

---

[33] Nicola Nixon, "Cyberpunk: Paving the Ground for Revolution, or Keeping the Boys Satisfied?," *Science Fiction Studies* 19 (1992): 219–35.
[34] Dick Hebdige, *Subculture: The Meaning of Style* (London: Methuen, 1979).
[35] William Gibson, *Distrust that Particular Flavor* (New York, Penguin, 2012), 10.

capital, resource extraction, and other global forms of exploitation (as, indeed, did Le Guin and others before them). But, in emphasizing the ability of a digitally savvy youth culture to disrupt this system, such authors presented a form of revolutionary – if on occasion nihilistic – praxis allied with anti-Reaganite and anti-Thatcherite punks.

And yet, as I have noted elsewhere,[36] the gender and racial politics of many of the early pieces of cyberpunk undermined these goals. Sharon Stockton notes that the classic cyberpunk hero is someone who "is removed entirely from problems of influence and given the status of prime mover, of pure subject in a world of pure object, of phallic projection into a feminized matrix that approximates the universe."[37] Nixon further states that the "corporate collectives" that Gibson's heroes fight against, especially in his earlier work, are figured as an orientalist, usually Japanese, threat, arguing, in effect, that Gibson's works – however unwittingly – reproduce the "yellow peril" narratives of Nowlan's Buck Rogers.[38] Likewise, in comparing Zion, the Black separatist community in Gibson's novel, to the author's earlier depiction of the Lo Teks in "Johnny Mnemonic" (1981), Delany has said:

> [I]t speaks directly from "the political unconscious" of the cyberpunk subgenre that, as soon as [Gibson] specifically "darkened" the Lo-teks' image and re-presented it in the form of the Rastas, they lost all their oppositional charge – hell, all their physical strength – all their cultural specificity, their massive group presence, and their social power to escape the forces of multinational capitalism.[39]

As Santesso suggests of the effects of SF's pulp tropes, cyberpunk thus seems unable to remove itself completely from the capitalist matrices of power. Such authors as Octavia Butler and Nalo Hopkinson, drawing on wider literary and cultural traditions, obviously counter such trends, as discussed in the next section, but in the mainstreaming of cyberpunk, it looked as if SF would close out the twentieth century with hacker heroes all too easily co-opted into neoliberalism's governing mantra of "disruptive

---

[36] Jason Haslam, *Gender and Race in American Science Fiction: Reflections on Fantastic Identities* (New York: Routledge, 2015), 135.
[37] Sharon Stockton, "'The Self-Regained': Cyberpunk's Retreat to the Imperium," *Contemporary Literature* 36.4 (1995): 589.
[38] Nixon, 224–5.
[39] Delany, quoted in Mark Dery, "Black to the Future: Interviews with Samuel R. Delany, Greg Tate, and Tricia Rose," in *Flame Wars: The Discourse of Cyberculture*, ed. Mark Dery (Durham, NC: Duke University Press, 1994), 197. These interviews were originally published as part of a special issue of *South Atlantic Quarterly*.

innovation."[40] The 1999 film *The Matrix* is a self-aware exemplar of this conundrum, depicting racial and gendered revolutions that play on the dual meaning of that word: Both transformative and repetitive, twentieth-century SF seemed forever stuck in the matrices of its own making.

Enter the Twenty-First Century: Futurity's Revenge

That revolving logic is also a risk of the structure of this chapter, in that it offers a politically inflected version of a traditional narrative of SF literary history that centers now canonical works of SF's dominant subgenres. I have tried to mitigate such problems throughout the chapter by gesturing in each section to works that seem to fall outside such "mainstream" SF genealogies, and which serve to critique the more regressive elements of the mainstream genre. Of course, this bears its own risk: Readers would be forgiven for seeing in this an attempt to "recover" SF by allowing for a more avant-garde depth model that includes such important figures as Du Bois and Ellison. The intended goal, however, as the section on the New Wave should suggest, is that these "other" voices have always been central to SF, and so any genealogy should also start with them. Indeed, in the past decade or more, significant publishing and critical attention has focused on these traditions, with much of that work dedicated to futurisms that run directly counter to the silencing forms of the pulps. Afrofuturisms, Africanfuturisms, Indigenous futurisms, Latinx futurisms: All of these and more point to futures built on a heteroglot of voices.

The importance of Octavia Butler in this transformation, from the late 1970s to the turn of the millennium, is more significant than can be stated: I have not included her in the overview of periods in part because her work is given extensive treatment elsewhere in this volume, but also because her novels and stories – with their focus on Black feminist politics, ecological awareness, and assertion of the centrality of difference – exceed and transform the field of SF even as she wrote firmly within it. The same can be said of Caribbean-Canadian author Nalo Hopkinson, whose *Brown Girl in the Ring* (1998) and such stories as "Something to Hitch Meat To" (from her 2001 collection *Skin Folk*) point to the ways in which the

---

[40] On Clayton Christensen's concept of "disruptive innovation" and neoliberalism, see Christopher Newfield, "'Innovation' Discourse and the Neoliberal University: Top Ten Reasons to Abolish Disruptive Innovation," in *Mutant Neoliberalism: Market Rule and Political Rupture*, ed. William Callison and Zachary Manfredi (New York: Fordham University Press, 2019), 244–68.

political strategies of Gibson's "street" are better tied to the multiplicity of cultural and racialized politics of the modern cityscape.

And as we entered the twenty-first century, Black authors, and specifically Black women authors, as well as Indigenous authors, Latinx authors, and other racialized and minoritized groups, have indeed become more visible and central to the entire field of SF, which had all but silenced their voices for so long. Much work has been done to resurrect this alternative genealogy of SF; as Alondra Nelson notes, while "Afrofuturism" maybe have been coined in 1993, "the currents that comprise it existed long before."[41] Central to this effort has been a series of anthologies, starting with Sheree R. Thomas's revolutionary *Dark Matter* anthologies (2000 and 2004) and including Nalo Hopkinson and Uppinder Mehan's *So Long Been Dreaming: Postcolonial Science Fiction and Fantasy* (2004), Grace Dillon's *Walking the Clouds: An Anthology of Indigenous Science Fiction* (2012), Bill Campbell and Edward Austin Hall's *Mothership: Tales from Afrofuturism and Beyond* (2013), Nisi Shawl's *New Suns: Original Speculative Fiction by People of Color* (2019), and many others. Likewise, N. K. Jemisin, Nnedi Okorafor, and Cheri Dimaline, among many other Black and Indigenous writers and writers of color, have seen their works rightly feted within and beyond SF circles in the first two decades of the twenty-first century, even as the voices of retrenchment have tried to push back.[42]

These forms of futurist thinking, in which those previously and currently marginalized voices not only continue but thrive in a future that looks decidedly different from both Gernsback's pulps and Gibson's cyberspace, also forged new spaces throughout the twentieth century, however. From Hopkins and Schuyler to Ellison, Delany, Butler, and beyond, Afrofuturism is a primary example whose presence allows for an entirely different genealogy for twentieth-century SF, one that we can read back through as a history seemingly subsumed but that nonetheless influenced all of the SF that grew alongside it and that came later.

A nearly perfect metonym – and as much a causal agent – for this parallel development of various SF worlds is a figure already much

---

[41] Alondra, Nelson, "Introduction: Future Texts," *Social Text* 20.2 (2002): 14. Afrofuturism was coined by white critic Mark Dery in the chapter "Black to the Future: Interviews with Samuel R. Delany, Greg Tate, and Tricia Rose," cited earlier.

[42] In SF fandom, conservative reactionary voices reached public notice around 2015 during attempts to derail the Hugo awards. For an overview, see David M. Higgins, *Reverse Colonization: Science Fiction, Imperial Fantast, and Alt-Victimhood* (Iowa City: Iowa University Press, 2021), 4–10.

discussed above: Samuel R. Delany. With an oeuvre covering more than the past half-century (although not always in SF), as an author explicitly engaged in political writing (especially on issues of sex, race, gender, and class), and as one who has connections to earlier pulp authors, the New Wave, cyberpunk, and Afrofuturism (the term being coined in an interview with him and other creators), Delany points to the multiple realities of SF's political possibilities. Take the issue of climate change and the recently coined SF subgenre of "cli-fi" that discusses it.[43] Arguably, Delany has been dealing with this global phenomenon since his earliest writing: *Nova* (1968) involves a quest for a new form of energy and energy extraction. The novella "We, in Some Strange Power's Employ, Move on a Rigorous Line" (originally published as "Lines of Power" in 1968), imagines a post-petroleum world where an international corporation provides power to everyone on Earth; this is a world where people work but have the time to be both pilots and poets, and where societies and systems (bureaucratic and otherwise) are gender, racially, and sexually inclusive. But still, Delany suggests, petroleum-fueled power (infra)structures continue to linger as forms of regressive resistance that nonetheless point to the cultural and social losses of a "one-world order" where individualism is on the wane as a political philosophy, in a way that echoes the labor and cultural losses of coal country in the current moment.

His most recent SF work, meanwhile, *Through the Valley of the Nest of Spiders* (2012), combines his "pornotopian" vision with his SF, tracing a near future running from the recent past (with Obama's election) through the next century. In the background, the reader will notice the transition to green energies, sustainable building materials, and so on. But, as Keguro Macharia has argued, this is primarily a novel "where black gay livability is possible and prized." The society depicted at the end of this magnum opus is also an explicitly science- and techno-phobic one; having seen the global devastations of earlier technophilia, the culture moves away from such solutions and toward social ones in which, Macharia writes, "possibilities for livability have been multiplied in materials ways."[44] The future Delany paints – one of differences and the pleasures and possibilities for care that they bring – provides its own response to the politics of twentieth-century

---

[43] Dan Bloom is generally credited with coining the term. See www.cli-fi.net/

[44] Keguro Macharia, "Rough Notes on Delany," *Gukira*, April 12, 2014, https://gukira.wordpress .com/2014/04/12/rough-notes-on-delany/. On Delany's pornotopian visions, including a discussion of Macharia's reading, see Matthew Cheney, *Modernist Crisis and the Pedagogy of Form: Woolf, Delany, and Coetzee at the Limits of Fiction* (London: Bloomsbury, 2020).

SF. Imagined futures have never been bound by the "ivory towers" of SF. Remember the sense of wonder created in those pulps, Delany seems to say, but forget any limitations on the futures they painted; instead, remember that there is yet hope in creating and inhabiting those many other futures and worlds outside those bounds, which also started so long ago.

CHAPTER 10

Western Fiction

Stephen J. Mexal

Over the past few decades, scholars of Western American literature have become increasingly dedicated to studying Western works by previously marginalized writers, including those by women, by queer writers, and by writers of color, particularly Native American, Latina and Latino, Asian American, and African American authors. They have taken similar pains to expand the temporal and geographic boundaries of what counts as "Western," enlarging its periphery far beyond settings that involve the nineteenth-century trans-Mississippi west.[1]

For scholars, in short, Western American literature is expansive. Today, when one speaks of it, one might be speaking about nearly any writer, writing about nearly any subject, set in nearly any time period, in any number of regions located west of the Atlantic coast.

The twentieth-century Western *genre*, though, is often not nearly so inclusive. Western genre fiction, with its horses and its endless vistas and its taciturn men with Stetson hats and guns – the thing many people likely still think of when they're asked to think of Western literature – was formed in the early twentieth century. If Western American literature today is broad and heterogeneous, the classic genre Western, especially as it existed for much of the twentieth century, is often not.

The use of the word "Western" as a noun synonymous with "Western genre fiction or film" (as in, "I read a great Western last week") is relatively new, dating only from the 1910s. Although it is possible to identify earlier antecedents, the genre Western was really born in the first half of the twentieth century. Because of its overwhelming popularity, Owen Wister's *The Virginian* (1902) is often pointed to as one of the earliest and most influential examples of the genre.

---

[1] Amy T. Hamilton and Tom J. Hillard, "Before the West Was West: Rethinking the Temporal Borders of Western American Literature," *Western American Literature* 47.3 (2012): 291.

In *West of Everything*, her influential study of Westerns, Jane Tompkins observes that the genre Western is distinguished by a few common characteristics. It is frequently set in the nineteenth century and in the American far west, and it is obsessed with men, the western landscape, animals, the presence or absence of women, and death. Within the genre, she writes, the west functions "as a symbol of freedom, and of the opportunity of conquest," seeming to promise an "escape from the conditions of life in modern industrial society," including limited labor opportunities, familial or personal obligations, and social injustice.[2]

Above all, though, the Western genre is fundamentally about the politics of individual freedom. Novels such as *The Virginian* (1902), *Riders of the Purple Sage* (1912), *Hondo* (1953), and, later, *Lonesome Dove* (1985) and *Blood Meridian* (1985) use the signs and symbols of the American west to ask questions about liberalism: what the individual owes to his neighbors or to the state, what the state owes the individual. In both its classic and revisionist forms, the popularity of the genre Western spans the twentieth century. And while Westerns written after the 1980s often use the conventions of the genre for deliberately critical, revisionist purposes, the genre remains a meditation on liberal individualism in America.

The western frontiers of North America have long been central to our collective political imagination. In 1689, John Locke tried to imagine what humans were like in a state of nature, before the invention of laws and monarchs. He hypothesized that the state of nature had been a "state of perfect freedom" in which individuals could conduct themselves as they saw fit, "without asking leave, or depending upon the will of any other man."[3]

Locke thought that this state of perfect natural freedom still existed in certain places, and he referred several times to the wilderness of America as an example of the state of nature. "Thus in the beginning all the world was America," he wrote.[4] Locke's ideas would form the core of what would eventually be called liberalism: a political philosophy premised on the essential and inalienable freedoms of the individual. As midcentury political scientist Louis Hartz once put it, freedom, American-style, is often simply a "nationalist articulation of Locke."[5]

[2] Jane Tompkins, *West of Everything: The Inner Life of Westerns* (New York: Oxford University Press, 1992), 4.

[3] John Locke, "The Second Treatise of Government," in *The Selected Political Writings of John Locke*, ed. Paul E. Sigmund (New York: W. W. Norton, 2005), 18.

[4] Ibid., 38.

[5] Louis Hartz, *The Liberal Tradition in America* (New York: Harcourt, Brace, 1955), 11.

Some contemporary political theorists have pointed out that political identification, often thought of as something historical or demographic, is in fact best grasped in the realm of the aesthetic. Fiction and history, after all, share a common reliance on narrative. They both convey truths relevant to a given group by telling stories. As historian F. R. Ankersmit explains, political identification is a consequence of aesthetic identification.[6] It requires an act of imagination. Someone has a sense of peoplehood chiefly because they are first able to imagine themselves as an actor within that people's narrative self-fashioning.

In short, narratives and aesthetics matter when it comes to political identification. But due to the centuries-old link between the western borders of America and the imagination of individual freedom, certain narratives have arguably carried more political implications than others. Multiple US presidents, for example, have sought to acquire political power by draping themselves in the trappings of the American frontier west.[7]

Western genre fiction, in other words, is often speaking in a particular political language. And, more often than not, that language is used to make claims about the unbounded freedoms of the individual. The motif, seen in countless Western stories, novels, and films, of the protagonist who stands outside the formal apparatus of the legal system, undertakes violent action to correct some transgression, and as a result is recognized as some kind of lone hero, some Emersonian Übermensch, is perhaps the subtext of nearly every classic genre Western. In a Western state of nature, this motif seems to say, true individual liberty can at last be found. Many classic genre Westerns seem to imagine that a lone man with a gun is little more than a Jeffersonian natural aristocrat by another name.

Broadly speaking, the twentieth century saw two opposing trajectories for the Western. The first trajectory, seen in the classic genre Western, is one of wild popularity in the first half of the twentieth century, followed by slow decline in the second. The classic genre Western tends to reproduce what Richard Slotkin calls the frontier myth, or the belief that "the conquest of the wilderness and the subjugation or displacement of the Native Americans ... have been the means to our achievement of a

---

[6] F. R. Ankersmit, *Aesthetic Politics: Political Philosophy Beyond Fact and Value* (Stanford, CA: Stanford University Press, 1996), 47.

[7] See David A. Smith, *Cowboy Presidents: The Frontier Myth and US Politics Since 1900* (Norman: University of Oklahoma Press, 2021).

national identity."[8] In its classic form, the Western is a generic container for romantic stories that are largely white, male, and rural, and that tend to uncritically embrace the myth of settlement and conquest.

The second trajectory, in contrast, rose in the final few decades of the twentieth century and can be seen in the emergence of stories exploring the racial and ethnic diversity of the west, stories that critically engage western history, and stories that are, perhaps above all, skeptical of the once-dominant frontier myth.[9]

But while these two trajectories have opposing impressions of the tropes of the Western genre – one uncritically embracing; the other skeptical and revisionist – politically, both are about the same individualist subtext. Nearly every Western story asks a simple question: What does it mean to be free?

For decades, Owen Wister's novel *The Virginian* (1902) has been hailed as the antecessor of the genre Western. It is a novel that is fairly obsessed with political freedom and the rights of the individual. The core conflict of the novel arises when the titular unnamed protagonist hangs several cattle rustlers, including his onetime friend Steve, because, we are told, courts of law refused to convict the rustlers. The novel suggests that the Virginian is absolutely justified in executing these men. Even though the tools of democratic civil governance, including the legal system, have not found these men guilty (let alone determined that they should be put to death), the novel nonetheless unambiguously concludes not just that the Virginian was correct to execute them in a moral sense, but also that he was somehow justified to do so in a civil and legal sense as well.

At multiple points in the novel, the narrator and other characters contemplate the nature of freedom and the instruments of civil government. The "Declaration of Independence," the narrator muses at one point, "acknowledged the *eternal equality* of man" and freed a spirit of "true aristocracy," one founded on a Darwinian battle for supremacy: "Let the best man win! That is America's word. That is true democracy. And true democracy and true aristocracy are one and the same thing."[10] This comment, which serves as a kind of thesis statement of the novel's politics, is not terribly complicated. It rotates the dreamworld of American

[8] Richard Slotkin, *Gunfighter Nation: The Myth of the Frontier in Twentieth-Century America* (Norman: University of Oklahoma Press, 1998), 10.
[9] See David M. Wrobel, "The Literary West and the Twentieth Century," in *A Companion to the American West*, ed. William Deverell (Oxford: Blackwell, 2004), 460–80.
[10] Owen Wister, *The Virginian* (New York: Penguin, 1988 [1902]), 95.

freedom, turning it from a horizontal landscape of liberal democracy into a vertical tournament of aristocracy.[11]

In the novel, the American west is a space in which that "true aristocracy" is determined through conflicts in which men prove their superiority. The most lucid explanation of this belief comes in the aftermath of the Virginian's lynching of the rustlers. Wister gives one character, a ranch owner and legal expert named Judge Henry, the role of explaining this dynamic to the reader. Judge Henry's task is to demonstrate to the other characters (as well as to Wister's readers) that the Virginian's actions are somehow justified in a legal or political sense, given that those actions have not been sanctioned by any legal or political body. In acquitting the rustlers, the juries, the Judge argues, "into whose hands we have put the law," have been "not dealing the law" correctly. As a consequence, "ordinary citizens" must "take justice back into [their] own hands where it was at the beginning of all things." This action should not be understood as a defiance of the law, he cautions, but rather as an assertion of the animating spirit of democracy: "the fundamental assertion of self-governing men, upon whom our whole social fabric is based."[12] In the novel, "self-governing" is not a democratic term of art but a valorization of an aristocratic individualism: every man his own government, every man his own army.

Wister's *Virginian*, published at the dawn of the twentieth century, neatly sets out the central political mythos of the genre Western: that the American west is a space in which white men can rediscover the foundational freedoms of the state of nature. For men such as the Virginian, it suggests, those freedoms are something akin to liberty before liberalism: an older, pre-governmental individualism that suggests, in its darker implications, that the individual liberty of one person can be justly measured by the degree to which its exercise restricts the freedom of another.

Ten years after Wister, Zane Grey's bestselling *Riders of the Purple Sage* (1912) solidified the popularity of the genre Western. As Lee Mitchell puts it, Grey's novel "all but single-handedly confirmed the shape of a powerful new narrative form."[13] Set in 1871 in southern Utah, one of the book's central conflicts involves a group of powerful Mormon polygamists trying to convince Jane Withersteen, the wealthy daughter of one of those

[11] Stephen J. Mexal, *The Conservative Aesthetic: Theodore Roosevelt, Popular Darwinism, and the American Literary West* (Lanham, MD: Lexington, 2021), 296–300.

[12] Wister, 281–2.

[13] Lee Mitchell, *Westerns: Making the Man in Fiction and Film* (Chicago: University of Chicago Press, 1996), 123.

polygamists, to marry into the church. Jane, in turn, is trying to prevent a gunfighter and cowboy named Jim Lassiter from taking revenge on that same group of Mormons, whom Lassiter blames for killing his sister.

Although scholars have focused on its representations of femininity and domesticity, as well as its portrayal of the Church of Jesus Christ of Latter-Day Saints, the novel is also – and perhaps more obviously – engaged with fundamental questions of law and political liberalism.[14] Law, in the novel, is not framed as a democratic tool for negotiating competing claims to justice. It is instead an articulation of power. Jane thinks of the "law and might" represented by Lassiter's guns, for instance.[15] And although the historical Mormon migration to Utah had begun in the mid-1840s in part due to their status as a persecuted minority group, in the novel's 1870s milieu, characters speak of the all-encompassing power of "Mormon law."[16] In Grey's novel, law in the west is always undemocratic: the byproduct of either the quasi-governmental force of the church or the unlegislated will of the gunslinger.

To underscore this theme, Grey reinvents a concept first used in Adam Smith's *The Theory of Moral Sentiments* (1759): the invisible hand. For Smith, the invisible hand was a metaphor for economic liberalism. The individual, acting in his own self-interest, inadvertently creates an invisible hand that assists the public interest. In contrast, in *Riders of the Purple Sage*, the invisible hand is framed as the collective, yet anti-public, will of the church. "I fear that invisible hand," one character says, going on to clarify that he means the "Bishop . . . He's the law."[17] Far from valorizing liberal individualism, here the metaphor of the invisible hand is a kind of illiberal specter, haunting all who find themselves outside the church.

Like *The Virginian*, *Riders of the Purple Sage* is a classic genre Western. And despite *Riders*'s unease with the illiberal power of the church, both novels are wholly unironic in their romantic attraction to a certain undemocratic, individualist western dream: namely, that the force of law is subordinate to the law of force. "Where would any man be on this border without guns?" Lassiter asks at one point. "Gun-packin' in the West since the Civil War has growed into a kind of moral law. An' out here on this border it's the difference between a man an' something not a man."[18] This

[14] See Cathryn Halverson, "Violent Housekeepers: Rewriting Domesticity in *Riders of the Purple Sage*," *Rocky Mountain Review of Language and Literature* 56.1 (2002): 37–53; William R. Handley, "Distinctions without Differences: Zane Grey and the Mormon Question," *Arizona Quarterly* 57.1 (2001): 1–33.

[15] Zane Grey, *Riders of the Purple Sage* (New York: Grosset & Dunlap, 1912), 219.   [16] Ibid., 10.

[17] Ibid., 20.   [18] Ibid., 157.

is a hard and violent kind of individualism – a lone man facing down an entire community and being hailed as a hero for it – but it is also perfectly in keeping with one of the foundational political myths of the genre Western: that for a certain kind of white man, the nineteenth-century American west is a space for the fullest and purest exercise of liberal selfhood. If *Riders* asks readers to choose between the unelected power of the church and the unelected power of a quickdraw cowboy, it's clearly not supposed to be much of a choice.

Grey followed *Riders of the Purple Sage* with dozens of other Western genre novels, eventually making him one of the wealthiest writers in America. The dazzling popularity of the novel, coupled with the rising commercial potential of Western genre films, encouraged publishers to invest in the burgeoning Western genre.

Louis L'Amour, an enthusiastic reader of Grey's novels as a boy, grew up to become a writer who capitalized on that expanded investment in the Western genre, coming of age at a time when the popularity of Western genre fiction was inseparable from the popularity of Western genre films. After one of L'Amour's first published stories, "The Gift of Cochise," appeared in *Collier's* magazine in 1952, the film rights to the story were purchased by actor John Wayne. A screenplay was written by James Edward Grant, and the resulting film, *Hondo*, would be released in 1953. While the film was being shot, L'Amour wrote a novel based on Grant's screenplay – that is, he wrote a novel based on a screenplay based on his own short story – which was published that same year.[19]

Although it was only his second published novel, and he went on to write dozens of other books and to become one of the bestselling American authors of the second half of the twentieth century, L'Amour's *Hondo* (1953) remains one of his best-known works, perhaps due in part to its clear connection to the Western film genre. (As well as, perhaps, to Wayne's endorsement on the first edition of the book, splashed across the front cover: "Best western novel I have ever read – John Wayne.")

Like L'Amour's other novels, *Hondo* is not generally well regarded among literary critics. Yet it is worth briefly observing its remarkable popularity, its symbiosis with the rise of the midcentury Western genre film, and its simplistic view of freedom and violence in the American west. As John D. Nesbitt writes, in *Hondo*, the "highest values are to survive

---

[19] Michael T. Marsden, "Louis L'Amour's *Hondo*: From Literature to Film to Literature," *Literature/Film Quarterly* 27.1 (1999): 16.

with honor, to pass on what one has learned, and to die well."[20] The novel leaves little room for historical complexity. Although the protagonist, Hondo Lane, is part Indian, the central drama inescapably involves defending the homestead property rights of a virtuous white woman against the encroachments of hostile Apache.

In the novel, the American southwest is a space of liberty but also looming danger, a depiction that lends the region a mythic political resonance. Over two centuries before L'Amour, John Locke felt that the state of nature, that wellspring of individual freedom, could still be glimpsed on the frontiers of America. But Locke also felt that liberal selfhood was not necessarily universal. This was likely why he suggested that certain types of criminals should be viewed as "wild savage beasts with whom men can have no society nor security."[21] Even in Locke's state of nature, freedom did not mean freedom for everyone.

In *Hondo*, racial difference poses a similar unbridgeable gulf, the kind that seems to preclude the normal tools of liberal governance – contracts or ownership rights, for instance – from negotiating difference. One character is reminded that "you will always be a white boy," even if he tries to live with Indians.[22] Another insists on essential racial difference, saying that "Indians can smell white people."[23] In warning the female protagonist about the security of her homestead, Hondo cautions: "If they [i.e., the Apache tribe] rise there won't be a live white in the territory."[24]

While whites are not blameless in the conflict – Hondo admits that "we broke that treaty" with the Apache – the novel nevertheless has a bleak and violent vision of individual liberty.[25] Its sense of individual freedom is not universal, but tightly limned by racial identity and a war for survival. Freedom exists only for those who can win it. In short, its liberalism is basically illiberal. "The Apache knew his hour was past," L'Amour writes. "He knew the white men would take even his last stand, but it was not in him to knuckle under. He would fight, sing his death song, and die."[26] In *Hondo*'s depiction of the American southwest, individual liberty cannot exist for everyone, everywhere. The novel instead offers a fantasy of freedom won through the gun – a country for white men.

In recent decades, scholars of Western American literature and film have shown increasing interest in what is often called the "post-Western" genre.

---

[20] John D. Nesbitt, "Change of Purpose in the Novels of Louis L'Amour," *Western American Literature* 13.1 (1978): 68.
[21] Locke, 21.   [22] Louis L'Amour, *Hondo* (New York: Bantam, 2019 [1953]), 103.
[23] Ibid., 31.   [24] Ibid., 28.   [25] Ibid., 28.   [26] Ibid., 146.

These are post–World War II works that seem to participate in the conventional Western genre while at the same time never fully belonging to it. As Neil Campbell writes, such works go "beyond the traditional Western while engaging with and commenting on its deeply haunting assumptions and values."[27] Some examples of this phenomenon from the last quarter of the twentieth century arguably include the works of Larry McMurtry, including his novel *Lonesome Dove* (1985).

Not unlike L'Amour's *Hondo*, a version of *Lonesome Dove* was first written as a screenplay, coauthored by McMurtry himself. The film remained unproduced until McMurtry eventually turned the screenplay into a Pulitzer Prize-winning novel, when it was adapted into a television miniseries. Partly as a result of the series, McMurtry felt that audiences seemed to misunderstand the anti-mythic, critical elements in the novel.[28] Yet, as Cordelia Barrera puts it, McMurtry's work nevertheless "disrupts a traditional frontier mythology" and "effectively deconstructs the Western genre."[29] In *Lonesome Dove*, this disruption of the frontier myth takes a few different forms, including a symbolic reworking of the liberal right to movement.

Lonesome Dove is a sprawling epic set in the 1870s, but one particular character's demise is illustrative. At one point, Augustus "Gus" McCrae, a former Texas Ranger and cowboy, is injured in a battle with a group of Blackfeet warriors. He escapes, but his leg, pierced by two arrows, turns gangrenous and has to be amputated. After his other leg becomes infected, too, Gus decides against having it amputated as well. He thinks it better to die than to live without the full freedom of movement. He has, he decides, "walked the earth in my pride all these years," and "[i]f that's lost, then let the rest be lost with it."[30] The value of being alive, in his view, is connected to an inalienable freedom of movement. "I like being free on the earth," he declares, adding, "I'll cross the hills where I please."[31] Given a choice between living with symbolic restrictions on his liberty (that is, having both legs amputated and being unable to "walk the earth"), on the one hand, and dying, on the other, he chooses death.

[27] Neil Campbell, *Post-Westerns: Cinema, Region, West* (Lincoln: University of Nebraska Press, 2013), 31; see also Jesús Ángel González, "New Frontiers for Post-Western Cinema: *Frozen River, Sin Nombre, Winter's Bone*," *Western American Literature* 50.1 (2015): 51–5.
[28] Mark Busby, *Larry McMurtry and the West: An Ambivalent Relationship* (Denton: University of North Texas Press, 1995), 178–200.
[29] Cordelia E. Barrera, "Written on the Body: A Third Space Reading of Larry McMurtry's *Streets of Laredo*," *Western American Literature* 48.3 (2013): 233.
[30] Larry McMurtry, *Lonesome Dove* (New York: Simon & Schuster, 2010 [1985]), 795.
[31] Ibid., 798.

Gus's death serves as an ironic commentary on how the genre Western has historically conflated liberal autonomy with white masculinity. Like countless white men before him, Gus sees unrestricted freedom of movement as his birthright. For him, "being free" means being able to "cross the hills where I please." And in terms of the principles of classical liberalism, he is basically correct about the Lockean foundations of freedom of movement.

Yet, unlike much pre-World War II Western genre fiction, McMurtry's novel seems to recognize how an unthinking conflation of whiteness, masculinity, and individual freedom has resulted in deeply illiberal outcomes. In the classic genre Western, the freedom to move without impediment often slid into the freedom to conquer without consequences. In contrast, Gus's death serves as a symbolic repudiation of that illiberal fantasy. He is, he seems to realize, a man out of time. "Imagine getting killed by an arrow in this day and age," he says. "It's ridiculous, especially since they shot at us fifty times with modern weapons and did no harm."[32] In the novel's revisionist imagination, if Gus's attitude toward unrestricted individual liberty for white men is anachronistic, then, appropriately, so is his mode of death.

With *Lonesome Dove*, McMurtry seemed eager to turn a clear eye toward dismantling some long-cherished myths of individual freedom in the American west. Decades later, fittingly enough, he would continue this project by coauthoring the screenplay for the 2005 film adaptation of Annie Proulx's short story "Brokeback Mountain" (1997).

Proulx's story concerns a same-sex love affair between two ranch hands, Ennis Del Mar and Jack Twist, who first meet when hired to care for a flock of sheep on the fictional Brokeback Mountain in 1960s Wyoming. Like other revisionist Western writers, Proulx invokes the longstanding myth of individual freedom in the west, only to undercut that myth by reminding readers how limited that freedom really was.

In the story, their love affair is secretive, and Jack is ultimately killed in what we are led to conclude is a hate crime. Yet despite these clear markers of unfreedom, Proulx nonetheless frames Brokeback Mountain as a kind of individualist refuge: a space where Ennis and Jack can be their true selves, without impediment. She updates one of the oldest signifiers in the Western political imagination – the conflation of Western space with individual freedom – by complicating it. In one part of the rural west,

---

[32] Ibid., 798.

they are terribly unfree. But in another part of the west, Brokeback Mountain, the space itself becomes a metonym for individual liberty.

In what the narrator calls the "imagined power of Brokeback Mountain," Jack twice refers to the mountain itself as not just the symbol of but also the seeming source of the conditions that led to their love affair.[33] "Old Brokeback got us good and it sure ain't over," he says at one point, as if the actual mountain had somehow ensnared their hearts.[34] When it becomes clear that the two will never be together permanently and openly, Jack mourns the loss by saying, "[W]hat we got now is Brokeback Mountain" – again using the mountain as a metonym for the freedom they once enjoyed there.[35] The story's revisionist view of the genre Western seems clear: While the rural space of Brokeback does signify a unique individual freedom to Jack and Ennis, it is only because they have been denied that freedom elsewhere in the west, and elsewhere in America.

Although McMurtry would not coauthor the adapted screenplay for *Brokeback Mountain* until the early twenty-first century, in the 1980s arguably his nearest contemporary in reimagining the genre Western was Cormac McCarthy, whose magisterial *Blood Meridian* (1985) was published the same year as *Lonesome Dove*.

Blood Meridian is remarkable in part for its angular, Faulknerian prose, but also for its unremittingly shocking violence. Set after 1848, the year the Treaty of Guadalupe Hidalgo ended the Mexican–American War and ceded the bulk of the territory composing the modern American west from Mexico to the United States, the novel offers a stark, nearly nihilistic exploration of violence. As Susan Kollin puts it: "Unlike the classic Western, *Blood Meridian* does not offer a region whose promise and possibility were somehow lost at a certain point in history, but a West fully corrupted from the moment Anglos arrived."[36] In its post-Western imagination, the frontier myth is reframed as a horrific testament to human depravity.

Early on, the novel's nominal protagonist joins a filibuster organized by the aptly named Captain White, a racist and imperialist who is bent on seizing additional territory in Mexico. Proclaiming "[t]here is no government in Mexico," White wraps their violent project in a cloak of

[33] Annie Proulx, "Brokeback Mountain," *The New Yorker*, October 13, 1997, 85.   [34] Ibid., 78.
[35] Ibid., 83.
[36] Susan Kollin, "Genre and the Geographies of Violence: Cormac McCarthy and the Contemporary Western," *Contemporary Literature* 42.3 (2001): 562.

paternalist imperialism.[37] They are emissaries of good governance, White asserts, merely "the instruments of liberation in a dark and troubled land."[38] In short order, though, their party is slaughtered and White's severed head is found floating in a jar of mescal.

Yet McCarthy does not frame White's demise as some kind of moral comeuppance. In the novel, violence does not signify much of anything. No character or ethnic group in *Blood Meridian* is unequal to its symmetrical expanse of bloodletting. Violence seems amoral in the novel, even pedestrian. It simply *is*.

In the classic genre Western, the landscape is a kind of game field upon which humans try to establish supremacy, with the prize frequently being mastery of the land itself. There is a clear hierarchy: One human is the hero, another the villain, and a basic anthropocentrism typically places both above the land and horses and other animals.

In *Blood Meridian*, though, there is a discomfiting equality. No human, animal, or landform is held above any other. "In the neuter austerity of that terrain all phenomena were bequeathed a strange equality," the narrator observes. "[I]n the optical democracy of such landscapes all preference is made whimsical and a man and a rock become endowed with unguessed kinships."[39] That "optical democracy" is one in which differences between subjects and objects are leveled into a flat plane. Human life and human freedom are not assigned any special value.

In setting his story in what he calls "the bloodlands of the west," McCarthy turns the conventional Western almost exactly on its head.[40] The traditional genre Western told stories of liberal individualism loosed from the tether of democracy: a land of disconnected individuals, usually white men, galloping over rocks and streams and proving their place in a universal hierarchy through the barrel of a gun. *Blood Meridian*, though, is almost exactly the opposite. In emphasizing the flattened "optical democracy" of the west, it reimagines the nineteenth-century American west as a nightmare of ruthless equality without any individual rights at all: of democracy without liberalism.

Because of the historical and philosophical connections between the imagination of individual liberty and the imagination of the western frontiers of North America, the genre Western has long had clear political implications. In 1893, historian Frederick Jackson Turner famously

---

[37] Cormac McCarthy, *Blood Meridian, or the Evening Redness in the West* (New York: Vintage, 1992 [1985]), 34.
[38] Ibid., 34.   [39] Ibid., 247.   [40] Ibid., 138.

asserted a link between liberal individualism, democracy, and the concept of the American frontier, concluding that "frontier individualism has from the beginning promoted democracy."[41]

Whether that's true or not, it seems fair to conclude that stories about the American west have long had a particular political purchase. That purchase seems especially apposite to the genre Western, at least as it existed in its classic form in the early to mid-twentieth century. Novels such as Wister's *The Virginian*, Grey's *Riders of the Purple Sage*, and L'Amour's *Hondo* valorize a kind of tournament liberalism, seeming to view the American west as a new state of nature, a place where a man with a gun enjoys a fantasy of absolute freedom, of being able to fully enact his will upon the world.

Not surprisingly, perhaps, those genre Westerns have often been associated with icons of the modern Republican Party. Theodore Roosevelt was close friends with Wister and was thanked by name in *The Virginian*.[42] Dwight D. Eisenhower counted Zane Grey among his favorite novelists.[43] While in office, George H. Bush once quoted Grey in a speech.[44] Ronald Reagan awarded Louis L'Amour a Congressional gold medal, the first novelist to be given that honor.[45] While there are likely a number of reasons for the seeming affinity those men had for Wister, Grey, and L'Amour, at least one is because the classic genre Western tends to dramatize a hard kind of individualism. By the twentieth century, that individualism was increasingly associated with the political right.

Yet the genre Western is not some static monolith. In the final few decades of the twentieth century, a new generation of writers began crafting revisionist, post-Western reconsiderations of the classic genre Western. McMurtry, McCarthy, Proulx, and others used the signs and symbols of the pre-World War II genre Western to tell new stories about freedom in America. In revisiting the Western, they also infused it with a new political energy. Their west was no longer solely a romantic playground for virtuous white men with guns. On the contrary, their reimagination of the genre Western seemed electrified by the knowledge

[41] Frederick Jackson Turner, "The Significance of the Frontier in American History," in *The Frontier in American History* (New York: Henry Holt, 1921), 30.

[42] Wister, xxx.

[43] Maxine Benson, "Dwight D. Eisenhower and the West," *Journal of the West* 34 (1995): 59.

[44] George H. Bush, "Remarks at the Presentation Ceremony for the Achievement Against All Odds Awards: May 3, 1990," *Weekly Compilation of Presidential Documents* 26.18, May 7, 1990 (Washington, DC: Office of the Federal Register), 712.

[45] Edwin McDowell, "Publishing: Congress Honors Louis L'Amour," *New York Times*, September 23, 1983, C20.

that the frontier myth was too often a cover story for a conquest. In their works, liberal individualism, the animating political philosophy of the classic genre Western, is not a transcendent universal good. Instead, it is a troubled historical artifact, a belief now freighted with a history of violence.

CHAPTER II

Literary Realist Fiction

Matthew Shipe

In "Writing American Fiction," an essay originally published in *Commentary* in 1960, Philip Roth observed how "the American writer in the middle of the twentieth century has his hands full in trying to understand, describe, and then make *credible* much of American reality. It stupefies, it sickens, it infuriates, and finally it is even an embarrassment to one's own meager imagination."[1] Roth's remarks would seem prescient as the tumult of the 1960s unfolded – it is striking that he would make this argument three years before the assassination of John F. Kennedy – but they more broadly reflect the pressure many writers faced when trying to capture the turbulent and, at times, incoherent nature of American life during the twentieth century. "How naïve I was in 1960 to think that I was an American living in preposterous times! How quaint," Roth elaborated in a 2018 interview given only a few months before his death from congestive heart failure, suggesting how the dizzying and often infuriating nature of American life continued to flummox the writer's imagination in the opening decades of the new millennium. "But then what could I know in 1960 of 1963 or 1968 or 1974 or 2001 or 2016?"[2]

Indeed, "Writing American Fiction" helps illuminate the challenges facing American writers who embraced realism as their literary mode as they endeavored to somehow reflect the contours and texture of American life in a period in which the nation was relentlessly redefining itself. Toward the end of his career, John Updike noted that his "only duty was to describe reality as it had come to me – to give the mundane its beautiful due."[3] Updike's emphasis on "the mundane" marks one

---

[1] Philip Roth, "Writing American Fiction," in *Why Write? Collected Nonfiction 1960–2013* (New York: Library of America, 2017), 27.

[2] Charles McGrath, "No Longer Writing, Philip Roth Still Has Plenty to Say" [interview with Philip Roth], *New York Times*, January 16, 2018, www.nytimes.com/2018/01/16/books/review/philip-roth-interview.html

[3] John Updike, *The Early Stories, 1953–1975* (New York: Alfred A. Knopf, 2003), xv.

prominent strand of American realism, and his influence can be felt in such writers as Ann Beattie, Andre Dubus, Richard Russo, Anne Tyler, Richard Ford, Lorrie Moore, and Jonathan Franzen, novelists whose work frequently focused on the travails and discontents of American middle-class, largely white, families. That said, American literary realism is not so much a unified approach to recording the reality of American life – writers as diverse and dissimilar as Edith Wharton, Willa Cather, John Steinbeck, Richard Wright, Mary McCarthy, James Baldwin, Marilynne Robinson, Chang-rae Lee, and Raymond Carver could all be accurately described as practitioners of realism – and the political implications of their work are as varied as the writers who produced them. In her landmark study of realism's place in American letters, Amy Kaplan argues how realism radically evolved over the course of the twentieth century:

> From a progressive force exposing the conditions of industrial society, realism has turned into a conservative force whose very act of exposure reveals its complicity with structures of power. These reversals accompany changes in the historical understanding of American capitalism, from a class-based system structured by the relations of production to a culture of consumption and surveillance which sweeps all social relations into a vortex of the commodity and the spectacle.[4]

Kaplan's argument nicely captures how realism transformed over the course of the twentieth century, from a potentially progressive force – how William Dean Howells's *A Hazard of New Fortunes* (1889), Theodore Dreiser's *Sister Carrie* (1900), and Edith Wharton's *The House of Mirth* (1905) expose the conditions of modern urban life – to one with a more complicated political legacy.[5]

As Kaplan suggests, realist novels during the first half of the twentieth century were often explicitly political in their intent, an engagement that reached its apex in the 1930s and 1940s as writers responded to the horrors of the Great Depression and the impending threat of fascism. Novels such as Erskine Caldwell's *Tobacco Road* (1932) and John Steinbeck's *The Grapes of Wrath* (1939) documented the economic devastation that the Great Depression triggered, while works like Sinclair Lewis's *It Can't Happen Here* (1935), which imagined a United States taken over by a fascist dictator, exposed the looming threat posed by Nazi Germany and the rise of European fascism. Considering the art and literature of the

---

[4] Amy Kaplan, *The Social Construction of American Realism* (Chicago and London: University of Chicago Press, 1988), 1.
[5] Kaplan's study focuses on *A Hazzard of New Fortunes*, *The House of Mirth*, and *Sister Carrie*.

1930s, Morris Dickstein observes how novels such as *The Grapes of Wrath* reflected "a message of solidarity, or common responsibility for the nation's well-being" that reinforced the political vision of Roosevelt's New Deal programs.[6] While Steinbeck would drift to the right in the wake of World War II, *The Grapes of Wrath* in many ways has become synonymous with a brand of realistic fiction that remains tethered to a specific political agenda.

In contrast to the more politically engaged fiction that emerged in the 1930s and 1940s, midcentury realists – a group that includes Ralph Ellison, Saul Bellow, John Cheever, Bernard Malamud, Eudora Welty, John Updike, James Baldwin, Flannery O'Connor, Joyce Carol Oates, Philip Roth, and Joan Didion, to name but a few – largely eschewed the overt political agendas that had propelled, and some would say burden, the social realist fiction of the earlier period and instead turned inward for their subjects. Indeed, the writers who emerged in the aftermath of the war largely adopted an elevated notion of literature, seeing it as a spiritual force that was inimical to the strictures of political ideology. Recalling the early years of his career in a 1973 self-interview, Philip Roth noted how, as an aspiring novelist during the 1950s, he had

> imagined fiction to be something like a religious calling, and literature a kind of sacrament, a sense of things I have had reason to modify since. Such elevated notions aren't (or weren't back then) that uncommon in vain young writers; they dovetailed nicely in my case with a penchant for ethical striving that I had absorbed as a Jewish child, and with the salvationist literary ethos in which I had been introduced to high art in the fifties, a decade when cultural, rather than political, loyalties divided the young into the armies of the damned and the cadre of the blessed.[7]

In *I Married a Communist* (1998), the second installment of his celebrated American trilogy, Roth revisits this perspective, giving it to a literature professor, Leo Glucksman. Glucksman had inspired that novel's narrator, the novelist Nathan Zuckerman, to abandon his love of writers such as Norman Corwin, whose explicitly political radio dramas the young Zuckerman (and Roth) had savored, and to adopt a literary aesthetic that embraced nuance and contradiction. As Glucksman instructs the ambitious Zuckerman:

---

[6] Morris Dickstein, *Dancing in the Dark: A Cultural History of the Great Depression* (New York: W. W. Norton, 2009), xxi.

[7] Philip Roth, "On *The Great American Novel*," in *Reading Myself and Others* (New York: Farrar, Straus and Giroux, 1975), 77–8.

Politics is the great generalizer ... and literature the great particularizer, and not only are they in an inverse relationship to each other – they are in an *antagonistic* relationship. To politics, literature is decadent, soft, irrelevant, boring, wrongheaded, dull, something that makes no sense and that really oughtn't to be. Why? Because the particularizing impulse *is* literature. How can you be an artist and renounce the nuance? But how can you be a politician and *allow* the nuance? As an artist the nuance is your *task*.[8]

Roth's notion of literature's spiritual capacity and his inclination for ambiguity and irony can be felt in many of his contemporaries' work, much of which displayed a deep skepticism toward any fiction that expressed an overt political agenda. The approach to literature that Roth describes here – a belief that art should be divorced from politics – was largely influenced by the literary education that Roth's generation experienced during the early 1950s; the New Critics' emphasis on close reading and their rejection of the overtly political fiction of the previous generation shaped the sensibility of the generation of writers who came of age in the 1950s. "We were all very personal then, sometimes relentlessly so, and, at that point where we either act or do not act, most of us are still," Joan Didion recalled of the lack of political activism that shaped her experience at the University of California Berkley during the early 1950s. "I suppose I am talking about just that: belonging to a generation distrustful of political highs, the historical irrelevancy of growing up convinced that the heart of darkness lay not in some error of social organization but in man's own blood."[9]

The distrust of political fiction that Didion and Roth highlight can be felt keenly in Ralph Ellison's *Invisible Man* (1952), one of the landmark novels of the postwar period. Much like J. D. Salinger's *The Catcher in the Rye* (1951), the other essential *bildungsroman* to come out of the decade, *Invisible Man* offers a searing indictment of how the United States has repeatedly betrayed its democratic ideals. The novel depicts American society as essentially a rigged game designed to disabuse, and even destroy, African Americans. Through the course of the novel, Ellison's anonymous protagonist repeatedly discovers how American society operates to manipulate and harm him as he escapes the cruelties of the Jim Crow South only to find hi mself ensnared in the equally unfair and cruel racism that permeates New York City. Central to the narrator's

---

[8] Philip Roth, *I Married a Communist* (Boston, MA: Houghton Mifflin, 1998), 223.
[9] Joan Didion, "Morning After the Sixties," in *The White Album* (New York: Farrar, Straus and Giroux, 1979), 206.

education is his experience with a political organization named the Brotherhood – inspired by Ellison's experience with the American Communist Party in the 1930s and early 1940s – as the group manipulates him into trying to recruit the denizens of Harlem into their movement. By the end of the novel, Ellison's narrator becomes disillusioned by the group's rhetoric, coming to believe that he was simply being manipulated once again to work against his own self-interest for the amusement of a white audience. As the narrator concludes of his experience with the Brotherhood, equating it with his other experiences with white America throughout the novel:

> For all they were considered, we [African Americans] were so many names scribbled on fake ballots, to be used at their convenience and when not needed to be filed away. It was a joke, an absurd joke. And now I looked around a corner of my mind and Jack and Norton and Emerson merge into one single white figure. They were very much the same, each attempting to force his picture of reality upon me and neither giving a hoot in hell for how things looked to me. I was simply a material, a natural resource to be used.[10]

The uncertainty toward politics that Ellison expresses throughout *Invisible Man*, however, does not mean that the novel is somehow apolitical, nor was Ellison alone in his skepticism of communism, reflecting a larger disappointment with the Party that many left-leaning artists of his generation felt in the wake of the discovery of Stalin's atrocities as well as the anti-communist hysteria fueled by the House Committee on Un-American Committee hearings of the late 1940s and the McCarthy hearings of the early 1950s. Despite its indictment of American life and of leftist politics, *Invisible Man* ultimately remains a hopeful book that advocates for the democratic ideals that the nation was founded upon, even as it acknowledges how the nation has never been governed by those ideals. Considering the novel thirty years after its publication, Ellison reflected how, in writing it, he had hoped that it "could be fashioned as a raft of hope, perception and entertainment that might help us afloat as we tried to negotiate the snags and whirlpools that mark our nation's vacillating course toward and away from the democratic ideal."[11] Ellison's notion of how literature might help others navigate the uncertainties and absurdities of American life captures how many of the realist writers of his generation responded to the politics of their era. Deeply informed by the

---

[10] Ralph Ellison, *Invisible Man* (New York: Vintage, 1995 [1952]), 508.   [11] Ibid., xx–xxi.

realities and the contradictions of the Cold War, the realistic writers of the 1950s and 1960s had to straddle the often uncomfortable line of asserting the claims of freedom and liberty that were central to the United States's ideological battle with the Soviet Union while also recognizing and critiquing the racial, economic, and political inequality that threatened to destabilize the idealized vision of itself that the United States attempted to project to the rest of the world. As Louis Menand has argued:

> In the first two decades of the Cold War, many people therefore believed that art and ideas were an important battleground in the struggle to achieve and maintain a free society. Artistic and philosophical choices carried implications for the way one lived one's life and for the kind of polity in which one wished to live it. The Cold War charged the atmosphere. It raised the stakes.[12]

Indeed, much of the most memorable realistic fiction of the 1950s and 1960s critiqued the empty consumerism and emphasis on conformity that seemed to define American life in the decades after World War II. Novels such as Salinger's *The Catcher in the Rye*, Sloan Wilson's *The Man in the Gray Flannel Suit* (1955), and Philip Roth's *Goodbye, Columbus* (1959) exposed what Salinger's teenaged protagonist Holden Caulfield diagnoses as the "phoniness" of the adult world. Following the troubled teenager over the course of a weekend after he leaves his prep school, *The Catcher in the Rye* became one of the most successful novels to emerge in the postwar era as it captured the tensions and uncertainties of the postwar nation. Holden critiques the blatant hypocrisy of the adult world he encounters. "Pencey was full of crooks," Holden declares of the prestigious prep school that has just expelled him. "Quite a few guys came from these very wealthy families, but it was full of crooks anyway. The more expensive a school is, the more crooks it has – I'm not kidding."[13] Holden's overwhelming distrust of the adult world – throughout the novel he decries all the phonies and hypocrisy that he witnesses – reflects the tenuous and, at times, contradictory rules that permeated American society during the early 1950s amid the fervor ignited by McCarthyism. Considering the novel's reflection of the era's politics, Alan Nadel has argued how Holden, with his memorable "red hunting hat," strives

---

[12] Louis Menand, *The Free World: Art and Thought in the Cold War* (New York: Farrar, Straus and Giroux, 2021), 6.
[13] J. D. Salinger, *The Catcher in the Rye* (New York: Little, Brown and Company, 1991 [1951]), 4.

to become the good Red-hunter, ferreting out the phonies and the sub-
versives, but in doing so he emulates the bad Red-hunters, those who have
corrupted the conditions of utterance such that speech itself is corrupt.
Speech, like, veracity, like the Soviets, like atomic power, has a dual nature,
one that implicates the speaker equally with the spoken, allowing only a
religious resolution to the closeted life of containment and the web of
contradictions that makes it impossible to keep the narrative straight.[14]

Nadel's more allegorical reading of *The Catcher in the Rye* illuminates how
Holden's confused confession reflects the contradictions of the early Cold
War era, which demanded suspect Americans to assert constant declara-
tions of their loyalty; early on, Holden boasts how he is "the most terrific
liar you ever saw in your life" while he constantly tries to persuade readers
that his narrative is truthful.[15]

The novel's uncertain conclusion, with Holden sequestered away in a
mental hospital, illustrates the difficulties of navigating a world where the
political rules no longer make sense. To be an adult in Holden's mind is to
be a "phony," an agent who enacts only trauma. Desperate to avoid that
fate, he instead slips away into seclusion. "If you want to know the truth,"
Holden confides in the novel's famous conclusion, "I don't *know* what
I think about it. I'm sorry I told so many people about it. About all I know
is, I sort of *miss* everybody I told about."[16] Holden's final reflection
acknowledges the painful limitations of his narrative. By having confessed
his story, Holden has been able only to acknowledge, however obliquely,
the loss that he has experienced – namely, the death of his younger
brother, Allie, but there are also several references to sexual violence against
children – without healing that trauma. Literature, in other words, can
expose the instability and hypocrisies of the postwar nation.[17] The implication is that the only sane option is to retreat from public life, as Salinger
did in the wake of his final published short story "Hapworth 16, 1924"
in 1965.

In contrast to Salinger's focus on urban life – Holden's misadventures
take place within the confines of Manhattan – a great many of the realist

---

[14] Alan Nadel, *Containment Culture: American Narratives, Postmodernism, and the Atomic Age*
(Durham, NC and London: Duke University Press, 1995), 71.
[15] Salinger, 16.   [16] Ibid., 213–14.
[17] The most explicit of these is Holden's recollection of a date with Jane Gallagher, whose alcoholic
stepfather may have abused her. Sexual violence is implied in the suicide of James Castle, a
classmate of Holden's at an earlier prep school, and in Holden's encounter with his former
English teacher, Mr. Antolini. "That kind of stuff's happened to me about twenty times since
I was a kid. I can't stand it," Holden reflects, having rushed out of Mr. Antolini's apartment after
his former teacher has petted Holden's head in the middle of the night. Salinger, 78–9, 193.

writers of the 1950s and the 1960s took the burgeoning suburbs as the location for, and sometimes the subject of, their fiction. The emergence of the suburbs in the 1940s and 1950s radically reoriented American family life, as multigenerational homes became a thing of the past, and drastically reshaped the nation's larger cities, as middle-class white families left larger urban areas en masse for the bucolic promise of the newly created suburbs. As Leerom Medovoi has noted:

> The Cold War suburbs transformed not only the basic terms of race, but also those of family, gender, and sexuality through its [sic] prevailing ethos of domesticity. As it removed people from the city, Fordism [the model of mass production and consumption introduced by Henry Ford] eroded the institution of the extended family, erecting in its place a streamlined nuclear family, the new atomic unit of postwar consumer society characterized by ownership of a home, at least one automobile, a television set, refrigerator, washer and dryer, and much more.[18]

In Roth's debut novella, *Goodbye, Columbus* (1959), the young narrator, Neil Klugman, who has grown up in the urban confines of Newark, finds in his affluent girlfriend's basement refrigerator a perfect synecdoche for the economic (and, for Neil, sexual) riches contained within the suburban home. "I opened the door of the old refrigerator; it was not empty," Neil recalls of Brenda Patimkin's basement icebox.

> No longer did it hold butter, eggs, herring in cream sauce, ginger ale, tuna fish, an occasional corsage – rather it was heaped with fruit, shelves swelled with it. There were greenage plums, black plums, red plums, apricots, nectarines, peaches, long horns of grapes, black, yellow, red, and cherries, cherries flowing out of boxes and staining everything scarlet. And there were melons – cantaloupes and honeydews – and on the top shelf, half of a huge watermelon, a thin sheet of wax paper clinging to its bare red face like a wet lip. Oh Patimkin! Fruit grew in their refrigerator and sporting goods dropped from their trees![19]

Despite the comforts offered by the Patimkins' home, Neil finds an emptiness in their suburban existence and the conformity that middle-class life would seem to require, his skepticism marring his relationship with Brenda. Late in the novella, Neil encounters some women, now mothers, with whom he had gone to high school, noting how they,

---

[18] Leerom Medovoi, *Rebels: Youth and the Cold War Origins of Identity* (Durham, NC and London: Duke University Press, 2005), 18.
[19] Philip Roth, *Goodbye, Columbus and Five Short Stories* (Boston, MA: Houghton Mifflin, 1959), 43.

compared suntans, supermarkets, and vacations. They looked immortal sitting there. Their hair would always stay the color they desired, their clothes the right texture and shade; in their homes they would have some Swedish modern when that was fashionable, and if huge, ugly baroque ever came back, out would go the long, midget-legged marble coffee table and in would come Louis Quatorze. There were the goddesses, and if I were Paris I could not have been able to choose among them, so microscopic were the differences. Their fates had collapsed them into one.[20]

Neil's depiction of the banality of suburban life remains typical of how many realist writers portrayed the burgeoning suburbs, a place that seemed to embody the conformity and the consumerism that had become touchstones of postwar American life. In *Revolutionary Road* (1961), Richard Yates chronicles Frank and April Wheeler, whose marriage violently falls apart in the picture-perfect environment of their suburban enclave. "The Revolutionary Hill Estates had not been designed to accommodate a tragedy," Yates writes toward the novel's conclusion, when April has died after trying to abort an unwanted pregnancy. "Even at night, as if on purpose, the development held no looming shadows and gaunt silhouettes. It was invincibly cheerful, a toyland of white and pastel houses whose, bright, uncurtained windows winked blandly through a dappling of green and yellow leaves."[21] Yates's description of the "invincibly cheerful" suburban space captures the larger political critique that propels *Revolutionary Road* and so much of the realistic fiction set in the suburbs, suggesting how these superficially ideal spaces mask the violence and the debilitating emphasis on conformity that shaped American life in the opening decade of the Cold War.

John Cheever's short stories also chronicle the newly minted suburban lifestyle, his fiction chronicling the drinking and adultery that would soon become synonymous with suburban fiction. "It was one of those midsummer Sundays when everyone sits around saying, 'I *drank* too much last night,'" Cheever writes in the opening of "The Swimmer" (1964), his most famous story. "You might have heard it whispered by the parishioners leaving church, heard it from the lips of the priest himself, struggling with his cassock in the *vestiarium*, heard it from the golf links and the tennis courts, heard it from the wildlife preserve where the leader of the Audubon group was suffering from a terrible hangover."[22] The story chronicles the middle-aged Neddy Merrill as he swims all the pools of his suburban

---

[20] Ibid., 96.   [21] Richard Yates, *Revolutionary Road* (New York: Vintage, 2000 [1961]), 323.
[22] John Cheever, *The Stories of John Cheever* (New York: Alfred A. Knopf, 1978), 603.

neighborhood in an attempt to navigate his way back home, his journey becoming more surreal and dark as it becomes obvious that Neddy has suffered a series of severe financial and personal failures. "The Swimmer" concludes with Neddy arriving back home to find himself locked out. "He shouted, pounded on the door," Cheever writes in the story's final sentence, "tried to force it open with his shoulder, and then, looking in at the windows, saw that the place was empty."[23]

The bleakness of "The Swimmer" is typical of Cheever's fiction, its emphasis on the emptiness and the excesses of suburban life. In "O Youth and Beauty!" (1953), a frustrated wife accidentally shoots and kills her vainglorious middle-aged husband as he attempts to recreate his younger, more athletic days by jumping over his living room furniture, a jarring conclusion that reflects how the surreal frequently interrupts Cheever's largely realistic fiction. The politics of the early Cold War creep into "The Brigadier and the Golf Widow" (1964), as the story chronicles the downfall of Charlie Pastern, who builds a bomb shelter in the backyard of his suburban home. "It bulks under a veil of thin, new grass," Cheever writes of the shelter in the story's opening paragraph, "like some embarrassing fact of physicalness, and I think Mrs. Pastern set out the statuary to soften its meaning."[24] The Pasterns' bomb shelter nicely illuminates how politics infiltrate Cheever's fiction, the shelter a visible reminder of how the realities of the Cold War shape the seemingly protected confines of suburbia.

The atomization of American life – the loosening of the social fabric – captured in Cheever's fiction can also be felt in the "dirty realism" that emerged in the 1970s and 1980s. As embodied by the short stories of Raymond Carver, "dirty realism" eschewed the middle-class enclaves that define Cheever's work to explore the nation's underclass. While politics rarely intrude into his fiction, Carver's stories, written in a pared-down prose style, reflect the fragmentation of American culture in the aftermath of the 1960s. "Nothing was going right lately," Carver writes in the opening of "Jerry and Molly and Sam" (1972), which chronicles an unfaithful husband's decision to abandon the family dog.

> [Al] had enough to contend with without having to worry about a stinking dog. They were laying off at Aerojet when they should be hiring. The middle of the summer, defense contracts let all over the country and Aerojet was talking of cutting back ... If your number was up, that was that – and

> there was nothing anybody could do. They got ready to lay off, and they laid off. Fifty, a hundred men at a time.[25]

The economic insecurity that shapes Al's existence in the story is a recurring theme in Carver's fiction: His stories chronicle a nation without a safety net to protect many of its citizens, a lack of protection that leads to a sense of impotence and alienation within his mostly male protagonists. "Later, after things had changed for us," Jack, the narrator of "Feathers" (1982), confesses in the story's final section, talking about the unspecified trauma that reshaped his marriage, "and the kid had come along, all of that, Fran [his wife] would look back on that evening at Bud's place as the beginning of the change. But she's wrong. The change came later and when it came, it was something that happened to other people, not something that could have happened to us."[26] A similar sense of dissolution characterizes Ann Beattie's fiction, whose stories and novels follow the Baby Boomers as they navigate the moral and political ambiguities of post-1960s America. "She had run away from home when she was younger and when she returned, things were only worse," Beattie writes of Penelope, the protagonist of "Colorado" (1976), whose tendency to drift through life is characteristic of the sense of ennui that looms over Beattie's characters. "She had flunked out of Bard and dropped out of Antioch and the University of Connecticut, and now she knew that all colleges were the same – there was no point in trying one after another. She had traded her Ford for a Toyota, and Toyotas were no better than Fords."[27] Like Carver's stories, Beattie's fiction is rarely explicitly political, but the careful chronicling of her characters' various and constantly shifting domestic arrangements nevertheless captures the shifting social and political mores of her generation, illuminating how the political and cultural upheaval of the 1960s reshaped American life.

A more expansive history of the United States' postwar experience emerges in John Updike's fiction. Less sardonic than Yates or Cheever, Updike lovingly captured the texture, the lived reality, of middle-class American life. "This is America, where we take everything in, tacos and chow mien and pizza and sauerkraut, because we are only what we eat, we are whatever we say we are," the narrator of the short story "How to Love America and Leave It at the Same Time" (1972) muses as he takes his

---

[25] Raymond Carver, *Collected Stories*, ed. William L. Stull and Maureen P. Carroll (New York: Library of America, 2009), 116.
[26] Ibid., 376.   [27] Ann Beattie, *The New Yorker Stories* (New York: Scribner, 2010), 90.

family on a cross-country trip.[28] In his most celebrated work, the Rabbit Angstrom series – *Rabbit, Run* (1960), *Rabbit Redux* (1971), *Rabbit Is Rich* (1981), *Rabbit at Rest* (1990), and the novella "Rabbit Remembered" (2001) – Updike chronicled the life and times of Harry "Rabbit" Angstrom, a former high-school basketball standout turned middle-class Toyota salesman.[29] Taking place over the course of five decades, the Rabbit series traces American culture as it moved from the conservatism of the Eisenhower years, through the revolutions of the 1960s, to the impending collapse of the Soviet Union and the end of the Cold War, whose presence had shaped Harry Angstrom's adult life. While politics remains in the background of the first Rabbit novel – in many ways, *Rabbit, Run* counters the fantasy of Jack Kerouac's *On the Road* (1957) that one can easily escape the confines of domestic life, as Harry attempts and fails to leave his marriage and young family – it emerges more forcefully in the tetralogy's latter installments.[30] "I *don't* think about politics," Harry exclaims in *Rabbit Redux*, as his resentment toward the antiwar movement has put him out of step with his more liberal wife (Updike himself bristled at the rhetoric of the New Left and of the antiwar movement). "That's one of my Goddam precious American rights, not to think about politics."[31] The novel concludes with Harry's home being burned down by his neighbors, who are outraged that he has housed an African American radical, Skeeter, and his young white lover, an upper-class hippie runaway named Jill, in his suburban home. More so than any other work of fiction to come out of the late 1960s, *Rabbit Redux* captures the chaos and uncertainty that defined those years, as the political and cultural consensus that had shaped American life after World War II seemingly crumbled overnight.

The final two Rabbit novels are broader in scope as they chronicle the sense of exhaustion and fragmentation that defined American culture in the wake of the 1960s. Both personal and national exhaustion are

---

[28] John Updike, *Collected Early Stories*, ed. Christopher Carduff (New York: Library of America, 2013), 774.

[29] Both *Rabbit Is Rich* and *Rabbit at Rest* won the Pulitzer Prize for Fiction; the latter also won the Howells Medal. "Rabbit Remembered" revisits the Angstrom clan a decade after Harry's death at the end of *Rabbit at Rest*.

[30] In his introduction to the tetralogy, Updike makes this connection to Kerouac explicit: "Jack Kerouac's *On the Road* came out in 1957 and, without reading it, I resented its apparent instruction to cut loose; *Rabbit, Run* was meant to be a realistic demonstration of what happens when a young American family man goes on the road – the people left behind get hurt." See John Updike, *Rabbit Angstrom: A Tetralogy* (New York: Everyman's Library, 1995), xii.

[31] Ibid., 304.

expressed in the opening sentences of *Rabbit Is Rich*, which takes place during the 1979 oil crisis: "Running out of gas, Rabbit Angstrom thinks as he stands behind the summer-dusty windows of Springer Motors display room watching the traffic go by on Route 111, traffic somehow thin and scared compared to what it used to be. The fucking world is running out of gas."[32] By the time of *Rabbit at Rest*, Harry Angstrom feels himself and his nation to be belated, their best days behind them. Unmoored by the end of the Cold War and with a heart damaged by a lifetime of overconsumption, Harry feels as if his life – and, by extension, the life of his country – lacks the vitality that had once defined it. "Do you ever get the feeling," Harry asks the young secretary of the Toyota dealership he used to manage, "now that [George] Bush is in, that we're kind of on the sidelines, that we're sort of like a big Canada, and what we do doesn't much matter to anybody else? Maybe that's the way it ought to be? It's kind of a relief, I guess, not to be the big cheese."[33] More broadly, the gnawing sense of depression that Harry experiences throughout *Rabbit at Rest* reflects the alienated political sensibility that governs Updike's later work. In novels such as *Roger's Version* (1986) and *Toward the End of Time* (1997), Updike's characters mourn the consequences of the neoliberal state while also clinging to a wary pragmatism that the American experiment will continue, if not exactly flourish.

The ambivalence toward the American project that colors Updike's late fiction is deepened in Chang-rae Lee's *Native Speaker* (1995) and Jonathan Franzen's *The Corrections* (2001), two novels that deftly capture the social and political crises that the United States encountered as it emerged from the Cold War. Considering the fate of the large "social novel" in "Why Bother?," an essay originally published in *Harper's* magazine in 1996 under the title "Perchance to Dream," Franzen observed:

> The current flourishing of novels by women and cultural minorities shows the chauvinism of judging the vitality of American letters by the fortunes of the traditional social novel. Indeed, it can be argued that the country's literary culture is healthier for having disconnected from mainstream cultures; that a universal 'American' culture was little more than an instrument for the perpetuation of a white, male, heterosexual elite, and that its decline is the just desert of an exhausted tradition.[34]

---

[32] Ibid., 623. [33] Ibid., 1374–5.

[34] Jonathan Franzen, "Why Bother?," in *How to Be Alone* (New York: Farrar, Straus and Giroux, 2002), 79.

Indeed, Lee's *Native Speaker* would help usher in a flourishing of Asian American literature as the novel captures the fractious debates over multiculturalism that emerged in the 1990s. The book follows Henry Park, a first-generation Korean American who works as an industrial and political spy, as he is assigned to follow John Kwang, a successful Korean American businessman who aspires to become mayor of New York City. Like the eponymous narrator of Ellison's *Invisible Man*, Park remains acutely aware of his double-consciousness as he finds himself always slightly on the outside of American society. At the beginning of the novel, his estranged wife, Leila, writes him a list of the reasons why she is leaving their marriage, accusing him of being a "B+ student of life," an "illegal alien," and a "neo-American."[35] The novel, like *Invisible Man*, ends on a hopeful note, with Henry, having given up his career as a spy, and Leila reconciled and Leila working with young ESL students who are attempting to learn English. "Now, [Leila] calls out each one as best as she can," Lee writes in the novel's final sentence, "taking care of every last pitch and accent, and I hear her speaking a dozen lovely and native languages, calling all the difficult names of who we are."[36]

A similar optimism ultimately informs Franzen's *The Corrections*, which in many ways offers a caustic overview of the travails that defined American life in the 1990s. Published in the immediate aftermath of the September 11 terrorist attacks, *The Corrections* reflects the anxieties – concerns over globalism, the rise of the pharmaceutical industry, the proliferation of the internet – that permeated American culture at the end of the millennium. "The madness of an autumn prairie cold front coming through. You could feel it: something terrible was going to happen. The sun low in the sky, a minor light, a cooling star. Gust after gust of disorder," Franzen writes in the novel's opening sentence, suggesting the sense of things falling apart that develops throughout the novel.[37] Focusing on the tribulations of a Midwestern family, the Lamberts, whose aging patriarch, Alfred, is suffering from Parkinson's disease, *The Corrections* relays a family's encounter with the forces of globalism and modern medicine, the novel exposing the larger systems that determine one family's existence. In particular, the novel captures the now dominant logic of neoliberalism, which, among other things, had put a renewed emphasis on free-market capitalism and had shaped how many individuals

[35] Chang-rae Lee, *Native Speaker* (New York: Riverhead Books, 1995), 5.   [36] Ibid., 349.
[37] Jonathan Franzen, *The Corrections* (New York: Farrar, Straus and Giroux, 2001), 3.

imagined their bodies and their relationships to one another.[38] Franzen's critique of neoliberalism emerges most clearly in his characterization of the eldest Lambert child, Gary, who becomes fixated on managing his own mental well-being in a vain attempt to convince himself that he is not clinically depressed:

> [Gary] had a spring in his step, an agreeable awareness of his above-average height and his late-summer suntan. His resentment of his wife, Caroline, was moderate and well contained. Declines led advances in key indices of paranoia (e.g., his persistent suspicion that Caroline and his two older sons were mocking him), and his seasonally adjusted assessment of life's futility and brevity was consistent with the overall robustness of his mental economy. He was not the least bit clinically depressed.[39]

Indeed, Franzen's novel beautifully renders how the logic and language of the markets and of the pharmaceutical world have infiltrated our sense of ourselves and each other. Nevertheless, *The Corrections* ends on a hopeful note, as Enid Lambert, who had long suffered in her marriage to Alfred, moves forward with her life after he dies from Parkinson's: "She was seventy-five and she was going to make some changes in her life."[40] It's an ending that suggests the guarded optimism that in many ways defined American life during the 1990s and suggests the realist novel's capacity for chronicling the political and cultural changes that emerged at the end of the millennium. More broadly, *The Corrections* suggests how the realist novel could do more than just conserve the texture of American life; it could also equal its postmodern brethren in illuminating how large political and economic forces determine our lives. Like the bulk of the realistic fiction highlighted in this chapter, *The Corrections* resists the urge to promote a political agenda, but instead uses the strictures of realism – the desire to render reality in all its complications and contradictions – to reflect the wider political realities that determine the tenor of American life.

---

[38] Rachel Greenwald Smith offers an illuminating reading of *The Correction*'s relationship to neoliberalism; my argument is indebted to her work. See Rachel Greenwald Smith, *Affect and American Literature in the Age of Neoliberalism* (Cambridge: Cambridge University Press, 2015), 1–11.
[39] Franzen, *The Corrections*, 137–8.   [40] Ibid., 566.

CHAPTER 12

Immigrant Fiction

Heather Hathaway

The twentieth century was *the* century of immigration to the United States. Three main waves comprise this hundred-year span. The first took place between 1880 and 1924 and consisted primarily of European immigrants, who entered through Ellis Island on the East Coast; and of Asian immigrants, who entered through Angel Island on the West. The second wave ranged from 1924 to 1965 and was much smaller than the first, largely due to shifting political views toward immigrants, which resulted in legislation that significantly restricted the flow of newcomers. The third wave was triggered in 1965 by another change in both national attitude and policy, and it lasted into the early decades of the twentieth century.

Indeed, the United States prides itself as being "a nation built by immigrants," as the George W. Bush Center puts it, or as the nation harboring more immigrants than any other, according to the Brookings Institute.[1] At the same time, however, the immigrant in American society has forever been politicized, regardless of the newcomer's status as documented, undocumented, refugee, asylum seeker, green card holder, or "naturalized" citizen. Historians have analyzed the political implications of who assimilates, who adapts, when and why. Lawyers have explored the politics surrounding the granting and denial of citizenship to immigrants. Political scientists have studied the relationship between immigrants, voting practices, and elections. Cultural studies scholars have debated the appropriate metaphor for immigration. Is it a "melting pot," the term used during the first half of the twentieth century to describe the processes by which immigrant groups meld into a mythological "America"? Or is it a "salad bowl," the term used in the latter half of the century to describe the processes by which individual groups maintain distinct ethnic or immigrant identities? For all these reasons, immigration is a perennial political

---

[1] See www.bushcenter.org/publications/resources-reports/reports/immigration.html; www.brookings.edu/product/our-nation-of-immigrants/

focus of Congress: fifty-five immigration-related acts or laws were passed between 1900 and 2000.

Immigrant literature reflects political realities through its portrayal of how migration to the United States brings success for some and marginalization for others. The genre confronts the myth that all newcomers enjoy equal potential to achieve the "American Dream" by exposing how racialization, the process of assigning individuals to categories based on characteristics such as skin color or facial features, significantly determines inclusion or exclusion. Here, I first highlight the conventions and tropes that defined immigrant literature as a genre between 1880 and 1924. Next, I discuss how Cold War political ideologies shaped the political uses to which immigrant literature was put at midcentury. And finally, I illustrate how, since 1965, immigrant writing has shifted from demonstrating the immigrant's civic virtues to working as a powerful political tool through which to instigate social change.

1880 to 1924

Between roughly 1880 and 1924, rapid industrialization created job opportunities that drew approximately 30 million newcomers to the United States. By 1920, immigrants comprised nearly fifteen percent of the US population. Patterns of chain migration, wherein one community member immigrated first and was followed by others, resulted in ethnic groups clustering by region. Scandinavians, for example, generally settled in the Dakotas and Minnesota. Austrians and Germans settled in Wisconsin, central Minnesota, Iowa, Illinois, and Pennsylvania. Italians established themselves in New York, New Jersey, Connecticut, and Rhode Island. Canadian immigrants settled in Maine and along the US–Canada border.[2] These groups were predominantly racialized as white.[3]

Groups racialized as non-white also migrated to the United States during this period. Chinese immigrants who had arrived in the 1850s to work on the transcontinental railroad were followed by immigrants from other Asian countries, the majority of whom settled on the West Coast. Mexicans moved to Texas, Arizona, New Mexico, and Southern California. Black immigrants from the Caribbean also moved to the

[2] Ran Abramitzky and Leah Boustan, "Immigration in American Economic History," *Journal of Economic Literature* 55.4 (2017): 1311–45.
[3] Noel Ignatiev, among other scholars, has discussed at length the processes of racialization during this period. See Noel Ignatiev, *How the Irish Became White* (New York: Routledge, 1995).

United States, following Black southerners to northern cities during the Great Migration.

Where these immigrants settled and among whom, in addition to how they were racialized, played a significant role in their ability to assimilate. Black immigrants from the Caribbean faced discrimination from both whites and African Americans. Nativist groups targeted Asian immigrants whom they blamed for deflating wages, and in 1882 the first of numerous Chinese Exclusion Acts was passed by Congress. By 1907, the Dillingham Commission was formed to assess the impact of immigrants on the economy. Growing numbers of newcomers from eastern and southern Europe, which the Commission deemed less assimilable than those from western and northern Europe, led to the imposition of literacy tests and quotas by country of origin. In 1924, Congress passed the Johnson–Reed Act, which capped annual immigration to two percent of the number of immigrants, per country, who were living in the United States as of the 1890 census. Given that the majority of immigrants in 1890 were from northern and western Europe, these nations were favored. Whereas in 1910 over a million newcomers entered the United States annually, just fourteen years later the flow was reduced to 150,000.[4]

These developments took place within the Progressive Era of American politics, during which the government believed that it had a role in easing social and economic problems emerging from industrialization and urbanization. The rapid rise in immigrants was seen as contributing to social ills such as crowded tenements, the growth of communicable illnesses, low wages, and long hours for workers. Muckraking writers led the charge for reform and many used the novel to persuade the reading public. Upton Sinclair's 1906 exposé of the meatpacking industry, *The Jungle,* for example, realistically portrayed the tragedies experienced by a family of Lithuanian immigrants in Chicago at the hands of big business. Sinclair's goal was to educate readers about the exploitation of immigrant laborers, but the public was more horrified by his depiction of contamination in the food industry.

Hamilton Holt, the editor of the progressive journal *The Independent,* used non-fiction to demonstrate the virtues of immigrants and the perils they faced. The title of *The Life Stories of Undistinguished Americans, As Told by Themselves* (1906) deliberately included "as told by themselves" to emphasize the veracity of the narratives. These autobiographies revealed the power of racialization in withholding or securing one's potential to

---

[4] Abramitzky and Boustan, 1317.

climb the economic and social ladder. Those who were racialized as white, such as the "Swedish Farmer," the "Polish Sweatshop Girl" or the "French Dressmaker," experienced the stereotypical American rise from rags to riches. Those who were racialized as non-white, however – both immigrant and US-born alike – such as the "Japanese Servant," the "Chinaman," the "Indian" or the "Negro Peon," recounted exploitation, discrimination, and physical violence absent from the other narratives.

By 1917, fictionalized autobiographies along the lines of the true stories collected by Holt emerged as a subgenre of immigrant literature and established the conventions and tropes that would dominate immigrant writing until midcentury. These tales typically begin by narrating the immigrant's difficult journey by ship from an agrarian and slow-paced life in Europe to the bustling New World. Upon arriving in the United Sates, the protagonist is taken aback by the modern city and the wonders of technology, such as electric lights and streetcars. After enduring exploitation as a "greenhorn," a status demonstrated by the immigrant's Old World clothing, poverty, and lack of language skills, the newcomer acquires the tools of assimilation: American clothing, money, and knowledge of English. Through diligence, optimism, and ingenuity, the immigrant slowly ascends the class ladder and achieves the American Dream. This subgenre resembles the rags-to-riches stories by Horatio Alger, but in the immigrant narratives, hard work rather than good works proves to be the path to success.[5]

Abraham Cahan's 1917 novel *The Rise of David Levinsky* adheres to these literary conventions. Cahan, a socialist, immigrated to the US from Lithuania in 1882. He became a leader of socialist movements in New York and the editor of the Yiddish-language newspaper the *Jewish Daily Forward*. In *The Rise of David Levinsky*, Cahan describes his protagonist as arriving in America, feeling disoriented and alone. Levinsky is soon befriended by a kinsman who loans him money and buys him a new suit. Levinsky starts out as a poor peddler but, over time, he learns the ways of the New World, masters the language, and establishes a profitable business making cloaks – which he sells, of course, to other newly arrived immigrants. By the novel's close, Levinsky has achieved all the markers of capitalist – and, by association, "American" – success.

---

[5] For Alger, "good works" involved ethical acts of honesty or generosity, but more often than not, the street urchin is saved by an older male benefactor, leading some scholars to trace a pedophilic undercurrent in the novels.

Below the surface, however, lingers a shadow narrative. Levinsky feels no personal reward in attaining the American Dream, as is reflected in the novel's final chapter, "Episodes of a Lonely Life." Although Levinsky has been metaphorically reborn through immigration, that transformation also leaves him feeling part of no people or place. He abandoned the virtuous religious practices that sustained him in Lithuania for "book-learning" in the United States, a secularization that satisfied his mind but crushed his soul. He betrayed fellow immigrants who worked for him and stifled their efforts to achieve fair pay and protection through unionization, cutting him off from his community. In the hands of the socialist reformer Cahan, the process of Americanization under capitalism leaves one lonely and alienated from both home and host cultures.

Writing by women during this first phase of mass migration shows how gender shaped the immigrant's experience. In 1920, passage of the Nineteenth Amendment secured women's suffrage. Against the backdrop of the first wave of US feminism, Polish American Anzia Yezierska, in her 1925 fictionalized autobiography *Bread Givers*, presented how this political context affected the values of a white female immigrant. Sara Smolinsky, the novel's protagonist, seeks not the wealth of David Levinsky but rather education and independence from her oppressive father and from the stultifying cultural traditions of the past. Reb Smolinsky believes, for example, that it his right, as a Jewish patriarch, to live on the wages of his daughters and wife so that he can devote himself to the study of the Torah. Sara's sisters seek to escape this exploitation through marrying suitors they love. Reb Smolinsky undermines the relationships, however, and arranges unions that provide financial security for himself but make his daughters miserable. Sara rejects reliance on the patriarchy, whether it is symbolized by a father or a husband. She moves out, attends night school, and eventually supports herself through teaching. As in Cahan's tale, however, Sara's transformation comes with personal loss. Her mother dies after she moves out and, at the novel's end, a suitor pressures her to take in and care for her father as he ages. In *Bread Givers*, Yezierska shows the ways in which the cultural traditions of the past, expectations of female domesticity and care work, and the precarity of living as a single working woman combine to lock immigrant women into economic structures of dependence that thwart their quests for autonomy.

These issues were even more burdensome for non-white female immigrants. Writer Edith Maude Eaton, a Chinese immigrant who also wrote under the name Sui Sin Far, recounts these travails. Eaton's mother was Chinese and her father British. Born in England, she lived her adult life in

Canada and the United States and devoted her writing to the experiences of Chinese Americans, often in reference to the discriminatory laws established by the Chinese Exclusion Acts. Her articles were published regularly in Montreal newspapers and a selection of these were collected in her 1912 collection, *Mrs. Spring Fragrance*. Eaton highlights the oppression experienced particularly by Chinese American women, whose rights and opportunities were even more limited than those of Asian men, thus demonstrating how race- and gender-based discrimination doubly conspired against female immigrants of color.

Black immigrants and writers from the Caribbean infused nationalist movements into American politics during the Progressive Era. Hubert Harrison, from St. Croix, was a key organizer of the Socialist Party of America. Nevis immigrant Cyril Briggs founded the Black communist journal *The Crusader* in 1918. Jamaican Marcus Garvey led the Universal Negro Improvement Association (UNIA), which advocated a form of Black nationalism to link people of African descent across continents. Writers Claude McKay, from Jamaica, and Eric Walrond, from Guyana, contributed to these efforts. McKay worked as a journalist and coeditor of Max Eastman's socialist publication *The Liberator*. Walrond edited Garvey's *Negro World*, the journal of the UNIA, from 1921 to 1923. Both writers used literature as a means of exposing and protesting injustice.

McKay is well known for his poem "If We Must Die," but three of his novels – *Home to Harlem* (1928), *Banjo* (1929), *and Banana Bottom* (1933) – are equally political.[6] While in Jamaica, McKay learned about Fabianism, and, upon arriving in the United States, he explored various leftist political movements including socialism and communism. He came to define himself as an "internationalist" rather than hew to a specific ideology, but the concerns of 1930s radicals are addressed in his fiction. His novels emphasize the dignity of the poor and of laborers, for example, whether they be prostitutes, peasants, or production workers. Through his character Ray, a Haitian immigrant in *Home to Harlem*, McKay probes the alienation experienced by Black immigrant intellectuals in the United Sates whose achievements, like his own, were circumscribed by anti-Black racism and xenophobia.

Eric Walrond directs his aim specifically toward US imperialism. *Tropic Death* (1926) consists of interrelated stories set in the Panama Canal Zone

---

[6] See Heather Hathaway, *Caribbean Waves: Relocating Claude McKay and Paule Marshall* (Bloomington: University of Indiana Press, 1999).

and, as the title suggests, it exposes the political agenda undergirding US supervision of the project: racial capitalism. The American military established a racial caste system that deemed Black workers "unskilled," regardless of their actual abilities, and paid them in silver, while white workers were considered "skilled" and paid in gold. In "Panama Gold," Walrond sardonically comments on this by describing a Black laborer who is permanently disabled while working on the Canal and, thus, is unable to support himself for the remainder of his life. "Subjection" describes the violence inflicted upon Black workers by members of the supervising American military. In "The Wharf Rats," Walrond condemns the disposability of Black life under American and British imperialism through his portrayal of two young Trinidadian men who are killed by sharks while diving for coins tossed into the water by white tourists from a cruise ship. Throughout *Tropic Death*, Walrond exposes how US economic investment in the Canal was dependent upon race-based segregation, exploitation of laborers, and desecration of the land, all in the name of "progress."

The initial period of twentieth-century immigrant writing in the United States laid the foundations of the genre for the remainder of the century. Themes of citizenship, "belonging," racial capitalism, and xenophobia thread through all that was written later, as do the literary tropes characterizing the early non-fictional and fictionalized immigrant autobiographies published during the period. But the writings produced during the second and third waves of immigration are also distinctively shaped by the unique historical circumstances and political ideologies that characterize each period, allowing us to see how the political arc of immigrant writing shifts from one of civic affiliation toward individual autonomy.

1924 to 1965

Strict national quotas established by the Immigration Act of 1924 effectively ended the first wave of immigration to the United States, and these restrictions remained in place until the passing of the Hart–Celler Act in 1965. The percentage of foreign-born people declined from fourteen percent in 1920 to five percent by 1970.[7] Domestically, the politics of immigration changed too, resulting in policy changes that often contradicted the rationale on which previous acts had been based. Regulations on Mexican immigration provide just one illustration of this. Between

---

[7] Abramitzky and Boustan, 1320.

1929 and 1936, for example, in response to the labor crises of the Great Depression, the United States engaged in a campaign to deport Mexican immigrants who were perceived as taking jobs away from American citizens. In 1942, however, the depletion of the labor force caused by soldiers shipping off to World War II led to a need for labor. Consequently, the Bracero Agreement was developed to allow single Mexican men to enter the US as short-term contract workers in agriculture and industry. By 1953, concerns about employment for soldiers returning from Korea combined with uncontrolled migration across the US–Mexico border to lead to a crackdown on Mexican immigrants; even as the Bracero Program continued to recruit temporary workers, "Operation Wetback" actively deported them.

Cold War political ideologies shaped other immigration policies during the period. Because China, the Philippines, and India were US allies during World War II, for instance, various laws during the 1940s repealed elements of the Asian Exclusion Acts. Cold War anxieties about the spread of communism led to the development of "containment" as the dominant foreign policy. Its goal was to contain Soviet geopolitical expansion, including through military intervention in susceptible nations. "Containment" also influenced immigration policy and domestic culture. The 1952 McCarran–Walter Act, for example, opened immigration by quota to all countries, including newly independent postcolonial nations that the US government deemed vulnerable to communist takeover. Domestically – and this means, literally, home life – "potentially danger-ous social forces" could be "tamed" through the establishment of a gendered hierarchy in which the father enforced normative values and behaviors to achieve a harmonious consensus in the family, which served as a metaphor for the nation.[8] Dissent was not tolerated. The popular 1950s and 1960s television shows *Leave It to Beaver* and *My Three Sons*, for example, embody this ethos. Immigrant literature during the period reflects that, in Cold War America, consumerism, homogeneity, and heteronormativity reigned.

The publication history of Japanese American writer Toshio Mori's 1949 story cycle *Yokohama, California* demonstrates the influence of "containment culture" on one group of immigrants. Mori admired Sherwood Anderson's 1919 *Winesburg, Ohio*, a story cycle about an average white community in the Midwest, and throughout the 1930s he

[8] Elaine Tyler May, *Homeward Bound: American Families in the Cold War Era* (New York: Basic Books, 1988), 14.

crafted tales that offered a comparable portrayal of an average Japanese American community on the West Coast. Mori depicts the residents of "Lil' Yokohama" as average Americans. They love the great American pastime of baseball, admire American movies and stars, are invested in their children's education, and support themselves and serve the community through ownership of small businesses. They also practice Buddhism, eat ethnic foods, and have Japanese names. These factors are not portrayed as being in tension with one another. A small press in Idaho contracted with Mori to publish *Yokohama, California* in 1941. The release was stalled, however, by the war and the subsequent incarceration of Japanese Americans between 1942 and 1946. When the collection finally appeared in 1949, two stories had been added that reveal just how drastically the political climate in the United States had changed for this immigrant community.

The first story, "Tomorrow Is Coming, Children," was written while Mori was incarcerated in Topaz, the War Relocation Center in Utah. In it, Mori recounts the experience of a Japanese woman's immigration to the United States and he generally follows the literary conventions of early twentieth-century white immigrant narratives. The woman arrives by ship and, alongside her fellow travelers, eagerly awaits a glimpse of San Francisco, "the golden city of dreams." Recalling the trope of needing to dress like an American to become one, when she disembarks in "her best kimono," her husband tells her she must never wear it again because she, in his words, "look[s] like a foreigner . . . You must dress like an American. You belong here." She struggles with loneliness because she cannot speak English. She and her husband face violence from their white neighbors. But, in the end, she tells her grandchildren that she wants to be buried in America because she now feels that she truly does "belong here."[9] The poignant irony, of course, is that the grandmother narrates her life story from the confines of a Japanese American prison camp.

When *Yokohama, California* was published in 1949, "Tomorrow Is Coming, Children" was placed first in the collection. Whether Mori or the press made this decision is unclear, but the effect of the story's placement is not. Opening the collection with a classic immigrant narrative emphasizing the rise from rags to riches through optimism and industry does the political work of defining Japanese Americans as being just like all other immigrant groups who had successfully become integral parts of the American social fabric. So, too, does the second story added in 1949,

---

[9] Toshio Mori, *Yokohama, California* (Seattle: University of Washington Press, 1985 [1949]), 17, 20.

"Slant-Eyed Americans." This story portrays a Japanese American family's reaction to the bombing of Pearl Harbor. As they face fear, shame, and discrimination based solely on their ancestry, their faith in the United States stands. Not only is their firm footing as Americans proven by one son's service in the US military, but the mother insists that, in the midst of World War II, "America is right. She cannot fail. Her principles will stand the test of time and tyranny."[10] Mori's writing is characteristically subtle and complex, but this story is patriotic to the point of verging on jingoism, making it seem out of place in the collection. By adding these two stories to *Yokohama, California*, Mori and his publishers changed the point of the text. Whereas before the war it offered a slice of Americana that illustrated the successful assimilation of an immigrant community into the great American melting pot, after the war it was transformed into a defense of that immigrant community's very presence.

The Cold War politics of containment were complemented by a seemingly antithetical foreign policy of engagement, primarily with non-communist nations in Asia.[11] President Dwight D. Eisenhower believed that one effective way to bridge differences between East and West involved personal interaction among individuals. Describing his People-to-People program, for example, he stated: "[I]f we are going to take advantage of the assumption that all people want peace, then the problem is for people to get together and to leap governments – if necessary to evade governments – to work out not one method but thousands of methods by which people can gradually learn a little bit more of each other."[12] Eisenhower envisioned programs such as the establishment of sister cities, pen-pal exchanges, and international sports and arts events as venues through which to achieve this political goal.

Like containment, engagement was intended to thwart communism. Politicians advocating this ideology understood that America's history of xenophobia and economic imperialism risked alienating emerging post-colonial nations where they sought to encourage the development of capitalist democracies, not communism. An educational and outreach initiative was required, and literature became one of the means by which cross-cultural "interaction" could be achieved. American readers could be introduced to other cultures by immigrant writers.

[10] Ibid., 132.
[11] See Christina Klein's outstanding study of this. Christina Klein, *Cold War Orientalism: Asia in the Middlebrow Imagination, 1945–1961* (Berkeley: University of California Press, 2003).
[12] See www.eisenhowerlibrary.gov/research/online-documents/people-people-program

A *New York Times* review of Pardee Lowe's *Father and Glorious Descendant* (1943) emphasizes the political work that literature was made to do during the 1950s: Reviewer Helena Kuo states that, though Chinese herself, she "could never quite understand the Chinese in San Francisco – they were too American and too Chinese. Mr. Lowe explains them."[13] Carlos Bulosan's fictionalized autobiography about Filipino farm workers during the Depression, *America Is in the Heart* (1946), did similar cultural and political work, as is suggested by its selection by *Look* magazine as one of the fifty most important works of American literature.[14] Chinese immigrant C. Y. Young's novel *The Flower Drum Song* (1957) was so popular that Richard Rodgers and Oscar Hammerstein II transformed both it and Margaret Landon's novel *Anna and the King of Siam* (1944) into Broadway musicals that were perceived as providing insight into foreign lands and cultures, regardless of the inaccuracy of their representations.

The State Department took an active role in using immigrant literature during the period to advance its foreign policies abroad. Jade Snow Wong's popular memoir, *Fifth Chinese Daughter* (1950), for example, was translated into several Asian languages by the US government. In 1953, the State Department enlisted Wong for a four-month speaking tour of Asia to promote the fact that a rags-to-riches story was indeed possible for Chinese in America. "I was sent," Wong wrote, "because those Asian audiences who had read translations of *Fifth Chinese Daughter* did not believe a female born to poor Chinese immigrants could gain a toehold among prejudiced Americans."[15] The government similarly co-opted the work of second-generation Japanese American immigrant Miné Okubo. Her graphic memoir of the Japanese American incarceration, *Citizen 13660* (1946), was promoted by the government to demonstrate that this particular immigrant group, who shortly before had been demonized as the enemy, had been transformed by their imprisonment into patriotic American citizens.[16] Neither Wong's nor Okubo's work presents as sanguine an image of the United States as the State Department claimed.

---

[13] Helena Kuo, "Son and Illustrious Parent; *Father and Glorious Descendant*" [book review], *New York Times*, 11 April, 1943, 19.
[14] Klein, 227. By 1954, however, Bulosan was targeted as a communist during the McCarthy era and his work was diminished in the public's eye.
[15] Jade Snow Wong, "Introduction to the 1989 Edition," in *Fifth Chinese Daughter* (Seattle: University of Washington Press, 1989), viii.
[16] Greg Robinson, "Birth of a Citizen: Miné Okubo and the Politics of Symbolism," in *Miné Okubo: Following Her Own Road*, ed. Greg Robinson and Elena Tajima Creef (Seattle: University of Washington Press, 2008), 159–78.

Not all immigrant literature fitted the government's agenda, however. Second-generation Japanese American writer John Okada's 1957 novel *No-No Boy*, for example, was not as easily exploitable. *No-No Boy* explores the postwar fallout of decisions made by Japanese American men to enlist or to refuse to be drafted into the military during the incarceration. These decisions divided Japanese American communities within the prison camps. Some Nisei eagerly joined the military out of obligation as American citizens. Others felt that their incarceration indicated that they were not seen as "true" Americans and they refused. Some parents took pride in their children's military service while others felt betrayed by the United States and sought repatriation to Japan. Okada's novel confronts the tensions surrounding patriotism and politics that affected this immigrant community's struggles in midcentury America, and, as such, his book received only nominal attention upon its original publication.

Immigrant literature, and particularly that about Asia or by Asian American writers, was employed to advance both of the midcentury political ideologies of containment and engagement. On the one hand, literary scholars might consider this somewhat advantageous in that fiction was perceived to be a notable cultural asset for education and persuasion. On the other, both writers and their works were put to propagandistic purposes that defied the aesthetic complexity and nuance of the writing itself. The next generation of immigrant writers learned from this example.

1965 to about 2000

In 1965, the Immigration and Nationality Act was passed. It eliminated the country-specific quotas that had been imposed in 1924 and raised immigration caps from 150,000 to 270,000 entrants annually. Seventy percent of those places were allotted to family members of American citizens, twenty percent were allotted to employers seeking workers possessing specific skills, and five percent were allotted to refugees.[17] The Cuban Adjustment Act of 1966, the Chinese Student Protection Act of 1992, and the Nicaraguan Adjustment and Central American Relief Act of 1997 offered additional refuge to people fleeing political persecution and violence. Although these and other policy changes allowed the number of immigrants entering the United States to return to its peak flow during the early period of the twentieth century, the demographic characteristics of the newcomers shifted considerably.

---

[17] See https://immigrationhistory.org/item/hart-celler-act/

Compared with immigrants arriving in 1907, the 2010 census showed that newly arrived immigrants spoke more English, were better educated, and came from non-European nations.[18] Most significantly, however, the majority were racialized in the United States as non-white: fifty-one percent of immigrants in the United States in 2010 were Latin American and twenty-eight percent were Asian. Immigrants from the Middle East and Africa contributed to the mix, so that, during the first two decades of the twenty-first century, approximately 650,000 non-white immigrants entered the United States each year.[19]

These demographic shifts affected immigrant politics in the United States. As people of color, recent arrivals simultaneously recognized that the United States provided opportunities unavailable in their home countries but also called out the racial capitalism that formed the root of American history and culture. The containment and engagement ideologies that had dominated the Cold War era gave way in the 1960s and 1970s to domestically focused liberationist and Civil Rights movements, many of which were led by immigrant activists. César Chávez and Dolores Huerta spearheaded the United Farm Workers Union. Chinese, Japanese, Korean, and Southeast Asian activists joined forces to establish the Asian American movement, a coalition-based program that worked on specific initiatives, such as the Japanese American Redress movement, and on trans-Asian resistance to US militarism globally. The Third World Liberation Front brought multiple oppressed groups together to demand curricular change in the American educational system, leading to the development of Black and ethnic studies programs in universities across the United States. These programs provided important new contexts in which to teach immigrant literature, which both echoed and revised previous conventions and tropes of the genre.

Political philosopher Michael J. Sandel describes the liberal arc of twentieth-century America as one in which "the civic or formative aspect of politics has largely given way to the liberalism that conceives of persons as free and independent selves, unencumbered by moral or civic ties they have not chosen."[20] Immigrant literature from the later years of the twentieth century follows this arc precisely. If early twentieth-century

---

[18] "Remembering Ellis Island's Busiest Day: How Has Immigration Changed Since 1907?," New American Economy Research Fund, April 16, 2019, https://research.newamericaneconomy.org/report/immigration-1907-v-2017/

[19] Abramitzky and Boustan, 1320.

[20] Michael J. Sandel, *Democracy's Discontent: America in Search of a Public Philosophy* (Cambridge, MA: Harvard University Press, 1996).

immigrant writing sought to represent civically minded assimilating capitalists, late twentieth-century literature tells stories of non-representative
individuals whose experiences and allegiances cannot be codified into given
formulae. Four works by second-generation Barbadian American Paule
Marshall, written between 1959 and 1991, beautifully illustrate the political arc of the twentieth-century immigrant novel in the United States.

Marshall's first novel, *Brown Girl, Brownstones* (1959), is a fictionalized
autobiography that both echoes themes of previous immigrant writing and
revises traditional tropes as it narrates the life of Selina Boyce, a second-
generation Barbadian American teenager coming of age in Brooklyn. Like
Abraham Cahan, Marshall pointedly analyzes what is lost and gained by
aspiring West Indian immigrants in the United States, among them Silla,
Selina's mother, who pursued the "Almighty Dollar" so single-mindedly
that she risked sacrificing her humanity. Like Anna Yezierska and Maude
Eaton, Marshall vividly conveys how Selina's talents, ambitions, and
desires for independence are dually blunted by the sexism and racism of
her own community and of larger American culture. Like her fellow
Caribbean immigrants, Claude McKay and Eric Walrond, Marshall
exposes the emasculating power of US imperialism through her portrayal
of Selina's father, Deighton. Like John Okada, Marshall explores the
cultural dislocation experienced by immigrants who could not assimilate
because of color, cultural ties, or constitution. But Marshall concludes her
novel by looking forward rather than back as she depicts Selina not only on
the cusp of her own liberation but looking toward the newly independent
Black nations in the Caribbean and Africa that were simultaneously
liberating themselves from oppressive pasts.

Marshall's second work, a collection of interrelated stories titled *Soul
Clap Hands and Sing* (1961), shifts focus from the domestic to the
international sphere. Whereas *Brown Girl, Brownstones*, in Marshall's
own estimation, was an "attempt at a revolutionary statement in individual
rather than political terms," *Soul* was an attempt to "take up [the] dual
theme of the emerging third world and a moribund West."[21] Through
four stories set in Brooklyn, Barbados, British Guiana, and Brazil, Marshall
typifies the "emerging third world" through Black female characters and
the "moribund West" through aging male figures who struggle with the
changing and challenging societies by which they are surrounded.

Marshall engages this theme further in *The Chosen Place, the Timeless
People* (1969). Here, she explores the neocolonialist incursion of the

---

[21] Paule Marshall, "Shaping the World of My Art," *New Letters* 40.1 (1973): 97–112.

United States into the Caribbean. Written in the context of the feminist, Black Power, and Pan-African movements, the novel centers around the fictional Caribbean Bourne Island, half of which is mired in poverty and half of which has been built into an American tourist destination by corrupt local politicians. Into this setting Marshall brings an American non-profit "development" organization funded by a self-serving white female philanthropist from Philadelphia's Main Line. Marshall subtly suggests that the woman's investment in the "modernization" of Bournehills is grounded in the same condescending liberal concept of "racial uplift" that motivated Gilded Age northerners' engagement with Blacks during the Great Migration. Marshall brilliantly portrays the novel's powerful Black female protagonist, Merle Kinbona, defending her community against exploitation by white Americans and crooked Caribbean businessmen. Kinbona relies on the spirit of Bournehills's folk hero, Cuffee Ned, the leader of the island's nineteenth-century slave revolts, as she navigates the challenges facing her community. Through *The Chosen Place, the Timeless People*, Marshall revolutionizes the immigrant novel from one written about the immigrant's role in America to one about the immigrant's role in saving her community from American neoliberal agendas.

Marshall's last novel, *Daughters* (1991), updates her analysis of the vexed relationship between the Caribbean and the United States. She uses familial structures as metaphors through which to examine the debilitating dependency that developed between Caribbean nations and the United States, their new "Mother Country," since the emancipation movements of the 1960s. The novel is set on the fictional island of Triunion and depicts the political campaign of Primus Mackenzie, a Triunion native running for office. He is aided in his pursuits by his wife, Estelle, a Black activist from South Carolina. Linking the two is Ursa, their daughter, a social scientist who works in New York to improve Midlands City, a Black community decimated by the development of a highway. Through their family dynamic, Marshall exposes the Reaganite politics that jointly undergirded the domestic colonization of Black communities in the United States and the international colonization of the Caribbean. Again, in *Daughters*, Marshall portrays Black women as relying on the model of their ancestors – in this instance, Cuffee Ned and his "co-conspirator" and comrade in arms, Congo Jane – to thwart racist, classist, and sexist structures of dependency and oppression.

Throughout the twentieth century, immigrant writers have consistently used fiction as a political tool through which to demonstrate their allegiance to the United States, their adopted home, as well as to call out its shortcomings. From the rags-*to*-riches plots characterizing the first era of mass migration to the United States, to the rags-*versus*-riches critiques of inequality dominating the century's end, immigrant literature follows the arc of liberalism that shaped the century. It has morphed from works that seek to prove the immigrant's civic commitment to American ideals to those that seek to expose the imbalance between power and justice implicit in them. As such, twentieth-century immigrant writing in the United States reveals as much about politics as it does about literature and literary history.

CHAPTER 13

Gothic Horror Fiction

Kevin Corstorphine

The topic of politics and genre fiction is fraught territory to explore. Very often the charge of a work being 'political' is used pejoratively, but it reveals more about the critic than intended; in this case, it is likely that it simply does not align with their own politics. In discussions of Gothic horror fiction, the fields of gender, race, and class are often the subjects of critical attention, with the assumption that such attention can reveal social 'anxieties'. A certain tendency in academia has been to cast individual texts in binary political terms, such as reactionary/progressive or conservative/liberal. None of this is necessarily reflective of the inherent complexity of an individual author's politics and how this translates into storytelling – if anything, it might undermine the claim of any given work's aspiration towards terms such as 'art' or 'literature', reflective of the expression of a unique vision. Debates about the role of the novel within mass culture and the idea of 'popular' as a fiction category are thus bound up with discussions of politics and horror. This chapter explores some of the ways in which American horror novels have been placed within politics and how we might assess their evolving content and critical interpretation. The term 'Gothic' is used here to denote a continuation of a European publishing phenomenon that arose (not entirely coincidentally) at the same time as the United States was founded as a republic. Novels such as Ann Radcliffe's *The Mysteries of Udolpho* (1794) and Matthew Lewis's *The Monk* (1796) presented a faux-medieval setting replete with supernatural suggestion or actual events. Fred Botting ties the 'Gothic fascination with a past of chivalry, violence, magical beings and malevolent aristocrats'[1] to the political upheavals characteristic of the late eighteenth century, specifically the French Revolution – and, we might add, the American. The notion of Gothic, Botting writes, 'resonates as much with anxieties and fears

---

[1] Fred Botting, 'In Gothic Darkly: Heterotopia, History, Culture', in *A Companion to the Gothic*, ed. David Punter (Oxford: Blackwell, 2000), 3.

concerning the crises and changes in the present as with any terrors of the past'.[2] The aesthetics of the Gothic changed in the move to the New World, with authors such as Charles Brockden Brown and Nathaniel Hawthorne, as Alan Lloyd-Smith points out, 'substituting the wilderness and the city for the subterranean rooms and corridors of the monastery, or the remote house for the castle'.[3] More than this, however, 'certain unique cultural pressures led Americans to the Gothic as an expression of their very different conditions'.[4] These pressures, which might include the legacy of Puritan attitudes to sexuality and human nature, as well as cultural guilt over Native American genocide and African slavery, have led Leslie Fiedler to make the startling assertion that 'the American novel is pre-eminently a novel of terror',[5] and that even 'our classic literature is a literature of horror for boys'.[6]

Fiedler's charge against the whole of American letters is perhaps a wider matter, but the assumption remains that the Gothic genre, which moves through the magazine tradition of the weird tale in the early twentieth century and is repackaged as the horror novel in the second half, is inherently juvenile and sensationalist. Where the British Gothic novel had been associated with a corrupting influence on the minds of young women, the American horror tradition moves in the twentieth century towards a presumed (but not always valid) association with young men. Dale Bailey, for example, claims that 'males under the age of thirty or so . . . form the primary audience for the kind of fiction publishers market as horror'.[7] Darryl Jones likewise points out that 'operating at one perceived limit of popular culture, horror is often characterized as a debased if not unhealthy genre'.[8] This, however, does not preclude the possibility of a political reading of the Gothic. Jones cites the Marquis de Sade's 1800 description of the Gothic novel as 'the necessary fruit of the revolutionary tremors felt by the whole of Europe',[9] explaining that:

> [N]ot only is de Sade referring to what has become a traditional conception of the Gothic novel as an ideologically and aesthetically radical or

[2] Ibid., 3.
[3] Alan Lloyd-Smith, *American Gothic Fiction: An Introduction* (New York: Continuum, 2004), 4.
[4] Ibid., 4.
[5] Leslie Fiedler, *Love and Death in the American Gothic Novel* (Funks Green, IL: Dalkey Archive Press, 1997), 26.
[6] Ibid., 29.
[7] Dale Bailey, *American Nightmares: The Haunted House Formula in American Popular Fiction* (Bowling Green, OH: Bowling Green State University Popular Press, 1999), 52.
[8] Darryl Jones, *Horror: A Thematic History in Fiction and Film* (London: Arnold, 2002), 127.
[9] Ibid., 9.

revolutionary form in which societal taboos are examined and violated . . . but also to the ways in which the systems, not only of thought and identity but ultimately of power and government, which were to shape late eighteenth-century political history insinuate themselves into Gothic novels.[10]

If the content of the Gothic novel is transgressive, however, that does not necessary imply that it takes a political stance; instead, it may simply reflect contemporary political construction of identity – here, specifically the portrayal of a fantastical and barbarous Catholic Europe. This in turn 'allowed a British audience conversely to identify itself as Protestant, rational, ordered, stable, and modern'.[11] If the same logic and trajectory can be extended to the American context, then it should likewise be possible to use the form as a gauge of national feeling, however fantastical the events might seem. Despite the sophistication of many readings of Gothic short stories and novels, and the recognition of their often profound insights – for example, of human psychology in Edgar Allan Poe – the lurid sensationalism of much Gothic writing is inherently suited to a popular audience and should not be discounted when thinking about the relationship between literature and politics.

Lloyd-Smith puts the tension between disreputability and popularity at the heart of a history of the Gothic in the United States:

> Widely reviled as infantile, depraved, and potentially corrupting, American Gothic appealed to the popular audience in a rapidly growing readership, itself a consequence of private circulating libraries, the development of cheap printing methods, and an explosive growth in magazine production and consumption at the beginning of the nineteenth century . . . a concern with the behavior of the people, the dominant political force in the new American democracy, increased general interest in what had been dismissed as below polite consideration.[12]

The American Gothic, then, is rooted in the democratic project of the United States itself, and its concerns reflect this new form of society. The focus of the Gothic, in a process that continues throughout the twentieth century, is turned towards the violent, aberrant, and grotesque in everyday life, as opposed to the exotic locales of the British Gothic novel, bound up in a Romantic fascination with travel, ruins, and the aesthetics of the sublime. What, though, is the political implication of the American Gothic, besides a focus on the demos itself (rather than a corrupt aristocratic or monastic elite), and what kind of political order does it endorse?

---

[10] Ibid., 9.   [11] Ibid., 9.   [12] Lloyd-Smith, 25.

To return to the set of binary political oppositions set up earlier, Chris Baldick and Robert Mighall have posited the original Gothic novels as falling in neither of these camps. '[A]lthough Gothic Criticism wishes such novels to be excitingly subversive or, failing that, to be scandalously reactionary, the sad truth is that they are just tamely humanitarian: they creditably encourage respect for women's property rights, and they imply that rape, arbitrary imprisonment and torture are, on the whole, a bad thing.'[13]

If this translates across the Atlantic, then the American Gothic novel might be, if not strictly bourgeois, then what the twentieth century's most successful practitioner of the form, Stephen King, has called 'neither more nor less than an agent of the status quo'.[14] He specifically invokes US politics by claiming that 'monstrosity fascinates us because it appeals to the conservative Republican in a three-piece suit who resides within all of us. We love and need the concept of monstrosity because it is a reaffirmation of the order we all crave as human beings.'[15] King's own writing does tend to reinscribe the essential rightness of 'American' values such as family, decency, and hard work, but only after spectacularly disturbing them through monstrosity that is often quite insidiously woven into 'normal' American life. Glennis Byron writes of Victorian novels such as Robert Louis Stevenson's *Strange Case of Dr Jekyll and Mr Hyde* (1886), where 'evil is sinuously curled around the very heart of the respectable middle-class norm'.[16] Similarly, for King, evil is both fantastical and banal at the same time; in his world, the evils of bullying and abuse are as likely to appear as the supernatural forces they are imaginatively aligned with. King's assumptions about politics are those of his baby boomer generation: injustice is bad, but the fundamental order of American society is not irredeemable. Jones, citing King's autobiographical *On Writing* (2000), notes that 'in Stephen King's cultural imagination, it is forever about 1961, or should be, and he is very aware of his own propensity for both anti-authoritarianism and nostalgia: "In my character, a kind of wildness and a deep conservatism are wound together like hair in a braid."'[17] King's novels are prolific and varied, but the 'typical' King storyline features troubled but essentially decent people banding together to defeat some kind of evil, either newly emergent in society or representative of some ancient force. King's status in the publishing phenomenon of the horror

---

[13] Chris Baldick and Robert Mighall, 'Gothic Criticism', in Punter, 227.
[14] Stephen King, *Danse Macabre* (London: Warner, 1993), 56.   [15] King, *Danse Macabre*, 55.
[16] Glennis Byron, 'Gothic in the 1890s', in Punter, 137.   [17] Jones, 138.

novel as well as his wider cultural presence make his work essential to understanding twentieth-century American Gothic horror, but his political stance, while a useful yardstick, is not the only way to look at the genre. Examples of his work are examined in more specific detail later in this chapter, but it is first important to take a more chronological look at the development of the American Gothic horror novel across the twentieth century, as well as some relevant parallel developments in American politics.

Twentieth-century American Gothic horror and its critical reception have both been bound up with psychoanalytic theory, particularly the Freudian notion of the return of the repressed, which lends itself easily to a literature of haunted places and imaginations. Jerrold E. Hogle credits Fiedler with using Freud to lend credibility to writing previously dismissed as unworthy of critical attention. Hogle, however, also notes how it was Marxist theory that allowed Fiedler to view the American mind as still 'haunted' by the Old World political hierarchies that it had overthrown. Citing Anna Sonser, he points out how this critical tradition has made 'both past and recent examples of US Gothic show, under a hyperfictional guise, that "American identity always comes back to social relations that are simultaneously economic and cultural"'.[18] At the start of the twentieth century, the prime economic and cultural issue facing the United States, as expressed in Gothic literary production, was that of the failure of Reconstruction. Authors such as Poe (albeit not an explicitly political writer) had provided a template for what would be termed the Southern Gothic, which would become the dominant critical reference point for the term 'Gothic' in the US, at least when applied to respected literary forms. While there was a parallel thriving tradition of what is now often termed 'weird' fiction (after H. P. Lovecraft's definition), this was largely associated with the pulp magazines. The Southern Gothic, on the other hand, intersected in more obvious ways with contemporary literary fashions, most prominently modernism, and is the mode most readily associated with the novel form. As Charles L. Crow points out, 'the modernist project, with its experiments in time and consciousness, was well suited to Southern Gothic's concern with history and guilt'.[19] The South's secession from the Union and the question of racial politics following

---

[18] Jerrold E. Hogle, 'The Progress of Theory and the Study of the American Gothic', in *A Companion to American Gothic*, ed. Charles L. Crow (Oxford: Wiley Blackwell, 2014), 7.

[19] Charles L. Crow, 'Southern American Gothic', in *The Cambridge Companion to American Gothic*, ed. Jeffrey Andrew Weinstock (Cambridge: Cambridge University Press, 2017), 146.

emancipation allowed authors such as William Faulkner and Erskine Caldwell to write intensely specific and personal novels that nonetheless showed the traces of a contested past.

Writing about these authors, Louis Palmer suggests 'that we see the form of Southern Gothic that emerges in the 1930s as a liminal discourse, one that occupies a space between solidly defined locations of class and race. Furthermore, it is a discourse that, like its medieval counterpart, the original Gothic art, uses the body as a grotesque signifier for material conditions.'[20] Faulkner especially 'deliberately appropriated the Gothic tradition'[21] in a novel such as *Absalom, Absalom!* (1936), which features a manor house metaphorically haunted by the ghosts of the past, family secrets (specifically racial mixing), incest, and murder. Nonetheless, the effect is not one of horror as such. Discussing the character of Quentin, who witnesses the burning of the Sutpen family's manor and the deaths of those within, Max Putzel writes: 'If the Gothic tale is intended to make us shiver deliciously at some imagined horror, that is certainly not what we feel as Quentin lies shaking bone-chilled in his dormitory bed.'[22] Faulkner's writing is centred on the human specificity as well as on a broader engagement with the identity of the South. Ambrose Bierce, in his short story 'The Death of Halpin Frayser' (1891), describes how his protagonist 'grew to such manhood as is attainable by a Southerner who does not care which way elections go'.[23] Bierce's satirical comment is an important reminder that the Southern Gothic, even decades later, cannot be anything but political. Southern Gothic frequently links the past to the present and portrays the attempt to move forward as frequently impossible, even when it is necessary. Flannery O'Connor's *Wise Blood* (1952) tackles the subject of religion in this way, as war veteran Hazel Motes sets himself up as a preacher in his new 'Church without Christ' in an attempt to abandon the notions of sin and guilt. It descends into a grotesque, and distinctly Gothic, chain of events that involves murder and self-blinding.

The relationship between the Southern Gothic and what we define as a Gothic horror novel is a complex one, and the Southern Gothic mode continues to feed into the genealogy of horror. Despite this, the Southern Gothic remains a distinct form characterized by themes drawn from classic

[20] Louis Palmer, 'Bourgeois Blues: Class, Whiteness, and Southern Gothic in Early Faulkner and Caldwell', *The Faulkner Journal* 22.1/2 (2006–7): 120–39, here 137.

[21] Ibid., 121.

[22] Max Putzel, 'What Is Gothic about Absalom, Absalom!', *Southern Literary Journal* 4.1 (1971): 18.

[23] Ambrose Bierce, 'The Death of Halpin Frayser', in *American Gothic from Salem Witchcraft to H. P. Lovecraft: An Anthology*, ed. Charles L. Crow (Oxford: Wiley-Blackwell, 2013), 220.

Gothic, but it retains a quality (or aspiration) to high literary form, complex characterization, and social commentary as essential elements. It can be distinguished from the sensationalist, exploitative, and escapist characteristics of what we might call the horror novel.

While Southern Gothic continues to influence the aesthetics and tone of popular fiction, as well as film and television, and has notable literary descendants, for example in the work of Cormac McCarthy, the horror novel has been formed from a different stream of the American Gothic tradition. In the United States especially, the Gothic found its natural home in the nineteenth century in periodicals, where the short story form condensed the narrative but also enabled great inventiveness in the hands of the best writers, such as Poe. In the first half of the twentieth century, horror became somewhat split from literary culture, notably modernism, although the connections between the themes and techniques of the authors concerned continue to be re-examined. Both responded to a rapidly changing world and to the necessary political upheavals brought about by a century of war and the collapse of the great European empires. These changes, of course, would put the United States at the forefront of global politics, but the fear and loathing engendered by any change can be seen in horror writing, particularly that of H. P. Lovecraft. Lovecraft published few novel-length works, and even those were serialized and can only really qualify as novellas, such as *At the Mountains of Madness* (1936) and the posthumously published *The Case of Charles Dexter Ward* (1941). Nonetheless, it is essential to consider the influence his work has had on subsequent authors who have adopted not only the specifics of his 'weird' style of writing but also a worldview that impacts on the politics of their fiction. Discerning these politics is a task that often falls to the literary historian, to infer from the author's personal beliefs the political leaning of the fiction, or to analyse the fiction itself in context. In the case of Lovecraft, this has caused considerable friction between critics who have claimed that Lovecraft was a xenophobe and racist, impacting on a reading of his work, and those who argue, as prominent Lovecraft scholar S. T. Joshi has consistently insisted, that he should be judged simply as a man of his time. This strikes at a core issue in examining the horror novel and politics: whether the very existence in the text of a monstrous 'Other' is inherently a political representation, or if it can be seen as either simply fantastical or appealing to some primal fear, universal to humankind.

Lovecraft's racial prejudice has been much noted, particularly in the context of his private correspondence, although also in early poetry and in

short stories such as 'He' (1926), where the lack of whiteness evident in a
New York overrun with immigrants is portrayed as inherently horrific:

> The throngs of people that seethed through the flume-like streets were
> squat, swarthy strangers with hardened faces and narrow eyes, shrewd
> strangers without dreams and without kinship to the scenes about them,
> who could never mean aught to a blue-eyed man of the old folk, with the
> love of fair green lanes and white New England village steeples in his
> heart.[24]

The fear of New York City and the immigrants that impacted on its
changing dynamics at the start of the twentieth century lines up with
Lovecraft's own life and views, and in this case the fiction can reasonably
be read as reflective of his nativist and conservative politics. Michel
Houellebecq reads this as feeding directly into his paranoid invocation of
place: 'a fundamental figure in his body of work – the idea of a grand,
titanic city, in whose foundations crawl repugnant nightmare beings'.[25]
Like Joshi, Houellebecq (whose own novels attack both liberalism and
corporatization) attempts to distance this attitude from a specific manifestation of racism and towards a generalized misanthropy. The fear of
sinister non-white Others and an appeal to a rural idyll of blue-eyed white
folk, however, is clearly very difficult to separate from the racial politics of
Germany at the time (with Lovecraft expressing an early admiration for
Hitler) – and, of course, of a segregated and often nativist United States.
Elsewhere in his work, there is a consistent fear of racial mixing, notably in
'The Shadow over Innsmouth' (1936), where villagers of a small New
England town are found to have been interbreeding with fish-like creatures
known as 'Deep Ones', producing a distinct 'Innsmouth look'.[26] The
parallels with contemporary eugenics and notions of racial purity are not
only clear but directly addressed in the text, with references to influence
from 'queer ports in Africa, Asia, the South Seas, and everywhere else',[27]
leading Steffan Wöll to read the village as 'a signifier for the crisis of the
American immigrant society and melting pot narratives of the 1920s'.[28]

It is important to note the enormous influence of Lovecraft on subsequent horror authors, because of the way in which these aesthetics and

---

[24] H. P. Lovecraft, 'He', in *H. P. Lovecraft: The Complete Fiction*, ed. S. T. Joshi (New York: Barnes &
Noble, 2008), 332–3.
[25] Michel Houellebecq, *H. P. Lovecraft: Against the World, Against Life*, trans. Dorna Khazeni
(London: Gollancz, 2005), 103.
[26] H. P. Lovecraft, 'The Shadow Over Innsmouth', in Joshi, 821.   [27] Ibid., 810.
[28] Steffan Wöll, 'The Horrors of the Oriental Space and Language in H. P. Lovecraft's "The Shadow
over Innsmouth"', *Zeitschrift für Anglistik und Amerikanistik* 68.3: 241.

sentiments feed through so strongly, for example in the abject terrors of an author such as Stephen King. The novel *It* (1986), for example, centres on a malevolent evil threatening the small town of Derry, Maine. Most prominently appearing in the form of a clown called Pennywise, the creature is in fact a shapeshifter, originally from outer space, echoing Lovecraft's immensely powerful and malign alien beings such as the iconic creature of 'The Call of Cthulhu' (1928). If the mythology of the horror novel is rooted in early twentieth-century fears of invasion and miscegenation, then this presents a deep challenge to its claims to a kind of benign, even apolitical, liberal humanism. Despite the shadow he casts over American horror, Lovecraft is only one author, and the tendency towards a fearful othering goes back further in the Gothic horror tradition. Tabish Khair argues that the Gothic, originating in a well-educated and cosmopolitan social scene in eighteenth-century England, was largely about the ways in which these authors responded to 'a world of many invasions, ambiguities, uncertainties, all of which were brought home to them not only by their knowledge of Empire but also by the physical presence of Empire in metropolitan spaces in England'.[29] Thus, the non-white Other becomes a locus of fear, even if this fear is displaced into fantastical forms of monstrosity. It is perhaps because of this characteristic of the Gothic mode that while it does not always engage overtly with political discussions, social change and questions of identity and belonging are never far below the surface of its seemingly escapist narratives.

The horror novel as a distinct entity arises in the postwar United States as a response to the social and political circumstances of the time. Cold War fears of a communist invasion, either physical or ideological, are evident in popular films of the time, for example *Invasion of the Body Snatchers* (1956), where the invading enemy replaces humans with alien 'pod people'. The film can be read as an allegory for the Soviet threat, or conversely for the stifling social conformity that arose in the US in opposition to it. Horror novels, too, in juggling their roles as genre fiction and as a response to the social conditions they arise within, often show an ambivalent attitude. Richard Matheson's *I Am Legend* (1954) is a good example of this. Ostensibly a vampire novel, it is filled with racially coded undertones that reflect its writing on the cusp of the Civil Rights era. *I Am Legend* takes its cue from the blending of science fiction and horror that characterized weird fiction, giving pseudo-scientific explanations for the

[29] Tabish Khair, *The Gothic, Postcolonialism and Otherness: Ghosts from Elsewhere* (Basingstoke: Palgrave Macmillan, 2015), 41.

vampire myth and grounding it in a world built up around the character of its protagonist, Robert Neville. Tormented by the death of his wife and daughter, and seemingly alone, Neville barricades himself in his house at night and goes on daytime missions to destroy as many vampires as he can while they sleep. The threshold of Neville's house becomes not only a physical barrier but an ideological one, a barrier against contamination, not so much by the vampire plague (he is immune) as by what the infected humans represent. The way in which Neville is described gives some clues as to what he might be afraid of:

> He was a tall man, thirty-six, born of English-German stock, his features undistinguished except for the long, determined mouth and the bright blue of his eyes, which moved now over the charred ruins of the houses on each side of his. He'd burned them down to prevent *them* from jumping on his roof from the adjacent ones.[30]

Especially in the immediate postwar period, it is difficult to claim such a purposefully Aryan hero as an ideologically neutral protagonist. Not only that, but the inflected '*them*' in this context is more usually seen in implied racist discourse. In addition, the vampires are continually categorized by Neville as 'dark' or 'black', despite them being described elsewhere as bloodless and pale. Early on in the novel, Neville feels dejected: 'He sank down on the couch and sat there, shaking his head slowly. It was no use; they'd beaten him, the black bastards had beaten him.'[31] In the end, Neville is captured by a group of vampires who have developed a medication to curb their symptoms, and who have come to see him as the true monster, due to his daytime killing sprees. If we do read Neville's story as one of the dominant order of white supremacy being replaced by a new one, then it is a change that the narrative tentatively embraces, or at least portrays as inevitable: 'and the dark men dragged his lifeless body from the house. Into the night. Into the world that was theirs and no longer his.'[32]

If horror tends to avoid taking a direct political stance, it does at least cling to a certain reliance on conservative values in order to set up a dichotomy of normal versus monstrous in the text. As US society shifted in the cultural upheavals of the 1960s, the most successful horror novels dramatized these conflicts in oblique yet spectacular fashion. As young Americans protested against the Vietnam War, racial injustice, and restrictive sexual mores, mainstream horror novels moved away from the

[30] Richard Matheson, *I Am Legend* (London: Gollancz, 2002), 8. [31] Ibid., 29–30.
[32] Ibid., 153.

speculative excesses of the weird tradition (which continued to flourish in cult fandom and comic books) and drew on older American obsessions with the intrusion of evil into the everyday. In one direction of this impulse, a novel such as Robert Bloch's *Psycho* (1959) gives a secular vision of evil. Here, seemingly mild-mannered Norman Bates has developed a split personality, internalizing a twisted version of his mother's persona, driving him to murder. Bates, like the tired motel he runs, situated on a stretch of road outdated by the construction of the new interstate highways, is trapped in an old value system that no longer serves him in a changing world. His shame over his lack of a nuclear family and over his own sexuality is what marks him out as deviant. Similarly, Shirley Jackson's *The Haunting of Hill House* (1959) has its protagonist Eleanor Vance driven insane by an inability to take advantage of the possibilities opening up for a young woman in American society; she is driven instead to a dangerous identification with a seemingly haunted house. The idea that someone might be dangerously different, but living among us, is clearly tied to Cold War fears of subversion, but also harks back to nineteenth-century Gothic writing. Nathaniel Hawthorne's 'Young Goodman Brown' (1835) depicts a young man going into the forest at night and discovering that his respectable Puritan community is engaged in devil worship. This is something he has been complicit in through his motivations from the start, but he is nonetheless disturbed to find that his peers, and specifically his wife, have been involved in this heresy all along. Hawthorne's short story is ambiguous in its presentation of the reality of the supernatural, but Paul J. Hurley reads this as a wilful act: 'Goodman Brown sees evil wherever he looks. He sees it because he wants to see it.'[33] This pessimistic tone is one that characterizes much Gothic horror writing in the 1960s and into the 1970s, or certainly those works that strike a chord with a wide readership – notably, popular novels such as Ira Levin's *Rosemary's Baby* (1967) and William Peter Blatty's *The Exorcist* (1971).

Bailey argues that it is at this point in American literary history that the horror novel is cemented as a recognizable entity, noting that 'writers like William Peter Blatty, Ira Levin, and Stephen King ... not insignificantly, would soon come to identify themselves as genre writers, horror writers, in a way that would have been alien to most of their predecessors'.[34] King has become one of the world's bestselling authors and his work has both a cult

---

[33] Paul J. Hurley, 'Young Goodman Brown's "Heart of Darkness"', *American Literature* 37.4 (1966): 418.
[34] Bailey, 47.

following among genre fans and a wide readership, as well as many successful film adaptations produced from his work. Despite drawing consistently on horror, and specifically on many of the authors mentioned here, King's concerns, across dozens of novels and hundreds of short stories, are broad. Don Herron points out that, from the start, King has embedded into his work 'important adult concerns about politics, relationships, or economics, which invest an otherwise popular novel or film with serious intent'.[35] *The Shining* (1977) is a good example of his engagement with broader themes such as the nuclear family, masculinity, and the meaning of work within the American capitalist system. The protagonist, Jack Torrance, is an aspiring playwright who has lost his job teaching English after assaulting a student in frustration. He has suffered from alcoholism and the trauma of an abusive past at the hands of his father. He takes a caretaking job looking after the Overlook Hotel in the Rocky Mountains over winter, taking along his wife Wendy and young son Danny. The hotel transpires to be a kind of 'psychic battery'[36] that has stored all of its own past traumas, such as mafia killings and drug overdoses, as well as the previous caretaker's brutal murder of his own family. These 'ghosts', bound up with the presence of the hotel itself, torment Jack and eventually possess him, driving him to attempt to kill Wendy and Danny. The plot is complicated by Danny's psychic power, the 'shining' of the title, which allows him to read minds and to see into the past and the future. Politically, the novel comments on the aspirations and realities of the United States, with the hotel reflecting both the grandeur and the seediness of the capitalist American Dream. Despite the prevalence of social commentary in his work, the marketing of King as a horror genre author tends to flatten out and conceal this aspect. He has even complained about this misunderstanding in interviews, writing of his novel *Needful Things* (1991) – in which a junk shop owner sells people whatever they desire most, but for the hidden cost of their soul – that 'I thought I'd written a satire of Reaganomics in America in the eighties' but that this was lost on most readers and reviewers.[37]

---

[35] Don Herron, 'Stephen King: The Good, the Bad, and the Academic', in *Kingdom of Fear: The World of Stephen King*, ed. Tim Underwood and Chuck Miller (San Francisco: Underwood-Miller, 1986), 133.

[36] King, *Danse Macabre*, 297.

[37] Lisa Rogak, *Haunted Heart: The Life and Times of Stephen King* (London: JR Books, 2009), cited in Kelly Konda, '*Needful Things* at 25: Reflecting on Castle Rock's "Final" Story', *We Minored in Film* [online] https://weminoredinfilm.com/2018/08/26/needful-things-at-25-reflecting-on-castle-rocks-final-story/

The racial politics of the United States are perhaps the clearest indicator of what constitutes horror. Given that the historical horrors of the African American experience transcend fictional ghost stories, this has an impact on how we might read the fiction. The idea that the typical horror narrative is rooted in a particular kind of white suburban experience is pointed out by Bailey in a discussion of Eddie Murphy's 1983 comedy show *Delirious*. Murphy's jokes point out the absurdity of the white protagonists in films such as *The Amityville Horror* (1979) and *Poltergeist* (1982) who refuse to accept what is happening and flee their clearly haunted houses. Bailey notes that 'the subversive horror of the routine grows from our shared awareness of a central but unpleasant truth of American culture: blacks live in a fundamentally different world from whites and the foreclosed possibilities of that world do not allow the haunted house story to operate by its usual rules'.[38] In fact, it is in the horror novel's very avoidance of unpleasant social realities that a conservative tendency to maintain the status quo might well predominate. Horror, however, can be used to comment on the past and to instigate social change in the present. Toni Morrison's *Beloved* (1987) stands out as an example of late twentieth-century Gothic horror writing with a clear social conscience. Morrison uses the framework of the ghost story to present a novel about the agony of the past. *Beloved* is based not on myth, but on the real-life story of Margaret Garner, who killed her own daughter rather than have her returned to slavery. Sethe, who has been enslaved in the past, has to reckon with her own repressed guilt and trauma when a woman whom she believes to be a flesh-and-blood incarnation of her deceased daughter returns to her. *Beloved* is undeniably Gothic and has much of horror in it, but it defies the codified conventions of the horror genre novel to produce something more politically engaged and potentially transformative.

The transgressive potential of Gothic horror novels has perhaps been present throughout their production. Clive Barker, creator of *Hellraiser* (1987), views the true nature of the horror novel as that of the imaginative power of the fantastical, rather than the conventional narrative structure that bounds it. Writing about King, he claims: '[I]f we once embrace the vision offered in such works, if we once allow the metaphors a home in our psyches, the subversion is under way.'[39] Gina Wisker points to the potential of horror narratives as 'a vehicle for imaginative change, equality,

---

[38] Bailey, 49.   [39] Clive Barker, 'Surviving the Ride', in Underwood and Miller, 59.

rewriting forms and relations of power'.[40] This has certainly proved to be the case in the twenty-first century, where the writing of H. P. Lovecraft, for example, has been both reimagined and critiqued in novels such as Victor LaValle's *The Ballad of Black Tom* (2016), Matt Ruff's *Lovecraft Country* (2016), and Paul La Farge's *The Night Ocean* (2017). Without diminishing the vastly different perspectives offered by Gothic horror novels through oversimplification, the most accurate way to summarize their politics might not be so different from any other form of fiction. The Gothic horror novel reflects, and often actively exploits, the fears of society at any given time. In its compulsive focus on bringing the repressed and the abject to the surface, and often showing a disregard for notions of good taste, it has proven to be particularly revealing of truths that are politically unpalatable and yet crucial to examine.

[40] Gina Wisker, *Horror Fiction: An Introduction* (New York: Continuum, 2005), 10.

CHAPTER 14

Postmodern Metafiction

Rob Turner

> Doubt is our product, since it is the best means of competing
> with the 'body of fact' that exists in the minds of the general public.
>
> Brown & Williamson Tobacco Corporation,
> on smoking and public health (1969)[1]

Since the leaking of this infamous memo, half a century ago, our political
culture has been shaped by a tide of misinformation and bullshit. From the
repeated efforts to dispute the scale (and even the existence) of a human-
induced climate emergency, to the 'alternative facts' that Kellyanne
Conway offered to Chuck Todd on NBC back in 2017, the weaponization
of doubt by the (far) right is wearily familiar. Against this backdrop, with
fabulists crawling off the page and into power, the appetite for postmodern
metafiction has steadily waned. As Jeet Heer put it in *The New Republic*,
the US elected its 'First Postmodern President' with Donald Trump.[2]
Does anybody still want to read John Barth?

Of course, there were those voicing unease with postmodernism long
before the election of the forty-fifth president. Back in 2008, Zadie Smith
noted the widespread view that 'the American metafiction that stood in
opposition to Realism has been relegated to a safe corner of literary history,
to be studied in postmodernity modules, and dismissed, by our most
famous public critics, as a fascinating failure'.[3] Others have been more
explicit about the political impulse that spurred this shift. David James, in
the introduction to his study of contemporary anglophone fiction, dis-
misses the work of postmodern novelists such as Barth, writing of the need

---

[1] Cited in Naomi Oreskes and Erik M. Conway, *Merchants of Doubt* (London: Bloomsbury, 2012),
34.
[2] Jeet Heer, 'America's First Postmodern President', *The New Republic*, 8 July 2017.
[3] Zadie Smith, 'Two Paths for the Novel', *New York Review of Books*, 20 November 2008.

to 'reinvigorate modernist aesthetics in response to politically abortive metafiction'.[4]

Concerns about the slipperiness of metafiction, and its alleged politics, were being raised even during the supposed heyday of the form. In the mid-1980s, for instance, Leslie Silko wrote a damning review of Louise Erdrich's second novel, *The Beet Queen* (1986), in which she claimed that

> Erdrich's 'metafictional' devices are ... an outgrowth of academic, post-modern, so-called experimental influences ... Self-referential writing has an ethereal clarity and shimmering beauty because no history or politics intrudes to muddy the well of pure necessity contained within language itself.[5]

Across seven pages, Silko goes on to attack *The Beet Queen* as solipsistic, disengaged, and conservative. Crucially, however, at no point is she troubled with the issue of whether the events depicted in Erdrich's book are *literally true*. Despite the tempting overlap with contemporary post-truth debates, the critical question of the politics of metafiction is not simply reducible to the need to guard readers against 'alternative facts'; realist fictions, after all, are still fictions. Instead, Silko urges us to consider the workings of 'language itself', and what she goes on to call the 'oddly rarefied place' of the metafictional novelist's psyche.[6]

To grasp the roots of this peculiar style, the supposedly diseased plant from which Erdrich is said to be an 'outgrowth', it is worth turning back to the essay that gave the form its name. In the opening chapter of his first non-fiction book, *Fiction and the Figures of Life* (1970), William H. Gass turns his attention to the 'metatheorems' that can be found in contemporary mathematics and logic, before finding an analogy in the recent fictions of 'Borges, Barth, and Flann O'Brien'. These dizzying texts are constructed, he points out, from 'forms of fiction [that] serve as the material upon which further forms can be imposed. Indeed, many of the so-called antinovels are really metafictions'.[7] As well as coining the term (and offering a mini-canon of metafictional authors), Gass's essay also contains an early glimpse of the strange, rarefied mode of literary authorship that so troubles Silko:

[4] David James, *Modernist Futures: Innovation and Inheritance in the Contemporary Novel* (Cambridge: Cambridge University Press, 2012), 10.
[5] Leslie Marmon Silko, [Untitled review of *The Beet Queen*], *Studies in American Indian Literatures* 10.4 (1986): 177–84, here 177–9.
[6] Ibid., 180.
[7] William Gass, 'Philosophy and the Form of Fiction' in *Fiction and the Figures of Life* (New York: Alfred A. Knopf, 1970), 24–5.

Before us is the empty page, the deep o'er which, like God, though modestly, we brood. But that white page, what is it? Perhaps it is the ideally empty consciousness of the reader – a dry wineskin or a *tabula rasa*. And if, as authors, we think this way, then what we want is a passive mind and, as in love, an utterly receptive woman.[8]

Fusing authorial godliness with the purity of a blank page, the act of writing is transformed by Gass into an erotic vision of individual sublimity, leading to (male) mastery over an imagined (and femininized) reader. Within a few pages, the fantasy has darkened further, as he teases out the implications of such an omnipotent position: '[I]f Mary sickened, the cause was God, and if Mary died, it was God who called her Home . . . In the *story* of Mary, if Mary dies, the novelist killed her.'[9]

There is a comic edge to these lines, but Gass's sexualization of literary production picks up a misogynistic thread that runs through his early writings.[10] These uglier elements of his work may not seem relevant to the politics of metafiction more broadly, but similar power fantasies can be seen lurking within many canonical metafictions. During the 1970s and 1980s, for instance, most critics joined Linda Hutcheon in taking *The French Lieutenant's Woman* by the British writer John Fowles (a text that made a huge impact in the US) as 'one of the best metafictional examples' and a 'model' for the form.[11] Throughout that book – with its tellingly possessive title – the author is held up as a supreme presence, asserting control over the page. As Brian McHale points out:

> [W]hat is ultimately real in the ontological structure of *The French Lieutenant's Woman*, if not the author's performance in creating that world? The author occupies an ontological level superior to his world; by breaking the frame around his world, the author foregrounds his own superior reality. The metafictional gesture of frame-breaking is, in other words, a form of superrealism.[12]

---

[8] Ibid., 12–13.   [9] Ibid., 18–19, emphasis added.

[10] In 'Philosophy and the Future of Fiction', the 'sequel' to the essay cited above, Gass offers the following anecdote concerning his early work: 'I once conceived that the body of the text of one of my books, *Willie Master's Lonesome Wife* [1968], was the body of a woman. Thus when you opened the text and entered it, you were entering a woman. Northwestern University Press, the publisher, didn't know what was happening. I thought we should put a condom in as a bookmark so that you would be able to enter the book safely. Since the basic character was a woman of low morals, this might very well have been needed.' William Gass, 'Philosophy and the Future of Fiction', *Syracuse Scholar* 1.2 (1980): 10.

[11] Linda Hutcheon, *Narcissistic Narrative: The Metafictional Paradox*, 2nd edition (Waterloo: Wilfried Laurier University Press, 2013 [1980]), 57.

[12] Brian McHale, *Postmodernist Fiction* (London: Routledge, 1987), 197.

According to McHale's 'superrealist' reading, the seemingly destabilizing touches that disrupt a metafictional text like *The French Lieutenant's Woman* – such as the celebrated moment in the thirteenth chapter when Fowles admits that '[t]his story I am telling is all imagination. These characters I create never existed outside my own mind' – serve, in fact, to illustrate the author's omniscient position, and to assert his mastery.[13]

Shortly after Fowles's book was published, Robert Scholes joined the small chorus of American critics celebrating this kind of authorial self-elevation, writing of an elite circle 'working in the rarefied air of metafiction', an admiring phrase that unwittingly anticipates Silko's attack on Erdrich.[14] Across the early 1970s, a canon of white, male American writers came to inhabit this lofty space. Scholes borrowed Gass's terminology, but others reached for other (dramatically capitalized) neologisms: 'For me,' Richard Federman announced in 1975, 'the only fiction that still means something today is that kind of fiction that tries to explore the possibilities of fiction ... the kind of fiction that constantly renews our faith in man's imagination and not in man's distorted vision of reality ... This I call SURFICTION.'[15]

Surveying the American metafictions (and surfictions) of the 1970s, it becomes clear that the task of reading such texts politically requires close attention to the unstated power relations that underlie the authors' repeated claims to 'superrealism' and mastery. Across these early self-reflexive trips through 'man's imagination', a recycled god complex crops up repeatedly. Every now and then, the worn trope is played for comic effect: in Kurt Vonnegut's *Breakfast of Champions* (1973), for instance – as McHale points out – the narrator can be seen 'flaunt[ing] his godlike omniscience by quoting bust, waist, and hip measurements for every female character, and penis length and diameter for every male character'.[16] Towards the end of the book, Vonnegut's debased god barges into the fictive world, and speaks directly to his protagonist, Kilgore Trout:

> Count Tolstoi freed his serfs. Thomas Jefferson freed his slaves. I am going to set at liberty all the literary characters who have served me so loyally during my writing career ... Arise, Mr. Trout, you are free, you are *free*.[17]

[13] John Fowles, *The French Lieutenant's Woman* (London: Vintage, 2012 [1969]), 103.
[14] Robert Scholes, 'Metafiction', *Iowa Review* 1.4 (1970): 115.
[15] Richard Federman, ed., *Surfiction: Fiction Now ... and Tomorrow* (Chicago: Swallow Press, 1975), 7.
[16] McHale, 210.   [17] Kurt Vonnegut, *Breakfast of Champions* (New York: Dell, 1973), 293–4.

Once again, we find the fantasy of absolute authorial mastery. But here it is joined by something else: a nightmarish history is peeking through the godly facade. This is a mastery with deep roots, as a white, heterosexual, American male indulges himself by controlling (and toying with releasing) his indentured subjects.

As the metafictional master dissolves into a benevolent plantation owner, the essential whiteness of this model becomes unmistakable. There are echoes here of a longer history of authorial control and political power, a line that can be traced back to the modernist era. T. S. Eliot, for example, famously felt that Joyce's use of Homeric myth was 'simply a way of controlling, of ordering, of giving a shape and a significance to the ... anarchy that is contemporary history'.[18] Even more striking, perhaps, is the case of William Faulkner and his imagined Yoknapatawpha, a fictional reimagining of his home county of Lafayette, Mississippi. As the author explained in a 1956 interview:

> I discovered that my own little postage stamp of native soil was worth writing about and that I would never live long enough to exhaust it ... It opened up a gold mine of other people, so I created a cosmos of my own. I can move these people around like God.[19]

The image of a white southerner, owning a 'gold mine of other people', can be read as a troubling precursor to Vonnegut, anticipating his winking association between author-gods and plantation owners.

Examining the whiteness of the postmodern canon, Madelyn Jablon notes that, in their influential studies of metafiction, 'theorists such as Robert Scholes, Patricia Waugh, and Linda Hutcheon omit reference to the tradition of self-consciousness in black fiction'.[20] The issue is not solved, however, simply by adding Black writers to an existing list of names: as we have seen, the whiteness of the form is embedded in its central assumptions and methods. 'It is the challenge of the black tradition to critique this relation of indenture,' Henry Louis Gates, Jr. points out: 'I once thought our most important gesture [was] to *master* the canon of criticism, to *imitate* and *apply* it, but I now believe that we must turn to the black tradition itself to develop [new] theories.'[21]

---

[18] T. S. Eliot, *Selected Prose*, ed. Frank Kermode (London: Faber & Faber, 1975), 177.
[19] Philip Gourevitch, ed., *The Paris Review Interviews. Vol. 2* (Edinburgh: Canongate, 2007), 57.
[20] Madelyn Jablon, *Black Metafiction: Self-Consciousness in African American Literature* (Iowa City: University of Iowa Press, 1997), 3.
[21] Henry Louis Gates, Jr., 'Canon-Formation and the Afro-American Tradition' in *Afro-American Literary Study in the 1990s*, ed. Houston A. Baker, Jr. and Patricia Redmond (Chicago: University of Chicago Press, 1989), 25.

Outlining his alternative tradition, one of the Ur-metafictions that Gates identifies is *The Interesting Narrative of the Life of Olaudah Equiano* (1789), drawing attention to the trope of the 'Talking Book' and highlighting the fact that Equiano 'allows it to function as an allegory of his own act of fashioning an Anglo-African self out of words. Equiano's usage amounts to a fiction about the making of a fiction.'[22] Gates demonstrates that African American literary and musical cultures are built upon an 'extraordinarily self-reflexive tradition, a tradition exceptionally conscious of its history', and he proceeds to trace lines of influence from Equiano's foundational act of linguistic self-fashioning to the central role that textual production plays in Black autobiographies of the following century, such as *Narrative of the Life of Frederick Douglass, an American Slave*.[23]

As we head back to the postmodern era with this model in mind, it is worth noting (in passing) that, by the 1980s, the self-reflexive tradition Gates describes had become almost ubiquitous in the lyrical techniques of early hip-hop. More than other forms of popular song, rap foregrounds self-narration and self-fashioning, as heard in the real-time accounts of an MC's skill that will make or break an onstage battle ('Ain't another MC who can rhyme like this / Not your mother or your father, aunt, brother, or your sis').[24] Intricately self-reflexive (and quasi-metafictional) gestures can be found in the grooves of mid-1980s rap albums, such as the surreal 'Talking Book' account of a rhyme snaking through sonic technology on the opening cut of LL Cool J's debut, *Radio* (1985): 'Circulating through your radio, non-stop / I'm lookin' at the wires behind the cassette / And now I'm on the right, standing on the eject / Wearing light blue Pumas, a whole lotta gold.' These lyrical snippets are a reminder of the strength of the African American self-reflexive tradition in the postmodern era, a fact that Gates recently acknowledged in a new introduction to a reissue of *The Signifying Monkey*: 'through the hip-hop generation of musicians, formal signifying is alive and well'.[25]

Turning back to prose metafictions, though, there remains the very real question as to how this self-reflexive tradition can speak back to the grand

---

[22] Henry Louis Gates, Jr., *The Signifying Monkey: A Theory of African American Literary Criticism. 25th Anniversary Edition* (Oxford: Oxford University Press, 2014 [1988]), 171.

[23] Henry Louis Gates, Jr., 'Introduction to *The Signifying Monkey*' [1988], reprinted in Winston Napier, ed., *African American Literary Theory: A Reader* (New York: NYU Press, 2000), 339–47, here 343.

[24] Kool Moe Dee, performing live at Harlem World's Christmas Celebration, December 1981.

[25] Gates, *The Signifying Monkey*, xxxiii.

fantasies of (white) authorial control discussed above. In early studies, most accounts of postmodernist fiction included no Black writers; if space was made for a single name, it tended to be Ishmael Reed, and even his inclusion was often seen as precarious.[26] Discussing Reed's work, back in 1974, Neil Schmitz saw his books as being awkwardly poised between traditional and innovative formal modes:

> To turn from the stiffening form of the traditional novel . . . only to fall into [the] elaborate glosses of metafiction is an artistic fate Reed has taken great pains to avoid. And therein lies the problem that has informed his subsequent fiction.[27]

In any case, for Reed himself, the association with canonical postmodernists was unwelcome. Seeing his publisher's attempts to link *Mumbo Jumbo* with the work of white writers, the novelist sent Doubleday a furious letter in September 1972, demanding that 'allusions to people like Burroughs, Golding and Vonnegut in ad copy cease. I have nothing in common with the gentlemen; it is made to look as if they are masters and I their apprentice.'[28] Crucially, the discussion turns immediately to the question of mastery, as Reed reiterates his steadfast opposition to (white) authority, something that had already led him to drop out of formal education a decade earlier. As he put it: 'I just didn't want to be a slave to somebody else's reading lists.'[29]

For Reed, the goal is not to reject individual authorial mastery *as such*. (Indeed, it is almost the opposite: he is refusing to be subordinated to other authors.) According to bell hooks, this position falls short. Writing in the first issue of the *Postmodern Culture* journal, she looks back to modernist master narratives and suggests that, during the 1960s, 'black power movements were influenced by perspectives that could be easily labelled modernist. Certainly many of the ways black folks addressed issues of identity conformed to a modernist universalizing agenda.'[30] Querying this, she points to a more profound rejection of mastery:

[26] Scholes's *Fabulation and Metafiction* (1979) touches on Reed's *The Last Days of Louisiana Red* (1974); Hutcheon omits Reed from *Narcissistic Narrative: The Metafictional Paradox* (1980) but includes a brief discussion of his work in *The Politics of Postmodernism* (1989).
[27] Neil Schmitz, 'Neo-HooDoo: The Experimental Fiction of Ishmael Reed', *Twentieth Century Literature* 20.2 (1974): 126.
[28] Ishmael Reed, 'Letter (September 1972)', cited in John K. Young, *Black Writers, White Publishers: Marketplace Politics in Twentieth-Century African American Literature* (Jackson: University Press of Mississippi, 2006), 71–2.
[29] Ishmael Reed, interviewed by John O'Brien [1972], in Bruce Dick and Amritjit Singh, eds, *Conversations with Ishmael Reed* (Jackson: University Press of Mississippi, 1995), 28.
[30] bell hooks, 'Postmodern Blackness', *Postmodern Culture* 1.1 (1990).

> If radical postmodernist thinking is to have a transformative impact then a
> critical break with the notion of 'authority' as 'mastery over' must not
> simply be a rhetorical device, it must be reflected in habits of being,
> including styles of writing ... This is not a reinscription of modernist
> master narratives of authority.[31]

The challenge of negotiating postmodernism as a Black writer is not
simply to swap names or replace reading lists (tellingly, Reed's 1972 letter
continues, 'I tried to make my influences clear by publishing the biblio at
the back of the book'); instead, hooks insists that a fundamentally new
mode of writing must be developed, extending all the way down to the
level of the sentence.

Returning to 1970s metafiction with this manifesto in mind, there is
one standout text that might be seen to enact, stylistically and methodo-
logically, a 'critical break with the notion of "authority" as "mastery over"'.
As hooks herself has remarked, '*Thank god there was Samuel Delany
there.*'[32] Delany's *Dhalgren* (1975), a work of surreal science fiction,
remains the most ambitious (and expansive) metafictional experiment of
its age, yet it has been marginalized or ignored, even in recent studies of
the form.[33] In light of this relative obscurity, it is perhaps worth giving a
brief account of the text: *Dhalgren*'s blurred plot follows a nameless
protagonist into a fictional Midwestern city, Bellona, where an unexplained catastrophe has occurred. As the book unfolds – or, more properly,
disintegrates – this confused hero dabbles with poetry, writes a journal,
and spends time having sex and hanging out with street gangs. Text slowly
overlaps with text, time scrolls forward and back, pronouns shift, and we
drift through a burned-out cityscape that feels like it could almost be
another planet, or the dying Detroit.

The continued near absence of *Dhalgren* from the critical discussion of
postmodern metafiction may reflect some lingering doubts in the academy
(at least until fairly recently) upon being presented with texts perceived as
genre fiction. Delany himself has remarked on this, noting that such
'worrying about the purity of the genres on any level is even more futile

---

[31] Ibid.
[32] Adam Fitzgerald, 'Don't Romanticize Science Fiction: An Interview with Samuel Delany', *Literary Hub*, 4 December 2017.
[33] Delany's novel is absent from the classic surveys of metafictional form (Hutcheon and Scholes), and, more surprisingly, from the pages of the leading studies of Black self-reflexive fictions (Gates and Jablon). This gap may close with time; *Dhalgren* receives two fleeting mentions in the most recent book-length account of American metafiction, Josh Toth's *Truth and Metafiction: Plasticity and Renewal in American Narrative* (New York: Bloomsbury, 2021), 118, 130.

than worrying about the purity of the races'.[34] On a more pragmatic level, the gap might also simply reflect the scale of the book (the first edition runs to 879 pages). In his influential account of the form, Scholes insists that 'when extended, metafiction must either lapse into a more fundamental mode of fiction or risk losing all fictional interest ... Metafiction, then, tends towards brevity.'[35] Abandoning this call for concision, Delany takes obvious delight in 'risk[ing] losing all fictional interest', cheerfully unpicking any sense of authority or unity. The disorder even extends to the printed book itself: as Teresa Ebert has observed, the novel exists in a state of flux, with the writer making numerous changes in subsequent reprintings over the years, additions and deletions that 'destabilize the text and emphasize its postmodern preoccupation with the on-going *process* rather than the finished *product*'.[36]

What makes *Dhalgren* such a key text in re-examining the politics of postmodern metafiction, though, isn't its scale or its perplexing editorial history; it's the fact that the text is so committed to asking the question of what self-reflexive writing means for an American living outside the 'rarefied air' of the canon. 'I am black,' Delany announced in an essay published within a few months of the novel. 'I have spent time in a mental hospital, and much of my adult life, for both sexual and social reasons, has been passed on society's margins.'[37] Elsewhere, in a pseudonymous review of his own novel, he makes the point even more directly: 'Delany's basic precept is that today there is no social center; and Delany's hero is a socially marginal naïf, in a world where there are only margins.'[38]

In this self-review (itself a kind of metafiction), Delany invites us to reconsider the opening of *Dhalgren*, using the passage to distance his work from the mastery exhibited by the high modernists:

> The novel begins with a clear recall of the myth of Daphne. But when, in the next scene, Kid, about to discuss the incident with the truck-driver who

---

[34] Samuel R. Delany, Sinda Gregory, and Larry McCaffery, 'The Semiology of Silence', *Science Fiction Studies* 14.2 (1987): 134–64, here 142.

[35] Scholes, 'Metafiction', 106–7.

[36] Teresa L. Ebert, 'The Convergence of Postmodern Innovative Fiction and Science Fiction: An Encounter with Samuel R. Delany's Technotopia', *Poetics Today* 1.4 (1980): 91–104, here 101. Ebert admits (in a footnote on p. 101) that Delany has corresponded with her, trying to stress the relatively low-level nature of his revisions and alterations. He has since, however, made even more changes to the text.

[37] Samuel R. Delany, 'Of Sex, Objects, Signs, Systems, Sales, SF, and Other Things' [1975], in *Straits of Messina* (Seattle: Serconia Press, 1989), 50.

[38] K. Leslie Steiner [Delany], 'Some Remarks Toward a Reading of Dhalgren' [1975], in *Straits of Messina*, 89.

has given him a lift, thinks, 'No, the Daphne bit would not pass–', we suspect Delany is also telling us that we cannot discuss this novel as though it were a contemporary *Ulysses*, i.e., a novel with a coherent referent myth ... It won't pass.[39]

Where Eliot had celebrated Joyce's use of myth as providing 'a way of controlling [the] anarchy' of contemporary history, Delany clearly rejects this. In his metafiction, things will not cohere. The poet-hero starts to unspool before our eyes, derailed by amnesia, aphasia, and drugs, as the prose snaps into little fragments and chattering spirals: 'how many different meanings could reside in one gesture. The thought prickled through his stuttering ering ing mind.'[40] The broken type in this line is fairly typical: Delany is preoccupied by the (near-infinite) obstacles to accurate representation, including the struggle to reproduce vernacular dialects. At one point, his protagonist wonders how what he calls the 'mauled and apocopated music' of a Black character's voice could be 'fixed to a page with roman letters and standard marks of elision? He decided: It can't.'[41]

In the final pages of *Dhalgren*, the book starts to decay yet further, bristling with marginal notes and crossed-out words, as Delany replicates the cacophonous *mise-en-page* of his hero's contradictory 'plague journal'. Picking gingerly at this material in his self-review, the novelist feigns surprise at 'what a substantial amount of the machinery of this very long book [is] given to debunking the traditional authority on which ... various textual privileges are founded'.[42] The heap of inconsistencies and oddities slowly erodes our sense, he notes, of a 'real recounting of real happenings written by a real person in real time'.[43] Rather than sitting, with Gass, before an 'empty page, the deep o'er which, like God, though modestly, we brood', this spiralling text leaves the reader with a feeling of helplessness before its messy paper chaos. The effect is hypnotic, and overwhelming. As Bunny, a male erotic dancer, remarks to Delany's metafictional hero: 'You've written a beautiful book – though I don't understand a line.'[44]

Returning to the founding issue of *Postmodern Culture*, and to bell hooks's manifesto for postmodern Blackness, it is worth acknowledging another, less frequently cited, essay from the same volume. Joining the call for a chorus of new and oppositional voices, Kathy Acker's 'Dead Doll Humility' offers a stinging response to the power trips of white heterosexual author-gods:

---

[39] Ibid., 65.   [40] Samuel R. Delany, *Dhalgren* (London: Vintage Books, 2001 [1975]), 184.
[41] Ibid., 205.   [42] Steiner [Delany], 61.   [43] Ibid., 63.   [44] Delany, Dhalgren, 579.

The writer's voice is the voice of the writer-as-God. Writer thought, Don't want to be God; have never wanted to be God. All these male poets want to be the top poet, as if, since they can't be a dictator in the political realm, can be dictator of this world ... Decision not to find this own voice but to use and be other, multiple, even innumerable voices.[45]

The political point is clear. Once more, a line is drawn connecting mastery and authorial godliness to maleness, and, ultimately, to fascism. Delany, too, shares this view (despite the fact that he identifies as a man), telling Takayuki Tatsumi in 1986 that he sees his literary project as seeking to 'blow open the whole literary game, the game in which the white–male–heterosexual position is assumed to be the particular dream-outside-of-history in which, today, everyone could, of course, live comfortably and, there, be Masters of History – if only we'd all leap ever so lightly into it'.[46]

Like hooks, Acker has cited Delany as an influence, seeing his 1970s writings as having 'carved in literary geography a pathway between novel-writing and poetry', while also managing to escape the 'outdated laws and regulations of bourgeois realism'.[47] The same impulse can be found running through her late metafictions. In 'The Killers' (1993), Acker recounts an unsettling dream, characteristically overlaying this material with autobiographical fragments and snippets of pop culture. And then, just as she seems to be drawing to a close, she turns to the relationship between her words and realism:

> what I've just told you, though each little bit was real or had happened, has nothing to do with realism ... Why bother with the lie of realism? ... By letting you see through my own eyes, I give you my viewpoints, moral and political ... those who practice realism want to limit their readers' percep-tions, want to limit perceptions to a centric – which in this society is always a phallocentric – reality.[48]

For Acker, the essential appeal of her anti-realist mode is that it takes the trouble to make tangible the particular 'viewpoints, moral and political' from which she writes, rather than veiling them behind the false univer-sality enjoyed by a white–male–heterosexual subject position.

As we have seen, however, realism is alive and well in the present era. Perhaps surprisingly, the hunger for the real (and realism) that Zadie

[45] Kathy Acker, 'Dead Doll Humility', *Postmodern Culture* 1.1 (1990).
[46] Takayuki Tatsumi, 'Interview with Samuel R. Delany', *Diacritics* 16.3 (1986), 26–45, here 43.
[47] Kathy Acker, 'On Delany the Magician' [1996], in Samuel R. Delany, *Trouble on Triton: An Ambiguous Heterotopia* (Hanover, NH: Wesleyan University Press, 1996 [1976]), ix.
[48] Kathy Acker, 'The Killers' [1993], in *Biting the Error: Writers Explore Narrative*, ed. Mary Burger, Robert Glück, Camille Roy, and Gail Scott (New York: Coach House Books, 2004), 16–18.

Smith sensed in the 2008 zeitgeist can be detected in some contemporary metafictions. The Nigerian-born, US-based author Chimamanda Ngozi Adichie's *The Thing Around Your Neck* (2009) includes a short story titled 'Jumping Monkey Hill' that exemplifies this peculiar trend. Narrating a week in the life of a fictional author – Ujunwa Ogundu – Adichie's tale concerns the difficulty of producing new work at a writers' retreat. Ogundu's story-in-progress (concerning a fictional protagonist named Chioma) is included as a text-within-a-text, nested within Adichie's, and the two layers mirror one another, tracing repeating patterns of male oppression. Towards the end of the frame narrative, the heroine is challenged about the believability of her work by the organizer of the writers' retreat, and she bursts into defiant laughter, declaring that her tale was entirely true: "'The only thing I didn't add in the story," she said with her eyes on Edward's face, "is that after I left the Alhaji's house, I got into the jeep and insisted that the driver take me home."'[49] The two layers are collapsed into one, and the story snaps shut: fiction is shown to have sprung directly from life.

In her study of 'Jumping Monkey Hill', Daria Tunca points out that this *mise-en-abyme* effect is grander than it initially appears. She identifies two further layers to the metafiction: Adichie's own experience with a male award administrator back in 2003, and the short story ('Lagos, Lagos') that she composed on that occasion.[50] The climactic authentication of Ogundu's work-in-progress is thus mirrored by Adichie's own life and work outside the text, reiterating her central claim to truth. In the years following this oddly realist metafiction, Adichie went on to publish a mini-manifesto, titled 'To Instruct and Delight: A Case for Realist Literature' (2012). Noting her lifelong aversion to pulp and science fiction, this essay offers a political defence of realism (the 'bourgeois' fiction dismissed by Acker), claiming that the mode offers a route to warmly humanist governance:

> This is part of realist literature's magic: that we are able to thrill to the magnificent diversity in the world. [It can] remind us of how similar we are, in the midst of our differences . . . I sometimes wonder whether it might be a good idea to send a package of books of realist literature to every prime minister and president in the world.[51]

---

[49] Chimamanda Ngozi Adichie, *The Thing Around Your Neck* (London: Fourth Estate, 2009), 114.

[50] Daria Tunca, 'The Danger of a Single Short Story: Reality, Fiction and Metafiction in Chimamanda Ngozi Adichie's "Jumping Monkey Hill"', *Journal of Postcolonial Writing* 54.1 (2018): 69–82.

[51] Chimamanda Ngozi Adichie, 'To Instruct and Delight: A Case for Realist Literature', Commonwealth Foundation, 2012.

In light of the contemporary debates with which this chapter began, Adichie's optimism might be read – following her vocal relief at the result of the 2020 presidential election – as aligning with our post-Trump moment, a period that has, for some, renewed belief in the familiar values of liberal centrism. And yet, of course, this neat, symmetrical return to realism and centrism can also be read as a comforting slip back into old truisms ('how similar we are, in the midst of our differences'). Global crises and systemic injustices are allowed to creep on, or so the argument goes, even as the quality of books on presidential bookshelves improves.

There are, however, contemporary American metafictions that buck this trend. Before closing, it is worth turning to a series of experimental novellas that resist the idea of placing realist credos at their core. Renee Gladman, in her recent *Calamities* (2016), describes herself as being trapped inside a broken world, 'trying to look at it, but it was lying on my face, making it hard to see. The world was made up of layers, one encompassing the other, and it smelled like onion. I didn't want to think that the world was an onion [but] I couldn't deny what I was smelling.'[52] In darkly comic terms, Gladman's strange world-onion can be read as a twin to the layered *mise-en-abyme* found in texts such as Adichie's. Here, though, the underlying point is very different:

> I was a part of something that formed a sphere of folds, where one fold lay organically next to another, each one thicker as you moved outward, away from the core, though onions have no true core, or rather, no core that survives our trying to reach it. And that was why I thought it was difficult to understand this world. You dislodged the thing you were trying to find, and whenever you moved, it moved.[53]

Adichie's text orbited around the disclosure of truth, but Gladman's *Calamities* contains nothing tangible. Truth – and the self – is elusive, and it recedes even as the writer reaches out for it.

This is the perilous state that Gladman explores across her series of Ravicka fictions, published across the last decade with the Dorothy project (a radical feminist press). Making use of invented languages, (mis)translations, and surreal shifts of tone and location, these books are not quite science fiction, although they often brush against it. 'They were not aliens, and this cathedral was not another planet,' she insists in the first volume, *Event Factory* (2010), before adding, 'remembering this took a great deal of discipline'.[54] By the end of the fourth novella, *Houses of Ravicka* (2017),

[52] Renee Gladman, *Calamities* (Seattle: Wave Books, 2016), 91.   [53] Ibid., 91.
[54] Renee Gladman, *Event Factory* (St Louis: Dorothy, 2010), 58.

her imagined city is seen contorting into new shapes, scrambling communities and leaving the narrator as a kind of textual refugee: 'Was I visible? Did I migrate? Could I be of some use to the city?'[55] Amidst all the existential and architectural turmoil, the shifting terrain is endlessly reflected by the page itself: 'you were in language, you were in a thinking text: pages were walls that enclosed you, the ground was the floor of the book, the horizon of the sentence'.[56]

The rifts and fissures in Gladman's work are, clearly, more disorienting than those of more stable contemporary (meta)fictions, such as Adichie's. To read this anti-realist surface as a retreat to the supposedly 'politically abortive' strategies of postmodernism, though, would be a mistake. In the 'Afterword' to her fourth (and most recent) Ravicka novella, Gladman insists that she is preoccupied, throughout these books, with the question of how 'one survives the atrocities of the political and social present'.[57] Her answers are all provisional and fleeting, an approach that bears the stamp of the most lasting postmodern American metafictions.[58] Like Delany and Acker, Gladman refuses fantasies of control, even as she captures (often in frightening detail) the precarity of life lived out of control, at the edge of crisis.

---

[55] Renee Gladman, *Houses of Ravicka* (St Louis: Dorothy, 2017), 131.   [56] Ibid., 116.
[57] Ibid., 149.
[58] The list of 'Acknowledgements' at the end of *Event Factory* concludes by extending 'deepest thanks ... most especially to Samuel R. Delany, for *Dhalgren*' (p. 129). Gladman's engagement with the paradox of control also hints at the influence of another text from 1975, the autobiographical metafictions of the French semiotician, *Roland Barthes by Roland Barthes*. As Barthes writes, towards the end of that book, 'Is it not the characteristic of reality to be *unmasterable*? And is it not the characteristic of system to *master* it? What then, confronting reality, can one do who rejects mastery?' *Roland Barthes by Roland Barthes*, trans. Richard Howard (New York: Hill and Wang, 1977 [French edition, 1975]), 172.

PART III

Case Studies

CHAPTER 15

Herland *(1915): Charlotte Perkins Gilman*

Cynthia J. Davis

Charlotte Perkins Gilman (1860–1935) was a writer and reformer who reached the height of her fame during the Progressive Era, although she never fully identified with Progressivism. Nor did she identify as a feminist, believing the emergent movement to be too narrowly focused on suffrage and personal liberation. She was an early enthusiast of socialism – particularly British Fabianism and the American variant, known as nationalism, inspired by Edward Bellamy's utopian novel *Looking Backward* (1888) – provided that socioeconomic change resulted from gradual evolution, not revolution. When asked, she described herself as a humanist and (self-taught) social scientist, best equipped to diagnose what ailed the social body. Although she would not have put it this way, her diagnosis amounted to a more systemic version of what had ailed her personally. She thus centered her activism on correcting the gendered expectations and domestic conventions that had made marriage and motherhood so unhappy for her from the first and that she fictionalized in works such as her best-known short story, "The Yellow Wall-Paper" (1892). Gilman thus anticipated second-wave feminism in making the personal political.

A tireless lecturer and prolific author, she published numerous poems, essays, and works of both fiction and non-fiction devoted to critiquing existing methods of enforcing gender divides that she believed were artificially and erroneously created in the first place. As her utopian fiction makes clear, however, her vision of a world where this "unnatural" divide no longer pertains is a society that would retain numerous other established hierarchies, which she naturalized.[1] Espousing an organic social

---

[1] Charlotte Perkins Gilman, *Herland* [1915], reprinted in *Herland, The Yellow Wall-Paper, and Selected Writings*, ed. Denise D. Knight (New York: Penguin, 1999), 1. Gilman wrote two additional utopian novels, *Moving the Mountain* (1911) and the *Herland* sequel, *With Her in Ourland* (1916).

philosophy from her early days as an activist, she grounded her politics in the domain of biological existence, initially endorsing a laissez-faire approach based on her belief that natural laws, tendencies, and processes that weren't interfered with would inevitably work to facilitate the progressively complexifying and meliorative course of evolution. But the more she came to believe that humans had deviated from this evolutionary civilizing process, the more ardently she advocated for an interventionist approach resembling what Michel Foucault termed "biopolitics," especially in the productive sense of wielding power to develop, improve, impose order on, and preserve (but also when necessary destroy) life.[2] By the time Gilman wrote *Herland* (1915), she was tying the relative "health and vitality" of a given nation to the relative "health and vitality" of its members, basing her assessments on the extent of degeneracy and impurity she detected in the social body under examination and prescribing drastic cures as needed.[3] In addition to her advocacy of biopower, her 1915 utopian novel reveals its author's conservative tendencies; these tendencies certainly increased as she aged and soured on the prospect of sweeping social reform, but they had been there all along, even in her most seemingly radical theories of gender.

Herland is undoubtedly a political novel in the broadest sense, delineating as it does a set of ideas, principles, and processes governing the organization of the eponymous "two-thousand-year-old feminine civilization" along with the decisions made by its denizens.[4] Just as important to *Herland*'s politics, however, is its author's distinctive take on the word. Her definition resembles Hannah Arendt's conception of politics as "no less than ... the work of man," so long as the gendered and generic connotations of "man" are understood to be in tension.[5] Politics in theory, Gilman believed, "is in no way masculine; neither is it feminine, save in this: that the tendency to care for, defend and manage a group, is in its origin maternal."[6] Within what she called our man-made world, however, masculine meddling had mistakenly relegated these maternal tendencies to the background, to the detriment of human progress. The damage from

[2] Michel Foucault, *The Birth of Biopolitics: Lectures at the Collège de France, 1978–1979*, ed. Michel Senellart, trans. Graham Burchell (Basingstoke and New York: Palgrave Macmillan, 2008), 2.

[3] Kyla Schuller, *The Biopolitics of Feeling: Race, Sex, and Science in the Nineteenth Century* (Durham, NC and London: Duke University Press, 2018), 2.

[4] Gilman, *Herland*, 135.

[5] Hannah Arendt, *The Human Condition* (Chicago and London: University of Chicago Press, 2018 [1958]), 206.

[6] Charlotte Perkins Gilman, *The Man-Made World, or Our Androcentric Culture* (New York: Charleton Company, 1911), 210.

this interference included its adverse impact on natural laws and evolutionary processes that, she believed, along with the sociologist Lester Frank
Ward, might otherwise have been consciously improved by human intelligence in its modern advanced state.[7] Western civilizations had been so
"marred" by this "constant obtrusion of an ultra-masculine tendency" that,
she concluded, their representatives could no longer muster the "devotion
and efficiency" necessary for the intelligent planning for the future that
made a utopia like Herland possible.[8]

Our male progenitors' most grievous error in her view was forcing their
female contemporaries to enter into an "abnormal sexuo-economic relation" with them.[9] This egregious and "unnatural" deviation from the
"natural process of social advancement" had ultimately resulted in that
devolutionary anomaly, the housewife, whose enforced specialization in
"sex-functions" in exchange for economic protection and ensuing "mor-
bid" feminine dependence sharply distinguished her not only from females
of other species but also from the "male of our species," who "has become
human, far more than male."[10] The "excessive sex-distinction in the
human race" might seem "perfectly natural" to some, but for Gilman it
was an aberration she devoted her career to correcting.[11] By the time she
began calling it out, this unnatural "sex-distinction" had in her estimation
grown so injuriously excessive that it threatened to "check and pervert the
progress of the race" and cause even advanced nations to "fail."[12] It was the
current incarnations of femininity and masculinity among what she called
the "higher races" that most concerned her, since she considered these
deviations to be the primary deterrents to what she defined as "racial
advancement and higher civilization."[13]

In lieu of a man-made and hence unnatural world, Gilman sought to
bring into being the far more natural and proper world order that she

---

[7] Ward embraced "telic" or planned evolution, believing that the level of intelligence humans had
attained by his lifetime made it possible for them – and for representative governments on their
behalf – to facilitate human and social progress.

[8] Gilman, *Man-Made World*, 211.

[9] Charlotte Perkins Gilman, *Women and Economics* (Boston, MA: Small, Maynard, and Company,
1898), 23.

[10] Gilman, *Herland*, 26, 39, 30, 43.   [11] Ibid., 40, 81.

[12] Gilman, *Women and Economics*, 37, 73. "Race" was a slippery term in Gilman's lexicon. At times,
she used it to denote the human race; at others, the white race with which she identified and that
she occasionally implicitly and increasingly explicitly equated with the human race. More often than
not, she seemed incapable of envisioning the progress of the one apart from the other.

[13] Ibid., 29; Gail Bederman, *Manliness and Civilization: A Cultural History of Gender and Race in the
United States, 1880–1917* (Chicago: University of Chicago Press, 1995), 156. Bederman's chapter on
Gilman's gender politics persuasively roots them "in the white supremacism of 'civilization'" (122).

believed would have existed had masculine desires not "left their heavy impress" on the course of human history.[14] Excepting its all-female population, *Herland* depicts what Gilman believed the modern world would look like had "Mr. Man" not gotten "into the saddle" at some early point on the road from savagery to civilization and had he not initiated the "Great Divergence" between human males and females, which struck Gilman as the most "catastrophic change in all nature."[15] Yet she also believed that there was still time to right this wrong evolutionary turn. Advanced civilizations could get back on track by repudiating androcentrism and centering their politics instead around an "older, deeper, more 'natural' feeling, the restful reverence which looks up to the Mother sex" – a reverence that is not just the prevailing affect in Herland but the defining principle of its organic social order.[16]

Believing the "man-made world" to be harmfully unnatural, Gilman plays up the "naturalness" of a highly evolved world like Herland. Indeed, throughout her polemical writings, Gilman urges a return to nature, albeit one bearing little resemblance to her contemporaries' chest-thumping promotion of testosterone-enhancing outdoor activities and adventures (a masculinist project on which I will elaborate). The nature Gilman wanted us to rediscover instead dates back to a time before any such chest-thumping began, a time predating "this root error about men and women" that has for "age after age" during this "short stretch we call 'history'" prevented evolution from running its natural course, keeping "the *real* elements of humanity" from emerging.[17] For Gilman, as for many utopian thinkers, what ought to be real is the ostensibly utopian, and what is currently "real" is "false," the result of a racial failure to progress according to an evolutionary plan, so "shackled, chained, blinded" had those meant to advance been by an androcentric culture that never should have developed.[18]

As the next section clarifies, Gilman remained invested in established social hierarchies, including those of race, sexuality, and status, even as she fundamentally challenged a world order that had erroneously boosted men above women. Her challenge was reinforced by the emergent social science informing her organic social philosophy and her gender politics in particular. She acknowledged a large debt to Ward, whose "gynaecocentric theory" she considered "the greatest single contribution to the world's

---

[14] Gilman, *Man-Made World*, 234.
[15] Charlotte Perkins Gilman, "With Her in Ourland," *The Forerunner* 7.11 (November 1916): 291.
[16] Gilman, *Herland*, 129.   [17] Gilman, *Man-Made World*, 258–9.   [18] Ibid., 206–7.

thought since Evolution."[19] Ward's theory held that life was "originally and essentially female," given its origins in an act of cellular parthenogenesis.[20] Although neither a feminist nor an activist, Ward posited that "it must be from the steady advance of woman rather than from the uncertain fluctuations of man that the sure and solid progress of the future is to come."[21] Gilman took Ward's theory and ran with it, grounding her reform agenda in this female origin story while making parthenogenesis the secret to Herland's survival. Ward gave her license to proclaim woman "the mother of the world," to insist that women deserved to advance to their rightful "full place" as such, and to seek to jumpstart this restoration process by imagining for readers of *Herland* what a world of mothers mothering the world might look like.[22]

Another formative influence on Gilman's utopian thinking was Patrick Geddes and J. Arthur Thomson's influential *Evolution of Sex* (1889), especially its argument that evolutionary progress beginning at the cellular level was *not* based on Darwinian struggle and strife. Instead, the co-authors concluded that life sprang from an "organic sociality" which boded well for the future of multicellular organisms like humans. "[I]t is possible," they surmise, "to interpret the ideals of ethical progress, through love and sociality, co-operation and sacrifice, not as mere utopias contradicted by experience, but as the highest expressions of the central evolutionary process of the natural world."[23] What was a hypothesis for Geddes and Thomson became the foundational premise of *Herland*.

Viewing literature as an extension of her politics – or, as she put it, as a hammer "to drive nails with" – across her didactic fiction Gilman sought to give form to her vision of a world where her proposed reforms had been embraced and implemented.[24] "Our Past we cannot help," she once wrote. "Our Present slips from us in the making. Only the Future can be

---

[19] Quoted in Cynthia J. Davis, "His and Herland: Charlotte Perkins Gilman 'Re-presents' Lester F. Ward," in *Evolution and Eugenics in American Literature*, ed. Claire Roche and Lois Cuddy (Lewisburg, PA: Bucknell University Press, 2003), 77.

[20] Lester F. Ward, "The Past and Future of the Sexes," *Independent*, March 8, 1906, 542.

[21] Lester F. Ward, "Our Better Halves," *Forum* 6 (1888): 275.

[22] Gilman, *Women and Economics*, 248.

[23] Patrick Geddes and J. Arthur Thomson, *The Evolution of Sex* (London: W. Scott, 1889), 311–12. This section on Gilman's influences, along with the subsequent analysis of her investment in eugenics, draws on comparable discussions in both Davis, "His and Herland," 73–88, and Cynthia J. Davis, *Charlotte Perkins Gilman: A Biography* (Stanford: Stanford University Press, 2010), 251, 299ff.

[24] Quoted in Davis, *Charlotte Perkins Gilman*, 130.

molded."[25] For good or for ill, this idea of a malleable future forged around her distinctive take on a prelapsarian organic past shaped both her politics and her political novels, *Herland* chief among them.

In the remaining pages, I unpack precisely what Gilman meant by a better world as dramatized in her 1915 utopian novel. A quick summary first for those unfamiliar with the plot: *Herland* tells the story of three American men who are exploring a "great river" in some unspecified tropical land. There, they learn about a sheltered country populated for the past two millennia exclusively by women, thanks to parthenogenetic reproduction.[26] Although told by their local guides that this is "No Place for men," the three explorers determine amid an imperialist age to make the uncharted territory "our find."[27] They soon venture into what Terry, the boorish expedition leader and an acknowledged "man's man," anticipates will be a land filled with "just Girls and Girls and Girls," "Peacherinos" ripe for the picking.[28] Instead, they are captured and subsequently schooled in the superiority of Herland to Ourland on nearly all counts. All three men wind up marrying Herlanders. In the end, the chivalrous Jeff remains behind in Herland; the unreformed sexist, Terry, is summarily expelled; and the narrator, a comparatively enlightened social scientist named Van, prepares to embark on a journey with his wife, Ellador, to see the larger world, setting up the following year's alarmist sequel, *With Her in Ourland* (1916), serialized, like *Herland*, in Gilman's one-woman magazine, *The Forerunner*.

Utopian fiction is predicated on contrasts, including those between here and there, the present and the future. *Herland* spotlights distinctions both between and within gender categories. Although scholars who rediscovered the novel in the 1970s typically interpreted its approach to gender differences as a "playful deconstruction of patriarchal thought," as Thomas Peyser has astutely observed, its approach more closely approximates an inversion of "that thought."[29] In other words, *Herland* doesn't so much challenge established gender binaries as flip them. Accordingly, the novel resorts to stereotypes when depicting its male characters while simultaneously casting them as inessential creatures of convention. The female characters in *Herland*, by contrast, are unfailingly portrayed as productive, high-minded, public-spirited, and forward-looking workers and builders,

[25] Charlotte Perkins Gilman, "What May We Expect of Eugenics?," *Physical Culture* 31 (March 1914): 219.

[26] Gilman, *Herland*, 4.   [27] Ibid., 7.   [28] Ibid., 11, 9, 17.

[29] Thomas Peyser, "Reproducing Utopia: Charlotte Perkins Gilman and *Herland*," *Studies in American Fiction* 20.1 (1992): 14.

evincing the "clear intelligence and dependableness" that even the insightful Van originally "assumed to be masculine qualities."[30] By inverting conventional understandings of masculinity and femininity, Gilman suggests that supposedly fixed and essential gender attributes are instead both fluid and socially constructed. Still, this inversion leaves in place a gendered antithesis that she elsewhere sought to attenuate in the interest of revealing an underlying common humanity – at least among the whites whom she identified as the most racially advanced group.

In *Herland*, the most illuminating contrast is arguably the one drawn between Herlander women and what Van refers to as "our women at home."[31] Even though the two societies being compared in *Herland* are contemporaneous, the differences between their female populations are nonetheless temporal in nature, reflecting Gilman's belief that conventional American women of a certain class are erroneously and regrettably stuck in time, having failed to evolve as planned, and that women like the Herlanders represent what *should* be our present and could be our future. Their differences are also attributed to the contrast between Herland's matriarchal culture and Ourland's patriarchal culture – even though, as discussed shortly, there are aspects of patriarchal culture that Gilman appeared perfectly content to replicate in her utopian matriarchate.

In nearly every point of comparison between the two female populations, the Herlanders come out ahead. Whereas "*our* women" are often criticized for "being so personal," for instance, Herlanders' preferred pronoun is not "I" but "'We' and 'we' and 'we.'"[32] The cult of domesticity that included many middle-class American women among its members was decried by Gilman as a key source of personal unhappiness and social dysfunction, helping to explain why her utopian Herlanders do not even have a word for "home" in their vocabulary and need to ask for its definition.[33] Perhaps the sharpest contrast lies between the two countries' respective approaches to mothering. Gilman clarifies that the American mothers, who are "kept in the home to care for the children," are nothing like Herland's mothers, for whom the "maternal instinct" was "raised to its highest power."[34] Where the myopic mothers back home are said to devote their maternal energies exclusively to "their private families," Herland's "Mothers of the Future" direct their capacious maternal energies toward building up "their country and race" through their children, a set

---

[30] Gilman, *Herland*, 70.   [31] Ibid., 75.   [32] Ibid., 125.   [33] Ibid., 62, 95.   [34] Ibid., 59.

of evolutionary reformist priorities that resemble Gilman's own.[35] Her positioning of these "race mothers" as exemplary is indicative of what Alys Eve Weinbaum calls Gilman's "maternalist racial nationalism," where women serve as the "primary agents" of racial and national purity and superiority on account of their expansive maternal capacities.[36]

It is their depersonalized, farsighted approach to mothering that qualifies Herlanders in Gilman's mind as "women *plus*."[37] Indeed, her endorsement of "race-mothering" helps explain why she retains the category "woman" in a novel otherwise interested in making gender identity seem incidental. "They don't seem to notice our being men," Jeff observes. "They treat us – well – as they do one another. It's as if our being men was a minor incident." Similarly, near the end of his Herland stay, Van concludes, "We were now well used to seeing women not as females but as people."[38] Herlanders, according to Gilman's taxonomy, are at once women, mothers, people, and human beings, but neither females nor conventionally feminine. They are, to use her preferred characterization, "human women," a phrasing that conveys her desire to meld the two terms whose divergence she holds responsible for a host of contemporary problems.[39] She even coins a term, "womanness," to capture this unique blend, substituting this neologism for the conventional term, "womanliness," which could risk connoting the exaggerated femininity she deplored.[40] Her invented word encapsulates the humanizing-of-women progress that she sought to instantiate in contemporary gender politics, a transformation that would make mothering no longer an obstacle to women's advancement but instead, once properly redefined and expansively reoriented, its vehicle. Excessive femininity should be rued as an evolutionary mishap, Gilman insisted; its opposite, the elevated status that Herland's "ultra-women" have achieved through their visionary "race-mothering," should be exalted as the right and proper evolutionary culmination of our maternal origin story.[41]

Focused intensely on the progress she wanted to see unfold along gender lines, Gilman never lost sight of potential setbacks. A strong reaction

---

[35] Ibid., 58, 95–6. Gilman advances comparable albeit more extensive critiques of both conventional domesticity and traditional mothering in treatises such as *The Home* (1903) and *Concerning Children* (1900).

[36] Gilman, *Herland*, 95; Alys Eve Weinbaum, *Wayward Reproductions: Genealogies of Race and Nation in Transatlantic Modern Thought* (Durham, NC and London: Duke University Press, 2004), 62, 78.

[37] Gilman, *Herland*, 127.   [38] Ibid., 32, 135.   [39] Ibid.,128.   [40] Ibid., 127.

[41] Ibid., 59.

against women's advancement during her lifetime turned on a contentious discourse surrounding the gendering of both civilization and culture. For her part, Gilman believed that the energy constituting the "main current of social life" was inherently "maternal" and that it was only through the unintended "maternalizing of man" on behalf of his female dependents in an androcentric culture that civilization had advanced at all.[42] As she saw it, then, civilization was primarily a function of the protective "tendencies of the female," which were powerful enough to subvert even the "naturally destructive tendencies of the male."[43] This explains why the three Americans are quick to pronounce this land of Hers "a *civilized* country!" from the moment they arrive.[44] Even the curmudgeonly Terry concedes that the women there are all "highly civilized," although he has the hardest time squaring this observation with the absence of male influence.[45]

Gilman's association of civilization with distinctly female energies and efforts could be seen as signifying what the historian Ann Douglas would later controversially describe as "the feminization of American culture" over the course of the nineteenth century. But where Douglas joined certain nineteenth- and early twentieth-century male cultural commentators in regretting the perceived replacement of a foundational, stern, and masculine Calvinist culture by a "debased" sentimental, female-centered consumer culture, Gilman in *Herland* and elsewhere assigns a positive value to a culture handed over to women, although admittedly only after she had dramatically redefined what it meant to be a woman.[46] At the century's turn, a number of prominent white men lamented the sapping of national virility as evidence of cultural effeminacy, attenuation, and decline, which they believed could be corrected only through a vigorous remasculinization of the culture.[47] Opposing the "savage impulse towards domination" informing these virilizing efforts, Gilman insisted that the "reproduction of perfectly good savages is not the business of humanity. Its business is to grow, socially; to develop, to improve."[48] No wonder, then, that *Herland* ends with the expulsion of the brutish Terry, who acts on his boast that women enjoyed "being *mastered*" by attempting to rape his new

[42] Gilman, *Women and Economics*, 126–7.   [43] Ibid., 128.   [44] Gilman, *Herland*, 13.
[45] Ibid., 27.
[46] Ann Douglas, *The Feminization of American Culture* (New York: Farrar, Straus and Giroux, 1998 [1977]), 6.
[47] See Michael Kimmel, *Manhood in America: A Cultural History* (New York: Free Press, 1996). Additionally, I summarize this remasculinizing project in my monograph, *Pain and the Aesthetics of US Literary Realism* (Oxford and New York: Oxford University Press, 2021), 9–12.
[48] Daniel E. Bender, "Women's Empires: Gynaecocracy, Savagery, and the Evolution of Industry," *American Studies* 51.3–4 (2010): 72; Gilman, *Man-Made World*, 215.

Herland wife.[49] More disturbing still to Gilman was what the historian Gail Bederman describes as some of the contemporaneous masculinist project's more ardent proponents' insistence "that to avoid the decline of civilization, sexual differences must be upheld and even increased, lest the two sexes become more alike and thus more like uncivilized savages."[50] This line of argument upends Gilman's own take on the relation between sexual difference and civilized progress, as direct a challenge to her reform arguments as she faced at the time and an important context for understanding her countervailing attempts to equate a society where conventional sexual differences are made to appear both unnatural and unnecessary with the utopian apex of civilization.

Dedicated primarily to contesting contemporary notions of male supremacy, Gilman's utopian novel holds other key variables constant. In other words, it is male supremacy more or less exclusively that *Herland* challenges, not white supremacy, established socioeconomic hierarchies, or heteronormativity.[51] From the outset, the novel hastens to assure us that Herlanders are not "savages" like the native guides who have led the three explorers to this uncharted "Woman Country," which is populated by "white" women of "Aryan stock" who have descended from "the best civilization of the old world."[52] The xenophobia and white racial pride that had become keynotes for Gilman around the time of *Herland*'s composition had long been important elements of her commitment to racial advancement: As early as 1898, she was proclaiming "Anglo-Saxon blood" the "most powerful expression of the latest current of fresh racial life from the north."[53] Increasingly throughout her body of work, Gilman took white supremacy for granted as the basis of all advanced civilizations, Herland included.

If Herlanders have yet to attain evolutionary perfection, it is because they have yet "to re-establish a bi-sexual state for our people," by which they mean reproduction through heterosexual coupling instead of through parthenogenesis.[54] In this one area, they acknowledge that they fall short of utopia, having remained in their own eyes "only half a people."[55]

---

[49] Gilman, *Herland*, 129.   [50] Bederman, 137.
[51] Numerous scholars have commented on Gilman's racism and her investment in white supremacy specifically. In addition to Bederman, Peyser, and Weinbaum, see, for example, Bernice L. Hausman, "Sex Before Gender: Charlotte Perkins Gilman and the Evolutionary Paradigm of Utopia," *Feminist Studies* 3 (1998): 489–510; Jennifer Hudak, "The 'Social Inventor': Charlotte Perkins Gilman and the (Re)Production of Perfection," *Women's Studies* 32 (2003): 455–77.
[52] Gilman, *Herland*, 6, 55.   [53] Gilman, *Women and Economics*, 147.   [54] Gilman, *Herland*, 88.
[55] Ibid., 98.

This investment in what Gilman calls "bi-sexuality" proves the scholar Lynne Evans's point about how the "erasure of men from Herland society put an end to heterosexual relations" but failed to "eradicate heteronormativity"; indeed, Herlanders eagerly (yet chastely) pursue heterosexuality, believing that it would expedite, in the short term, the reproduction of children, which they consider their great work as a nation, and, in the long term, their civilization's continued evolution beyond its already highly advanced state.[56] That said, heterosexual unions are the *only* form of intermixing endorsed in *Herland*: Although the three marriages are praised for advancing Herland to the next stage of civilization, other marital "combination[s] of alien races, of color, caste or creed" are construed as impeding that advance, since the objections to them, we are told, are "well-founded."[57]

The secret to Herland's superiority, we soon learn, lies in its intentional practice of eugenics, whose emergence in the early twentieth century Foucault explicitly connected to the rise of biopower. Although initially skeptical of what she characterized in 1910 as "the science of the improvement of the human race by better breeding," Gilman soon embraced eugenics as a necessary biopolitical prophylactic.[58] By 1914, she was declaring that society had a fundamental right "to arrest its own decay"; two years later, she contended that anyone with "a proper regard for human life" would support "instant measures to check the supply of feeble-minded and defective persons, and further measures to prevent the reproduction of unfortunates."[59] No longer did she assume that evolution, once back on track and left unchecked, ought to eventually right the wrongs of the unnatural man-made world. By the time she wrote *Herland*, she was convinced that progress required the deliberate exercise of biopower.

Modeling the active intervention in biological processes that Gilman was now promoting, the Herlanders respond to the pressure of population by deliberatively deciding to create only as many people as their "country

---

[56] Ibid., 88; Lynne Evans, "You See, Children Were the – the Raison d'Être": The Reproductive Futurism of Charlotte Perkins Gilman's Herland," *Canadian Review of American Studies* 44.2 (2014): 305. Evans cites Lee Edelman's *No Future: Queer Theory and the Death Drive* (Duke University Press, 2004) on the importance of the figure of the child to heteronormativity and argues convincingly that Herland exemplifies the "reproductive futurism" that Edelman critiques.

[57] Gilman, *Herland*, 121.

[58] Charlotte Perkins Gilman, "Prize Children," *The Forerunner* 1.5 (May 1910): 10.

[59] Gilman, "What May We Expect of Eugenics?," 219; Charlotte Perkins Gilman, "The Sanctity of Human Life," *The Forerunner* 7.5 (May 1916): 128–9.

will support."[60] Their devotion to becoming "Conscious Makers of People" leads them to practice "negative eugenics," making it their "first business to train out, to breed out, when possible, the lowest types," by which they mean "unfit" and hence undesirable potential mothers along with their possible offspring.[61] Gilman approvingly contrasts what she characterizes as their thoughtful, intentional, and restrained approach to mothering with other nations' dreadful "sense of helpless involuntary fecundity, forced to fill and overfill the land, every land, and then see their children suffer, sin, and die, fighting horribly with one another."[62] She suggests that it is only through a comparable eugenical approach to populations – where those she identified as inherently superior would play an active role in determining their own advancement while simultaneously keeping supposedly inferior others literally down and out, where she felt they belonged – that any society could ever achieve its civilized promise.

The United States had become for Gilman the most disappointing cautionary tale in this regard. Instead of living up to its initial promise as a "Splendid Child," the country is compared in the sequel to *Herland* to an "idiot child" whose body was "bloated and weak" due to "crowding injections of alien blood."[63] Far from celebrating the foundational American precept of *e pluribus unum*, by 1916 Gilman was repeatedly and vehemently criticizing policymakers for failing to prioritize "Quality" over "quantity" in matters of immigration.[64] Her utopian imagination could not envision a world that allowed for the flourishing of *all* human beings, no matter their race, ethnicity, country of origin, socioeconomic status, sexual orientation, or physical, mental, and neurological condition; indeed, such a world now seemed to her more dystopian than utopian. Instead of looking forward like the forerunner she claimed to be, she increasingly indulged in a nostalgia for a dehistoricized, speculative account of the past, a time before she believed it all went wrong. For her, the trouble began with the prehistoric, unnatural, and "unprecedented dominance of the male," only to be followed thousands of years later by the dragging, devolutionary weight of the "hopeless substratum of paupers and degenerates" that she blamed for her country's decline in her own lifetime.[65] Gilman's challenges to established gender conventions may

[60] Gilman, *Herland*, 69.   [61] Ibid., 69, 83, 69.   [62] Ibid., 69.
[63] Charlotte Perkins Gilman, "With Her in Ourland," *The Forerunner* 7.11 (November 1916): 29; "With Her in Ourland," *The Forerunner* 7.5 (May 1916): 123.
[64] Quoted in Davis, *Charlotte Perkins Gilman*, 301.
[65] Gilman, *Man-Made World*, 7; *Herland*, 68.

have been both lauded and criticized in her own day for their radicalism, but underlying that apparent radicalism was a conservatism that fundamentally informed her politics, which increasingly amounted to a reactionary biopolitics, including in the one area, the politics of gender, where she sought the most dramatic changes to the status quo.

CHAPTER 16

It Can't Happen Here *(1935): Sinclair Lewis*

Christopher Vials

> Everyone, including Doremus Jessup had said in 1935, "If there ever
> is a Fascist dictatorship here, American humor and pioneer indepen-
> dence are so marked that it will be absolutely different from anything
> in Europe" ... All that was gone, within a year after the [dictator-
> ship], and surprised scientists discovered that whips and handcuffs
> hurt just as sorely in the clear American air as in the miasmic fogs
> of Prussia.
>
> Sinclair Lewis, *It Can't Happen Here* (1935)

The phrase "it can't happen here" has become instantly recognizable in the
United States. It generally appears in the titles of opinion columns, think
pieces, and blogs, and to read the phrase is to instantly know that a dire
warning of a nascent American fascism is forthcoming. More to the point,
the phrase serves as a now familiar caution against naivety, prodding
Americans for their false hope that US liberal institutions will automati-
cally protect them from a budding authoritarian dystopia in their own
backyard. Writing in June 2020, for instance, Salman Rushdie wrote in
the *Washington Post*: "In my most recent novel, *Quichotte*, I characterized
the present moment as the 'Age of Anything-Can-Happen.' Today I say,
beware, America. Don't believe that it can't happen here."[1] Rushdie was
writing about Trump and his similarities to authoritarian leaders in the
recent history of India and Pakistan, and his piece uses the phrase "it can't
happen here" in a remarkably typical way. That is to say, since the
publication of Sinclair Lewis's novel *It Can't Happen Here* in 1935, the
phrase has served as an instantly recognizable, ironic rebuke to the
assumption that fascism is fundamentally alien to "the American Way."
It has become a commonsense rebuttal to the presumed *foreignness* of

---

[1] Salman Rushdie, "I've Seen Dictators Rise and Fall: Beware, America," *Washington Post*, June 3,
2020, www.washingtonpost.com/opinions/2020/06/03/salman-rushdie-ive-seen-dictators-rise-fall-
beware-america/

fascism to the United States. Yet Rushdie, like so many others who use it, does not mention the source text that initially launched it into the public sphere.

The idea of fascism as an international as well as a *domestic* threat has been at the heart of a distinct US antifascist tradition since the 1930s, with Sinclair Lewis's novel standing out as the literary urtext of this impulse. This tradition sees fascism not as something located merely in Europe or Asia, nor as something made impossible by a culture in which democratic liberalism is hegemonic; rather, it is an international, cultural force that is also nascent *within* US institutions, and that becomes particularly visible at times of crisis. Its bases – xenophobic nationalism, militarism, racism, anti-Marxism – reside "here" as well, and these fundamentals need only effective political mobilization and the proper historical conditions to congeal into a fascist movement, or even a fascist state. As such, to fight fascism has not meant restoring the status quo, but opposing the institutional and ideological roots of exclusion and hierarchy, roots that are as American as they are German or Italian. As Lewis's character Karl Pascal exclaims about the novel's totalitarian President Buzz Windrip, "Buzz isn't important – it's the sickness that made us throw him up that we've got to attend to."[2]

Lewis's novel is evoked far more than read, but revisiting it is instructive. Rereading *It Can't Happen Here* in the twenty-first century reveals not simply the origin of a phrase, but an expansive and surprisingly complex debate about the nature of American fascism illustrative of the US public sphere in the 1930s and 1940s. Chillingly, there has become almost no need to say "it can't happen here" after the presidency of Donald Trump and the authoritarian shift he brought about in US mainstream politics. As fascism has become de-exoticized in the public imagination, the phrase has lost much of its force as a provocation against complacency. But revisiting Lewis's source text remains valuable for gauging the distinct contours of American fascism, and even its limitations are instructive. On the one hand, the novel gives us a remarkably prescient reading of the complex class dynamics and populist coalitions that remain crucial to understanding white nationalist politics and successful neofascist movements. It also strikingly captures the nature of American fascist rhetoric and how it is registered by those outside the fascist "base." On the other hand, in projecting white Midwestern farmers as the main site of resistance, it also shows the serious limitations of the early twentieth-century socialist

[2] Sinclair Lewis, *It Can't Happen Here* (New York: New American Library, 2005), 109.

populism that animated Lewis's political imagination. I will conclude with a reflection on possibilities and constraints of populism as an antifascist political frame.

When he sat down to write *It Can't Happen Here*, Sinclair Lewis's literary fame was well established, although his star was beginning to fade. He won the Nobel Prize for Literature in 1930, mostly for novels such as *Main Street* (1920), *Babbitt* (1922), *Arrowsmith* (1925), and *Elmer Gantry* (1927), but his two novels in the first half of the Depression decade – *Ann Vickers* (1933) and *Work of Art* (1934) – were not as well received as his earlier work. As can be seen from the (incomplete) timeline above, he wrote lengthy works with impressive speed, yet *It Can't Happen Here* was hastily composed even by Lewis's standards. He churned out the 400-page first edition in only two months and did not regard the end product as his best work. Lewis quipped to a friend, "It's a bad book, but at least it gives Doubleday a chance finally to make some money on me."[3] That it did. While it did not revive his waning literary reputation, its topicality quickly placed it on the bestseller list. Most reviewers did not see *It Can't Happen Here* as Lewis's most well-crafted novel, but centrist, liberal, and left-wing critics alike praised its analysis of fascism and lauded its relevance to American life. Despite its critical treatment of communists, even the communist press touted Lewis's chilling work. It was adapted for the stage in 1936 through a grant from the Federal Theatre Project (FTP), and the stage adaptation met with both critical and commercial success. Produced in English, Yiddish, and Spanish, the FTP production ran for 260 weeks (a five-year run) and was viewed by hundreds of thousands of people, many of whom had never been to the theater in their lives.[4] Although production companies have perennially revived the play, the political rise of Trump recently inspired renewed interest in the novel and its theatrical adaptation. Berkeley Repertory Theatre produced *It Can't Happen Here* again in 2016 and partnered with over forty theaters across the country to air it as a four-part radio play in the fall of 2020. Penguin Books also reissued the novel in the quite deliberate year of 2017.

When *It Can't Happen Here* first appeared in 1935, Hitler had been in power in Germany for only two years, and Mussolini in Italy for thirteen. Mussolini's power grab in 1922 drew little interest from the international left outside of Italian immigrant communities, but Hitler's seizure of a

---

[3] Mark Schorer, *Sinclair Lewis: An American Life* (New York: McGraw Hill, 1961), 611.
[4] Richard Lingeman, *Sinclair Lewis: Rebel from Main Street* (New York: Random House, 2002), 408, 415.

technologically advanced, military powerhouse nation eleven years later suddenly catapulted "fascism" to the forefront of international headlines. To many Americans, particularly on the left, it was a source of anxiety – to others, inspiration. In 1934, the media mogul William Randolph Hearst began touting the virtues of Hitler and Mussolini within his expansive newspaper and newsreel networks after touring Nazi Germany; he saw these regimes as offering a model for dealing with strikes and other "Red" provocations on his side of the Atlantic. Meanwhile, in that same year, the anti-Semitic priest and father of right-wing radio, Father Charles Coughlin, founded his pro-fascist *Social Justice* magazine, while his weekly, nationally broadcast, political sermons enjoyed one of the largest audiences on the airwaves.[5] Also in 1934, news broke of an outlandish plot hatched by millionaire bankers to overthrow President Franklin Roosevelt and his New Deal administration in a *coup d'état* using a secret army of military veterans (the plot was foiled in its infancy when General Smedley Butler went public after the plotters tried to enlist him). To be sure, Roosevelt remained quite popular, and the president crushed his Republican opponent in the 1936 election even as his rhetoric and his New Deal policies swung much more openly to the left. Electorally, the political right remained in the wilderness through the 1930s. But the left's very insurgency, combined with a vast and unpredictable undercurrent of explicitly pro-fascist sentiment, raised credible fears of a right-wing authoritarian backlash in the making.

Lewis learned much of what he knew about fascism abroad from his second wife Dorothy Thompson, a prominent journalist who had covered Germany extensively and had been one of the few individuals to personally interview Adolf Hitler. Born in rural Minnesota in 1885, he apprehended it from a framework supplied by the populist and socialist movements of his Midwestern social milieu of the late nineteenth and early twentieth centuries. After graduating college, Lewis joined the Socialist Party of America in 1911, the constituency of which included industrial workers and the lingering remnants of the populist farmers' movement (or at least the farmers' movement's more radical edge). Although he stopped paying dues within a year, he retained the general, democratic socialist and populist orientation of the Socialist Party for the rest of his days. For instance, while he kept aloof from radical causes in his later years, he

[5] Chris Vials, *Haunted by Hitler: Liberals, the Left, and the Fight against Fascism in the United States* (Amherst: University of Massachusetts Press, 2014), 42.

confided to a friend in 1948 that he still considered himself a socialist because government ownership of industry was simply "more efficient." Dorothy Thompson considered her husband "an old-fashioned populist," likely of the socialist variety represented by Eugene V. Debs or Robert La Follette.[6]

It Can't Happen Here centers on a small-town, Vermont newspaper editor named Doremus Jessup and his fight against the American fascist regime of President Buzz Windrip and his successors. In the style of a realist historical novel, the narrative cuts back and forth between the national political scene and the lives of ordinary protagonists; in its course, real historical figures interact with its fictitious characters. Emerging from within the Democratic Party, Windrip is a folksy populist who handily defeats Roosevelt in the Democratic primary and wins the presidential election of 1936. He quickly concentrates executive power to himself and banishes all political parties save for a new one his administration has created, called "The American Corporate State and Patriotic Party" (referred to as "the Corpo"). Before and after taking power, he uses a uniformed militia – the Minute Men (or MMs) – to brutalize the opposition, much like the Blackshirts in Italy and the Brownshirts in Nazi Germany. As both a political movement and a state, the Corpo's rhetoric is recognizably right-wing: Corpo leaders and rank-and-file members consistently speak of restoring traditional American values, reviving the nation's martial glory, intensifying white supremacy, halting immigration, and eviscerating the influence of Jews, foreigners, intellectuals, and the political left in public life.

As in historical fascism, the regime sets up party institutions that parallel established state bodies such as the judiciary, the police, and the educational system, and these new "Corpo" institutions eventually supplant the older ones. Two years after taking power, the Corpo government imposes the death penalty on dissenters and has established a system of concentration camps all over the country. Meanwhile, from the town of Fort Beulah, Vermont, Jessup gradually turns his quiet outrage into action, publishing an underground, anti-government newspaper called *Vermont Vigilance*, an act that eventually lands him in one of the regime's concentration camps for a time. Toward the end of the novel, the government goes through several violent leadership changes, becoming more and more brutal with each new ruler, and whole sections of the country rise in revolt, mostly in

[6] Lingeman, 378, 512; Schorer, 178.

urban centers and rural areas in the Midwest and on the West Coast. The end of the novel finds Jessup once again working with the resistance, called the New Underground, which is locked in an uncertain war of attrition against parts of the country that still consent to the rule of the fascist state.

One of the real insights of *It Can't Happen Here* is the way it captures the distinct nature of American fascist speech and how it registers with people whom it fails to interpellate. In the wake of the Trump presidency, Lewis's portrait of the demagogue Buzz Windrip now reads as being uncannily prescient. In addition to the xenophobic nationalism and explicit politics of Corpo rhetoric (to which I return momentarily), the underlying persona that delivers these politics appears to its opponents as banal, unintelligent, and brazenly dishonest. Before Windrip takes power, while he is still a senator campaigning for the presidency, the antifascist Jessup attends one of his speeches, and Lewis describes it as follows: "watching Senator Windrip, [Jessup] could not explain his power of bewitching large audiences. The Senator was vulgar, almost illiterate, a public liar easily detected, and in his 'ideas' almost idiotic ... his humor the sly cynicism of a country store."[7] Windrip persistently appears to his opponents as an open, obvious charlatan whose ideas are clearly vacuous; to underscore his status as a con man, Lewis tells his readers that Windrip was once a salesman at traveling medicine shows. (These shows were common in the late nineteenth century, in the wild days before the Food and Drug Act of 1906. Traveling medicine salesmen were generally understood to be scam artists who preyed on gullible or desperate rural people.) Lewis tells us that Windrip "redeemed himself, no doubt, by ascending from the vulgar fraud of selling bogus medicine, standing in front of a microphone, to the dignity of selling bogus economics, standing on an indoor platform under mercury-vapor lights in front of a micro-phone."[8] Before he became a US senator, the future dictator was merely a corrupt machine politician devoted to enriching his cronies; once he assumes dictatorial power, his regime is predictably riddled with "graft." He despises the press because it sees through his chicanery, and he projects his own qualities onto journalists when accusing them of "lies."[9]

Lewis reminds us here of a perennially observed aspect of fascist speech: that is, in addition to its cruelty and xenophobia, it appears to the unconverted as fundamentally idiotic and obviously disingenuous. As Hannah Arendt observed of the Nazi functionary Adolf Eichmann:

---

[7] Lewis, 70.   [8] Ibid., 69.   [9] Ibid., 34.

"He was genuinely incapable of uttering a single sentence that was not a cliché" (her book on Eichmann was accordingly subtitled *A Report on the Banality of Evil*).[10] Likewise, Lewis's source Dorothy Thompson wrote, after her personal interview with Hitler, that his "social and economic theory is, to a half-way educated person a tale told by an idiot … what he says, read next day in cold news print, is usually plain nonsense."[11] Fascism's failure to interpellate the formally educated is no doubt fueled by its anti-intellectualism, a hallmark trait of this strand of right-wing politics that has marked it from the outset.

But linked to its perceived "idiocy" is its sloppiness – its brazen dishonesty. Contemporary philosopher Jason Stanley has noted that "[r]egular and repeated obvious lying is part of the process by which fascist politics destroys the information space."[12] This lying is arguably fueled by the epistemology of privilege, and, more specifically, by a politics that violently embraces that privilege. That is, the fascist speaker wants something to be true even though they fear that it is not; yet they believe they can make it come true by asserting it over and over in public. They do so because their subject position has allowed them to get away with this rhetorical Ponzi scheme in the past. Even though many around them can "see right through them," the materiality of their privilege has forced others to defer to their authority; meanwhile, others who embrace that same privilege are encouraged by it and respond accordingly. If fascists successfully convert the state into a fascist regime, Stanley warns us that the "fascist leader can replace truth with power, ultimately lying without consequence."[13] The epistemology of violently embraced privilege drives fascists to ever more reckless behavior, fueling their romantic notion that miracles can be brought about through sheer belief, their salvation won through an eventual "triumph of the will." Of course, the fascist is only dimly aware of his personality structure: as Theodor Adorno and his team of Berkeley-based psychologists reminded us, a profound aversion to self-reflection is a fundamental feature of what they called "the authoritarian personality."[14]

---

[10] Hannah Arendt, *Eichmann in Jerusalem: A Report on the Banality of Evil* (New York: Penguin, 2006), 48.

[11] Dorothy Thompson, *I Saw Hitler!* (New York: Farrar and Rinehart, 1932), 29.

[12] Jason Stanley, *How Fascism Works: The Politics of Us and Them* (New York: Random House, 2018), 57.

[13] Ibid., 57.

[14] T. W. Adorno, Else Frenkel-Brunswik, Daniel Levinson, and R. Nevitt Sanford, *The Authoritarian Personality* (New York: W. W. Norton, 1982), 163–4.

Lewis's dystopia also provides insights into the nexus of race and class that fuels what is called "white nationalist" populism. The fictional Corpo state follows Windrip's rhetoric in that its policies are explicitly anti-Semitic, anti-Black, and anti-immigrant, mobilizing the resentments of the white working class and middle class alike. Racial homogeneity and white, Christian supremacy are central to its drive for national renewal and its cult of tradition. They are also central to the regime's professed populism, which Lewis spends much of the narrative debunking. In his presidential campaign, Buzz Windrip promises to redistribute wealth and even give every white Christian laborer $5,000 a year. His xenophobic economic plan is based on autarky: He rejects international treaties that entangle the nation with foreigners in favor of an 'America First' policy of domestic production.[15]

Yet Windrip is incredibly shrewd when it comes to political power, and he clearly understands wherein it lies. Lewis takes pains to show how bankers and industrialists support Windrip because of his promise to restore order and crack down on "Reds." They understand his populism only as a ruse to secure power, and their intuition is correct. Like the historical Nazi regime, which took the "socialism" out of National Socialism by murdering the leaders of its largely working-class Brownshirt movement (the Sturmabteilung or SA) in 1934, the Windrip regime also silences its genuinely plebian supporters. Bishop Prang, for example, who leads "The League of Forgotten Men," an anti-Semitic movement of the dispossessed that seeks the nationalization of the banks, is put in jail after it becomes clear that no nationalization is forthcoming. The Corpo government ultimately serves the interests of capital by out-lawing the left and stripping the rights of unionized workers. It affirms the right of private property, limiting its economic critiques to the financial sector only, which it racializes as Jewish by making the word "Jewish" an inseparable prefix of the word "banker." This latter move follows a long-standing pattern of racializing economic grievances on the far right, bracketing off finance as parasitic, Jewish, and "international," while venerating manufacturing, farming, and mining as the productive labor of the nation. The fascist is thereby allowed to preserve a faith in capitalism by preserving the fantasy that vital sectors of capitalism (finance and international trade) can be exorcised from it.

Although capitalists ultimately benefit from the Windrip regime, the novel refuses to reduce fascism to a mere capitalist conspiracy. *It Can't*

[15] Lewis, 90.

Happen Here emphasizes the ways in which middle- and working-class white men are agents of authoritarianism, and how capitalists themselves are generally not the ultimate power brokers of a fascist movement. The character Shad Ledue – who stands in for the plebian supporters of Windrip in the novel – eagerly supports the state and becomes its chief representative in his small town because it taps into his hatred of Blacks and "elites" (which the regime redefines as Jews, communists, and sophisticates). Support for the Corpo movement and the regime gives him some "benefits": It allows him the libidinal pleasure of personally brutalizing Jews, African Americans, and leftists, and he materially advances (for a time, at least) when he is made commissioner for Northern Vermont, quite an advance from his earlier position as handyman. Although it restores capitalism, the Windrip regime successfully interpellates people such as Ledue precisely because its driving logics are not strictly economic. Ultimately, its rhetoric is fueled by a complex desire for *national renewal* based on racial homogeneity, white Christian supremacy, patriarchy, and a simplistic cult of tradition. Once in power, it hardens and intensifies all existing social hierarchies by means of extreme violence. In all, *It Can't Happen Here* uses antifascism to explore how racism and religious bigotry can be mobilized through nationalist rhetoric in ways that bring short-term gains for working-class and middle-class white men, and, whether intentionally or not, how capitalism can benefit in the process.

Lewis's reading of fascism was by no means atypical of his generation. Contrary to what many scholars have assumed about the 1930s, the left had a robust and sometimes generative debate about the nature of fascism in that decade, and the analysis did not always lead to simple class reductionism. To be sure, that debate included a crude analysis, especially common before 1935, that I have called elsewhere the "puppet master theory" of fascism: that is, the notion that big business was the true power behind the thrones of Hitler and Mussolini, and that businessmen secretly pulled the strings of fascist demagogues. The puppet master theory rendered race and gender epiphenomenal, disavowed the very real investments of working- and middle-class people in fascism, and gave opponents few tools to combat the specific appeals of fascist nationalism. But a more productive view was equally common: the "gangster theory." Born of a generation immersed in noir detective fiction, the gangster theory held that, although traditional elites enabled fascism, they could not control its direction once the new authoritarian state was created, causing real friction within the class coalitions that initially supported the fascist power grab. As Italian antifascist exile Vincenzo Vacirca wrote in 1933: "Fascism in Italy now takes towards capitalism the position of certain gangsters, hired by some American manufacturers for strike breaking purposes, of whom they cannot rid themselves and who blackmail them without mercy."[16] Though refracted through popular culture, this reading of the class politics of fascism is in line with the views of many contemporary historians of fascism, who also tend to see the upper classes more as enablers of fascism, not its primary agents. Like Sinclair Lewis and so many other liberals and leftists in the 1930s, fascism's historians also tend to view the rich as unable to control the largely middle-class authoritarians once they take control of the state.

The gangster theory informs the plotline of *It Can't Happen Here*. Its capitalist characters fully support Windrip and his regime for his promises to crack down on labor agitation and Reds, but once the Corpo state is fully consolidated, they complain about a lack of autonomy. For instance, Medary Cole, a local manufacturer, complains to Jessup about the regime's official militia, the Minute Men (called "Minnie Mouses" by their opponents), and how they enforce the regime's autarchy and war economy: "I'm getting awful sick of having these Minnie Mouses dictate where I have to buy my gunnysacks and what I can pay my men ... We pay them and pay them big to bully us. It don't look so reasonable as it did in 1936."[17] This gangster theory was quite common in the Socialist Party circles that informed Lewis's analysis, and it became widespread in communist ones as well after the Party's shift to its Popular Front line in 1935. It also informed the modernisms of Dashiell Hammett, Orson Welles, and Bertolt Brecht. This narrative of fascism's class politics said little about race, gender, or nationalism, but because it suggested that non-economic motivations drove fascists, it opened the door, at least partially, to generative questions about their many other driving forces. For one thing is also clear among scholars of fascism: Unlike many conservatives, economics bores fascists. Economics is not their "mobilizing passion," to borrow a phrase from historian Robert Paxton.[18] Rather, they are driven primarily by fantasies of national renewal, racial hierarchy, militarism, and (male) violence.

In the novel, racism, xenophobia, and anti-Semitism are always on the minds of the fascist characters, revealed through their many statements and slurs, as well as in the many practices they pursue. The latter include the

---

[16] Vials, 75–80.   [17] Lewis, 205.
[18] Robert Paxton, *The Anatomy of Fascism* (New York: Alfred A. Knopf, 2004), 41.

full disenfranchisement of African Americans, the banning of Jews from public places, allowing the poor whites of the Minute Men militias to extort or confiscate Black- and Jewish-owned businesses, and the murdering of Black and Jewish professionals. In its rendering of anti-Black racism, Lewis's portrait of fascist dystopia is much more detailed than more contemporary instances of the genre, such as Margaret Atwood's *The Handmaid's Tale* (1985) or Philip Roth's *The Plot Against America* (2004), in which racism against people of color barely figures in their authors' authoritarian projections.

Be that as it may, the narrative's limitations become abundantly clear in its rendering of the resistance. *It Can't Happen Here* figures communists who are brave and courageous but also overly dogmatic: The Communist Party cannot offer resistance on account of its own sectarianism. Instead, the New Underground, led by former Republican candidate Walt Trowbridge, dynamically organizes small farmers in the Northwest, Midwest, and the Dakotas. These areas, Lewis writes, were "the part of America which had always been most 'radical' ... It was the land of the Populists, the Non-Partisan League, the Farmer-Labor Party, and the La Follettes."[19] The liberated zones are organized as farmers' "co-operatives," and, despite the Republican label, Trowbridge mouths anti-corporate sentiments at the end of the novel that make him sound much more like a socialist of the older populist mode.[20]

This nostalgic return of the populist farmers' movement was pure fantasy even in the 1930s, a decade when the largely urban, multiethnic, multiracial Communist Party USA was clearly rising as the most dynamic force on the left, while the Socialist Party of America was in distinct decline. Just as today, the left during the Depression was primarily concentrated in the cities. In exceptions such as rural Alabama, it was driven by African American workers and sharecroppers, as Robin D. G. Kelley has shown,[21] or by striking Mexican or Filipino farmworkers on the West Coast, not by the white Midwestern yeomen imagined by Lewis. The author does, in fact, include African American and Jewish resistance in the novel: Jews form an urban guerilla wing of the New Underground, and African Americans defend their land and rights with guns, fists, and knives at a number of points in the narrative. But his projection of the rural Midwest as the main site of resistance reveals the limits of his white

[19] Lewis, 371.   [20] Ibid., 366.
[21] Robin D. G. Kelley, *Hammer and Hoe* (Chapel Hill: University of North Carolina Press, 1990).

populist imagination, and at a time when contemporary history furnished him with ample evidence that its course was trending in quite different directions.

Populism, as historian Michael Kazin has shown, is neither intrinsically left-wing nor right-wing. Rather, it is a set of politics that envisions a virtuous majority of ordinary people beset by self-serving, undemocratic elites who have corrupted some better way of life that existed in the past. This description now sounds like a pithy summation of reactionary politics, but populism was not always a narrative of the dominant order. Before 1945, populism was mainly employed by the left – namely, the populist farmers' movement, the early Socialist Party, the labor movement – yet was increasingly claimed by the political right after the war. The past they looked back to included earlier instances of the labor movement, a free soil republic of small farmers, artisanal production, and egalitarian strains they saw in the American Revolution. In Lewis's 1930s, populism was up for grabs, claimed by the left (the Popular Front and the Congress of Industrial Organizations) and the right (Father Coughlin's "Christian Front").[22] Its fluid status is reflected in the novel in that it animates both the Minute Men militia and the opponents of the regime. Its protagonist, Doremus Jessup, after all, is inspired to fight fascism not by contemporary communists abroad, but by American abolitionists and revolutionaries such as Thaddeus Stevens, John Brown, Ethan Allen, and, problematically, Thomas Jefferson.

Ultimately, *It Can't Happen Here* exposes the dangers of populism while also showing us the limits of using populism to fight populism. Lewis's dystopian sketch illustrates how the political right can easily use this mode to cement cross-class alliances of white Christians against "parasites" above and below, diverting their class resentments toward people of color, religious minorities, and only a small section of the elite. Unintentionally, he also illustrates how its majoritarianism, when used by the left, can flatten and homogenize the experiences of different groups of workers and subjects, ultimately ignoring the very real democratic resistance and contributions of the racialized. At its best, populism can aid the fight against fascism by redirecting a recognizable political frame away from the right (the Popular Front) and by re-instilling faith in the democratic capacities and shared interests of a classed majority

---

[22] Michael Kazin, *The Populist Persuasion: An American History* (Ithaca, NY: Cornell University Press, 1995).

("the 99 percent" of Occupy Wall Street). Its "backward glance" can highlight how fascism corrupts hard-won gains wrought by social movements and democratic struggles of the past. But its narrative of shared interest cannot be blind to the historical reality of racial and gender hierarchies dividing "the people," and majoritarian modes always carry this danger. At the end of the day, populism may not be enough to ensure that it doesn't happen here.

CHAPTER 17

All the King's Men (1946): Robert Penn Warren

Jonathan S. Cullick

Among political novels in US literature, *All the King's Men* is "the land-mark against which all other such novels are now judged and [it] remains the most significant."[1] Based loosely on Huey P. Long, the governor (1928–32) and US senator (1932–5) of Louisiana, the novel's plot is set in the frame of 1936–9 with flashbacks to the narrator's idyllic youth and his protagonist's emergence in politics. Young reporter Jack Burden meets political neophyte Willie Stark in the summer of 1922 and follows his trajectory in state politics over the subsequent years. Ambitious but initially an ineffective campaigner, Stark rises in public stature by freeing himself from the political establishment and asserting his own populist voice. Having educated himself in law, he self-educates in politics, intui-tively evolving from a policy wonk to a demagogue. Once in office as Governor Stark, he retains his populist ideals but uses graft and intimida-tion to implement his policies. Eventually, his corruption becomes more gratuitous than functional; he commits adultery and attempts to cover up his son's scandalous behavior. His political world begins to collapse when he desires to build something free from corruption – a hospital to serve the poor. These events are narrated by Jack Burden, who follows Willie's rise as a reporter but eventually joins Willie's administration as an aide and opposition researcher. Jack's own story forms the core of the novel as much as the story of the man he follows.

Jack's – or anyone's – following of Willie stands at the center of the novel's political themes. This is a novel not only about the leader, *the king*, but also about the devotion of the followers, *the king's men and women*. While Stark's populist program garners widespread support in his eco-nomically poor state, it is what Stark says and how he says it that attracts

---

[1] Harold Woodell, "From Huey Long to Willie Stark: Louisiana Politics in AKM," in *Songs of the New South: Writing Contemporary Louisiana*, ed. Suzanne Disheroon Green and Lisa Abney (Westport, CT: Greenwood Press, 2001), 68.

attention. His charisma is magnetic. The political rhetoric in *All the King's Men* positions this novel as a historical and contemporary case study of American populism and demagoguery.

Before the 1930s setting of *All the King's Men*, populism in the US had a brief history as a formal political movement. In the 1890s, the rising People's Party, an agrarian movement of southern and western farmers, put forward their own presidential candidate for the Democratic Party nomination: William Jennings Bryan. The People's Party faded after Bryan lost the general election of 1896. Although populist impulses within political parties have occasionally arisen since then, no populist political party has re-emerged.

As an orientation or style in US politics, however, populism has had a much broader history. Populism in the US had its earliest voices in Thomas Jefferson, Andrew Jackson, and Abraham Lincoln. Populist voices were heard at the turn of the century in the founding of the American Federation of Labor (1886) and the National Association for the Advancement of Colored People (1909), in the 1920s and 1930s radio broadcasts of Father Charles Coughlin, in the Congress of Industrial Organizations (founded in 1935) and the New Deal of the 1930s, in the Cold War Senate hearings of Joseph McCarthy in the 1950s, in the 1960s segregationist campaigns of George Wallace, and in the turn to the right in US politics throughout the 1970s and 1980s. During the second decade of the twenty-first century, populist voices have been heard on the left in the policy positions of Bernie Sanders, and on the right in the rallies and tweets of Donald J. Trump.[2]

National Review writer Michael Brendan Dougherty defines populism as "a political style that locates the legitimacy of political action and reform in ordinary people directed primarily against what it sees as elite groups or corrupted elite institutions." *New York Times* columnist Ross Douthat defines populism as "a political tendency that tries to rally voters around issues and ideas that have broad mass appeal that are excluded from or

---

[2] For a historical survey of populism and its characteristics, see Michael Kazin, *The Populist Persuasion*, revised edition (Ithaca, NY: Cornell University Press, 2017). For surveys of the intellectual style of populism, see Jon Meacham, *The Soul of America: The Battle for Our Better Angels* (New York: Random House, 2018); Richard Hofstadter, *Anti-Intellectualism in American Life* (New York: Random House, 1963); and Hofstadter's outstanding essay, "The Paranoid Style in American Politics," *Harper's*, November 1964, 77–86, https://harpers.org/archive/1964/11/the-paranoid-style-in-american-politics/

minimized in elite circles and debates; this is why you can have populisms of the left and of the right."[3]

These definitions accurately describe populism in US politics and in the novel *All the King's Men*. Populism may be defined further by its historical, political, psychological, and sociological characteristics. Any definition of populism must also include its rhetorical characteristics because we know that a political actor is populist through the way they talk. Populism may or may not be enacted in an elected politician's policy proposals, but it is always performed in language. Populism is flexible enough to course its way from the political left to the political right. In his classic study of populism, Michael Kazin defines it not as an ideology but as a "language of mass discontent." For sociolinguist Geoffrey Nunberg, populism is "as much a matter of style as substance": "Whoever's deploying it, the language of populism always involves a direct appeal to the emotions." Columnists David Brooks and George Will respectively describe populists as "defined by what they are against" as their "constant ingredient has been resentment."[4]

Wherever on the left–right political spectrum populism appears, it always performs a key rhetorical maneuver: It draws a line between those perceived to be *regular or real people* and those considered to be *the elite*. The populist's emotive rhetoric always invokes a binary social structure with the style and substance of grievance. The *people* are authentic and practical, the producers of society, mostly manual laborers, and overwhelmingly middle class and white (and usually depicted as male). The *elite* are artificial and effete, dependent on the labor of others, intellectual and condescending, profligate and manipulative. *The people* are small town, rural, and powerless. *The elite* are urban, cosmopolitan, and in power.[5]

All the King's Men embodies this populist binary and its rhetorical moves. A powerful moment in populist rhetoric appears at the novel's end, as Jack Burden investigates the events leading up to the assassination of Stark. At the public library, Jack runs into Sugar-Boy, Willie's driver

---

[3] Jane Coaston, Ross Douthat, and Michael Brendan Dougherty, "Can Republicans Make Populism Work Without Trump?," *The Argument*: New York Times [podcast], hosted by Jane Coaston, March 3, 2021, www.stitcher.com/show/the-argument/episode/can-republicans-make-populism-work-without-trump-82094736

[4] Kazin, *Populist Persuasion*, xi; Geoffrey Nunberg, "People Power; the Curious Fate of Populism: How Politics Turned into Pose," *New York Times*, August 15, 2004, www.nytimes.com/2004/08/15/weekinreview/people-power. Conservative columnists David Brooks and George Will are quoted in Henry Olsen, "Populism, American Style," *National Affairs*, Summer 2010, 4.

[5] Kazin, *Populist Persuasion*, 13–15.

and bodyguard. Sugar-Boy had grown up in a rough neighborhood, poor and bullied and no doubt headed for a life of street crime. With a stutter, Sugar-Boy also has difficulty speaking. Willie, who himself had come from humble origins, gave Sugar-Boy a job and self-respect. Wearing a business suit, with a .38 caliber revolver under his coat, and commanding the wheel of the governor's automobile, Sugar-Boy became the tough guy. But Willie gave him something else: a voice. What Sugar-Boy had difficulty saying, Willie could say for him. Now, directionless without Willie, Sugar-Boy reflects: "He could t-t-talk so good ... The B-B-Boss could. Couldn't nobody t-t-talk like him." "Sure," the sardonic Jack Burden replies, "he was a great talker." Sugar-Boy articulates why ordinary people are drawn to Willie as their representative in government.[6]

That magnetism is on display in the opening of the novel as Governor Stark and his aides are driving to his hometown for a photo op. To show the voters that he is a devoted family man with wholesome values, Stark will have his picture taken with his wife, son, and elderly father (despite his affairs and disconnection from all three). In a bit of comic relief, the dog Buck, who refuses to play the happy-to-see-his-master role in the photo session, is the only individual present with the good sense to avoid the whole political charade. On their way to this appointment, the Boss and his entourage stop at a drugstore for some cold drinks. Displayed on the wall above the soda fountain is a portrait of Stark, "a picture about six times life size," with the caption "My study is the heart of the people." A crowd of admiring supporters gathers at the drugstore and demands, "Speech, Willie, speech!" Jack Burden notes an indefinable transformation in Willie's expression and demeanor as he begins to address the crowd: "I'm not going to make any speech ... I didn't come here to make any speech. I came up here to go out and see my pappy, and see if he's got anything left in the smokehouse fit to eat. I'm gonna say: Pappy, now what about all that smoked sausage you wuz bragging about ..." What follows are remarks, punctuated with biblical quotations, in which Willie promises to fight for the common people against the powerful interests of the political establishment in the state capitol. Everything in Willie's impromptu speech – the simple vocabulary, the attack on elites, the exaggerated country accent – is classic populism.[7]

[6] Robert Penn Warren, *All the King's Men* (New York: Houghton Mifflin Harcourt, 1974 [1946]), 635.
[7] Ibid., 39, 9, 11, 14.

It is a style of public speaking that Willie started to cultivate years earlier in a hotel room one night after he experienced the failure of trying to explain policy to his audiences. His speeches had been filled with statistics and data points about tax and transportation programs. Audiences were yawning and Stark knew he was failing. In a pivotal scene in the novel, Burden advises Stark to stop boring his audience with issues and inspire them instead – to appeal to pathos and not logos, to make them feel like they are part of a movement:

> You tell 'em too much. Just tell 'em you're gonna soak the fat boys, and forget the rest of the tax stuff . . . Hell, make 'em cry, make 'em laugh . . . Or make 'em mad . . . It's up to you to give 'em something to stir 'em up and make 'em feel alive again. Just for half an hour. That's what they come for. Tell 'em anything. But for Sweet Jesus' sake don't try to improve their minds.[8]

Although some might protest that Burden's advice condescends to the voters, it is entirely valid. For the fictional Willie Stark and for real-life politicians, it works. Voters get motivated when they feel that they are part of something larger than themselves.

After Jack presents this reality to Willie, political aide Sadie Burke confronts Willie with another reality: He is being used by the political establishment. The morning after some late-night heavy drinking, Willie declares independence from the political establishment. He gives a break-out speech that employs Jack Burden's suggested populist speaking strategy. On the stage at a rally, Willie dramatically tosses aside the script that was written for him. Sharing his own sense of grievance with his audience, he identifies himself as a "hick" like them. Intuitively following an unwritten populist stylebook, Stark connects with his audience. He assures them that they are smarter and more informed than the elites, they don't need anyone to tell them anything, and that indeed they – not the elites – constitute the true embodiment of "the state":

> "I have a speech here," he said. "It is a speech about what this state needs. But there's no use telling you what this state needs. You are the state. You know what you need. Look at your pants. Have they got holes in the knee? Listen to your belly. Did it ever rumble for emptiness? Look at your crop. Did it ever rot in the field because the road was so bad you couldn't get it to market? Look at your kids. Are they growing up ignorant as you and dirt because there isn't any school for them?"

---

[8] Ibid., 108.

From this opening, Willie transitions into a story about his own life, starting with his beginnings as a "hick" to his current victimization by the elite political establishment: "'It's a funny story,' he said. 'Get ready to laugh. Get ready to bust your sides for it is sure a funny story. It's about a hick. It's about a red-neck, like you all, if you please. Yeah, like you.'" Stark brings his biography up to the moment when the elites tried to take advantage of him, just as they disrespect all the "hicks." Presenting himself as their representative – as their voice – he concludes his speech: "The truth is going to be told and I'm going to tell it." From this point forward, this is how Willie will greet his audiences: "'Friends, red-necks, suckers, and fellow hicks' ... And he would pause, letting the words sink in ... 'That's what you are. And me – I'm one, too.'" Eventually, Willie will get the crowd chanting "Nail 'em up!" – his promise to hold the elites in the state capitol accountable.[9]

This breakout speech demonstrates several elements of the populist style. First, the speaker – more educated, economically powerful, and politically connected than his audience – establishes a connection with those listening. Willie solidifies his identification with the agrarian voters. Second, the source of that shared connection is always grievance. Their resentments and Willie's become identical. Third – and most important for achieving public office, because the speaker has political access yet is still one of the people – the speaker tells them that he will be able to represent their interests. Willie promises that he will be their voice. He started out in life as a hick working in the dirt like them, but now he is working on the inside among the elite. However – and this is important – he assures them that he is not *of* the elite. The fourth element is the creation of a simple, emotional, combative, anti-elitist message: "Nail 'em up!"

A contemporary example illustrates the timelessness of these elements. In his acceptance speech for the nomination at the 2016 Republican National Convention, Donald J. Trump followed the formula articulated by Jack Burden and implemented by Willie Stark. Like Willie, he connected to ordinary voters, articulated their grievances and sense of powerlessness, and promised to use his power to be their insider agent:

> Every day I wake up determined to deliver a better life for the people all across this nation that have been neglected, ignored, and abandoned ... I have visited the laid-off factory workers ... These are the forgotten men

---

[9] Ibid., 135–6, 140, 142, 144.

and women of our country ... These are people who work hard but no longer have a voice. *I am your voice* ... I have joined the political arena so that the powerful can no longer beat up on people that cannot defend themselves. Nobody knows the system better than me, which is why *I alone can fix it.*[10]

Similar to Willie Stark's "Nail 'em up!" chant, Trump's contemporary populist rallies solicited audience participation with simple, syncopated, three-word slogans: "Build the Wall!" "Lock Her Up!" "Send Them Back!" "Stop the Steal!" Harold Woodell explains how these techniques work: "Warren has shown how the dynamics of demagoguery work to lead a man like Willie Stark to gain control of the masses through calculating techniques of manipulation. Following a pattern common to other powerful rulers, Stark" – and any other populist speaker – "identifies with the common people, understands their needs, attacks a common enemy, and uses his power to gain total control of state politics."[11]

What makes this kind of populist rhetoric perennially attractive are the socioeconomic conditions of a population that perceives itself to be vulnerable. The populist arises in fertile ground. Warren writes *All the King's Men* in the context of economic distress throughout the American South. Explaining the rise of Huey Long (and thus of Willie Stark), Woodell describes the degraded situation in Louisiana in 1880–1920:

> Politicians and powerbrokers developed a system of state governance like no other in the postbellum South ... The Pelican State crafted a social system in which all of the political power and most of the wealth rested in the hands of a privileged few, while the vast majority of the people languished in a forlorn condition of near servitude. Due to an arrogant, indifferent government, poverty levels ranked the highest in the United States while literacy levels and public services such as roads and health care were among the lowest.[12]

Twenty years after H. L. Mencken charged that the South was "almost as sterile, artistically, intellectually, culturally, as the Sahara Desert," President Franklin D. Roosevelt in 1938 called the South the "nation's #1 economic problem." There was in the US "an economic unbalance ... that can and must be righted."[13]

---

[10] Donald Trump, "Donald Trump's 2016 Republican National Convention Speech," *ABC News*, July 22, 2016, https://abcnews.go.com/Politics/full-text-donald-trumps-2016-republican-nationalconvention/story?id=40786529, emphasis added.

[11] Ibid.; Woodell, 72.   [12] Woodell, 68.

[13] H. L. Menken, "The Sahara of the Bozart," in *The American Scene: A Reader,* ed. Huntington Cairns (New York: Alfred A. Knopf, 1977 [1917]), 157–8; Franklin Delano Roosevelt, "Message to

Jack Burden refers to these conditions in the South to explain the rise of Willie Stark. In the novel's opening sequence, the car speeds down the new concrete highway that Governor Stark had built in this poor rural state. The first chapter describes silent sawmills abandoned by their absentee owners. Jack Burden says,

> This is a poor state, the opposition always screamed. But the Boss said: "There is a passel of pore folks living in it and no mistake, but the state isn't poor. It is just a question of who has got his front feet in the trough when slopping time comes. And I aim to do me some shoving and thump me some snouts."

Willie will take a little of his share along the way (greasing the wheels of government, as he says), but he will redistribute wealth to assist the poor.[14]

The *people versus elite* binary is explicitly addressed during a dinner party at Jack's family home in Burden's Landing, a hamlet of upper-middle-class professionals. A wealthy guest at the dinner party voices a conservative critique about the increasing taxation, regulation, and size of government – as well as the corruption – in Governor Stark's administration. Jack observes that everyone at the dinner party "assumed that even though I did work for Willie my heart was with them." Then he violates expectations by arguing that Willie got elected because the government has not been working and the fault, he implies, rests with some of the people in attendance at the party. As Jack says:

> Doesn't it all boil down to this? If the government of this state for quite a long time back had been doing anything for the folks in it, would Stark have been able to get out there with his bare hands and bust the boys? And would he be having to make so many short cuts to get something done to make up for the time lost all these years in not getting something done? I'd just like to submit that question for the sake of argument.[15]

This argument about popular discontent with the elites who have caused or ignored and benefited from poverty conditions is classic populism.

The poverty pervading the rural South has long been addressed in southern literature. Erskine Caldwell's *Tobacco Road* (1932) depicts the desperate conditions of sharecroppers, and although this novel and *God's Little Acre* (1933) could stereotype the poor as coarse and over-sexualized, he could also show their lives as poignant in their endurance. The poor

the Conference on Economic Conditions of the South," July 4, 1938, www.presidency.ucsb.edu/documents/message-the-conference-economic-conditions-the-south
[14] Warren, *All the King's Men*, 592.   [15] Ibid., 187.

whites in Harper Lee's *To Kill a Mockingbird*, Bob Ewell and his daughter Mayella, are depicted as violent and physically abusive, over-sexualized and falsely accusing a Black man of rape. Their depraved characteristics are contrasted with the well-respected Atticus Finch.

Beyond these stereotypes of "rednecks" or "hicks," the literature has offered an agrarian refiguration of rural southerners as doing the most noble work, God's work, farming. Agrarianism holds that cultivation of the soil provides independence, supporting individual liberty and self-reliance along with the social values of family, faith, and community. It is real work for real people, in contrast to the abstraction and artificiality of urban life, industrialism, and intellectual work. Agrarianism has been celebrated in US and southern literature since Thomas Jefferson called farmers God's chosen people in *Notes on the State of Virginia* (1785) and nineteenth-century southern writers such as Joel Chandler Harris, Thomas Nelson Page, William Gilmore Simms, and Henry Timrod extolled its virtues in contrast to city life. In *The Sound and the Fury*, *The Bear*, and the Snopes trilogy, William Faulkner depicts the tragic loss of family land and rural life following the destructive encroachment of commercialism and industrialism.

Warren himself was part of the group of Southern Agrarians based in Vanderbilt University. The group, which included Donald Davidson, Allen Tate, and John Crowe Ransom, published the manifesto *I'll Take My Stand: The South and the Agrarian Tradition* (1930). Warren's contribution, "The Briar Patch," was especially troublesome for implicitly supporting a segregated vision of agrarian life. An embarrassed Warren would later repudiate this essay implicitly in *Segregation: The Inner Conflict of the South* (1956) and explicitly in *Who Speaks for the Negro?* (1965), interviews he conducted with Black leaders of the Civil Rights Movement.[16]

But "The Briar Patch" is a reminder that in southern literature and US politics, the economic conditions of agrarianism and populism have a history of being articulated in racial terms. Kazin notes that "competing populist traditions have long thrived in the US." The *civic* tradition directs economic frustration upward toward corporate elites (e.g., Bernie Sanders). The *racial* tradition presents a "narrower and more ethnically restrictive" definition of "the people" as "real Americans" – "the patriotic (white) majority in the middle" between the corporate/academic elites above in

---

[16] Robert Penn Warren, "The Briar Patch" [1930] in *I'll Take My Stand* (Baton Rouge: Louisiana State University Press, 1977), 264; *Who Speaks for the Negro?* (New Haven, CT: Yale University Press, 2014), 10–11.

alliance with "the unworthy, dark-skinned poor below." This latter tradition of populism has been dominant.[17]

All the King's Men presents an all-white political world. The only Black laborers are men who Jack recalls working on the roadside (and Jack uses a racist term for them). Willie never addresses racial equality. However, the issue that puts Willie on the political map is his willingness to give a contract to a company that employs Black labor when it means being a responsible steward of the (white) taxpayers' money. The issue is the contract for construction of a new schoolhouse. Willie is outspoken in his support for the lower-bidding company that employs Black workers and his criticism of an overpriced sweetheart deal for a company that employs convict labor. The latter company gets the contract, the construction is substandard, and the result is a structural failure with children injured. Stark is hailed as a hero for his prophetic attempts to obstruct that contract. Back when the schoolhouse fight is at full volume, Jack's editor sends him to Mason City to investigate. Jack interviews locals who call Willie a "nigger-lover" for supporting the lower bid by the company employing Black carpenters, plasterers, and bricklayers. Jack explains: "Mason County, as I said, is red-neck country – and worse, some of the Negroes would be getting better pay, being skilled laborers." With this issue, Willie "became symbolically the spokesman for the tongue-tied population of honest men."[18]

Willie has a program for public healthcare, a hospital open to all, which will be his legacy. A Stark critic (one of those dinner party guests) protests this and other programs: "Free this and free that and free other. Every wool-hat jackass thinking the world is free. Who's going to pay? That's what I want to know? What does he [Governor Stark] say to that, Jack?" Jack's answer: "I never asked him." But, of course, we know the answer and so does the dinner party guest.[19] Huey Long was praised for providing infrastructure, public services, and assistance to both poor whites and Blacks in Louisiana. White conservatives criticized him for high taxation and business regulation.

Still, some liberal critics cited Huey Long for failing to pass any long-term legislation to improve labor, wages, or social conditions. Populism sometimes seems to be more rhetoric than reality. As Jane Coaston says, populism often manipulates voters more than it manipulates policy;

---

[17] Michael Kazin, "Trump and American Populism," *Foreign Affairs* 95.6 (2016), 17–24, here 17.
[18] Warren, *All the King's Men*, 85, 90, 95.   [19] Ibid., 185.

it makes promises but fails to show up.[20] With Willie Stark, however, Warren created an idealist who tries to transform rhetoric into policy. Willie does acknowledge that "there's some graft, but there's just enough to make the wheels turn without squeaking ... There never was a machine rigged up by man didn't represent some loss of energy." But when Stark says on his deathbed, "It might have been all different, Jack," we hear Coaston's critique and echoes of William Faulkner's Thomas Sutpen in *Absalom, Absalom!* uttering in bewilderment, "I had a design in my mind ... Where did I make the mistake in it?"[21] A man who would be king watches in disbelief as his self-created world crashes down around him. So strongly did Willie believe in his programs that he used corrupt and strong-arm tactics to accomplish his goals. Willie says that good things can be made out of dirt. He wants the hospital to be the exception to this rule, but even the hospital cannot be free from such a compromise of values. As Judge Irwin says at the dinner party, Stark understands that in politics one must break eggs to make omelets. The problem with this eggs-to-omelets approach is that neither the king's horses nor the king's men can undo the damage.

Alexander Hamilton was prescient about populism in Federalist #1: "Of those men who have overturned the liberties of republics, the greatest number have begun their career by paying an obsequious court to the people, commencing demagogues and ending tyrants."[22] *All the King's Men* leaves us with questions: Do we have no choice other than a play-by-the-rules-but-ineffective leader versus one who is effective but corrupt? If compromise is the grease that turns the wheels, is any liberal value immune from compromise or negation? Is any institution of liberal government secure against a constitutionally elected authoritarian? If there are no angels in politics, is there any hope for us mortals?

---

[20] Coaston, "Can Republicans Make Populism Work Without Trump?" Also see Joseph Blotner's comments on Huey Long: He "kept faith, by and large, with the people who elected him," giving the people (here quoting Arthur Schlesinger) "schools, hospitals, roads and public services." Notably, "Poor whites and even Negroes had unprecedented opportunities." However, Long still benefited personally from the contributions he took in from the plutocrats, and, as a result, beyond infrastructure, Long "left behind no record of social or labor legislation." Joseph Blotner, *The Modern American Political Novel 1900–1960* (Austin: University of Texas Press, 1966), 201.

[21] Warren, *All the King's Men*, 592, 603; William Faulkner, *Absalom, Absalom!* (New York: Vintage, 1990 [1936]), 212.

[22] Alexander Hamilton, "Federalist Number 1," in *The Federalist Papers*, ed. Clinton Rossiter (New York: Penguin, 1961).

CHAPTER 18

Invisible Man *(1952): Ralph Ellison*

Nathaniel Mills

The Vital Depths: *Invisible Man* and Political Epistemology from Below

Ralph Ellison's *Invisible Man* was published, to mainstream success and recognition, in 1952, and its reception was couched in the terms of the new liberal sensibility that had become hegemonic in the US political and cultural establishment. Postwar liberalism was organized by the affirmation of democratic political and pluralist cultural values, a reverence for the complexity of human nature and individual liberty that precluded programmatic resolutions to social problems, and the equation of radicalisms of the left and right as teleologically totalitarian. Its influential champion, in the early stages of the Cold War, was Arthur Schlesinger, Jr. The Harvard scholar of American political history sought to define liberalism outside the previously dominant terms of the 1930s and 1940s Popular Front, which had consociated backers of the Democratic New Deal and the pro-Soviet Communist left, and had approached social change through broadly collectivist framings of working-class and multiethnic solidarity. Schlesinger argued that the Cold War world required a more conservative program of democratic individualism and uncompromising opposition to Soviet or communist influence. In *The Vital Center* (1949), Schlesinger described human nature as marked by a tendency away from the responsibilities of individualism to the comforts and psychic outlets of tyranny. As a result, only American democracy, with its emphases on gradual reform, consensus-based decision-making, and the liberties of the individual, could address social needs while preserving individual freedom and difference against the totalitarian tendencies of radical alternatives.[1]

---

[1] For the historical and political contexts of Schlesinger's intervention, see Howard Brick and Christopher Phelps, *Radicals in America: The US Left Since the Second World War* (Cambridge: Cambridge University Press, 2015), 22–35; Stephen P. Depoe, *Arthur M. Schlesinger, Jr., and the Ideological History of American Liberalism* (Tuscaloosa: University of Alabama Press, 1994), 3–11;

Democracy had, however, to be defended with patriotic fervor if it was to triumph over the global spread of Soviet ideology. His trope for the radical defense of normative democratic processes was the vital center: a position to be maintained against right-wing and left-wing radicalism with uncompromising resilience. "[I]n a more fundamental sense," Schlesinger asks, "does not the center itself represent one extreme?" Liberalism, with the help of this trope, becomes a "fighting faith,"[2] an extremist manifestation of political moderation that, for instance, could support the persecution of US leftists, and imperialist military ventures abroad, in the name of combatting radical influence.

The *Vital Center* references what Thomas Schaub calls the "narrative of chastened liberalism" frequently invoked by US intellectuals and writers after World War II, a narrative of an exile's return to faith in American democracy occasioned by disillusion, thanks to Stalinism and Nazism, with radical politics.[3] This narrative could certainly fit the protagonist's journey in *Invisible Man*, through various institutions he learns to see as corrupted by the desire for totalitarian-like power, toward his concluding decision that his grandfather's cryptic deathbed advice instructs him to "affirm the principle on which the country was built." A positive review of the novel by Delmore Schwartz thus ran in the same 1952 issue of *Partisan Review* as the symposium "Our Country and Our Culture." An editorial preface to the symposium's individual contributions articulated *Partisan Review*'s participation in the new liberal discourse, arguing that American writers in large part no longer oppose their country as a "land of capitalist reaction." Instead, they adopt a new "affirmative attitude toward America," recognizing that "the democratic values which America either embodies or promises are desirable in purely human terms": Democracy "is not merely a capitalist myth" but offers the "only immediate alternative to Russian totalitarianism."[4] Schaub argues that, while *Invisible Man*'s treatment of racial injustice provides trenchant political critiques, the novel also synthesizes ahistorical or apolitical themes of individualism with a political sensibility largely loyal to the postwar liberal defense of the American project. Hence, establishment critics such as R. W. B. Lewis, Richard

Richard Aldous, *Schlesinger: The Imperial Historian* (New York: W. W. Norton, 2017), 122–3, 132–40.

[2] Arthur M. Schlesinger, Jr., *The Vital Center: The Politics of Freedom* (Boston, MA: Houghton Mifflin, 1949), 256, 245.

[3] Thomas Hill Schaub, *American Fiction in the Cold War* (Madison: University of Wisconsin Press, 1991), 7.

[4] "Our Country and Our Culture," *Partisan Review* 19.3 (1952): 283–5; Delmore Schwartz, "Fiction Chronicle: The Wrongs of Innocence and Experience," *Partisan Review* 19.3 (1952): 354–9.

Chase, and Stephen Spender extolled the novel for "going 'beyond'" antiracism and anti-capitalism.[5]

However, crucial differences between Ellison's novel and postwar liberal hegemony, as well as the particular if idiosyncratic investments of Ellison as a political thinker, can be suggested by juxtaposing *Invisible Man* and *The Vital Center*. Both texts use a spatial metaphor to introduce new schema for parsing the US political field. For Schlesinger, the vital center tropes his intentionally paradoxical relocating of the values of centrism to the polarized position of an extremism in order to create a new political spectrum. The trope thus throws political common sense out of joint by aggregating historically opposed discourses such as communism and fascism and isolating liberalism from its recent proximity to the left. In *Invisible Man*, Ellison similarly uses the trope of the depths or underground to excavate an epistemological vantage point from which he can re-examine American institutions according to new criteria: Does a sociopolitical institution act in a manner consistent with the intent of enacting social change based on its underlying values? And, if not, can its abandoned principles be rescued and repurposed? A political movement or institution of necessity uses a wide range of tactics and shifting strategic aims, but such choices must be grounded in an underlying commitment to sociopolitical alterity. If not, it effectively forsake their deeper vision of difference for cynical self-interest, for gains easily confined within the sociopolitical terrain of the present: It help maintain the status quo by reinforcing their place within it.[6]

To cite one example from the novel, Bledsoe, the college president, performs servility and gratitude to Norton to ensure Norton's continued financial support of the college. But he does so not as a means to a socially transformative end, not as a subversive strategy for achieving the college's racial uplift ideals of civic inclusion through education. Instead, he enacts stereotypical expectations of Black submission to help reproduce the structural racism that subjugates African Americans *because that system provides him with a secure and powerful location within it.* "It's a nasty deal and I don't always like it myself … But I've made my place in it and I'll have every Negro in the country hanging on tree limbs by morning if it means staying where I am." Like Ellison's famous description of the statue of the college's

[5] Schaub, 92, 113, 114.
[6] For a related reading of *Invisible Man* focused on its engagement with the political category of the utopian, see Nathaniel Mills, "Writing Brotherhood: The Utopian Politics of Ralph Ellison's *Invisible Man*," in *Lineages of the Literary Left: Essays in Honor of Alan M. Wald*, ed. Howard Brick, Robbie Lieberman, and Paula Rabinowitz (Ann Arbor: Michigan Publishing, 2015).

Founder, the surface-level manifestation of the college's vision of emancipation becomes indistinguishable from the reproduction of enslavement. The statue depicts the Founder holding the veil of social and ideological exclusion over a "kneeling slave," and the narrator cannot tell "whether the veil is really being lifted, or lowered more firmly in place; whether I am witnessing a revelation or a more efficient blinding."[7] The visual ambiguity bespeaks the absence of any subsurface key to its resolution: The underlying sociopolitical aim of "revelation" has been absorbed in its practice of complicity with Jim Crow and continued institutional "blinding."

John S. Wright characterizes Ellison's epistemological approach to political questions as a dialectical questioning rooted in a "black cultural tradition independent of political ideology," a questioning that in a "subterranean" manner interrogates the viability of social, political, and cultural theories with respect to the vicissitudes of African American experience.[8] I see a similarly idiosyncratic and subterranean analysis at work in *Invisible Man.* Postwar liberalism typically affirmed not only the ideal values of democratic equality and freedom, but the US state's current institutions as the best hope of eventually concretizing those values as social realities. Ellison's affirmation, to reference the Latin origins of the term, is more *radical,* a matter of redirecting the target of political commitment from surface-level institutional affiliation or defense to deep-rooted ethical and political values whose hope of material realization demands social transformation. The depths, for Ellison, locates a commitment not to extant if imperfect political processes as safeguards against extremism, but to fundamental principles – the inextricability of individual fulfillment, non-alienation, community, and equality, regardless of how each might be articulated in disparate political discourses – whose ethical demand for social fulfillment defines a transformative politics and serves as an evaluative metric of any institution ostensibly proclaiming them. Thinking politics from the depths, rather than the center, implies the radical uprooting of the surface alignments of American society.

Ellison from the Center, Right, and Left: *Invisible Man*'s Political Reputations

On the other hand, it was hardly surprising that Ellison and Schlesinger became friends when they met later in the 1950s:[9] Aspects of postwar liberalism certainly influenced *Invisible Man,* and it was arguably the

---

[7] Ralph Ellison, *Invisible Man* (New York: Vintage, 1995), 143, 36.
[8] John S. Wright, *Shadowing Ralph Ellison* (Jackson: University Press of Mississippi, 2006), 67–8.
[9] Arnold Rampersad, *Ralph Ellison: A Biography* (New York: Vintage, 2007): 524–5.

dominant ideological orientation of Ellison's celebrated postwar essays on culture and politics. Ellison also described his novel, upon its publication, using the ascendant liberal political terminology of the day. Accepting the 1953 National Book Award, he explained that, while he wanted to highlight "the inequalities and brutalities of our society," he sought to avoid the "narrow naturalism" of proletarian and protest fiction that, in its magnification of economic and racial oppression, generates only "unrelieved despair" about the state of the country. Instead, he sought to affirm American history and culture's "images of hope, human fraternity and individual self-realization."[10] Ellison, who had begun his literary career in the 1930s on the US Communist left, here performs for the literary establishment his own "chastened" turn from radical protest toward an "affirmative attitude toward America."[11]

The Black Communist literary left in 1952 accordingly denounced *Invisible Man* as an opportunistic sellout to the new political mood. Abner Berry, John Oliver Killens, and Lloyd Brown described it as a sensationalist potboiler teeming with sexual debauchery, excessive violence, anti-communist and racist stereotypes, and the phony universalism of what Brown called Ellison's "one-man-against-the-world theme."[12] Black Arts critics in the next decade, such as Larry Neal and Ernest Kaiser, saw Ellison as out of touch with contemporary Black life and, as a result, a purveyor of liberal political and European cultural and philosophical norms. Kaiser called *Invisible Man* "not a novel about Black protest or Black struggle against injustice, but a contrived novel ... for the existential notion that each person must solve his own problems individualistically and alone ... [T]he novel describes no Black's life as a whole ever lived anywhere in this country." Neal described the novel as "profound" but having "little bearing on the world as the 'New Breed' sees it ... We know who we are, and we are not invisible, *at least not to each other*."[13]

---

[10] Ralph Ellison, *The Collected Essays of Ralph Ellison*, ed. John F. Callahan (New York: Modern Library, 2003), 153.

[11] The most thorough excavation of Ellison's neglected early career as a leftist writer is Barbara Foley, *Wrestling with the Left: The Making of Ralph Ellison's* Invisible Man (Durham, NC: Duke University Press, 2010).

[12] Lloyd L. Brown, "The Deep Pit," *Masses & Mainstream* 5 (1952): 63; Abner W. Berry, "Ralph Ellison's Novel 'Invisible Man' Shows Snobbery, Contempt for Negro People," *Daily Worker*, June 1, 1952, 7; John O. Killens, review of *Invisible Man* in *Freedom* 2.6 (1952): 7.

[13] Ernest Kaiser, "A Critical Look at Ellison's Fiction and at Social and Literary Criticism by and About the Author," *Black World* 20.2 (1970): 81–2; Larry Neal, "And Shine Swam On," *Black Fire: An Anthology of Afro-American Writing*, ed. LeRoi Jones and Larry Neal (New York: William Morrow, 1968), 652. Neal would later offer a positive and influential political reevaluation of the novel in "Ellison's Zoot Suit," *Black World* 20.2 (1970): 31–52.

Scholars often read *Invisible Man* from within similar – though less stridently demarcated – streams of liberalism and radicalism, Black and Western political influences. For many, *Invisible Man* correlates American democratic processes and dominant political traditions with the tactics of Black leadership and epistemological resources of Black culture, often seeing the novel as anticipating Civil Rights-era Black political sensibilities.[14] T. V. Reed and John S. Wright link the novel's broadly democratic politics less to national political norms than to particular inheritances from Black culture and historical experience.[15] Other scholars echo midcentury Black radicals. Jerry Gafio Watts characterizes Ellison's democratic individualism as an elitism that led him to seek establishment credibility and downplay anti-Black oppression. Barbara Foley recovers the sophistication of Ellison's work as a Communist writer in the 1930s and early 1940s and argues that, in drafting *Invisible Man*, he reworked what started as an innovative proletarian novel into a near-formulaic anti-communist text.[16]

Invisible Man, however, often suggests its positive engagement with more radical political insights than critics – and Ellison's own carefully orchestrated public pronouncements – typically acknowledge. For example, the complicity of structural racism and capital emerges in multiple episodes as co-constitutive of the nation. Thus, Bledsoe warns invisible man: "When you buck against me, you're bucking against power, rich white folk's power, the nation's power – which means government power!"[17] American liberal cultural and political traditions are represented by Emerson's son, the white son of a wealthy trustee whose surname, suggestive alignment with Walt Whitman, and revelation of Bledsoe's letters of recommendation all position him within lineages of transcendentalism and abolitionism. But Emerson's son is compromised by the capitalist class location of that tradition: His wealth comes from his father's

---

[14] See, for instance, Danielle S. Allen, *Talking to Strangers: Anxieties of Citizenship since* Brown v. Board of Education (Chicago: University of Chicago Press, 2004); Timothy Parrish, *Ralph Ellison and the Genius of America* (Amherst: University of Massachusetts Press, 2012); Lucas E. Morel, "Ralph Ellison's American Democratic Individualism," in *Ralph Ellison and the Raft of Hope: A Political Companion to Invisible Man*, ed. Lucas E. Morel (Lexington: University Press of Kentucky, 2004) 58–90; and various essays on *Invisible Man* in two influential collections: *Ralph Ellison and the Raft of Hope* and *The New Territory: Ralph Ellison and the Twenty-First Century*, ed. Marc C. Conner and Lucas E. Morel (Jackson: University Press of Mississippi, 2016).

[15] T. V. Reed, *Fifteen Jugglers, Five Believers: Literary Politics and the Poetics of American Social Movements* (Berkeley: University of California Press, 1992), 58–86; Wright, 79–130.

[16] Jerry Gafio Watts, *Heroism and the Black Intellectual: Ralph Ellison, Politics, and Afro-American Intellectual Life* (Chapel Hill: University of North Carolina Press, 1994); Foley.

[17] Ellison, *Invisible Man*, 142.

global shipping empire, and his concern for the protagonist is also self-interested, as it involves a sexual exoticization of invisible man's Blackness that mirrors his father's colonial commodification of peoples and cultures. All he can offer invisible man, ultimately, is the opportunity to sell his labor power at Liberty Paints, where the racial whiteness of the entire American political edifice – and the secret of that whiteness being built on the exploitation of Black labor – is given allegorical exposition. The novel represents the social fabric of the nation as layered over by and reproduced through white racial dominance and economic exploitation. *Invisible Man*'s political sensibility is ultimately singular (perhaps Ellisonian is the best term), and it can be reconstructed in part by revisiting Ellison's thinking, in 1945, as he began writing.

Points of Origin: The Foundational Necessity of Illusions

Ellison famously described the inspiration for *Invisible Man* coming to him in rural Vermont, of all places. He was there during the world-historical turning point of August 1945, when, he would later claim, a voice within his mind spoke what would become the opening line of the novel: "I am an invisible man." Arnold Rampersad calls this story a "myth of origin,"[18] but Ellison's writings from this time give other indications about the concerns inspiring *Invisible Man*. In an August 1945 letter to his friend and supporter Ida Guggenheimer, Ellison described the sublimity of the Vermont landscape, noting that "[i]t is truly no land for the near-sighted or the narrowly self-centered." At the advent of the postwar era, Ellison was thinking not so much about the individual as about the need to rearticulate a spirit of responsibility for the collective betterment of humanity. When it came to political organizing around that responsibility, Ellison would decide that the white New England that carried the ethical and political conscience of nineteenth-century America was no longer up to the task. A few days following his letter to Guggenheimer, he wrote to Richard Wright and described a local community square dance, where the "anemic" music and "dismal" dancing suggested to him that New England had lost "a people's expression of its sense of life" and was no longer rooted in "the understructure, the mass base" of "gentility and sensitivity" upon which the "Golden Day" – literary critic Lewis Mumford's term for the nineteenth-century American literary renaissance and, to illustrate Ellison's conviction of New England's cultural decay, the name of the brothel in

---

[18] Rampersad, 194–5.

Invisible Man – had been founded.[19] New England, as Ellison found it in 1945, revealed no deeper sense of cultural purpose, much less one organized by the commitment to realizing ideals of democracy and equality.

At the same time, Ellison expressed his dismay that the previous institution in which he and Wright had invested their political hopes, the Communist Party of the United States, had also uprooted its maneuvers from bedrock principles. After Germany invaded the Soviet Union in 1941, the Party elected to support the Allied war effort. This meant moderating its domestic antiracist and anti-capitalist positions, which for Ellison and Wright amounted to a betrayal of Marxist principles and the working class. In the same letter to Wright, Ellison wrote that the Party leaders, who "want to play ball with the bourgeoisie" and abandon revolutionary commitment, "have no conscience." Like the Vermonters at the square dance, they were merely going through motions tied to no underlying ethos. But unlike Cold War liberals, who learned to see revolutionary ambition as inherently threatening to individual freedom, Ellison's objection is that the Communists abandoned their revolutionary ambition to work within the sociopolitical structures of racial capitalism. In an earlier August letter to Wright, Ellison emphasized the need to "offset the C.P. sell-out of our people; and I mean by this, both Negroes and labor." And Ellison is definitive about the future-looking principle any politics must express in its practice: "[T]here is no answer for Negroes certainly except some sort of classless society."[20] His perceptions that liberal New England and the Communist Party had lost touch with their respective roots inspired him to theorize the implications of such a development in *Invisible Man*: What happened when the practice of a given institution, movement, or an entire social order operated without any grounding in humane values and visions of a more egalitarian future? *Invisible Man* illustrates Ellison's answer in the dream the protagonist has immediately after falling through a manhole into the city's depths.

Invisible man dreams he is lying "*near where an armored bridge arched sharply away to where I could not see.*" He has been captured by a group of the novel's various political leaders, including Jack, Ras, Emerson, and Bledsoe. They castrate him, with Jack proclaiming: "Now you're free of illusions ... How does it feel to be free of illusions?" Invisible man replies, "*Painful and empty,*" but then indicates that his wasted genitalia represent

---

[19] Ralph Ellison, *The Selected Letters of Ralph Ellison*, ed. John F. Callahan and Marc C. Conner (New York: Random House, 2019), 190, 194–5; Rampersad, 192–3.

[20] Ellison, *Selected Letters*, 193–4, 188.

the entire "*universe*" of his castrators. All of these leaders pride themselves on having no "illusions": no deeply held principles or desires for utopian social change. Yet such illusions are the only vitality giving definition to political formations that, without foundational illusions, become, as invisible man has learned, interchangeable manipulators of human need. At the end of the dream, "*the bridge seemed to move off to where I could not see, striding like a robot, an iron man, whose legs clanged doomfully as it moved.*" The bridge *should* be a symbol for political movements as means to future ends, organizations that bridge the modern present to a better sociopolitical order. But this bridge has no end – it's not a bridge at all, not a tool for reaching a better world, but a trope for how illusion-free, merely mechanistic organizations perpetuate the destructive oppressions of the present. "*No, no, we must stop him!*" the narrator cries, as the bridge strides away.[21] Stopping those oppressions requires commitment to "illusions" of inclusive community and human worth and an accompanying responsibility for their sociopolitical implementation. In the atomic August of 1945, Ellison was wondering how such commitments might be reconstructed.

Exhuming the Principle: *Invisible Man*'s Underground Politics

When the narrator works at Liberty Paints, he is told that the Optic White shade he mixes – "as white as George Washington's Sunday-go-to-meetin' wig and as sound as the all-mighty dollar" – will be used to cover "a national monument" in Washington, DC. Brockway, a Black worker who makes the base of the paint, claims that it is "so white you can paint a chunka coal and you'd have to crack it open with a sledge hammer to prove it wasn't white clear through!"[22] Optic White is produced by Black labor: Brockway makes its base in the factory basement, and invisible man makes that chemical base white by adding a black chemical substance. Both processes are obscured by the surface-level whiteness of the final product: White supremacy and economic "soundness" in the US are interrelated products of the economic exploitation of Black workers whose humanity and demands for inclusion in the society they have built it buries and obscures. The paint then covers national monuments, suggesting how whiteness's economic and racial coordinates have buried or whitewashed the true founding ideals of the nation. Presumably, you would have to smash the monument with a sledgehammer to prove it was

---

[21] Ellison, *Invisible Man*, 569–70.   [22] Ibid., 201–2, 217.

possibly a monument to anything other than white supremacy and capitalism. In other words, Brockway's joke suggests that the inclusive principles submerged by the multiple socioeconomic implications of whiteness could be restored, although it would take a massive societal transformation guided by the institutional political equivalent of Brockway's sledgehammer.

This is what the Black man pushing a wheelbarrow of blueprints on the streets of New York seems to recommend to invisible man early in the novel. The man preserves blueprints for projects that were never built after "somebody done changed their plans." He sings an artful blues, and invisible man is struck by the man's skill: "God damn, I thought, they're a hell of a people!"[23] Reclaiming the blueprints, then, can be read as a political manifestation of the Black cultural ingenuity and artistry the man expresses. If political institutions "change their plans" and neglect their originary principles, then a Black political strategy could entail exhuming those principles from institutions that have abandoned them in practice.

The Brotherhood initially seems to be a vehicle for this strategy. It proclaims commitment to "a better world for all people" in which "the joy of labor shall have been restored." As a Brotherhood organizer, invisible man works toward making this "better world." His first speech, to a Harlem arena, rouses the transformative potential of the masses, but the leaders reprimand him for making "*incorrect*" political statements. When he undertakes further effective innovations – such as parades or introducing posters proclaiming the multicultural and interracial harmony of the Brotherhood's vision for the future – he is again checked: Brother Jack warns him, in an anonymous note, "*Do not go too fast* . . . you know that this is a *white man's world.*" Jack's note makes plain that, like Bledsoe, maintaining the present sociopolitical order, "the white man's world" and the Brotherhood's current place within it, is the leadership's real priority. Thus, invisible man's first meeting with Brotherhood leaders is at "an expensive-looking building in a strange part of the city" called the Chthonian, a name choice that reiterates the visual ambiguity of the Founder's statue.[24] The underworld of the Brotherhood – the deep commitment from which it operates – is not making "a better world for all peoples," but maintaining exactly what invisible man encounters at the Chthonian: the privilege and security of its leaders within the same racial-economic order that spatially segregates Manhattan. The cynical self-

[23] Ibid., 175–7.   [24] Ibid., 304, 349, 383, 299.

interest invisible man finds among the Brotherhood cadres is, effectively, the organization's underlying political vision.

Invisible man eventually realizes the truth about the Brotherhood's intentions, and, after he discovers that it has adopted a new strategy that deprioritizes its radical activism among African Americans, he roams Harlem in "dark glasses" and is mistaken for Rinehart, who seems to be, by turns, a local pimp, a numbers runner, and a storefront preacher. The invisibility of African American individuality in a racist society, depicted as the dehumanizing effect of structural racism in other episodes, here seems empowering: Rinehart's church celebrates "the Invisible" as an all-powerful deity, and its neon sign beckons passers-by to "BEHOLD THE INVISIBLE" and promises "I DO WHAT YOU WANT DONE!" This power suggests to invisible man the potential for subversively utilizing his racialized invisibility, for making his glasses not just a "disguise" but a "political instrument."[25]

He comes to equate "Rinehartism" with the "cynicism" of the Brotherhood. Since the Brotherhood sees Black constituents as only pliant tools for its machinations, invisible man will manipulate that invisibility "rine and heart," performing cooperation with its new strategy while working secretly to "[destroy] them, at least in Harlem."[26] However, during the climactic riot, invisible man concludes that the Brotherhood de-emphasized its community work in Harlem precisely to provoke such a cataclysm, to "murder" Harlem by letting socioeconomic contradictions lead to a politically unconscious eruption. "And I had helped," he decides, "had been a tool. A tool just at the very moment I had thought myself free. By pretending to agree I *had* indeed agreed, had made myself responsible for ... all ... whom now the night was making ripe for death."[27] His surface-level cooperation with the Brotherhood, because it was guided by nothing but unprincipled vengeance, merely furthered the Brotherhood's plans – by not standing for anything positive in his machinations, he has simply done what the Brotherhood wants done. Invisible man's realization here is central to Ellison's argument: If a political agent does not act in accordance with underlying affirmative values – an ethical blueprint for a better and inclusive society – then they ends up *reproducing* the current social order, becoming another "tool" of the status quo.

The riot thrusts two alternative political leaders to the fore. Dupre organizes a group of men to burn down their own tenement building. In a revision and reiteration of the novel's earlier eviction scene, at which

[25] Ibid., 482–96, 499.   [26] Ibid., 504–12.   [27] Ibid., 553.

invisible man succeeds in helping *stop* the unhousing of a Harlem couple, Dupre's followers force Black families from their homes. Dupre and his men have some sense that their destruction is a sociopolitical protest, but because it is rooted in no underlying plan for social change, their act merely replays the racial capitalist violence of eviction.[28] Ras changes his title to "Ras the Destroyer" and, "dressed in the costume of an Abyssinian chieftain," leads his followers into battle with the police. But Ras, too, has no vision of futurity beyond the immediacy of this violent clash, and is thus only lending a cultural nationalist guise to the erasure of Black life. Invisible man tries to persuade Ras's followers that they too are tools of Harlem's eradication: "They deserted you so that in your despair you'd follow this man to your destruction!"[29]

African Americans, invisible man learns, are continually betrayed by political organizations and movements, both white and Black, that act in their own self-interest rather than working to achieve concrete social change based on ethical and political illusions. So, at the end of the novel, he elects to stay underground to work through the complexities of the sociopolitical surface. He analyzes his grandfather's advice to relate to a racist nation in a subversive, underground manner: "agree 'em to death and destruction." His experience with Rinehartism and the riot suggests that merely performing allegiance to those in power is not what his grandfather meant. He instead concludes that this must mean that invisible man should "affirm the principle on which the country was built" and "the plan in whose name we had been brutalized and sacrificed."[30] Like the man with the blueprints rescuing neglected plans for better futures, invisible man must extract that principle from beneath its surface-level sociopolitical perversion and remake a politics on it. James Seaton observes that, although the Declaration of Independence's assertion of equality is "the most likely candidate" for the principle in question, the novel's epilogue does not explicitly identify it as such, enabling it to be parsed as "broader than any doctrine" and "not only an idea but also the aspirations and possibilities with which the idea was associated at the founding and since."[31]

The principle underlying the United States sociopolitical order in *Invisible Man* is not any actually existing historical form of that order – *Invisible Man* is not a call to defend the Cold War status quo against totalitarianism. Invisible man's grandfather, after all, derives his advice not from any fealty to extant US political structures but from his experience

[28] Ibid., 545–9.   [29] Ibid., 556–8.   [30] Ibid., 16, 574.
[31] James Seaton, "Affirming the Principle," in *Ralph Ellison and the Raft of Hope*, 25.

during Reconstruction, a blueprint for radical egalitarian social transformation undertaken in the wake of the Civil War and eventually defeated by white reactionaries. W. E. B. Du Bois explains that the Reconstruction program of the Black proletariat aspired to rectify the surface-level "pretensions of this republic" by remaking its social and economic bases, implementing cross-racial collectivity, and ending economic exploitation so that America "could really be a free commonwealth of freemen."[32] In 1945, Ellison referred to the southern overthrow of Reconstruction as "the counterrevolution of 1876," writing that the "return of the Southern ruling class to power ... pushed" the goal of racial equality "into the underground of American conscience," where it was subsequently "ignored." Around the time he was starting *Invisible Man*, the radical ambition and ethos of Reconstruction, buried in American political memory by racist reaction and cynical anti-democratic betrayals, contoured some of the transformative energies Ellison associated with exhuming and affirming the nation's principle. In his National Book Award speech, Ellison described the American ideal of democracy in utopian terms of belonging, as "love" and "man's being at home in the world."[33] Invisible man's grandfather imparts the necessity of political action being rooted in a commitment to actualizing this principle of community and human worth. Particular historical and institutional definitions of those values, such as civic equality, collectivity unabrogated by class exploitation, and Black cultural pride – the ostensible principles of the college, the Brotherhood, and Ras, respectively – all find expression in this expansive, associative sense of the submerged and repressed, yet ultimately foundational, ideal of political aspiration in America. *Invisible Man* advocates not the moderate pragmatism of vital center liberalism, but the broadly inclusive political passions – the dreams and illusions of freedom and community – that underwrite visions of alternative futures.

---

[32] W. E. B. Du Bois, *Black Reconstruction in America* (New York: Free Press, 1998 [1935]), 126.
[33] Ellison, *Collected Essays*, 148, 154.

CHAPTER 19

The Left Hand of Darkness *(1969)*: Ursula K. Le Guin

Tony Burns

Introduction

Ursula K. Le Guin's *The Left Hand of Darkness* is a classic example of a work of science fiction which is also a political novel.[1] It has to do with the politics of recognition. In it, a character named Genly Ai is an envoy of an interplanetary federation, the Ekumen, to the inhabitants of a planet named Gethen or Winter, containing two societies: Karhide and Orgoreyn. The occupants of the planet are human beings with a unique sexual physiology that differentiates them from members of the Ekumen, who are also human. Genly Ai's mission is to make the Gethenians aware of the existence of the Ekumen and to invite them to join it. The novel focuses on the relationship between Genly Ai and another character, Estraven, who at the beginning of the novel is the chief advisor, to King Argaven XV, the ruler of Karhide. Initially, their relationship is one of mutual suspicion. However, towards the end of the novel, in a trek over the Gobrin Ice, Genly Ai and Estraven come to trust one another. The barrier that initially existed between the worlds which these characters represent is broken down. As a result, although Estraven dies, Genly Ai succeeds in his mission.

The Politics of Recognition

The politics of recognition has to do with justice in interpersonal relationships. It involves the principle of equity, which states that equals ought to be treated equally. Le Guin suggests that it comes in three forms, all of which can be found in *The Left Hand of Darkness*. The first approach

---

[1] Ursula K. Le Guin, *The Left Hand of Darkness* (London: Gollancz, 2017). Hereafter referred to as *LHD*.

involves two individuals mutually recognizing one another as being unequals, or as being essentially different, and therefore as meriting differential treatment. This form reinforces the principles of order, hierarchy, and authority in any unequal society. Le Guin is critical of those who think in this way, especially if they attach importance to differences between individuals that she does not consider to be morally relevant (e.g. sex or gender) and use these differences as a justification for treating others in a manner in which they would not themselves wish to be treated, and which is therefore inequitable or unjust. Because of its exclusive focus on the principle of difference, rather than on that of sameness or identity, this approach may be characterized as a politics of *difference*.

The second approach differs from the first because it is egalitarian. It involves two individual human beings recognizing one another as equals, or as being essentially the same, despite the existence of any superficial differences that might exist between them (e.g. sex or gender). Given this assumption, the principle of equity demands that they should set aside these superficial differences. Justice demands that they ought to be treated, and to treat one another, in exactly the same way. Given their equality, differential treatment – or discrimination, in the unwelcome sense of the term – would not be morally justified. Advocates of this second approach do not value differences, which they tend to associate with undesirable forms of inequality. For that reason, this approach might be characterized as a politics of sameness or *identity*. Le Guin is sympathetic towards this approach but does not unequivocally endorse it.

The third approach, which is the one favoured by Le Guin, seeks to combine the insights of the first two approaches. Its advocates maintain that if two individuals are compared then it is clear that in some respects they will be the same or similar, and in other respects they will be different. In their view, both the similarities and the differences might be valued. We should not, therefore, think in either/or terms about the insights provided by the first two approaches. Rather, we should think in terms of both–and. To employ a phrase of the German philosopher, G. W. F. Hegel, whose views are of significance for those interested in the politics of recognition, this approach invokes the principle of *identity and difference*.[2]

---

[2] G. W. F. Hegel, *Hegel's Logic: Being Part One of the Encyclopaedia of the Philosophical Sciences*, trans. William Wallace (Oxford: Clarendon Press, 1975 [1830]), §103, 152; §116, 168; §121, 175; §123, 180; §214, 278.

Le Guin and the Politics of Difference: *Shifgrethor*

In *The Left Hand of Darkness*, the first form of the politics of recognition is associated with the concept of *shifgrethor*. Social relationships in Karhide and Orgoreyn, the two societies on the planet Winter, are ordered hierarchically. They are imbued with the principle of social inequality. In Karhide, especially, life is dominated by titles and rituals or codes of honour, which are associated with the demand for dignity and respect that superiors make of their subordinates. As Genly Ai, the envoy from the Ekumen, puts it, the word *shifgrethor* refers to the demand for 'prestige, face, place, the pride-relationship', which is 'the untranslatable and all-important principle of social authority in Karhide and all civilizations of Gethen'.[3]

According to Genly Ai, such things as vanity, pride, dignity, and status, or knowing and keeping to one's place or station in society, and demanding that others (especially one's subordinates) should do so as well, are central to social and political life on Gethen. As in Ancient China or Japan, or in French society before the French Revolution of 1789, this has to do with the notions of face and of saving face in situations where the demand for recognition from others may not be met. It is no accident that the society of Karhide is ruled by a king, Argaven XV.

Shifgrethor has the hallmarks of a social institution. Le Guin suggests that the hierarchical social relationships associated with it involve the exercise of a certain form of power by those who occupy superior positions in Gethenian society. This is reflected in the language they employ. Le Guin has Genly Ai observe that this is the language of 'those who rule men', or of those who occupy positions of authority in any hierarchical society: for example, 'kings, conquerors, dictators, generals'.[4] However, this form of power rests on manipulation and the engineering of consent rather than on coercive force. From this point of view, language is a rhetorical means of persuasion. Genly Ai comments at one point that Estraven 'had long practice in the evasions and challenges and rhetorical subtleties used in conversation by those whose main aim in life was the achievement and maintenance of the *shifgrethor* relationship on a high level'.[5] Likening *shifgrethor* to a game,[6] he says that there is a 'competitive, prestige-seeking aspect of it'.[7] The players of this game are involved in a 'perpetual conversational duel' with others, the purpose of which is to have

---

[3] Le Guin, *LHD*, 1, 13.   [4] Ibid, 3, 34.   [5] Ibid, 3, 33.   [6] Ibid., 8, 103, 105.
[7] Ibid., 3, 33.

their social position, especially their superiority and authority, recognized by others.[8]

Those who employ language in this way are never open, transparent, or clear about their meaning or their intentions when engaging in conversation with others. They are always mistrusting of others, whom they assume are trying to manipulate and control them. This is the case even when they are themselves honest, sincere, and well intentioned, with motives that are 'good', morally speaking. Individuals who play the game of *shifgrethor* are not necessarily dishonest, in the sense that they make statements that they know are untrue. For there is a difference between telling a lie and being evasive about the truth, especially if one refrains from telling the truth with good intentions. As Estraven says at one point, 'I think we shall have trouble learning how to lie, having for so long practiced the art of going round and round the truth without ever lying about it, or reaching it either.'[9] Towards the end of the novel, Genly Ai criticizes Estraven, whom he mistrusted at the beginning but who turns out to have been well intentioned and supportive of his mission all along, for engaging in such devious linguistic practices. What, he asks, was the point of all 'this intriguing, this hiding and power-seeking and plotting'?[10] Estraven's response is to acknowledge that 'my greatest error was, as you say, in not making myself clear to you'. However, by way of explanation, he points out that, like the other inhabitants of the planet Winter who play the game of *shifgrethor*, 'I am not used to doing so [making himself clear]. I am not used to giving, or accepting, either advice or blame.'[11] For anybody who did this would lose face.

Le Guin associates the notion of *shifgrethor* with the concept of 'manners', in contrast to that of 'morals'.[12] This distinction can also be found in the political thought of the eighteenth century and is central to the politics of recognition at this time. The ideas of Jean-Jacques Rousseau are important in this regard.[13] This is true especially of Rousseau's notion of *amour-propre*, in the *Discourse on the Origins of Inequality* (1755), which expresses very well the meaning of the concept of *shifgrethor*, as Le Guin understands it in *The Left Hand of Darkness*.[14] Life at the court of Louis XVI, in late eighteenth-century France, was dominated by the principle of

---

[8] Ibid., 3, 33.   [9] Ibid., 11, 150.   [10] Ibid., 4, 198.   [11] Ibid., 14, 199.
[12] Ibid., 1, 12, 8, 117–18.
[13] Tony Burns, *Social Institutions and the Politics of Recognition. Volume 2: From the Reformation to the French Revolution* (London: Rowman & Littlefield, 2020), 129–53.
[14] Jean-Jacques Rousseau, *Discourse on the Origin of Inequality*, trans. G. D. H. Cole (London: Dent, 1975 [1755]), 65–7.

manners, in the same way as in King Argaven XV's court in Karhide. In both cases social interaction is dominated by vanity, pride, and personal ambition, as well as by the demand for status, honour, dignity, respect, and prestige, all of which are associated with the names, titles, and labels that are characteristic of social inequality or of a superior position within a particular social hierarchy.

Le Guin and the Politics of Identity: Communication

The second, egalitarian form of the politics of recognition involves relationships of mutual respect between equals. This approach subverts the social hierarchy that is associated with the rituals of *shifgrethor* in Karhide society. It, too, is associated with a particular use of language. Here, however, language is not employed as a means of manipulation or rhetorical persuasion. Rather, it is considered to be a vehicle for the pursuit and communication of truth. As Genly Ai observes at one point, 'I was not duelling with Argaven, but trying to communicate with him.'[15] Genly Ai states that the essential purpose of the Ekumen is to support communication of this kind.[16]

Le Guin assumes that a precondition for such communication is that both parties should enter into a dialogue with one another. She emphasizes the fact that the envoy Genly Ai is sent to the planet Winter alone. For if he is isolated and alone, and therefore relatively powerless in his interactions with the local inhabitants, then, in such a situation, 'I must listen, as well as speak.' For this reason, any relationship into which he enters with an inhabitant of the planet he is visiting necessarily involves dialogue and not monologue. In Le Guin's view, this is part of what makes this relationship a moral as well as a political one. Genly Ai observes that 'the relationship I finally make, if I make one, is not impersonal and not only political: it is individual, it is personal, it is both more and less than political'.[17]

Genly Ai points out that such a relationship invokes the idea of 'not We and They' or 'I and It' but, rather, of 'I and Thou'.[18] In this respect, Le Guin's views resemble those of Ludwig Feuerbach[19] and of Martin Buber.[20] They also resemble the communicative ethics of Jürgen

---

[15] Le Guin, *LHD*, 3, 33.   [16] Ibid., 8, 117, 9, 135–6.   [17] Ibid., 18, 259.   [18] Ibid., 18, 259.
[19] Ludwig Feuerbach, *Principles of the Philosophy of the Future*, trans. Manfred Vogel, intro. Thomas E. Wartenberg (Indianapolis: Hackett, 1986 [1843]), §§54–63, 70–2.
[20] Martin Buber, *I and Thou*, trans. Ronald Gregor Smith (Edinburgh: T&T Clark, 1950 [1923]).

Habermas, for whom the notions of an 'ideal speech situation' and of
'distorted communication' are of particular importance.[21] Habermas's
'discourse ethics' highlights the importance of 'the universalisation principle', which is an alternative formulation of the principle of equity, or the
Golden Rule.[22]

Le Guin emphasizes the importance of trust. For language to be used as
an effective vehicle of communication, it is important that those who use it
not be suspicious of one another. For that to happen, however, it is
necessary that *shifgrethor* be set aside.[23] In *The Left Hand of Darkness*, this
is what happens, eventually, in the case of the characters Genly Ai and
Estraven. Over the course of the novel, especially in their trek over the
Gobrin Ice, they come to trust one another and to become friends (in the
Aristotelian sense of the term) .[24]

Le Guin associates the notion of communication with that of morals, as
distinct from that of manners. Rousseau's political thought exemplifies this
approach, which, being both humanistic and egalitarian, subverted what
Mary Wollstonecraft referred to as the 'unnatural distinctions' that existed
in eighteenth-century society.[25] As with Rousseau, there is an element of
strong cosmopolitanism in this second approach to the politics of recognition. On this view, which is influenced by the philosophy of Stoicism,
the principle of equity or the Golden Rule is a principle of natural law. As
such, it is valid universally, for all human beings in all societies everywhere,
irrespective of their determinate social identity. Those who respect this
principle of morality have no vanity or pride (*amour-propre*). They do not
believe that they are superior to others. Like Genly Ai, they have no
shifgrethor.[26]

Le Guin associates situations in which individuals do not mutually
recognize and respect one another, in accordance with the principle of
equity, with the concept of alienation. She suggests that there is a close
relationship between alienation and objectification, and therefore also
attempted enslavement. In her essay 'Science Fiction and Mrs Brown',
Le Guin insists that 'we are not objects. That is essential. We are subjects,
and whoever among us treats us as objects is acting inhumanly, wrongly,

[21] Jürgen Habermas, *Moral Consciousness and Communicative Action*, trans. Christian Lenhardt and
Shierry Weber Nicholsen (Cambridge, MA: MIT Press, 1990), 88, 113, 188–9.
[22] Habermas, 116–94.   [23] Le Guin, *LHD*, 6, 83–84, 11, 150, 14, 198.   [24] Ibid., 18, 248–9.
[25] Mary Wollstonecraft, *A Vindication of the Rights of Woman* (New York: Dover, 1996 [1792]),
145–54; see also Burns, *Social Institutions*, 194–206.
[26] Le Guin, *LHD*, 5, 48.

against nature.'[27] In 'American SF and the Other', Le Guin states that 'if you deny any affinity with another person or kind of person, if you declare it to be wholly different from yourself', then you have thereby 'denied its spiritual equality, and its human reality'. In so doing, 'you have made it into a *thing*, to which the only possible relationship is a power relationship', and not a moral one.[28] Le Guin associates power relationships with conflict, war, domination, exploitation, and oppression. In her view, alienation in this sense is a core theme of science fiction, as well as being one of the most fundamental problems of the political life of all human beings.

Central to Le Guin's fiction is the theme of barriers and walls, or the differences that separate those who are essentially equals from one another and that lead them to treat others unjustly by objectifying them. She suggests that 'building bridges' between those who appear at first sight to be completely different from one another is the solution to the problem of alienation. They must attempt to get past these differences and recognize the underlying essential equality that exists between them, and that could in principle unite them to one another. If this effort is successful, then they would no longer be aliens, strangers, or enemies. Rather, they would become friends. They would enter into a community or political society with one another. This theme lies at the very heart of *The Left Hand of Darkness*. This is Genly Ai's mission.

Feminism and *The Left Hand of Darkness*

Although there is disagreement about the significance of this particular form of identity politics for its plot, *The Left Hand of Darkness* has often been regarded as Le Guin's contribution to feminist science fiction.[29] Le Guin refers to the Gethenians, variously, as androgynous, ambisexual, or hermaphroditic. Most of the time they are neither male nor female. There is a monthly period in their life cycle (kemmer) when they become sexually active. During this period, an individual is either male or female. However, which of the two they will become is uncertain and cannot be predicted in advance. Genly Ai observes that, on Winter, 'normal individuals have no

---

[27] Ursula K. Le Guin, 'Science Fiction and Mrs. Brown', in *The Language of the Night* (New York: Harper Perennial, 1993 [1975]), 114.

[28] Ursula K. Le Guin, 'American SF and the Other', in *The Language of the Night*, 95, emphasis added.

[29] See, for example, Amy Clarke, *Ursula K. Le Guin's Journey to Post-Feminism* (Jefferson, NC: McFarland & Co., 2010).

predisposition to either sexual role in kemmer; they do not know whether they will be the male or the female, and have no choice in the matter'.[30]

It might be asked how these differences affect Genly Ai's mission. At one point, Le Guin has the character Tibe refer to Genly Ai and the other human beings living on the planets of the Ekumen as being sexual 'perverts'. According to Tibe, even the possibility that some (male) members of the human species might carry their sexual organs outside their bodies is 'a disgusting idea'. In conversation with Genly Ai, he says, 'I don't see why human beings here on earth [sic] should want or tolerate any dealings with creatures so monstrously different.'[31] If Genly Ai is to succeed in his mission, it is clear that such prejudice is an obstacle that must be overcome. The issue of how it might be overcome is central to the plot of the novel.

Le Guin's solution to this problem is to emphasize that, despite this difference, all human beings are fundamentally the same. In principle, therefore, these differences need not be something that permanently alienates the human beings of the Ekumen from those on the planet Winter. The gap that currently isolates and separates them from one another can be bridged. Regarding this issue, like all cosmopolitan thinkers, Genly Ai observes that, when interacting with the Gethenians, the Ekumen must appeal 'to their strong though undeveloped sense of humanity, of human unity'.[32]

As in the Ekumen, there is also a division of labour in Gethenian society. For example, children do exist there and they do have to be reared; the sick and the elderly do have to be cared for. However, on the planet Winter, this division of labour is not determined by either sex or gender. There, as Genly Ai notes in his report, 'anyone can turn his [sic] hand to anything'. The fact that 'everyone between seventeen and thirty-five or so is liable to be (as Nim put it) "tied down to childbearing," implies that no one is quite so thoroughly "tied down" here as women, elsewhere, are likely to be'. Morally speaking, the consequence of this is that, in Gethenian society, 'burden and privilege are shared out pretty equally'.[33] In short, unlike the societies of the Ekumen, including Earth (Terra), the principles of equity, or of simple reciprocity, and of human solidarity are respected on Winter. This is an old idea that can be traced back to Aristotle and the Greeks. It is the belief that, given the existence of the division of labour in society, and given also that all of those concerned are equals, then justice requires that, whatever the task may be, everyone

---

[30] Le Guin, *LHD*, 7, 91.   [31] Ibid., 3, 36.   [32] Ibid., 8, 99.   [33] Ibid., 7, 93.

should take turns performing it. So far as particular social roles and their duties are concerned, there should be rotation in office.

Advocates of the second approach to the politics of recognition – for example, Martha Nussbaum – are strong cosmopolitan thinkers.[34] They claim that the only things that really matter are the similarities between individual human beings, rather than the differences. According to Nussbaum, an identifier such as gender should be regarded as 'a morally irrelevant characteristic'.[35] Le Guin evidently had some sympathy for this view. Indeed, some of her critics have suggested that she is, straightforwardly, an advocate for it.

Le Guin and the Politics of Identity and Difference

Unlike the strong cosmopolitan advocates of the second approach, Le Guin does value the differences that exist between individual human beings. She advocates a third approach, associated with the notion of identity and difference. The principle underpinning this third approach is taken from Taoism. *The Left Hand of Darkness* is a Taoist work. This is perhaps best represented by the yin-yang symbol. During their trek over the Gobrin Ice, towards the end of the novel, Genly Ai shows this symbol to Estraven, pointing out that 'it is yin and yang'. He associates it with the idea that 'light is the left hand of darkness', an idea that gives the novel its title.[36] For Le Guin, the yin-yang symbol, and the opposition of darkness and light encapsulated within it, is representative of all similar dualities – for example, those of 'Light, dark. Fear, courage. Cold, warmth. Female, male.'[37] Like all good Taoists, Le Guin seeks to find a balance or equilibrium between such binary oppositions, a balance that takes each of them into account while refusing to make an either/or choice between them. In her view, they are not straightforward alternatives. Rather, they mutually complement one another. Le Guin regards the tension between such opposites as creative and productive. It is constitutive of the concrete existence, or the determinate identity, of all individual things.

From this point of view, in order for any individual thing to exist, there must be at least some differences between it and other things. If there were no differences at all, then everything would be submerged within the

---

[34] Martha C. Nussbaum, 'Patriotism and Cosmopolitanism', in *For Love of Country: Debating the Limits of Patriotism*, ed. Joshua Cohen (Boston, MA: Beacon Press, 1996), 3–20; see also Tony Burns, 'Nussbaum, Cosmopolitanism and Contemporary Political Issues', *International Journal of Social Economics* 40.7 (2013): 648–62.

[35] Nussbaum, 5.   [36] Le Guin, *LHD*, 19, 267.   [37] Ibid., 19, 267.

primordial 'soup' or the metaphysical 'stuff' out of which all individual things are composed. In the history of philosophy, this has been referred to in different ways. Some refer to it as 'Being' (Heidegger) whereas others refer to it as 'Matter' (Hobbes), or the one 'Substance' (Spinoza), or, more obscurely, the 'Absolute' (Hegel).

For those who think in this way, every individual thing is to be understood by reference both to what it is and also to what it is not – that is, its opposite or its negation. Without these differences, individual things could have no concrete existence at all. Hegel expresses this point very well when, citing Spinoza, he says that 'all determination is negation',[38] and when he refers to his 'Absolute' as 'the night in which, as the saying goes, all cows are black'.[39] This idea is important for Le Guin. It is illustrated in *The Left Hand of Darkness* by the episode in which Genly Ai is recognized as being the Ekumen's envoy on Karhide. As a result of that act of recognition, he says, 'I was set apart from those nameless ones with whom I had fled down a dark road and whose lack of identity I had shared all night in a dark room.' At that point, 'I was named, known, recognized; I existed.'[40]

Hegel expresses the same idea in a different way when he refers to a certain type of 'monochromatic' thinking that submerges all distinctions 'in the void of the Absolute, from which pure identity' or a 'formless whiteness' is produced.[41] In Le Guin's novel, this idea is captured by Genly Ai's observation, made during his trek with Estraven over the Gobrin Ice, that 'we stepped out of the tent onto nothing'. Estraven 'stood beside me, but neither he nor I cast any shadow. There was dull light all around, everywhere. When we walked on the crisp snow no shadow showed the footprint. We left no track.' There was 'nothing else at all. No sun, no sky, no horizon, no world. A whitish-gray void, in which we appeared to hang.'[42]

To capture this view that, for separate individuals to exist at all, there must be differences as well as similarities between them and others, Le Guin repeatedly employs the metaphor of a shadow in her writings. She discusses this shadow motif in an essay entitled 'The Child and the Shadow', where she connects it to the ideas of Carl Jung and the fairy tales of Hans Christian Andersen.[43] It can also be found in *A Wizard of*

---

[38] Hegel, *Hegel's Logic*, §91, 135.
[39] G. W. F. Hegel, *Phenomenology of Spirit*, trans. A. V. Miller (Oxford: Oxford University Press, 1977 [1807]), §16, 9.
[40] Le Guin, *LHD*, 8, 11.   [41] Hegel, *Phenomenology*, §51, 31.   [42] Le Guin, *LHD*, 18, 260.
[43] Ursula K. Le Guin, '*The Child and the Shadow*', in *The Language of the Night*, 54–67.

Earthsea, in which the character Master Hand observes at one point that 'to light a candle is to cast a shadow'.[44] The key point here is that, according to Le Guin, to claim that each individual thing necessarily casts a shadow is simply to say that it is defined as much by its negation or what it is not (as represented by its shadow) as by what it is. In comparison with the real things of which they are representations, shadows may be regarded as insubstantial. Here, one brings to mind Plato's simile of the cave in his *Republic,* in which shadows are mistaken for the real things of which they are the appearances.[45]

This is a philosophical idea that does not have anything specifically to do with the issue of social identity. However, it is evident that it does have an application there also. For example, a 'citizen', by definition, is 'not-a-slave', just as a 'slave' is 'not-a-citizen'. The suggestion here is that, for individual human beings to exist concretely, rather than as abstract moral persons, it is necessary that they possess a determinate social identity – for example, either as a citizen or as a slave. They must also, sociologically speaking, 'cast a shadow'. In *The Left Hand of Darkness,* Estraven says that *shifgrethor* 'comes from an old word for shadow'.[46] He also says that 'daylight's not enough. We need the shadows, in order to walk.'[47] Le Guin suggests that, although we can and should do without *shifgrethor,* we cannot do without shadows.

Le Guin points out that individual characters, such as Genly Ai and Estraven, might in certain circumstances be deprived of their social identity and in consequence become alienated or estranged from others within their own society. For example, this is what happens to Estraven when he is stripped of all his honorific titles and declared to be a traitor by King Argaven. Le Guin emphasizes that the circumstance in which Genly Ai and Estraven no longer cast shadows, when they are alone together on the Gobrin Ice, is one in which each of them no longer has a determinate social identity as a member of a particular society, with associated rights and duties. As Estraven observes, '[U]p here on the Ice each of us is singular, isolate, I as cut off from those like me, from my society and its rules, as he from his.' There is, he observes, 'no world full of other Gethenians here to explain and support my existence'. One consequence

[44] Ursula K. Le Guin, *A Wizard of Earthsea,* in *The Earthsea Quartet* (London: Penguin Books, 1993 [1968]), 288.
[45] Plato, *The Republic,* trans. H. D. P. Lee (Harmondsworth: Penguin Books, 1968), VII, 278–82.
[46] Le Guin, *LHD,* 18, 248.   [47] Ibid., 19, 267.

of this is that, so far as Estraven's relationship to Genly Ai is concerned, 'we are equals at last', but at the same time also 'alien' and 'alone'.[48]

Conclusion

At first sight, Le Guin appears to be straightforwardly an advocate of the second approach to the politics of recognition outlined earlier. She is a strong cosmopolitan thinker who suggests that we ought to value others *despite* the differences that exist between us and not *because* of them. Far from being a reason for celebration, therefore, differences of gender, for example, are thought to lie in the way of my entering into a moral relationship or a political community with others who are different from me in this respect. This has led some feminists to criticize what they take to be Le Guin's approach.[49] I have attempted to show that, although there is some evidence in *The Left Hand of Darkness* that supports this reading, there is also evidence that counts against it. Le Guin is a weak rather than a strong cosmopolitan thinker. In her view, it is not the case that the only thing that matters about us is the fact that we are human. Nor, therefore, is it the case that differences such as gender may be set aside as being morally irrelevant. To claim that Le Guin does not value these differences would be unfair. Nor would that view be consistent with her commitment to Taoism.

---

[48] Ibid., 16, 232.
[49] For discussion, see Clarke; and Ursula K. Le Guin, 'Is Gender Necessary? Redux', in *Dreams Must Explain Themselves: The Selected Non-Fiction of Ursula K. Le Guin* (London: Gollancz, 2018 [1988]), 36–45.

CHAPTER 20

If Beale Street Could Talk *(1974): James Baldwin*

Douglas Field

America has always felt the necessity of keeping its black male population under control. Behind every failure to make the police accountable in such killings is an almost gloating confidence that the majority of white Americans support the idea that the police are the thin blue line between them and social chaos.

Darryl Pinckney, "In Ferguson" (2015)[1]

The law is meant to be my servant and not my master, still less my torturer and my murderer. To respect the law, in the context in which the American Negro finds himself, is simply to surrender his self-respect.

James Baldwin, "A Report from Occupied Territory" (1966)[2]

In an article published in the *New York Times* in 2017, the authors drew attention to "the tragically chronic relevance of James Baldwin."[3] Since his death in 1987, Baldwin has become the most cited literary figure in the Black Lives Matter movement; his insightful comments on police brutality and racial injustice during the 1960s have become despairingly relevant again.[4] In the wake of the Ferguson protests in 2014, following the shooting of Michael Brown, an unarmed Black teenager, Baldwin's essays and interviews gained new traction across social media platforms. One interview in particular – "James Baldwin: How to Cool It" – first published in *Esquire* magazine over fifty years ago, has attracted widespread social media attention. In response to the interviewer's claim that the

---

[1] Darryl Pinckney, "In Ferguson," in *Busted in New York and Other Essays*, foreword by Zadie Smith (London: riverrun, 2019), 150.

[2] James Baldwin, "A Report from Occupied Territory" [1966], in *Collected Essays*, ed. Toni Morrison (New York: Library of America, 1998), 734.

[3] Wesley Morris and Jenna Wortham, "The Tragically Chronic Relevance of James Baldwin," *New York Times*, February 16, 2017, www.nytimes.com/2017/02/16/podcasts/the-tragically-chronic-relevance-of-james-baldwin.html

[4] See Melanie Walsh, "Tweets of a Native Son: The Quotation and Recirculation of James Baldwin from Black Power to #BlackLivesMatter," *American Quarterly* 70.3 (2018): 531–59.

police had demonstrated "a more permissive attitude" in their response to looters during recent riots, Baldwin replies, "I object to the term 'looters' because I wonder who is looting whom, baby." He added: "[Y]ou're accusing a captive population who has been robbed of everything of looting. I think it's obscene."[5] In Baldwin's fiction and non-fiction, the writer frequently overhauls the logic of the law, pointing to the ways in which white power has incarcerated Black Americans – mentally, physically, and psychically.

As D. Quentin Miller reminds us in his insightful book *A Criminal Power: James Baldwin and the Law*, "Virtually all of Baldwin's novels and plays have at their core a narrative of imprisonment, or police brutality, or police intimidation, or a rigged trial."[6] Baldwin's first novel, *Go Tell It on the Mountain* (1953), recounts how Richard, the biological father of the novel's protagonist, commits suicide shortly after his release from jail, where he had served time for a crime he did not commit, a theme that Baldwin addressed in his non-fiction. In "A Report from Occupied Territory" (1966), Baldwin analyzed the case of the "Harlem Six," a group of African American men put on trial, five of whom were later acquitted. "[T]he police are simply the hired enemies of this population," Baldwin concluded. "They are present to keep the Negro in his place to protect white business interests, and they have no other function."[7]

In Baldwin's work, including his final book, *The Evidence of Things Not Seen* (1985), an account of the Atlanta child murders that occurred between 1979 and 1981, the law is frequently depicted as corrupt. In "Down at the Cross: Letter from a Region in My Mind," first published in the *New Yorker* in 1962 and then published as *The Fire Next Time* the following year, Baldwin draws attention to the criminality "of white people, who had robbed black people of their liberty." And as white people "had the judges, the juries, the shotguns, the law," Baldwin points out that the law is inextricably bound to white power; it "was a criminal power, to be feared but not respected," Baldwin wrote, "and to be outwitted in any way whatever."[8] As he explained in his earlier essay, "The Discovery of What It Means to Be an American" (1959), "Every society is really

[5] "James Baldwin: How to Cool It," *Esquire*, July 1968, www.esquire.com/news-politics/a23960/james-baldwin-cool-it/

[6] D. Quentin Miller, *A Criminal Power: James Baldwin and the Law* (Columbus, OH: Ohio State University Press, 2012), 8.

[7] Baldwin, "A Report from Occupied Territory," 734.

[8] James Baldwin, "Down at the Cross: Letter from a Region in My Mind," *New Yorker*, November 17, 1962, www.newyorker.com/magazine/1962/11/17/letter-from-a-region-in-my-mind

governed by hidden laws, by unspoken but profound assumptions on the part of the people, and ours is no exception. It is up to the American writer to find out what those laws and assumptions are."[9]

As a writer and activist, Baldwin certainly rose to the challenge that he outlined in "The Discovery of What It Means to Be an American." In 1968, he organized a birthday party and fundraising event for Huey Newton, the incarcerated leader of the Black Panther Party. Two years later, Baldwin wrote an open letter to Angela Davis, who was awaiting trial for charges of conspiracy, kidnapping, and homicide.[10] And in London the following year, Baldwin joined a fundraiser for the Soledad Brothers, three African American men who had been accused of murdering a white prison officer in 1970.[11] Less well known is Baldwin's commitment to freeing Tony Maynard, Jr., an aspiring African American actor who had worked for Baldwin and who was wrongly convicted of first degree manslaughter in 1967 – his alleged victim, a decorated white Marine.[12] Charged with stealing a car in Hamburg, Germany, while touring in Europe with jazz musicians, Maynard was incarcerated while he awaited extradition to the United States on a trumped-up charge of homicide.[13]

While Maynard's arrest and acquittal are less well documented than the infamous case of Angela Davis, his incarceration became the foundation for the plot of *If Beale Street Could Talk* (1974), Baldwin's penultimate novel, and the subject of a 2018 film directed by Barry Jenkins. According to David Leeming, *If Beale Street* was a "'fictionalization' of Baldwin's literal and metaphorical concerns about American prisons," a reminder, as Shireen R. K. Patell puts it, of how "[l]iterature opens the cases that law deems closed."[14] As Baldwin explains in his long essay *No Name in the Street* (1972), in order to prevent Maynard's extradition from Germany to

[9] James Baldwin, "The Discovery of What It Means to Be an American" [1959], in *Collected Essays*, 142.

[10] James Baldwin, "An Open Letter to My Sister, Miss Angela Davis," *New York Review of Books*, January 7, 1971, www.nybooks.com/articles/1971/01/07/an-open-letter-to-my-sister-miss-angela-davis/

[11] Baldwin's speech, along with contributions by John Thorne, Penny Jackson, Howard Moore, David Udo, and J. Joshi, was published in the pamphlet *Speeches from the Soledad Brothers Rally*, Central Hall, Westminster, April 20, 1971 (London: Notting Hill Press, 1975).

[12] Olivia B. Waxman, "Is *If Beale Street Could Talk* Based on a True Story? The Answer Is Complicated," *Time*, February 22, 2019, https://time.com/longform/beale-street-could-talk-true-story/

[13] See James Baldwin, "No Name in the Street" [1972], in *Collected Essays*, especially 413–24.

[14] Cited by David Leeming in Waxman; Shireen R. K. Patell, "'We the People,' Who? James Baldwin and the Traumatic Constitution of These United States," *Comparative Literature Studies* 48.3 (2011): 356–87, here 357.

the United States, where he feared he would be murdered, Maynard's legal team needed to demonstrate that he was a political prisoner, a fact that Baldwin supported. "I agree with the Black Panther position concerning black prisoners," Baldwin wrote, "not one of them has ever had a fair trial, for not one of them has ever been tried by a jury of his peers. White middle-class America is always the jury, and they know absolutely nothing about the lives of the people on whom they sit in judgment."[15]

This chapter examines *If Beale Street Could Talk* in relation to Baldwin's views on the "criminal power" at the heart of the US judicial system. As Baldwin wrote in relation to Maynard's case, policing had become "political persecution" for African Americans during the 1960s through a series of policing and incarceration reforms.[16] By 1964, President Johnson highlighted crime as a national crisis, telling Congress and the nation in March 1965 that "streets must be safe" and "homes and places of business must be secure."[17] During 1965, as critics have noted, it was "the preservation of law and order" that seemed to eclipse the magnitude of the Civil Rights Act.[18] Recent historians of mass incarceration have shown the ways in which draconian prison sentences and police surveillance were inextricably linked to the Civil Rights Movement. Elizabeth Hinton points out: "The Johnson administration believed that African American men between the ages of fifteen and twenty-four, influenced by civil rights activists increasingly advocating for self-determination and community control, were primarily responsible for the unrest."[19] So much so, as Heather Ann Thompson explains, that, by the mid-1960s, "'a new doctrine' had emerged and the idea that 'civil rights demonstrations amounted to violence and created a climate of lawlessness' had become gospel to large segments of the American voting public."[20]

In 1965, President Johnson's "War on Crime" initiative resulted in substantial federal investment in police departments across the US, largely to curb the "criminal" activities of young African American men after the riots of Watts (1965) and Newark (1967). In the late 1960s, Baldwin

---

[15] Baldwin, "No Name in the Street," 421-2.   [16] Cited by Waxman.
[17] Cited by Heather Anne Thompson, "Why Mass Incarceration Matters: Rethinking Crisis, Decline, and Transformation in Postwar American History," *Journal of American History* 97.3 (2010): 703-34, here 729.
[18] See Elizabeth Hinton, "Why We Should Reconsider the War on Crime," *Time*, March 20, 2015, https://time.com/3746059/war-on-crime-history/
[19] Elizabeth Hinton, *From the War on Poverty to the War on Crime: The Making of Mass Incarceration in America* (Cambridge, MA: Harvard University Press, 2016), 13.
[20] Heather Ann Thompson, "The Racial History of Criminal Justice in the United States," *Du Bois Review: Social Science Research on Race*, 16.1 (2019): 221-41, here 228.

wrote how African American men were "corralled and controlled" in the wake of Richard Nixon's "Law and Order" campaign.[21] As Hinton explains, "The strategy of policing shifts from responding to actual crime to hunting for potential subjects." She adds: "You don't need to necessarily be doing something to raise suspicions."[22] This was certainly the case with Maynard, who, at over six feet tall and in his thirties, didn't match the police's description of the suspect, who was five foot eight and aged between eighteen and twenty-two.

As I explore shortly, Fonny's arrest for a crime he did not commit in *If Beale Street Could Talk* carries echoes of the fate suffered by Richard in *Go Tell It on the Mountain*. And while I stake the claim that Baldwin's novel responds to the draconian shifts in policing measures during the 1960s, it is important to remember that instances and allegations of police misconduct have a much longer history – a history, of course, that also stretches into recent and current events. Historians such as Thompson have shown how "law enforcement across the country single[d] out Blacks over Whites for arrest during and after the Second World War."[23] In *The Devil Finds Work* (1976), Baldwin recalls an incident that took place in Woodstock, New York, several years after Wright's story, when he was accosted by two undercover FBI agents. Noting that his color had already made him "conspicuous" in the small town, Baldwin concludes that the agents "frightened me, and they humiliated me – it was like being spat on, or pissed on, or gang-raped" – an incident that, as Maurice Wallace has argued, illustrates "the spectacular conditions of historical black masculine identity and the chronic effort to 'frame' the black male body, criminally and visually."[24]

If Beale Street Could Talk, one of Baldwin's least studied novels, recounts the story of the nineteen-year-old Tish and her relationship with Fonny, a sculptor and childhood friend. Told in flashbacks, the novel revolves around the couple's relationship, which is wrenched apart when Fonny is falsely accused of rape by Mrs. Rogers, who subsequently flees to Puerto Rico. Fonny awaits trial in the Manhattan Detention Complex known as "The Tombs," a notorious nineteenth-century jail, described in 1970 as a place where there was no access to telephones or medical care,

[21] Cited by Waxman.   [22] Ibid.   [23] Thompson, "The Racial History of Criminal Justice," 225.
[24] James Baldwin, "The Devil Finds Work" [1976], in *Collected Essays*, 547; Maurice Wallace, "'I'm Not Entirely What I Look Like:' Richard Wright, James Baldwin and the Hegemony of Vision; or Jimmy's FBEye Blues," in *James Baldwin Now*, ed. Dwight McBride (New York and London: New York University Press, 1999), 300.

and where beatings by guards were routine.[25] Like many of Baldwin's novels, *If Beale Street Could Talk* explores the power of love to withstand the punishing reality of racism in an environment where "the kids had been told that they weren't worth shit and everything they saw around them proved it."[26]

If Beale Street Could Talk, as Miller rightly notes, "represents the pinnacle of the incarceration motif in all of his fiction"; it is a novel in which Baldwin explores the damaging effects of racial profiling on the protagonists and their families.[27] Before Fonny is imprisoned, he meets up with his friend, Daniel, who was also arrested for a crime he did not commit. "They said – and they still *say* – I stole a car," Daniel tells Fonny. "Man, I can't even *drive* a car, and I tried to make my lawyer – but he was really *their* lawyer ... prove that, but he didn't."[28]Caught in possession of a small amount of marijuana, Daniel explains how "they said if I would plead guilty they'd give me a lighter sentence. If I *didn't* plead guilty, they'd throw me the book," a policing strategy that was not uncommon in the late 1960s.[29] A year before *If Beale Street Could Talk* was published, the state of New York had passed a series of punitive new drug laws that called for mandatory sentences ranging from fifteen years to life for possession of small amounts of narcotics.[30] Unlike Fonny, who survives his ordeal through the love of his family and Tish, Daniel is condemned to bitterness. White people, Daniel tells Fonny, "can do with you whatever they want," concluding that "[t]he white man's *got* to be the devil."[31]

In one of the few positive reviews of *If Beale Street Could Talk*, Joyce Carol Oates points to how the "system of oppression [in the novel is] closely tied up with the mind-boggling stupidities of the law."[32] As Hinton has documented, "This long War on Crime would eventually produce the contemporary atrocity of mass incarceration in America, distinguished by a rate of imprisonment far above all other industrialized nations and involving the systematic confinement of entire groups of citizens."[33] As has been well documented, President Nixon's campaign focused on "law and order"

---

[25] See Morris Lasker's obituary in the *New York Times*, December 28, 2009, www.nytimes.com/2009/12/29/nyregion/29lasker.html

[26] James Baldwin, *If Beale Street Could Talk* (London: Penguin, 1974), 48.   [27] Miller, 142.

[28] Baldwin, *If Beale Street Could Talk*, 122.   [29] Ibid., 122–3.

[30] See Hinton, *From the War on Poverty to the War on Crime*, 158; Thompson, "Why Mass Incarceration Matters," 707–8.

[31] Baldwin, *If Beale Street Could Talk*, 123–4.

[32] Joyce Carol Oates, "Review of *If Beale Street Could Talk*," *New York Times,* May 19, 1974, https://archive.nytimes.com/www.nytimes.com/books/98/03/29/specials/baldwin-beale.html

[33] Hinton, *From the War on Poverty to the War on Crime*, 2.

in order to win hearts and minds, and he acted on his campaign promises when he took office in 1969. Driven by an administration that believed in "black cultural pathology, rather than poverty, as the root cause of crime," Nixon gave financial support to local, undercover police squads, while giving the green light to begin the construction of new prisons.[34] And as Hinton makes clear, not only were young, low-income African American men arrested and incarcerated as a way of supposedly preventing future crime, but Nixon's administration encouraged surveillance of Black urban neighborhoods, a tactic that fostered what Thompson has called "the criminalization of urban space."[35]

In "Why Mass Incarceration Matters: Rethinking Crisis, Decline, and Transformation in Postwar American History," Thompson demonstrates how, during and after the Civil Rights era, urban inhabitants of color "became subject to a growing number of laws that not only regulated bodies and communities in thoroughly new ways but also subjected violators to unprecedented time behind bars."[36] Thompson's attention to the ways in which urban spaces were "criminalized to an unprecedented extent" illuminates the damaging effects of incarceration in Baldwin's penultimate novel, not just on Fonny but also on his lover. During Tish's visits to Fonny in jail, Baldwin contrasts the sacred space of her lover's loft – a place of sexual intimacy and love – with the dehumanizing glass wall of the prison visiting room. "I hope that nobody has ever had to look at anybody they love through glass," Tish muses, adding, "I couldn't touch him. I wanted so to touch him."[37] In Baldwin's narrative, the glass wall is a literal barrier that prevents Fonny and Tish from holding one another, but it also underscores the ways in which metaphors of incarceration cut across African American literature. In particular, Tish's references to the glass barrier separating her from Fonny carry echoes of W. E. B. Du Bois's developing theories on racial division. Whereas in *The Souls of Black Folk* (1903), Du Bois famously described the "veil" that obscured African Americans from whites, in his much later work, *Dusk of Dawn* (1940), the metaphor is radically revised so that African Americans are incarcerated in "a dark cave," behind "some thick sheet of invisible but horribly tangible plate glass."[38] In Du Bois's later work, as Thomas C. Holt observes, "The veil has become an imprisoning wall" – a reminder that, in Baldwin's

---

[34] Ibid., 21.   [35] Ibid., 22; Thompson, "Why Mass Incarceration Matters," 706.
[36] Thompson, "Why Mass Incarceration Matters," 708.
[37] Baldwin, *If Beale Street Could Talk*, 12, 13.
[38] W. E. B. Du Bois, *Dusk of Dawn: An Essay Toward an Autobiography of a Race Concept*, intro. Anthony Appiah (New York and Oxford: Oxford University Press, 2007), 103.

work, the prison functions as a material site of incarceration but also as a metaphor.[39] "There are two people you always find in prison," Baldwin wrote in his essay, "What Price Freedom?" (1964):

> the man in the prison and the man who is keeping him there. I, as the prisoner, have a terrible advantage since I have to understand by the time I am twelve the nature of the prison and your nature, since you are my warden, and then I have to figure out how to outwit you and how to lick you and I do, and I manage, very often anyway, to survive all your prisons.[40]

As Miller points out, in *If Beale Street Could Talk*, "[p]rison is the ultimate alienating space, but it falls along a continuum of such spaces."[41] Fonny and Tish attempt to create a sanctuary in Fonny's loft; but when they venture out, they are at the mercy of Officer Bell, a corrupt white policeman who controls public spaces through power and fear. As the couple walks into the streets, the police presence, as Miller notes, "connotes a threat rather than what it is supposed to connote: public safety."[42] Fonny is targeted by Officer Bell, both for moving downtown and also because "he had found his centre, his own centre, inside him: and it showed." "And if you're nobody's nigger," Tish explains, "you're a bad nigger."[43] And while *If Beale Street Could Talk* ends on a note of ambiguity – it is unclear whether or not Fonny has been released from prison – the novel succeeds in the ways that it humanizes the protagonists, moving them away from what the historian Khalil Gibran Muhammad has termed a "statistical discourse" about Black crime, one in which African Americans have routinely been blamed for their disproportionate incarceration.[44]

Early in his career, Baldwin reminded his readers that "literature and sociology are not one and the same; it is impossible to discuss them as if they were."[45] And while I am mindful of the pitfalls of reading Baldwin's fiction solely as a snapshot of the Nixonian "Law and Order" era, *If Beale Street Could Talk*, which explores the power of love in the face of a corrupt police and legal system, writes back to the statistical discourse that emerged during the 1960s and 1970s. As Hinton has shown, during this period,

---

[39] Thomas C. Holt, "The Political Uses of Alienation: W. E. B. Du Bois on Politics, Race, and Culture, 1903–1940," *American Quarterly* 42.2 (1990): 301–23, here 309.

[40] James Baldwin, "What Price Freedom?" [1964], in *The Cross of Redemption: Uncollected Writings*, ed. and intro. Randall Kenan (New York: Pantheon Books, 2010), 91.

[41] Miller, 143.   [42] Ibid., 144.   [43] Baldwin, *If Beale Street Could Talk*, 50.

[44] See Khalil Gibran Muhammad, *The Condemnation of Blackness: Race, Crime, and the Making of Modern Urban America* (Cambridge, MA: Harvard University Press, 2019).

[45] James Baldwin, "Everybody's Protest Novel" [1949], in *Collected Essays*, 15.

new ways of interpreting Black urban crime were not only "supported with federal funding" but were "grounded in cultural interpretations of racial inequality."[46] These policies not only "extended a long tradition of racially biased understanding of crime"; they also highlighted "the disparate rates of black incarceration as empirical 'proof' of the 'criminal nature' of African Americans."[47] Baldwin's writing on prisons – and *If Beale Street Could Talk* in particular – works powerfully as a discourse that resists and writes back to the state-sanctioned findings that equated Blackness with innate criminality. Baldwin's work underscores the ways in which "[l]-iterature accommodates the unsettled and unsettling nature of language, affords ambiguities free range, indulges the complex and nonclosural, and thus testifies to that which the law cannot admit into evidence."[48]

To conclude, I want to turn to one of Baldwin's lesser-known essays, "This Far and No Further" (1983), which was published in the prison magazine *Inside/Out* (later called *Time Capsule*).[49] Baldwin's essay begins with the premise that "the State creates the Criminal, of every conceivable type and stripe, because the State cannot operate without the Criminal," moving on to an argument that the criminal "may or may not be a Prisoner, and the Prisoner may or may not be a Criminal."[50] As Baldwin points out – echoing the ways in which the War on Poverty quickly morphed into the War on Crime – "rarely is the Prisoner someone who has managed to embezzle, say, two or three million dollars."[51] In Baldwin's logic, mass incarceration has little to do with rehabilitation; rather, incarceration is an extension of the state's need to scapegoat its citizens from low socioeconomic backgrounds, many of whom are people of color. Death row, Baldwin notes, "like the ghetto, is dark with dark faces."[52]

Midway through "This Far and No Further," Baldwin makes an oblique reference to a friend whom he visited in jail. And while Baldwin does not give many details, his recollection that he traveled 10,000 miles to visit his friend suggests that he may have been referring to Tony Maynard as he awaited extradition to New York from Hamburg.[53] In Baldwin's account, his friend had refused to work at the prison factories for the paltry prison wages. During a meeting with the prison warden, the author of *If Beale*

---

[46] Hinton, *From the War on Poverty*, 18.   [47] Ibid., 19.   [48] Patell, 357.
[49] Baldwin wrote two essays for *Inside/Out* (*Time Capsule*). "A Letter to Prisoners" (1982) is a much briefer piece, which is also collected in *The Cross of Redemption*, 247–9.
[50] Baldwin, "This Far and No Further," in *The Cross of Redemption*, 160–1, 161.   [51] Ibid., 161.
[52] Ibid., 163.
[53] New York to Hamburg is approximately 10,000 miles as a round trip. And while Baldwin was based in the South of France, he frequently stayed in New York City during the time of Maynard's imprisonment in Hamburg.

Street Could Talk is told that he must persuade his friend to cooperate if he wants him to have a fair hearing at his parole board, which Baldwin sums up as "a terrifying apprehension of crime and punishment!"[54]

In a statement reminiscent of his claim that the artist should always be "a disturber of the peace," in "This Far and No Further" Baldwin concludes: "It is the responsibility of the Artist perpetually to question the zealous State and the narcotized Society."[55] In works such as *If Beale Street Could Talk*, Baldwin anticipated the work of historians of mass incarceration, who also drew attention to how "it is the poor and the helpless who are incarcerated while the able and affluent fly away." Baldwin concludes, in a statement that has lost none of its relevance, that "it may be time to suggest that if the State depended less heavily on criminals, the Society would be burdened with fewer prisoners."[56]

---

[54] Baldwin, "This Far and No Further," 162.
[55] Eve Auchinloss and Nancy Lynch, "Disturber of the Peace: James Baldwin – An Interview," in *Conversations with James Baldwin*, ed. Fred L. Standley and Louis H. Pratt (Jackson: University Press of Mississippi, 1989), 171; Baldwin, "This Far and No Further," 163.
[56] Baldwin, "This Far and No Further," 163.

CHAPTER 21

The Monkey Wrench Gang *(1975): Edward Abbey*

Christopher K. Coffman

Edward Abbey's *The Monkey Wrench Gang* presents the adventures of four radicalized wilderness lovers in the desert of the American southwest. The novel is widely discussed as an important work in both the tradition of American nature writing and the development of American environmental consciousness and action. Yet, conversations about it are plagued by disagreements over the compatibility of its environmental vision with views found in other examples of American nature writing, by confusion regarding the exact nature of Abbey's political sensibilities, and by the novel's problematic blindness to the intersection of wilderness preservation with social justice platforms. However, the troubled criticism the work has generated in fact suggests the best approach to an appreciation of its politics – that is, via the intentionally inchoate formula its protagonists articulate: "Let our practice form our doctrine, thus assuring precise theoretical coherence."[1] This preference for intuitive action over organized political prescription is very much at the heart of the novel and among its greatest strengths; it allows Abbey not only to foreground a terrifically sympathetic agenda – if in some senses a tremendously inconsistent one – but also to exploit tensions deriving from some of the central paradoxes of environmental thought and nature writing.

Among the challenges one faces when approaching Abbey's work is the question of whether or not he should be regarded as a nature writer at all. Some critics assert that to do so is to misunderstand the novel. For Michael Potts, for instance, Abbey is instead a committed writer, one whose work employs the wilderness as a means to promote a particular political stance. From this perspective, Abbey's preoccupation with the wilderness is an expression of a dedication to freedom as a moral and political value; the wilderness is of interest not due to any inherent qualities or features, but

---

[1] Edward Abbey, *The Monkey Wrench Gang* (New York: Harper, 1975), 69.

because of its radical freedom from administration.[2] Readings like these accommodate points where Abbey sits uneasily alongside other nature writers, but they can be overstated. One difficulty this sort of argument encounters is that Abbey is hardly alone among major nature writers in scattering political material among the rolling rivers, saguaro, and field mice. One need look no further than the intersections of Henry David Thoreau's attitudes in *Walden* with those declared in his "Civil Disobedience" to recognize the commonalities among his environmental, moral, and political identities. Likewise, Rachel Carson's seminal *Silent Spring* would be, if not entirely worthless, at least severely diminished if we somehow excised its political content. On the other hand, arguments such as those Potts advances are by no means insubstantial, and, as Steven Vogel reminds us, Marx declared the very idea of a "nature" that is opposed to the "human" or the "social" evidence of a fundamental alienation.[3] For these reasons, careful consideration of Abbey's similarities to other nature writers is revealing as an approach to his politics.

The *Monkey Wrench Gang* does include an epigraph from Thoreau, but Abbey does not opt for a paean to the spirits of nature. Instead, he includes an obstinate assertion of urgency: "Now. Or never."[4] The exigency is related to a key difference Bill McKibben identifies when comparing Abbey and Thoreau: Thoreau's wilderness was the "profligate, fecund beauty of the Northeast," while Abbey's chosen land is the dry and hot desert. The novel's epigraph is, in this sense, not just impatience or a sense of political ultimacy, but a matter of having learned in an unforgiving landscape that the difference between life and death may be a moment's hesitation. As McKibben adds, this also makes the political, which largely remained only implicit in many earlier nature writers, much more evident in the case of Abbey.[5] So, set against the landscapes of the first Romantics or early authors who combined travelogues with nature writing, as did John Muir in his *My First Summer in the Sierra*, Abbey's wilderness can seem a matter of Darwinian competition rather than ennobling spiritualism. This is not the only difference between Abbey and his predecessors of

[2] Michael Potts, "Wildness and Wilderness: Anti-pastoralism and the Problematic Politics of Edward Abbey," *Australian Literary Studies* 30.2 (2015): 105–16, here 106–7.

[3] Steven Vogel, "On Nature and Alienation," in *Critical Ecologies: The Frankfurt School and Contemporary Environmental Crises*, ed. Andrew Biro (Toronto: University of Toronto Press, 2011), 187–205, here 196.

[4] Abbey, *The Monkey Wrench Gang*, xi.

[5] Bill McKibben, "The Desert Anarchist," *New York Review of Books*, August 18, 1988, www.nybooks.com/articles/1988/08/18/the-desert-anarchist/

this sort: When the comparisons turn to more recent nature writing, they reveal a more fundamental problem with the genre, one that is germane to Abbey's attitude to nature and to his politics.

Nature writing since World War II has shared more of Abbey's urgency than did earlier examples. Carson's *Silent Spring*, like Aldo Leopold's *A Sand County Almanac*, increasingly trades the celebratory wilderness sublime of Romanticism for more sober notes: As Rebecca Raglon argues, nature has lately been presented as a value under assault, and therefore best expressed with the eulogistic tones and elegiac modes that characterize writing about loss.[6] As nature's prowess has diminished in presentation, a felt need for its defenders to speak on its terms has also increasingly been evident. The shift in attitude pushes into the foreground problems of representation that have always been implicit in nature writing. Niklas Luhmann presented the paradox thus: How can the environmental movement effectively critique society if the language it has at its disposal and the audience it seeks to reach are of that society?[7] Likewise, Hannes Bergthaller asks whether the environmentalist can distinguish the biosphere from categories of social experience.[8] Phrased in this fashion, the point seems insurmountable, but, rather than proposing a resolution of the tension Bergthaller's constructionist question describes, critics such as Greg Garrard accept the challenge as a productive paradox, declaring the task of ecocriticism a matter of keeping "one eye on the ways in which 'nature' is always ... culturally constructed, and the other on the fact that nature really exists."[9] Therefore, we must expect a slippage between "nature" and "culture" to characterize works of writers such as Abbey, and to do so increasingly as the political content of the text becomes more explicit.

Such conditions are certainly explored in the novel, as in the passage dedicated to a conversation between George Hayduke and Bonnie Abbzug about the logging industry. Abbzug, while horrified by clear-cutting, considers that Americans do need lumber to build shelters. Hayduke proposes other options, describing increasingly unconventional visions of

---

[6] Rebecca Raglon, "Surviving Doom and Gloom: Edward Abbey's Desert Comedies," in *Coyote in the Maze: Tracking Edward Abbey in a World of Words*, ed. Peter Quigley (Salt Lake City: University of Utah Press, 1998), 168–83, here 168.

[7] Niklas Luhmann, *Ecological Communication* (Chicago: University of Chicago Press, 1989), 126.

[8] Hannes Bergthaller, "Paradox as Bedrock: Social Systems Theory and the Ungrounding of Literary Environmentalism in Edward Abbey's *Desert Solitaire*," in *Handbook of Ecocriticism and Cultural Ecology*, ed. Hubert Zapf (Berlin: De Gruyter, 2016), 105–22, here 105–6.

[9] Greg Garrard, *Ecocriticism* (London: Routledge, 2004), 10.

materials and methods, although also offering in conclusion a need for sturdier houses, like his "great-granpappy's cabin back in Pennsylvania." Abbzug, frustrated with the more impractical components of Hayduke's vision, responds, "All you're asking for is a counter-industrial revolution."[10] Hayduke is comfortable with the idea, and his advocacy of a reactionary return to pre-industrial culture celebrates an idealized version of our relation to the land and reminds readers that the wilderness is always tied to a network of sociopolitical conditions. As William Cronon has shown, American wilderness is no Edenic place, but can be understood as an historically produced value, a social construction that obscures a history of displaced populations, unjustly claimed territory, and bureaucratic regulation of space. These and other factors, all of which are typically hidden when one accepts the idea of an unpopulated wilderness, are suggested by Abbzug's question.[11] Ultimately, Hayduke grows frustrated with the more intractable portions of the argument and declares: "My job is to save the fucking wilderness. I don't know anything else worth saving. That's simple, right?"[12] It is not simple, of course, but both his vision of his grandfather's old cabin and his demand for simplicity recall us to Thoreau, a nature writer from an era when the question of industrialization's impact on nature was formulated on somewhat less complex terms.

Yet, the tension driving the conversation between Hayduke and Abbzug – between a recognition of a facilely defined, simple "wilderness" and a culturally constructed, ideological "wilderness" – is important to the novel's political value. On the one hand is Hayduke, a man of super-heroic action and little reflection. Hayduke's dedication to pragmatics repeatedly foregrounds a strong subjectivity, an autonomous self that has achieved a level of personal liberation through physical power and sheer contrariness. On the other is Abbzug, a problematically portrayed feminist who is the most urban, and urbane, of the central characters, and who most often calls the others to a pause with her meditations on the broader implications of their work. As David N. Cassuto explains, each of the protagonists of *The Monkey Wrench Gang* operate between these poles of conventional social life and radical environmentalism: Doc Sarvis largely lives a life of creature comforts, while his bank-rolling of ecotage redistributes his wealth in a fashion that resembles the renewable distribution of resources that

---

[10] Abbey, *The Monkey Wrench Gang*, 229.
[11] William Cronon, "The Trouble with Wilderness; or, Getting Back to the Wrong Nature," in *Uncommon Ground: Rethinking the Human Place in Nature*, ed. William Cronon (New York: W. W. Norton, 1996), 69–90, here 79.
[12] Abbey, *The Monkey Wrench Gang*, 229.

would be allowed by restitution of pre-industrial natural processes; likewise, the river guide Seldom Seen Smith makes his living leading tourists into the very land he wants to preserve from human interference.[13] In short, in the case of each main character there is a measure of conventional social attachment that inhibits entire dedication to the environment. This middle ground that Abbey creates, however, is exactly that space for political action, as to go too far in one's rejection of the social is to lose the self entirely, and thereby to lose the capacity for political contestation.

Such an issue is at the heart of Alexander Menrisky's argument that Abbey's central paradox is that the authentic subject cannot be reconciled to ecological interconnectivity.[14] Menrisky's insight links the political and the ecological: Both are means for connection, and both are necessary to us and subject to corruption. Abbey's characters are as suspicious of the total loss of self as they are of excessive self-preoccupation. Intriguingly, Abbey calls us away from the latter danger with reference to the Thoreauvian ideal of solitude: Even Hayduke, reflecting on the "old dream of total independence," recognizes that "[s]omewhere in the depths of solitude, beyond wildness and freedom, lay the trap of madness."[15] In the end, the middle ground Abbey's characters tread resembles the melting of boundaries between subject and nature for which many ecologists, including Lawrence Buell and Timothy Morton, argue. The perspective tips the balance away from the constructivist position of thinkers such as Luhmann and in the direction of a stance from which critiques of ideological codings of the wilderness may be mounted by groups of autonomous subjects.

For the most part, the resistance Abbey's protagonists mount is fairly humble: cutting down billboards, sabotaging construction equipment, removing surveyor stakes, and so forth. At the most extreme, a bridge is destroyed and a train that services a power station is derailed. Their ultimate ambition, however, is a much more powerful statement of environmental politics: the destruction of the Glen Canyon Dam. As Rob Nixon explains, big dams create three forms of diversion: Water is moved from one route to another; land is transferred from the powerless to the powerful; and attention is displaced to the technological.[16] Abbey's hatred

---

[13] David N. Cassuto, "Waging Water: Hydrology vs. Mythology in The Monkey Wrench Gang," *Interdisciplinary Studies in Literature and Environment* 2.1 (1994): 13–36, here 25–8.

[14] Alexander Menrisky, "The Ecological Alternative: Edward Abbey, The New Left, and Environmental Authenticity," *Criticism* 61.1 (2019): 51–71, here 76.

[15] Abbey, *The Monkey Wrench Gang*, 114.

[16] Rob Nixon, "Unimagined Communities: Developmental Refugees, Megadams and Monumental Modernity," *New Formations* 69.1 (2010): 62–80, here 79.

for the Glen Canyon Dam positions him in a lineage of Western authors who share his complaints, including John Muir's resistance to the flooding by damming of the Hetch Hetchy Valley and Wallace Stegner's work to preserve Dinosaur National Monument under similar conditions. As Cassuto argues, Abbey presents the hoarding of water behind dams not only as an environmental issue, but also, and perhaps more importantly, as a matter of power and finance. Rather than a well-intentioned accumulation of resources destined for equable redistribution among the needy, damming serves agribusiness.[17] What drives the exemptions and reallocations, however, is not merely political interest and financial greed, but a version of Manifest Destiny that envisions a green garden stretching from sea to sea, supporting itself with such technological sublimities as dams. In the face of that divine mandate, as Nixon explains, the populations and modes of life supported by the rivers that the dams redirect are displaced and erased, excluding them from participation in the political life of the nation. They thus form, in an inversion of Benedict Anderson's terminology, "unimagined communities."[18] The construction of more and larger dams, and the concomitant shifts in regulation of natural resources, was exacerbated after World War II, when dam construction worked hand in glove with Cold War techno-competition: The bigger the dam, presumably, the more powerful the government that installed it.[19] The connection between the energy industry, techno-military might, and environmental disaster is reinforced in *The Monkey Wrench Gang* when Abbey's protagonists encounter a strip mine on a mesa. Sarvis thinks

> of the plain of fire and of the oligarchs and oligopoly beyond: Peabody Coal only one arm of Anaconda Copper; Anaconda only a limb of United States Steel; US Steel intertwined in incestuous embrace with the Pentagon, TVA, Standard Oil, General Dynamics, Dutch Shell, I. G. Farben-industrie; the whole conglomerated cartel spread out upon half the planet Earth like a global kraken … its brain a bank of computer data centers, its blood the flow of money, its heart a radioactive dynamo, its language the technetronic monologue of number imprinted on magnetic tape.
> But George Washington Hayduke, his thought was the clearest and simplest: Hayduke thought of Vietnam.[20]

Sarvis's recognition that the interests of various governmental agencies and large businesses are irremediably entangled, here expressed in the terms of biblical corruption, pithily summarizes the typical political and financial factors driving the construction of dams. But Hayduke's simpler

---

[17] Cassuto, 13.   [18] Nixon, 63.   [19] Ibid., 65.   [20] Abbey, *The Monkey Wrench Gang*, 172.

formulation is perhaps even more powerful and revealing in its equation of a failed and brutal war and the machinery and techno-military politics of the American energy industry.

Abbey's assertions regarding connections among the energy business, agriculture, national and regional politics, and international military action may be broadly sketched, but they are no less effective for it. Furthermore, they help situate the politics of his novel in relation to both earlier and later literary texts. As Cassuto asserts, Abbey's recognition that the redistribution of access to natural resources that projects such as dams entail is a manifestation of the same sort of dynamic that drove the Dust Bowl-era migrations: "John Steinbeck, in *The Grapes of Wrath*, depicted starving Okies enjoined by agribusiness from planting subsistence crops on land purposely kept fallow."[21] Patricia Greiner makes a similar point about Steinbeck, and, further, recognizes its ancestry in texts such as Frank Norris's *The Octopus*, which pits the railroad, with its ties to industrial expansion, against the more sustainable land ethic of the ranchers who were displaced by rail lines.[22] These aspects of *The Monkey Wrench Gang* have done the most to connect it both to extraliterary political action and to a certain strand of more recent writing. Leslie Marmon Silko's *Ceremony* proves an intriguing successor: Like Abbey's novel, Silko's is preoccupied with the degree to which the freedom and wilderness of the West is challenged by government mismanagement of water. Also, just as Abbey's Hayduke regards the machines of environmental degradation through the lens of the military-industrial complex that shaped his traumatic years in Vietnam, so Silko's protagonist is a psychologically scarred World War II veteran whose experiences in the war reshape his understanding of the social and natural worlds to which he returns.

Silko's later *Almanac of the Dead* is even more closely connected to Abbey's work, and the point of intersection is especially intriguing. On March 21, 1981, an early incarnation of the environmental activist group Earth First! enacted a piece of guerrilla theater that was inspired by Abbey's novel: They unrolled a long, narrow sheet of black vinyl down the face of Glen Canyon Dam, creating the illusion of a dangerous crack in the structure. Abbey spoke approvingly of the event at the site, and he long maintained connections with the group, although never joining them officially. The action was recorded and edited into a 1982 film, *The*

[21] Cassuto, 18.
[22] Patricia Greiner, "Radical Environmentalism in Recent Literature Concerning the American West," *Rendezvous* 19.1 (1983): 8–15, here 9.

Cracking of Glen Canyon Damn [sic]. The lineage of the film undergoes a radical reformulation in Silko's *Almanac of the Dead*. In that novel, footage is shown of a group of "eco-warriors" who descend the face of the dam with "backpack[s] loaded with explosives." At the climax of the short film, "the giant video screen itself appeared to crack and shatter in slow motion, and the six ... figures ... disappeared in a white flash of smoke and dust. The entire top half of the dam structure ... folded over, collapsing behind a giant wall of reddish water."[23] So, while Abbey's characters only plan for the destruction of the dam, they inspired actual protests at the dam by Earth First!, whose documentary film of the staged actions was re-envisioned by Silko as having been a recording of the actual destruction of the dam viewed by characters in her novel. This chain of remediations, which shuttles between the literary and the extraliterary, may not help to explain the finer political points of Abbey's novel, but it does attest to the text's influence on political sensibilities and actions in and outside of fiction.

Silko's more violent vision of ecotage is entangled with other matters of social justice in *Almanac of the Dead*. However, the same might not necessarily be said of Abbey. Critics generally find that, while what he argues against is abundantly evident, that for which he contends is substantially less so. His work certainly has been a target for claims of racism, sexism, and class elitism. Abbey's alignment of wilderness appreciation with white males is a particular sticking point. Catrin Gersford, for instance, looks at both Abbey's construction of wilderness and his biography, and concludes that the former is male and Anglo-Saxon, while the latter is racist and misogynist to a degree that even sympathetic readers would find hard to recuperate.[24] Katrine E. Barber compares Abbey's activists with Silko's, and reaches much the same conclusion: Abbey's characters are largely male and white; Silko's are not, and, furthermore, they are more cognizant of the intersections between environmental justice and various matters of social justice.[25] Not all critics are in total agreement with such evaluations. Paul T. Bryant, for instance, argues throughout his essay on Abbey and gender that charging Abbey with sexism or misogyny

[23] Leslie Marmon Silko, *Almanac of the Dead* (New York: Penguin, 1991), 727.
[24] Catrin Gersford, *The Poetics and Politics of the Desert: Landscape and the Construction of America* (Amsterdam: Rodopi, 2009), 194.
[25] Katrine E. Barber, "Wisecracking Glen Canyon Dam: Revisioning Environmentalist Mythology," in *Change in the American West: Exploring the Human Dimension*, ed. Stephen Tchudi (Reno: University of Nevada Press, 1996), 127–43, here 142.

is problematic.[26] As a test case, then, one might consider the lack of strong female characters in *The Monkey Wrench Gang*. Abbzug, who is by far the most important female figure in the book, comes across as a girl Friday rather than a powerful heroine, and her role is most often defined by the male gaze. David Fenimore's assessment of Abbzug is much the same: She is largely presented in the very socially traditional terms of cook and object of sexual interest. Perhaps most revealingly, in terms of the question of Abbey's sexism, she is the character whose ability to perform tasks most often fails at the point of crisis.[27] Also, as Potts argues, as the only one of the novel's four central characters who is from the East Coast, Abbzug has different preferences than the others in terms of music, drugs, and books, and her tastes are mocked by her companions.[28] In these and in other ways, her character stands as an obstacle to those who would contend that Abbey is not sexist and his wilderness not gendered.

Against Abbey's example, we could weigh writers such as Gary Snyder and Arundhati Roy. As Greiner argues, Abbey's characters are primarily antagonistic in their motivations, and their lack of long-range visions for the coordination of actions means that they also fail to display the sort of interconnected awareness that is fundamental to the ecological sensibility. Snyder, on the other hand, offers in his poetry a vision of connectedness that very much appears informed by a sense of Leopold's land ethic and has the potential for a more equable and lasting response to environmental crisis.[29] Or, as Nixon has contended, we could look to the example of Roy. Her growth as a writer has had to account for neoliberal globalization, including the movement of the dam industry to the global South. As she has explained in her essay "The Greater Common Good," dams in such settings as the Narmada River valley, as opposed to those of the American desert southwest, greatly increase the chances of flooding in densely, rather than sparsely, populated areas. Under these conditions, it is impossible to ignore the imbrication of class and environmental politics, something Abbey largely neglects, even though he opposes dams as passionately as does Roy.[30]

The preceding paragraphs paint a rather dim picture of Abbey and his novel, yet they do so in part because the analysis focuses so narrowly on the representation of politics in *The Monkey Wrench Gang*. A more

---

[26] Paul T. Bryant, "Edward Abbey and Gender," in Quigley, ed., 226–41.

[27] David Fenimore, "Edward Abbey, *The Monkey Wrench Gang* (1975)," in *Literature and the Environment*, ed. George Hart and Scott Slovic (Westport, CT: Greenwood, 2004), 95–109, here 106.

[28] Potts, 113.   [29] Greiner, 14.   [30] Nixon, 67–8.

sympathetic view is possible if the evaluation shifts to the politics of representation. Cheryl Lousley has identified a widespread need for just such a shift: "the representational challenge" is "not the representation of nature, but ... how to make complex socio-ecological interactions socially viable as political concerns." From this point of view, the problem is not a matter of communicating environmental problems to audiences, but of revealing socio-ecological matters as an arena for political concern and action in the first place.[31] In light of this demand, Abbey's novel is somewhat more approachable.

One path to this alternate evaluation of the political consciousness of *The Monkey Wrench Gang* is the intuitive antagonism of the novel's characters. There is a good reason that Abbey's assertion that "growth for the sake of growth is the ideology of the cancer cell" is so frequently quoted.[32] As Harold Alderman argues, Abbey's politics are an unconventional anarchism: He loves personal liberty, the desert landscape, and the beautiful; he despises charismatic leaders, governments, and large movements.[33] Constitutionally suspicious of the Marxist notion that the masses are the home of virtue, Abbey is nevertheless a reactionary opponent of religions, states, and class categories.[34] In short, his spirit is that of uncompromising resistance and "perpetual rebellion," and his protagonist, Hayduke, is suited to the job: He is more powerful than anything around him except the desert itself, large like Pantagruel and idiosyncratic like Quixote.[35] From this perspective, it is clear, as Paul Slovic asserts, that the rhetorical intent of Abbey's text is that of a provocateur.[36] He is not attempting to present or to defend any particular platform, but to awaken us to our own wildness.[37] To put it more simply, if less strikingly: *The Monkey Wrench Gang* may ignore matters of social justice, but it does so because it is preoccupied with the more fundamental issue of getting readers to recognize that environmental degradation is a matter of political concern relevant to individual autonomy.

It is telling in this regard that, in addition to his other front matter, Abbey includes as an epigraph a definition of "sabotage" that traces its roots to the sabots (wooden shoes) thrown into the workings of machines,

---

[31] Cheryl Lousley, "Ecocriticism and the Politics of Representation," in *The Oxford Handbook of Ecocriticism*, ed. Greg Garrard (Oxford: Oxford University Press, 2014), 155–71, here 156–7.
[32] Edward Abbey, *One Life at a Time, Please* (New York: Holt, 1988), 21.
[33] Harold Alderman, "Abbey as Anarchist," in Quigley, ed., 137–49, here 138.   [34] Ibid., 140.
[35] Ibid., 142–3, 148–9.
[36] Paul Slovic, *Seeking Awareness in American Nature Writing: Henry Thoreau, Annie Dillard, Edward Abbey, Wendell Berry, Barry Lopez* (Salt Lake City: University of Utah Press, 1992), 110.
[37] Ibid., 112–13.

and he dedicates the book to Ned Ludd.[38] These opening pages thus situate the book's political content, with an anticipatory nod to Thomas Pynchon's 1984 essay "Is It OK to Be a Luddite?," in relation to populations marginalized by the early Industrial Revolution, deepening the history of the struggle Abbey presents, and also, if only to a partial degree, countering those who would accuse him of indifference to those among the disempowered who might benefit from the redistribution of water by damming. If Abbey's practice of environmentalism is, as Leo Mellor suggests, a form of celebrating individual self-determination, it is something from which people of all classes may profit, despite the protests of the collectivists.[39]

---

[38] Abbey, *The Monkey Wrench Gang*, vii, xiii.
[39] Leo Mellor, "The Lure of Wilderness," in *The Cambridge Companion to Literature and the Environment*, ed. Louise Westling (Cambridge: Cambridge University Press, 2014), 104–18, here 106.

CHAPTER 22

Ceremony (1977): Leslie Marmon Silko

Sandra M. Gustafson

Leslie Marmon Silko published her breakthrough novel *Ceremony* in March 1977, less than two years after North Vietnamese tanks entered the grounds of the presidential palace of Saigon, bringing an unofficial end to the US war in Vietnam. Even as the political atmosphere surrounding the Vietnam War helped shape Silko's novel, World War II provided its overt context. Centered on Tayo, a young veteran of the Pacific front, *Ceremony* is set in and around Laguna Pueblo, west of Albuquerque, New Mexico. When the reader meets Tayo, he is tossing and turning in his bed at the family's sheep camp, as voices wash over him like a flood: a man singing a love song in Spanish, promising to return; the voices of his Japanese captors, which segue into the Laguna voices of his uncle and his mother; and finally, "loud, loud music from a big juke box" with "flashing red and blue lights" recalling the colors of the American flag, which have the effect of "pulling the darkness closer."[1] Silko conveys all these elements of Tayo's experience with admirable compression, preparing the reader to engage with her protagonist's complex trauma. His suffering has its most immediate sources in the death of his cousin Rocky during the Bataan Death March in the Philippines and Tayo's own experiences in a Japanese prisoner-of-war camp. As the tale unfolds, it becomes clear that the roots of Tayo's trauma go much deeper than the war. They extend into his childhood and family history, the region's history of settler colonialism, and ultimately into the mythic realm where Silko locates the origins of what she terms "witchery," a dehumanizing yet all too human impulse toward violence.[2]

---

[1] Leslie Marmon Silko, *Ceremony* (New York: Penguin, 2006 [1977]), 5.

[2] Michelle Satterlee broke important ground on the subject of trauma in the novel in "Landscape Imagery and Memory in the Narrative of Trauma: A Closer Look at Leslie Marmon Silko's *Ceremony*," *ISLE: Interdisciplinary Studies in Literature and Environment* 13.2 (2006): 73–92. General studies include Allan Chavkin, ed., *Leslie Marmon Silko's Ceremony: A Casebook* (New York: Oxford University Press, 2002); and, for context, Joy Porter and Kenneth M. Roemer, eds.,

Silko has written about her familiarity with the effects of World War II on her family and the broader Laguna community. Her father, Lee Marmon, served a wartime tour of duty in the Aleutian Islands of Alaska, then returned to run the family trading post. In 1947, Lee Marmon's father gave him a camera and encouraged him to document life at the pueblo. The following year Leslie was born in Albuquerque; she grew up mainly at Laguna. Marmon's photographs of Laguna elders, ceremonies, and landscapes – and his success as a photographer – were factors influencing his daughter's literary career. Her work was further shaped by the Laguna stories that she heard and by the lingering effects of the war on some of the veterans in the community. In her preface to the thirtieth-anniversary edition of *Ceremony* published in 2006, Silko describes how she originally planned to write "a funny story" about "a World War II veteran whose family tried but could not keep him away from liquor." Her initial impulse toward comedy darkened as she considered the experiences of Laguna veterans who she knew, "many of whom were survivors of the Bataan Death March, cousins and relatives of mine who returned from the war and stayed drunk the rest of their lives." These men were "kind" and "available to us children," she writes, noting that "even as a child I knew they were not bad people, yet something had happened to them. What was it?"[3] Tayo's character emerged as a way to focalize the trauma and despair that Silko had long sensed in the veterans around her, and he gradually became the center of her novel.

In choosing a troubled World War II veteran as her central character, Silko followed the precedent of Kiowa writer N. Scott Momaday, whose *House Made of Dawn* (1968) won the Pulitzer Prize for Fiction in 1969. Momaday has been credited with launching the "Native American Renaissance" – Kenneth Lincoln's memorable term for the dramatic increase in novels written by Native Americans after Momaday's success. Momaday spent formative years living at Jemez Pueblo in New Mexico, some seventy-five miles northeast of Laguna. His novel follows the experiences of Abel, a Jemez veteran of World War II who has trouble reintegrating into pueblo life when he returns from the war. Suffering from alcoholism, Abel commits a murder and spends time in prison. After a difficult period living in Los Angeles, he returns to the pueblo by train, and, as he tends his dying grandfather, begins to reintegrate into his

---

The Cambridge Companion to Native American Literature (Cambridge: Cambridge University Press, 2006).

[3] Silko, *Ceremony*, xvi.

ancestral community. In addition to basic contours of characterization and setting, *Ceremony* echoes several of Momaday's main themes and plot elements. A partial list includes the following: the beauty of the desert region and the ceremonies that help humans maintain their place within it; difficult relationships between white and Indigenous people; alcoholism and its resulting violence; a main character who spends time in Los Angeles, then returns to the pueblo by train; and a concern with witches and witchery. Further, Silko incorporates elements from the Navajo Night Chant in the healing ritual that ultimately restores Tayo, in what amounts to a citation of Momaday's title phrase drawn from the Night Chant. But there are substantial differences in narrative style between the two works. Momaday initially draws his characters as small figures within a vast desert landscape, while Silko launches her novel from within the troubled mind of her central character. In certain ways, then, Silko's novel reads like a commentary on – even a diagnosis of – the root causes of the misery suffered by Momaday's protagonist Abel.

The differences between the novels by Silko and Momaday are, in part, generational. Momaday earned a bachelor's degree in English from the University of New Mexico in 1958 and went on to earn a PhD in English from Stanford in 1963, in an era when the New Criticism dominated the field of literary studies. By the time that Silko earned her undergraduate degree from the same department eleven years later, challenges to the dominance of the New Criticism had begun to emerge in the form of postmodern literature, post-structuralist theory, and political criticism.[4]

Stylistic and formal differences set their novels apart from one another. An early innovator, Silko employed a range of postmodern narrative techniques in *Ceremony*, including intertextual references to *House Made of Dawn*, fragments from Laguna tales, and metafictional elements, notably the convergence of the ceremony and the novel itself. Silko's first published fiction resembles Momaday's work more closely. While still an undergraduate, her story "The Man to Send Rain Clouds" (1968) appeared in what proved to be the final issue of the *New Mexico Quarterly*, a publication of the faculty and students at the University of

---

[4] A scandal that erupted in the University of New Mexico English Department in 1969, the year that Silko earned her bachelor's degree, conveys the political and intellectual climate at the time. The incident involved a Black teaching assistant named Lionel Williams who distributed "Love Lust," a sexually explicit poem by the Beat writer Leonore Kandel, to his freshman class. The episode stirred widespread debate on and off campus, eventually drawing the attention of the governor and legislature. Williams was fired, and the legal repercussions for academic freedom were intense and long-lasting. See https://timeline.unm.edu/item/lenore-kandels-love-lust.html

New Mexico.[5] She was awarded a Discovery Grant from the National Endowment for the Humanities for the tale, prompting her literary ambitions. Before turning to literature as a career, however, Silko intended to pursue the law. In her autobiographical introduction to the essay collection *Yellow Woman and a Beauty of the Spirit* (1996), Silko writes that, by her sophomore year in high school, she had determined to become a lawyer so that she could "seek justice."[6] Her interest in the law grew out of a suit against the state of New Mexico that the Pueblo of Laguna filed during her father's term as tribal treasurer. As a young child, she was intrigued by the witnesses who gathered in her family home to practice their testimony, which took the form of stories rather than legal documents. The tribe won its case, but the compensation was disappointing. The land was not restored, and there were sharply defined legal limits to its monetary value. Motivated by a sense of injustice, Silko completed her undergraduate studies and entered the University of New Mexico's American Indian Law School Fellowship program, but eventually she concluded that the American legal system was fundamentally flawed. The final straw came when she studied the case of a mentally disabled Black man who was put to death for the murder in 1949 of a white librarian after the US Supreme Court refused to stop his execution. Silko completed three semesters before leaving the program to "seek justice . . . through the power of stories."[7]

After leaving law school, she continued at the university for a time, studying photography and enrolling in graduate courses in the English department. In 1971, she moved to the Navajo reservation at Chinle to teach. Silko has observed that *Ceremony* reflects her experiences living and working among the Navajos, another parallel with Momaday's early years. Her inclusion of the Navajo healer Betonie, and his adaptation of the Night Chant ritual, is the most visible of these influences on the novel. Of her aborted legal career, she writes: "My time in law school was not wasted: I had gained invaluable insights into the power structure of mainstream society, and I continue to follow developments in the law to calculate prevailing political winds."[8]

The prevailing political winds were turbulent. Silko began her writing career at the height of the decolonization movements that were

---

[5] The story appeared under the name Leslie Chapman, her married name at that time, on pages 133–6 of vol. 38, no. 4 of *New Mexico Quarterly.*

[6] Leslie Marmon Silko, *Yellow Woman and a Beauty of the Spirit: Essays on Native American Life Today* (New York: Simon & Schuster, 1996), 18–20.

[7] Ibid., 20.   [8] Ibid., 20.

dismantling European empires throughout Africa, Asia, and the Americas. The intellectual and political sources of decolonization intersected with post-structuralism and leftist politics, while a role for anglophone fiction in the decolonizing project emerged with Nigerian author Chinua Achebe's acclaimed first novel, *Things Fall Apart* (1958). Momaday adopted ethnographic features reminiscent of Achebe's novels in his early work, including *The Way to Rainy Mountain* (1969), a blend of oral tradition, historical narrative, and poetic memoir, as well as *House Made of Dawn*. Silko took a different approach to decolonization in *Ceremony*, addressing the psychological impact of settler colonialism at an intimate psychological and familial level. She describes how the imposition of white beliefs and values has led to the self-debasing behavior of Tayo's mother, Laura. Seeking white acceptance, Laura goes with white boys and becomes addicted to alcohol, an intoxicant associated with white society. Alcohol tips the sexual adventurousness that Laura shares with the mythic Yellow Woman into prostitution and contributes to her untimely death. The theme of alcohol as a white tool of domination is one that Silko shares with both Achebe and Momaday; she provides a feminism-inspired focus on the way in which it impacts Indigenous women. The embedded story of Helen Jean, a young Native American woman picked up by Tayo's friends, fills in aspects of Laura's history and generalizes the experience of young Native women who seek a better life and become trapped in self-destructive patterns involving alcohol and sexual abuse.

By tying her narration closely to Tayo's point of view, Silko shrouds pivotal elements of the narrative (such as his mother's history) in mystery. These mysteries sometimes have a mythic function. The uncertainty surrounding Tayo's (white) father links him to both the Yellow Woman stories and the Christian God-man. At other times, the effect is to probe the psychic wounds that Tayo has suffered during his formative years. The lack of clarity surrounding Laura's life and death – which Silko supplements with Helen Jean's story – exemplifies this aspect of the narration.[9] The reader pieces together bits of Laura's story as they emerge in Tayo's memory; these pieces are highly colored by his emotional responses and form a picture inevitably centered on him. Early in Tayo's childhood,

---

[9] Post-structuralist philosopher Jacques Derrida developed the idea of the "supplement" in "Structure, Sign and Play" and *Of Grammatology* (both 1967). Robert Bernasconi defines the supplement as "an addition from the outside, but it can also be understood as supplying what is missing and in this way is already inscribed within that to which it is added" (*Jacques Derrida: Key Concepts*, chapter 3, available at https://grattoncourses.files.wordpress.com/2016/12/derrida-key-concepts-the-supplement.pdf).

Laura moved away from the pueblo with him under circumstances that are never clarified, presumably because Tayo was too young to absorb or remember them. He does recall other things about his early life. Passing through the town of Gallup on his way to meet Betonie, Tayo recalls living in a squalid encampment along an arroyo and accompanying his mother to bars. Tayo speaks briefly to his Uncle Robert about his recollections: "The traveling made me tired. But I remember when we drove through Gallup ... This is us, too, I was thinking to myself. These people crouching outside bars like cold flies stuck to the wall."[10] Most of Tayo's memories of Gallup are not conveyed through dialogue, however, but in third-person limited narration, filling in his world from his own perspective but not in his represented speech. The reader learns how, left to himself, Tayo would eat things he found on the barroom floor, learning quickly that ingesting cigarette butts would make him ill. At times he would fall asleep there, while his mother went off with a man. Elsewhere, he remembers the painful moment when his mother left him permanently with her sister Thelma and the extended family at Laguna; and he recalls standing at her gravesite, as his Uncle Josiah tries to comfort him. The reader shares Tayo's misery at his mother's death but never learns the specific cause and circumstances of it.

Josiah's love partially fills the void that her death leaves, but it cannot fully protect Tayo from his Auntie Thelma's emotional abuse, prompted by shame over her sister's behavior. In this matriarchal society, Thelma feels responsible for Laura's fate, and she is focused on restoring the family's position in the pueblo. This family orientation is in overt tension with Thelma's individualist understanding of her Catholic faith. Already in "The Man Who Would Send Rain," Silko had explored the uneasy blending of pueblo burial practices and Catholic beliefs. Thelma's Catholic faith emerges as a comparatively recent layer on the pueblo's deeply sedimented spiritual past. Her mistreatment of Tayo shapes the boy's perception that he holds a marginal place in the community, and this sense is reinforced by her celebration of her son Rocky, who is a full-blooded Laguna yet embraces white beliefs and values. Rocky endorses mainstream science even when it conflicts with local knowledge, plays football at his high school, plans to attend the university – and, pivotally, enlists in the army. Tayo enlists alongside Rocky, not because he believes in the war, but because Rocky tells the recruiter that Tayo is his brother, and this unprecedented claim of kinship momentarily overwhelms Tayo's

[10] Silko, *Ceremony*, 98–9.

better judgment. So desperate is Tayo for Rocky's acceptance that he forgets his promise to stay at Laguna and help Josiah with his cattle-breeding project. Josiah plans to hybridize drought-tolerant Mexican cattle with a stocky European breed, aiming to benefit the pueblo community, which suffers losses to their herds whenever one of the frequent droughts occurs. Tayo associates Josiah's unexplained death with the killing of Japanese captives in the Philippines. Josiah's loss further deepens and complicates Tayo's trauma, as does Tayo's belief that he has brought on the drought by cursing the tropical rain that fell as he struggled to get the wounded Rocky to safety.

Tayo's family arranges for him to meet first with Old Ku'oosh, a traditional Laguna healer, and then with the Navajo medicine man Betonie, whose hazel eyes reveal his Mexican ancestry. Throughout the novel, hazel-eyed characters – including Tayo himself as well as the Night Swan, the Mexican canteen dancer who becomes Josiah's lover and helps him arrange the purchase of the Mexican cattle – possess spiritual potency arising from the mixture of their backgrounds. Betonie conducts a healing ceremony based on the Navajo Night Chant, but he updates it to reflect the potential for change and growth. Betonie warns Tayo about the danger of adhering rigidly to tradition. "There are balances and harmonies always shifting, always necessary to maintain," Betonie tells him. "It is a matter of transitions ... the changing, the becoming must be cared for closely."[11] Entering into the ceremony, Tayo follows Betonie's instructions, watching the sky for the constellation that is reproduced as a full page in the novel.[12] This striking visual element of the text draws the reader into the reality of the ceremony unfolding around Tayo, who spots the constellation just after he encounters the woman Ts'eh. Ts'eh (who later tells him that she's a Montaño) is an avatar for the holy mountain Tsepina, whose English name is Mount Taylor. Following the stars, Tayo rides onto the mountain, intent on retrieving Josiah's stolen cattle from a white rancher, cutting through barbed wire to recover them. He completes this phase of the ceremony with the help of Ts'eh and Mountain Lion man, another semi-mythic character, who rescues him when he is injured and threatened by patrolling white cowboys. Having restored the cattle and himself to health by spending a summer gathering herbs with Ts'eh on the mesa, Tayo settles into life at the pueblo. He has made a place for himself there by recovering the cattle and repairing the community's relationship with the holy woman and the land. "You have seen her," Ku'oosh and the other old

[11] Ibid., 120.   [12] Ibid., 166.

men at the kiva cry after listening to his story. "We will be blessed again."[13] The rains have returned, ending the drought for the present. These intertwined historical, family, and personal factors shape Tayo as a representative individual who crosses social, geographic, and conceptual boundaries to create potent mixtures of races and cultures. Writing an anglophone novel that is also a healing ceremony, Silko offers hope for a decolonial politics that accepts hybridity, recognizes the sensitive work involved in transitions, and embraces Indigenous knowledge.

Even as Silko celebrates hybridization, transitions, and boundary-crossing, she recognizes that these processes have a dangerous side. The political significance of that danger emerges in yet another strand of this intricately woven novel. Tayo experiences vertigo and a palpable sense of threat when he first enters Betonie's hogan, where newspapers, calendars, and telephone books are laid out in concentric circles following the shape of the room, defying linear time and physical space. The misshapen boxes are jumbled together with Coke bottles, dried herbs, and sacks containing human hair. Tayo first diagnoses the danger as a personal threat tied to what he believes is his family's rejection of him; later, he interprets the foreboding as the futility of resisting white society. Betonie challenges these misreadings by telling the story of the "witchery" at the midpoint of the novel, as he prepares Tayo for the healing ceremony. Responding to Tayo's despair and skepticism about the power of "Indian ceremonies" to help him recover from "their wars, their bombs, their lies," Betonie insists that "the witchcraft" wants "us to believe all evil resides with white people" and to keep separate from them. This kind of "tribalism" is counterpro-ductive, for "it was Indian witchery that made white people in the first place." Recognizing this, he and Tayo have the power to "deal with white people, with their machines and their beliefs."[14]

The story that Betonie tells is set a "long time ago," when witches from around the world gathered for a "witches conference" north of Canoncito (a Navajo reservation east of Laguna). The witches started showing off and competing with one another, until an unfamiliar witch, of unknown origin and gender, spoke from the shadows. The witch told a story about the emergence of "white skin people" who grow away from the natural world and come to fear it. This new race of humans kills what it fears. Having conquered the world, the whites discover "rocks with veins of green and yellow and black" that they use to "lay the final pattern ... across the world and explode everything."[15] The other witches are frightened and beg

---

[13] Ibid., 239.   [14] Ibid.,122.   [15] Ibid., 127.

the speaker to call back the story, but the witch refuses, proclaiming: "It's already turned loose. It's already coming. It can't be called back."[16] This creation story presents Europeans as both a product of Indigenous magic and as a uniquely destructive force in world history. Animated by fear, white people seek to dominate the natural world, other human communities, and one another. Settler colonialism is one aspect of an unfolding pattern that denies limits and boundaries; with the invention of nuclear weapons, it now threatens to destroy the world.

Old Ku'oosh fails to fully heal Tayo because of his unfamiliarity with "white warfare – killing across great distances without knowing who or how many had died." Traditional healing rituals such as the scalp ceremony work only on warriors who come into immediate contact with their enemies. Tayo cannot even say for sure whether he has killed anyone. He reflects on the changes brought by military technology: "Ku'oosh would have looked at the dismembered corpses and the atomic heat-flash outlines" and concluded that "something close and terrible had killed these people. Not even oldtime witches killed like that."[17] Old Grandma is a bit more in touch with present realities, having witnessed the atomic flash from the nuclear test at White Sands, whose brightness penetrated the cataracts that have left her near-blind. The denouement of *Ceremony* centers on Tayo's recognition of a reality that until that moment had been too close for him to see. The pueblo is located in the Four Corners region, near Trinity site, where the first atomic bomb was tested, and Los Alamos labs, where it was developed; uranium from the Jackpile-Paguate uranium mine on Laguna land was central to the effort.[18] As Tayo makes his way to the mine – the source of the witchery – he recalls his grandmother saying of the White Sands test, "I thought I was seeing the sun rise again." This false dawn sharply contrasts with the true sunrise that is evoked through the Laguna sunrise ceremony that starts, ends, and punctuates the novel. Similarly, uranium is a false version of yellow pollen that figures in traditional ceremonies. The effect of nuclear weaponry has been to dissolve boundaries and draw humanity into a fatal connection: "The lines of cultures and worlds were drawn in flat dark lines on fine light sand, converging in the middle of witchery's final ceremonial sand painting.

[16] Ibid., 128.   [17] Ibid., 33–4.
[18] Kyoko Matsunaga, "Leslie Marmon Silko and Nuclear Dissent in the American Southwest," *Japanese Journal of American Studies* 25 (2014): 67–87.

From that time on, human beings were one clan again ... united by a circle of death."[19]

Silko's focus on nuclear weapons was broadly relevant to the politics of the 1970s. Anti-nuclear weapons activism became a prominent cause in the United States beginning with the Women Strike for Peace march in 1961. Four years later, the United States conducted its largest underground nuclear test at Amchitka, in the Aleutian Islands, near where Lee Marmon had been stationed; this test, and the history of Alaska's Indigenous population, created an improbable link to the Four Corners region. There was public resistance to the nuclear testing at the Amchitka site, tied to concerns over nuclear contamination and the danger of earthquakes and linked to protests against the Vietnam War. This opposition culminated in two attempts by Greenpeace vessels to interfere with the Cannikin test of 1971, which also withstood a Supreme Court challenge. The military shut down the site in 1973, the year that Silko moved with her family to Ketchikan on Revillagigedo Island – across the Bay of Alaska from the Aleutians – where she began writing *Ceremony*. In her preface to the thirtieth-anniversary edition of the novel, she writes that the island's climate (mild and rainy, caused by an oceanic effect known as the Kuroshio Current) left her depressed and homesick for the desert. Japan, of course, was the target of the only nuclear bombs ever detonated in an armed conflict. Coincidences and crosscurrents like these connections between Japan, Alaska, and the Four Corners region shaped the pattern of the novel that she eventually wrote.

The anti-nuclear weapons theme of *Ceremony* is linked to the novel's broader critique of war and violent conflict.[20] As noted earlier, Silko had already begun work on the novel when North Vietnamese tanks rolled through the gates of the presidential palace in Saigon, marking an unofficial end to a war that had spanned two decades and triggered the largest antiwar protests in US history. These protests had attracted prominent writers and intellectuals, including the poet Robert Lowell and novelist Norman Mailer. Lowell had spent time in prison as a conscientious objector during World War II, and he later wrote about the experience in the poem "Memories of West Street and Lepke" (published in *Life Studies*, 1959). Mailer had served in the Philippines during the war, and he

---

[19] Silko, *Ceremony*, 228.
[20] On *Ceremony* as it exemplifies the "peacebuilder's hermeneutic," see Sandra M. Gustafson, "Literature and Peace Studies," in *Peacebuilding and the Arts*, ed. Jolyon Mitchell, Giselle Vincett, Theodora Hawksley, and Hal Culbertson (Cham, Switzerland: Palgrave Macmillan, 2020), 217–33, especially 220–5.

was sent to Japan as part of the army of occupation. He fictionalized these experiences in his first novel, *The Naked and the Dead* (1948), which has certain thematic parallels with *Ceremony*: Silko has commented that "Norman Mailer was important" for her work.[21] In 1967, Lowell and Mailer were involved in the March on the Pentagon, and both men figure prominently in *The Armies of the Night: History as a Novel/The Novel as History* (1968), Mailer's account of the march that won both a Pulitzer Prize and a National Book Award.

These events offer a key to what are arguably the most disquieting aspects of Silko's novel: the presence of Emo, a Laguna veteran of the war, whose hatred for white people is matched by his envy of their world; and Tayo's decision not to rescue his friends Harley and Leroy as Emo tortures them to death. Emo's brutality, symbolized by the sack of Japanese teeth that he likes to shake while sharing war stories, provokes Tayo to his own act of violence when he jabs a broken beer bottle into Emo's belly. The long enmity between these young men predates the war and can be traced to Emo's resentment of Tayo's white heritage. Emo's envy of white society reflects his self-hatred and contempt for all things Native. He tortures Harley and Leroy in order to lure Tayo from hiding. Tayo's decision to embrace non-violence rather than to rescue his friends has two main facets: Harley and Leroy have conspired with Emo against Tayo; and Ts'eh has warned him that forces are gathering to push him into an act that would reinforce media narratives about the violence of drunken Indian veterans. If he had "jammed the screwdriver into Emo's skull the way the witchery had wanted," he would have completed "their deadly ritual for the autumn solstice"[22] rather than playing out his role in the life-giving ceremony in which Betonie has engaged him. Crucial to this conclusion are the disguising of Harley's and Leroy's deaths as the product of a car accident and the seemingly accidental death of Pinkie, the last member of the group, who is fatally shot by Emo. Emo himself leaves for California: "a good place for him," Tayo thinks.[23] The implication is that Emo fits into Hollywood narratives about violent Indians.

Tayo resists the pull toward violence and remains at Laguna, carrying on the stories and traditions and Josiah's plans for the cattle. Subordinating his "white" self to his "Laguna" self, he completes the ceremony,

[21] Robin Cohen, "Wovoka: An Interview with Leslie Marmon Silko," in *Leslie Marmon Silko's Ceremony: A Casebook*, ed. Allan Chavkin (Oxford and New York: Oxford University Press, 2002), 262.
[22] Silko, *Ceremony*, 235.   [23] Ibid., 242.

establishing new "balances and harmonies" in his community and in the culture at large. Silko's message echoes the work of Vine Deloria, Jr., a leading Native American intellectual and activist, who in 1974 had published the essay "Non-Violence in American Society," commenting on the era's social justice movements from the perspective offered by Richard Nixon's resignation. Deloria testified to "profound sadness" over the tragic fate of movement leaders such as Martin Luther King, Jr. and Malcolm X, but he concluded on a hopeful note, urging his readers to "see the waves of unexpected change sweeping over us as the result of non-violence of the past and see that it is time to build and plant." Silko wrote the preface to the thirtieth-anniversary edition of Deloria's *God is Red*, ending with a passage from his work beginning, "Who will find peace with the lands? The future of humankind lies waiting for those who will come to understand their lives and take up their responsibilities to all living things."[24] Giving narrative form to Deloria's message, the multiple strands of Silko's political thought considered here – the Native American Renaissance and decolonization, environmentalism, feminism, antiwar and anti-nuclear activism – are woven together in a story that is also a healing ceremony for readers. *Ceremony* aims to create a world where indigeneity emerges as the dominant force for a world at risk that is also a world in transition.

---

[24] Vine DeLoria, Jr., "Non-Violence in American Society" [1974], reprinted in *For This Land: Writings on Religion in America* (New York: Routledge, 1999), 44–50; *God is Red: A Native View of Religion* (Golden, CO: Fulcrum Publishing, 2003), vii–ix.

CHAPTER 23

Parable *Series (1993, 1998): Octavia E. Butler*

Claire P. Curtis

The flurry of attention given to Octavia Butler's *Parable* novels (*Parable of the Sower* and *Parable of the Talents*) after the 2016 presidential election noted Butler's prescience on a variety of issues: environmental degradation, declining public services, failing neighborhoods, untrustworthy police, and, most tellingly, a president with a penchant for scapegoating and a slogan about making America great again. The popular media celebrated Butler's series for her seemingly uncanny ability, "unmatched"[1] at capturing our times. Butler was praised for her predictive capacity, and media sources included the novels on their must-read lists for the year. But Butler did not understand herself to be predicting a far-flung future. Early in *Parable of the Talents*, Bankole, Lauren Oya Olamina's eventual husband, describes the characters' predicament as "caused by our own refusal to deal with obvious problems."[2] These are our problems to solve. The "obvious" problems (environmental, political, economic, sociological) were present in Butler's childhood in the 1970s (and before), and they are still present today. The *Parable* series is not simply a description of the ways in which things might go wrong; it is a diagnosis of what Bankole notes is our human "refusal" to confront such challenges. Read as dystopia, the *Parable* series should be seen as a series of warnings derived from Butler's experience. For Butler, *we* are the primary source of our problems. And yet the series is also a prescription for how we might accept responsibility and move forward. As an Afrofuturist, Butler creates an imagined future that is

---

[1] Abby Aguire, "Octavia Butler's Prescient Vision of a Zealot Elected to 'Make America Great Again,'" *New Yorker*, July 26, 2017; see also Maddie Crum, "A Dystopian Novelist Predicted Trump's Campaign Slogan in the 90s," *Huffington Post*, July 1, 2016, www.huffpost.com/entry/octavia-butler-predicted-make-america-great-again_n_5776d9dce4b0416464100242; "Sci-Fi Tried to Warn Us About Leaders Who Want to Make America Great," *Wired*, December 2016, www.wired.com/2016/12/geeks-guide-gerry-canavan/; Hephzibah Anderson, "Why Octavia E. Butler's Novels Are So Relevant Today," BBC, March 18, 2020, www.bbc.com/culture/article/20200317-why-octavia-e-butlers-novels-are-so-relevant-today
[2] Octavia Butler, *Parable of the Talents* (New York: Warner Books, 1998), 8.

not simply a description of American life, but also a possible direction for rethinking who we are and how we live.[3]

The Warner Books editions of both *Parable* novels include Butler's own biographical note: "I am a 53-year-old writer who can remember being a 10-year-old writer and who expects someday to be an 80-year-old writer." In *Parable*, Butler created a character, Lauren Oya Olamina, introduced on the day before her fifteenth birthday, who makes her last entry in *Talents* on the day before her eightieth birthday, as the first ships of Earthseed colonists are taking off for space. Olamina is a visionary, a community leader, and the founder of Earthseed, the religion whose goal is "to take root among the stars." Butler died before turning sixty (in 2006), but her fiction illustrates a capacity to understand the life of a child, middle-aged, and elderly person.

Butler saw herself and her characters into futures that seem unlikely at first glance. Born and raised in Pasadena, California, Butler was Black, poor, shy, and tall. Feeling a misfit and outside of the mainstream, she loved the imaginative reaches of science fiction as a child, even when she saw neither people like herself writing nor in those stories. Butler published twelve novels and eight short stories. The two *Parable* novels, published in 1993 and 1998, were part of a planned series of six, including the unpublished *Parables of the Trickster, Teacher, Chaos,* and *Clay.*[4] Only *Fledgling* (2005) and "The Book of Martha" (2003) were published after *Talents.* The world Butler created in the *Parable* series captured her imagination in her last decade.

Between the two *Parable* novels, in 1995, Butler was awarded the MacArthur "Genius Grant," which provided a financial security she had not previously experienced. *Parable of the Talents* won the Nebula Award for best science fiction novel in 1999.[5] Butler's *Parable* series intersects with multiple literary traditions: science fiction, African American literature more generally and the slave narrative more particularly, feminist literature, utopia and dystopia. Butler scholarship emerges from these traditions and their intersections.[6]

---

[3] In addition to the novels as written, there is now a graphic novel adaption by Damian Duffy and John Jennings of *Parable of the Sower* (Abrams ComicArts) and a forthcoming version of *Parable of the Talents,* as well as an opera by Toshi Reagon based on *Parable of the Sower.*

[4] Gerry Canavan, *Octavia E. Butler* (Chicago: University of Illinois Press, 2016), 147. These titles mirror the line from Earthseed: "God is Trickster, Teacher, Chaos, Clay" (199).

[5] Butler's short story "Speech Sounds" won the Hugo Award and "Bloodchild" won both the Hugo and the Nebula.

[6] For scholarship on Butler's work and African American literature, see Marlene D. Allen, "Octavia Butler's 'Parable' Novels and the 'Boomerang' of African American History," *Callaloo* 32.4 (2009): 1353–65; Madhu Dubhey, "Folk and Urban Communities in African American Women's Fiction:

Parable of the Sower follows Lauren Oya Olamina, a young Black woman of fifteen who leaves her family's walled neighborhood in Robledo, California in 2024 and embarks on a journey walking north, gathering people with her emerging religion, Earthseed, to the intentional community of Acorn that she founds in northern California. The novel is told only in Lauren's voice through her diary, the book that will later become "The Book of the Living." *Parable of the Talents* is narrated by Lauren's daughter, Asha Vere (originally named Larkin), and includes selections from Lauren's diary, Asha's father Bankole's writings, a few selections from her Uncle Marcus, and her own editorializing and analysis. Asha blames Lauren and her commitment to Earthseed for the destruction of her family and of the community of Acorn, whose children are kidnapped and adults enslaved. "If only my mother had agreed to go with my

Octavia Butler's *Parable of the Sower*," *Studies in American Fiction* 27.1 (1999): 103–28; Jasmine Noelle Yarish, "Seeding a Black Feminist Future on the Horizon of a Third Reconstruction: The Abolitionist Politics of Self-Care in Octavia Butler's *Parable of the Sower*," *Journal of Women, Politics and Policy* 42.1 (2021): 58–72; Diana Leong, "The Mattering of Black Lives: Octavia Butler's Hyperempathy and the Promise of the New Materialisms," *Catalyst: Feminism, Theory, Technoscience* 2.2 (2016): 1–35; M. Moreno, "Survival by Any Means: Race and Gender, Passing and Performance in Octavia Butler's *Parable of the Sower* and *Parable of the Talents*," in *Human Contradictions in Octavia E. Butler's Work*, ed. M. Japtok and J. Jenkins (Cham, Switzerland: Palgrave Macmillan, 2020), 195–212; Clarence Tweedy, "The Anointed: Countering Dystopia with Faith in Octavia Butler's *Parable of the Sower* and *Parable of the Talents*," *Americana: The Journal of American Popular Culture* 13.1 (2014).

For scholarship on feminist literature, see Patricia Melzer, "All that You Touch You Change: Utopian Desire and the Concept of Change in Octavia Butler's *Parable of the Sower* and *Parable of the Talents*," *FemSpec* 3.2 (2002): 31–52; Hoda Zaki, "Future Tense: Review, Parable of the Sower," *Women's Review of Books* (July 1994): 37–8; Derek Theiss, "Care Work, Age and Culture," *FemSpec* 15 (2015): 63–99; Anna Hinton, "Making Do with What You Don't Have: Disabled Black Motherhood in Octavia E. Butler's *Parable of the Sower* and *Parable of the Talents*," *Journal of Literary and Cultural Disability Studies* 12 (2018): 441–57.

For scholarship on science fiction, see Hee-Jung Serenity Joo, "Old and New Slavery, Old and New Racisms: Strategies of Science Fiction in Octavia Butler's Parables Series," *Extrapolation* 52.3 (2011): 279–99; Gregory Jerome Hampton, *Changing Bodies in the Fiction of Octavia Butler: Slaves, Aliens and Vampires* (Lanham, MD: Lexington, 2010).

For scholarship on utopia, see Peter Stillman, "Dystopian Critiques, Utopian Possibilities, and Human Purposes in Octavia Butler's Parables," *Utopian Studies* 14.1 (2003): 15–35; Tom Moylan, *Scraps of the Untainted Sky: Science Fiction, Utopia, Dystopia* (Abingdon: Routledge, 2000); Alex Zamalin, *Black Utopia: The History of an Idea from Black Nationalism to Afrofuturism* (New York: Columbia University Press, 2019).

For scholarship on political theory, see Lauren J. Lacey, "Octavia E. Butler on Coping with Power in *Parable of the Sower, Parable of the Talents*, and *Fledgling*," *Critique* 49.4 (2008): 379–94; Claire P. Curtis, *Postapocalyptic Fiction and the Social Contract: "We'll Not Go Home Again"* (Lanham, MD: Lexington, 2010); S. K. Dunning, "'Learn or Die': Survivalism and Anarchy in Octavia Butler's Parable of the Sower," in Japtok and Jenkins, eds.

For scholarship on environmental themes, see Brandon Jones, "Between Earth and Sky: Atmospheric Ambiguity in Octavia E. Butler's *Parable Series*," *ISLE: Interdisciplinary Studies in Literature and Environment* 27.4 (2020): 690–714.

father to live peacefully, normally in Halstead, it wouldn't have happened. Or at least it wouldn't have happened to us."[7]

The second novel thus complicates the first in both plot and structure. Lauren's narrative is challenged by Asha's objections to her mother's choices and to Earthseed as a movement. But the reader who comes to the novels through *Sower* might also see Asha's objections as a frustrating misreading of the very principles of Earthseed. Asha's perceptions of her family's history are equally problematic. Lauren's brother Marcus has lied to Asha about her mother's death and has lied to Lauren about knowing nothing about Asha's whereabouts. Asha resents that her mother never found her, while never fully acknowledging that one reason why she was not found was that Marcus hid that information from his sister.

Butler's work resists happy endings. But her ambiguous endings are themselves connected to a utopian impulse. Butler does not want the reader to imagine that we could arrive at a safe space, a place that somehow does not need to be changed. She asks for a certain kind of maturity from her reader. The lack of happy endings does not mean that there are not many possibilities for creating better worlds. But characters and readers are cautioned: Someone else is not going to produce a better world for us. We always need to be careful about who we follow. For Butler, embracing difficult projects can hone the talents needed for making a better world, even if the difficult project does not come to fruition. This utopian imagining is central to reading the *Parable* series politically.

In the afterword to the short story "The Book of Martha," one of the last pieces that she wrote, Butler declares that she does not believe in utopia. "It seems inevitable that my utopia would be someone else's hell."[8] Her character, Martha, has been asked to change humanity somehow – to make people more able to live without destroying one another and the Earth. Martha (like Butler, an African American fiction writer living in Seattle) declares that utopias do not work. But the *Parable* series is very much a part of the utopian literary and political tradition. The series does not set out a blueprint for a perfect society; rather, the two novels are "critical dystopias."[9] In a critical dystopia, the inklings of a better world are present while the problems of the current world are clearly outlined. All of

---

[7] Butler, *Parable of the Talents*, 202.
[8] Octavia Butler, "Book of Martha," in *Bloodchild and Other Stories* (New York: Seven Stories Press, 2005), 214.
[9] Moylan, 196.

Octavia Butler's fiction is political, but the *Parable* series is political in three particularly explicit ways.

The first way in which Butler's *Parable* series is political is that the world of politics, the external human forces that shape the world in which we live, is the constant background noise of the novels. The political and economic systems in which the characters move both deeply impact how they live and are also strikingly absent at the same time.

Robledo, Acorn, the members of Earthseed, the people traveling the highways of California searching for something better or safer – they are all subject to external forces. These forces often take the form of particular individuals acting badly: the "coyotes," who take advantage of the weak;[10] the guards of water stations, grocery stores, or Camp Christian, who take pleasure in terrorizing others. But these are not just bad people; they are the people who exploit external conditions to abuse others. Those external conditions include the absence of political authority in *Sower* or the presence of a president like Andrew Jarret in *Talents*. Political realities provide the opportunity for those motivated by hierarchy to cause pain. Here, we see a politics of power with little space for justice.

In neither novel is there such a thing as a public good or service. The United States in 2024 no longer supports public schooling, public water works, or public fire and safety agencies. There is no system of public transportation, no public library, no public hospital. We see no evidence of a local governing body – no mayor, no city council. Fire and police protection can be purchased, but the price is high and the protection minimal. These absences are hardly noteworthy for Lauren. She has never lived in a world where the larger public cared in any way about her well-being. And she has always lived in a world where the threats and risks of that external world have been present and growing worse.

People in Robledo rely on themselves and one another, but there is little they do (or seemingly can do) for the outside world. They provide a neighborhood watch and a small school (in Lauren's home). They grow much of their own food. So too in Acorn: They are self-sufficient and becoming more able to thrive in a challenging world. But Acorn, like Robledo, is not the safe space it is imagined to be. For Lauren's father and stepmother, Robledo is an oasis where the adults think they can wait out the depredations outside. For Lauren, Robledo is increasingly a kind of leaky prison, neither protected nor fulfilling. For Lauren, Acorn is the oasis – one that will be destroyed by external, politically supported forces.

---

[10] Octavia Butler, *Parable of the Sower* (New York: Warner Books, 1993), 181.

The absence of public services and local government does not mean that Lauren lives in a full-fledged state of nature. There is an extant federal government whose actions Lauren discusses, despite the declining status of the United States as a superpower.[11] The role of the federal government comes to a climax in the second novel, when the election of President Andrew Jarret energizes and legitimizes the Christian American forces that take over Acorn, enslaving its inhabitants, kidnapping their children, and raping and torturing their inhabitants. The opening journal entries of *Talents* outline Jarret's campaign and the psychological profile of those attracted to his vision for an America that can be "great again." Those "afraid and ashamed of their fear"[12] are drawn to the rhetoric of order and will ignore the terrible ways in which Jarret's followers will produce that order.

At this first, most basic political level, the *Parable* series offers a dystopian warning about possible futures and about the present. Responding to the undermining of the values of public services under Reagan, the novels warn about both power-seekers filling political vacuums and our own willingness to ignore the consequences.

The *Parable* series is political because of the relationship between the small communities of Robledo and Acorn and the larger political forces of the world in which they live. But at a deeper level, the novels are political in that they seek to answer the perennially political question: How can a group of individuals with disparate aims and interests live together peacefully? Robledo, Acorn, and finally Earthseed itself offer visions for *how* to live together.

Robledo, which Lauren rejects as a model for fruitful living together, presents a community trying to survive what it sees as a momentary lapse. The adults of Robledo wait and want to "return to normal." Lauren's father is the leader of the community in that he is their preacher, but each household supports and protects its own. Lauren's father does succeed in establishing the neighborhood watch and, at Lauren's suggestion, creates classes in a variety of survival skills. But Robledo is doing nothing more than holding on. Its model of living together is simply to hold on long enough, which it fails to do in part because its residents do not realize the degree to which external forces are against them. Robledo highlights that we must be vigilant against both leaders and communities of people seeking to divide and destroy, but also that we must be aware that ignoring external forces can lead to one's own destruction. Perceived as rich by the

---

[11] The decentering of the United States as a site of power mirrors the ways in which Butler uses alien encounters to decenter humanity from the universe.

[12] Butler, *Parable of the Talents*, 28.

surrounding squatters and individuals living without the meager protection the homemade neighborhood wall offers, and a target for the drug-
addicted "pyros" who seek to punish the rich and burn everything they
can, Robledo is vulnerable to external forces. When the community is
destroyed, Lauren leaves with two other Robledo survivors to head north.

Acorn, despite Lauren's own understanding of the problems of Robledo,
is simply a larger, more isolated, and more communal version of Robledo –
external forces will destroy it as well. Lauren is aware of those forces, and
she seeks to remind her community of the threats. But sometimes the
threat is simply overwhelming.

Lauren does create intentional systems of community to give Acorn an
internal strength that Robledo never had. These communal practices
include joining families as "change-sisters" or "change-parents," acknowledging that every family unit is fractured and that children, in particular,
need the love and attention – the explicit commitment – of multiple
adults. Schooling in Acorn is mandatory and requires both learning and
then teaching. The weekly Gatherings and the creed of Earthseed, in
contrast to Lauren's Baptist upbringing, tie the people of Acorn together
and help to prepare them for a hostile and changing world. Gatherings
present deliberative models of problem-solving where community members share, challenge, and question one another. New members are
expected to work, learn, teach, and participate. Lauren is referred to by
the children of Acorn as "Shaper," but Acorn is not hierarchical. All,
regardless of age or status, race or gender, who know something (a
language, a skill, a talent) share it with others, and decisions are made by
the votes of the community's members.

Earthseed is the real force of communal living in *Parable of the Talents*.
Its point is not to create one spatially isolated community but to spread its
message so that it can, eventually, "take root among the stars." Earthseed
will not reside in specific places and among specific people with a specific
worldview, like the Amish. Instead, Earthseed will open schools, train
doctors and engineers, provide scholarships, fund political campaigns. It
will seek to become a public good in a public that is hungry for a purpose
and a worldview. Lauren maintains that Earthseed will thrive only if it
spreads and realizes a model of community engagement that is both local
and expansive: to find people willing to care for children, to expand their
households to include the survivors of Acorn, to open their wallets and
their contact lists to others interested in the ideas of Earthseed.

The *Parable* series thus affirms the power of a communally oriented
worldview. "Earthseed is about preparing to fulfill the Destiny. It's about

learning to live in partnership with one another in small communities, and at the same time, working out a sustainable partnership with our environment."[13] This vision is important largely "for the people it encourages us to become."[14] It is, as is noted by most early adherents, a ludicrous aim. Lauren maintains her focus on it in part to provide a goal (a "positive obsession"[15]) that will require time, energy, intelligence, and working together toward a future they do not currently have. To bring about a world where taking root among the stars is possible means to radically change the world in which they live. Olamina's daughter might be right that the time and energy spent on building spaceships and discovering methods for cryo-sleep could have been spent on improving life on Earth. But the novels are not to be read as a how-to manual. What Asha Vere never sees are the ways in which the energy Earthseed puts into their Destiny does improve the lives of people here and now.

Beyond the internal practices of a community and the external conditions that affect it – but, in an important sense, prior to those practices – is the question of *who* is in the community. Butler's work in general wrestles with whether to create better worlds by changing the conditions of human community or by changing humans themselves. The *Parable* series illustrates what Butler calls the "human contradiction," the problem that the *Xenogenesis* novels seeks to solve through breeding with the alien Oankali and that "The Book of Martha" will solve through vivid, utopian dreams. The question is, then, how we live with this contradiction if change through alien reproduction or divine intervention is unlikely.

In the essay "The Monophobic Response,"[16] Butler describes the human contradiction as central to all science fiction:

> There is a vast and terrible sibling rivalry going on within the human family as we satisfy our desire for territory, dominance, and exclusivity. How strange: In our ongoing eagerness to create aliens, we express our need for them, and we express our deep fear of being alone in a universe that cares no more for us than it does for the stones or suns or any other fragments of itself. And yet we are unable to get along with those aliens closest to us, those aliens who are of course ourselves.

The world that Butler has created in the *Parable* series, a world drawn from the trajectory of the United States in the twentieth century and before, is one

---

[13] Ibid., 393.   [14] Ibid., 170.

[15] Octavia Butler, "Positive Obsession," in Bloodchild and Other Stories, 123–35.

[16] Octavia Butler, "Monophobic Response," in *Dark Matter: A Century of Speculative Fiction from the African Diaspora*, ed. Sheree Renee Thomas (New York: Warner Books, 2000), 415–16.

where certain bodies are seen as "alien" and thus as problems to be regulated or solved. Given their poverty, their race, their religious practice, or their mere inconvenience, these alien bodies are seen as being in need of external intervention. Christian America perceived the followers of Earthseed as heathens in need of re-education, stealing their children to be adopted away. Likewise, Christian America arrests people on the road who are seeking better opportunities. And, in *Sower*, the company town of Olivar will control its inhabitants through a new-old system of debt slavery, paying its worker inhabitants less than they need to survive, thus tying their bodies to the company.

But Butler's biopolitics goes beyond the control of the diversity of faces and histories that people these novels. One of the central facts about Lauren and a few other characters is that they have what Butler coins hyper-empathy syndrome.[17] The result of a parent's use of a drug to enhance intellectual performance, hyper-empathy syndrome allows Lauren and others to feel (or "share") the visibly apparent pleasure and pain of others. This form of embodied empathy is a risk. Those who are not sharers perceive it as a kind of strength and misunderstand the ways in which Lauren and others are impacted by the pain and violence happening to others. Butler was explicit about her desire to think through this embodied empathy to discover whether a world with such empathy would be a world of peace.[18] It would not.

To be recognized as a sharer is to reveal a way of having one's body controlled against one's will. In this way, hyper-empathy acts as a means by which the reader can understand the reality of living at the behest of the outside world. The close attention to the experience of being a sharer – the bodily and the psychological experience of feeling another's pain – is one way in which Butler emphasizes that the experience of being human is the experience of bodily vulnerability. Successful, or fruitful, community acknowledges that vulnerability and seeks both to make humans more resilient and to protect the vulnerable as well as one can. Failed communities imagine that they are invulnerable.

[17] For scholarship focusing on hyper-empathy, see Leong; Clara Escoda Agustí, "The Relationship between Community and Subjectivity in Octavia E. Butler's *Parable of the Sower*," *Extrapolation* 46.3 (2005): 351–9; Paula Barbra Guerrero, "Postapocalyptic Memory Sites, Damaged Space, Nostalgia and Refuge in Octavia Butler's Parable of the Sower," *Science Fiction Studies* 48.1 (2021): 29–45.
[18] Interview by Scott Simon with Octavia Butler in Conseula Francis, ed., *Conversations with Octavia Butler* (Jackson: University Press of Mississippi, 2010), 189–92.

Hostile or predatory humans (those motivated by hierarchy) in the *Parable* series feed on and seek to exploit that human vulnerability. These are the people motivated by hierarchy, by a desire to be more than, to have power over others. This last point is important for thinking about the politics of Butler's novels. While *Parable of the Sower* includes the requisite post-apocalyptic fictional scene of cannibalism, it does not make those cannibals (young and avoidable) the enemy. Enemies instead come in two forms: the opportunistic and the power-hungry. Life on the road is largely a matter of avoiding the opportunistic, the "coyotes" seeking out what they perceive to be weak and easy targets. Olamina notes that "they followed me because I seemed to be going somewhere";[19] this equally describes those who vote for Andrew Jarret.

But the power-hungry – like Jarret, like Cougar, the controller of the slave collar on Uncle Marcus – are people who desire to see others in pain. This desire is not one that Butler's characters can solve. They can avoid those who seek it (and Earthseed is filled with verses about avoiding such leaders). And they can empower the many who might go either way: toward Jarret out of fear, toward Olamina and Earthseed out of hope.

Hope for humans emerges out of a recognition of our tendency to hierarchy and a committed desire to resist that tendency.

> The human species is a kind of animal, of course. But we can do something no other animal species has ever had the option to do. We can choose: We can go on building and destroying until we either destroy ourselves or destroy the ability of our world to sustain us. Or we can make more of ourselves. We can grow up. We can leave the nest.[20]

Leaving the nest for Olamina means leaving Earth. Given what we know of the drafts for the future *Parable* novels in the series, humans bring themselves and their problems to space, and those colonies will present their own unique challenges. But the question remains: How does the human experience of hierarchy and intelligence produce a sustainable politics?

Conclusion

In his analysis of the unpublished *Parable* drafts, Gerry Canavan[21] notes that "the future is a social choice we make collectively." The future is unwritten, and Butler is not predicting a single possible outcome, but

---

[19] Butler, *Parable of the Talents*, 398.   [20] Ibid., 393.
[21] Gerry Canavan, "Eden, Just Not Ours Yet: On *Parable of the Trickster* and Utopia," *Women's Studies* 48.1 (2019): 59–75.

warning the reader of a variety of threats. Noting the prescience in Butler's description of the lies of Trumpian leaders should not obscure her warnings of what has *not* come to be. If we read the *Parable* series as setting out a political argument about how to live together, one that emphasizes a recognition of external threats, internal dynamics, and the people we can become, then we can recognize a more fundamental contrast between two models of political community. First is the model Butler argues against, under which a leader tells a community, "Follow me and these rules, and I (and the rules) will keep you safe." The second is the model that the novels advocate: "Join this worldview and work toward a different kind of future, and along the way commit to helping protect yourself and other members of this community." The *Parable* series explores this collective choice. A late chapter in *Talents* opens with this excerpt from *Earthseed: The Book of the Living*:

> Earthseed offers its own rewards – room
> for small groups of people to begin new lives and
> new ways of life with new opportunities, new
> wealth, new concepts of wealth, new challenges to
> grow and to learn and to decide what to become.[22]

This passage highlights all three of the political lenses described above. First, it emphasizes the unspoken larger world in which these new groups settle. The newness, repeated six times, is an affront, a challenge, a thorn, and an opportunity to the outside world. The second emphasis is the community itself, one dedicated to new ways of living that will challenge people to grow in new ways. The references to "new wealth" and "new concepts of wealth" suggest new communal practices, some yet untried, and others yet unthought. Finally, the passage focuses on the person: growing, learning, deciding *what* to become, not simply *who* to become. Butler's novels ask the reader to think about the people of these communities.

The *Parable* series is not a blueprint for a utopian world; the Destiny of Earthseed is not the key to peaceful politics. But Earthseed is better than the alternative. Working toward something that promotes work and learning, care for the vulnerable, and bettering oneself is surely a step in the right direction. "Tolerance, like any aspect of peace, is forever a work in progress, never completed, and, if we're as intelligent as we like to think we are, never abandoned."[23]

[22] Butler, *Parable of the Talents*, 357.
[23] Octavia Butler, "NPR Essay – UN Racism Conference," September 1, 2001, https://legacy.npr.org/programs/specials/racism/010830.octaviabutleressay.html

CHAPTER 24

The Underground Railroad (2016): Colson Whitehead

Bryan M. Santin

Judging by its status as a massive bestseller and its impressive list of top literary awards, Colson Whitehead's *The Underground Railroad* (2016) is one of the most significant American novels published in the first quarter of the twenty-first century. But it serves as the final, brief case study in this volume because it is also a Janus-faced text in American literary history that looks back toward the persistent political conundrums illuminated by twentieth-century American fiction and reconfigures them in generative ways for the twenty-first century. To date, all of Whitehead's novels exemplify not only a turn to popular genres inspired by an array of twentieth-century novelists discussed in previous chapters – from Ralph Ellison and Toni Morrison to Ursula K. Le Guin and Stephen King – but also an abiding interest in the paradoxes of the American liberal project.

The Underground Railroad represents a watershed moment in Whitehead's career-long, imaginative reassessment of the United States, as it evidences a profound confrontation with America's flaws via a prolonged, substantive engagement with American political history. Essentially, the novel poses, in the words of political scientists Melvin L. Rogers and Jack Turner, one of the foundational questions of African American political thought: whether "the harm and violence against black people is internal to [American democracy's] functioning, external to democracy and thus foreign, or external to it but nonetheless capable of being made consistent with democratic practices."[1] Like its generic twentieth-century predecessors – most notably, Ishmael Reed's postmodern satire *Flight to Canada* (1976), Octavia E. Butler's time-traveling SF tale *Kindred* (1979), and Toni Morrison's Gothic neo-slave narrative *Beloved* (1987) – Whitehead's meta-slave narrative critiques a

---

[1] Melvin L. Rogers and Jack Turner, "Political Theorizing in Black: An Introduction," in *African American Political Thought: A Collected History*, ed. Melvin L. Rogers and Jack Turner (Chicago: University of Chicago Press, 2021), 26.

naïve historical story of inevitable Black progress. It even flirts with the notion that American democracy and African American oppression are inextricable. But Whitehead also draws on various contemporary discourses, both academic and popular, to reject fatalistic narratives of inevitable injustice. Ultimately, although he privileges a Black perspective marked by affective pessimism, Whitehead shows how American normative myths can still be politically efficacious, even if Black Americans rarely experienced them as true for much of the country's history. Toward the end of the novel, one Black character reflects on America's abstract ideals and concrete crimes in a sentence that perfectly encapsulates this ambivalent mingling of affective despair and political hope: "Sometimes a useful delusion is better than a useless truth."[2]

To understand Whitehead's complex political vision in *The Underground Railroad*, one must first understand how Whitehead's political reflections evolved over the course of his career. In his early, pre-*Underground Railroad* novels, Whitehead's critiques of American culture and the US nation-state tend to lean toward ironic, light-hearted Horatian satire. In his speculative Black detective noir *The Intuitionist* (1999), a character's facial profile is described as "so banal and uncomplicated, so like this country."[3] In his metafictional postmodern tome *John Henry Days* (2001), Whitehead's Black folk hero John Henry watches the construction of a railroad track and thinks that the workers are building "the country mile by mile. This is the forging of a nation. This is some real hokey shit."[4] Toward the end of his corporate satire *Apex Hides the Hurt* (2006), a nomenclature consultant contemplates "America" as a marketing buzzword, noting that its ultimate meaning was merely "[w]hatever we dreamed" as a nation of neoliberal consumers.[5] In his autobiographical bildungsroman *Sag Harbor* (2009), the protagonist marvels at an ice cream shop's vast menu of toppings, "all kinds of wondrous things laid out in a gaudy pageant of gluttony American-style, freedom served as-you-like-it."[6] In a scene of comic foreboding in his post-apocalyptic zombie thriller *Zone One* (2011), a high-ranking political official basks in humanity's successful recapture of New York City, even though the country is about to be overrun (again) by the zombie hordes, as she asserts with blithe confidence:

---

[2] Colson Whitehead, *The Underground Railroad* (New York: Doubleday, 2016), 290.
[3] Colson Whitehead, *The Intuitionist* (New York: Anchor Books, 1999), 38.
[4] Colson Whitehead, *John Henry Days* (New York: Anchor Books, 2001), 40.
[5] Colson Whitehead, *Apex Hides the Hurt* (New York: Doubleday, 2006), 208.
[6] Colson Whitehead, *Sag Harbor* (New York: Doubleday, 2009), 105.

"This is America."[7] However, in *The Underground Railroad*, a mix between a steampunk SF novel and a second-generation neo-slave narrative, Whitehead's third-person omniscient narrator repeats this phrase almost exactly, but in an antebellum context that nullifies playful humor. Noting that slavecatchers were often "boys and men of bad character," the narrator makes a blunt, acidic assertion more characteristic of Juvenalian satire: "In another country they would have been criminals, but this was America."[8]

The arc of Whitehead's political thought is especially noteworthy because he delayed working on *The Underground Railroad* until later in his career, a decision that deepened the novel's critique. As he has admitted in interviews, Whitehead came up with the speculative premise of the novel – i.e., a real railroad mysteriously built underground that enslaved people used to escape their bondage – around 2000, but he did not write it because he "didn't feel mature enough or up to the task."[9] After determining that the novel would be thematically centered on big questions of "slavery, Americanness, and perseverance," Whitehead realized that he "wanted to stick to the truth of the black experience but not necessarily the facts," an ambitious allegorical experiment that would take years of reflection and study to capture effectively.[10] In addition to immersing himself in nineteenth-century slave narratives and in oral histories of enslaved people collected by the Federal Writers' Project, Whitehead read more recent scholarship that links American slavery to global capitalism, de-romanticizes heroic white sentimentalism embedded in earlier histories of the Underground Railroad, and emphasizes the fierce resilience of postbellum white supremacy into the twentieth century.[11] By grounding *The Underground Railroad* in primary documents of Black life and in an emerging historiography that privileges Black experiences, Whitehead reveals how a broad swath of American political history looks and feels from a distinctly African American point of view.

This perspective, rooted in Black affect and informed by an awareness of recurring racist persecutions in America, is built into the novel's unique, genre-hopping plot structure. In the major opening section, Whitehead

---

[7] Colson Whitehead, *Zone One* (New York: Doubleday, 2011), 208.
[8] Whitehead, *Underground Railroad*, 78.
[9] Colson Whitehead, "Colson Whitehead: Oprah, American History, and the Power of a Female Protagonist," interviewed by Stephenie Harrison, in *Conversations with Colson Whitehead,* ed. Derek C. Maus (Jackson: University of Mississippi Press, 2019), 109.
[10] Ibid., 113.
[11] Whitehead, *Underground Railroad*, "Acknowledgments." In this section, Whitehead mentions reading scholars such as Nathan Huggins, Stephen Jay Gould, Edward E. Baptist, Eric Foner, Fergus Bordewich, and James H. Jones.

utilizes a realistic prose style reminiscent of classic slave narratives, such as Frederick Douglass's *Narrative* (1845) and Harriet Jacobs's *Incidents in the Life of a Slave Girl* (1861), to introduce Cora, the young female protagonist who lives on the horrific Randall plantation in Georgia. However, as soon as Cora escapes with an older enslaved man named Caesar in the hope of finding the Underground Railroad, Whitehead deploys a sudden, fantastical twist. Instead of finding an archipelago of above-ground safe houses, Cora finds an underground train that functions like a proto-subway system for secret interstate travel. Before Cora boards the train, Lumbly, the local station agent in Georgia, tells her what to expect. "Every state is different," Lumbly says. "Each one a state of possibility, with its own customs and way of doing things."[12] Lumbly then adumbrates the allegorical significance of Cora's future episodic adventures: "If you want to see what this nation is all about, I always say, you have to ride the rails. Look outside as you speed through, and you'll find the true face of America."[13] Powerless to determine where she is headed, Cora first arrives in an alternate-history version of South Carolina. With its futuristic skyscrapers, modern medicine, and social welfare programs for free Blacks, South Carolina is a facade of racial progressivism. Lurking beneath the surface, though, are paternalistic programs of medical experimentation and of forced sterilization that allude to the infamous "Tuskegee Study of Untreated Syphilis in the Negro Male" and to racist practices in Progressive Era eugenics. In the next state, North Carolina, Cora must go into hiding in order to survive a genocidal political regime that has declared Black residency illegal and periodically implements this law by holding ritualistic public lynchings. Escaping to Tennessee, Cora inhabits a symbolic underworld in the form of a charred, post-apocalyptic wilderness destroyed by natural wildfires. In Indiana, Cora lives briefly in a secluded, all-Black utopian community, Valentine farm, that is eventually destroyed by its resentful white neighbors. The novel ends in uncertainty, poised between pessimism and optimism, as Cora seriously injures (and probably kills) the villainous Ridgeway before joining a Black caravan that is traveling by wagon to California.

When viewing the novel's plot from this zoomed-out perspective, the political implications are decidedly ambivalent. Although Cora does succeed in "achieving some measure of escape" in the end, as Derek C. Maus argues, it would be difficult to argue that she escapes "a [larger American] 'story' deeply rooted in White supremacy and lethal violence," as the novel

---

[12] Ibid., 70.   [13] Ibid., 71.

resists a "blueprint for a better future."[14] According to Yogita Goyal, Whitehead's rejection of a clear political solution on the level of plot is symptomatic of his complex experimentation with genre-mixing. The novel's various racist regimes, functioning like trans-temporal allegories, "acquire some of the ring of truth granted by the scaffold of the historical slave narrative [genre], even as they are tugged out of their own time, or harnessed from some future dystopia."[15] The result, Goyal argues, is a rich speculative novel that "does not relate the story of a fugitive slave's journey to freedom: it meditates on the very state of freedom and its possibility."[16] Like other key thinkers in the annals of Black political thought, Whitehead reconfigures celebrated concepts in American political theory – e.g., individual freedom, legal equality, constitutional rights, representative democracy, popular sovereignty – by contextualizing them within Black experiences across time.[17] This imaginative move tests not only the veracity of formal political concepts in the past, but also their future emancipatory potential. As Whitehead put it in an interview with Donna Seaman: "Why should [Cora] believe that there is any place of freedom when all she's witnessed her whole life is the brutality of the plantation? Yet she persists."[18] The reason for her perseverance, Whitehead continues, is because Cora remains animated not by (an entirely understandable) experiential fatalism, but by "impossible hope."[19]

A careful, more granular, close reading of Cora's symbolic encounters with the Declaration of Independence – one of the novel's crucial motifs – reveals a character arc that justifies her impossible hope in ways that a basic plot summary elides. While Cora never attains formalized legal freedom as that status would be understood within the traditional vocabulary of American political theory, she does achieve a form of historical awareness and political agency that catalyzes her pragmatic, hard-won optimism. Early in the novel, while Cora is still enslaved on the Georgia plantation, the omniscient narrator notes that a recently deceased enslaved boy,

---

[14] Derek C. Maus, *Understanding Colson Whitehead: Revised and Expanded Edition* (Columbia: University of South Carolina Press, 2021), 148.

[15] Yogita Goyal, *Runaway Genres: The Global Afterlives of Slavery* (New York: New York University Press, 2019), 133.

[16] Ibid., 135.

[17] For a recent, paradigmatic scholarly article on Black conceptual reconfiguration, see Michael Hanchard, "Contours of Black Political Thought: An Introduction and Perspective," *Political Theory* 38.4 (2010): 512–16.

[18] Colson Whitehead, "The Carnegie Interview: Colson Whitehead," interviewed by Donna Seaman, in Maus, ed., *Conversations with Colson Whitehead*, 157.

[19] Ibid., 157.

Michael, had been taught by his previous owner to memorize the Declaration. When Terrance Randall tells his brother James, who technically owns Michael, that he wishes to hear the enslaved boy recite the Declaration during a grotesque plantation "party," the Black boss Moses informs them both that Michael was killed by Connelly, the white overseer employed by the Randall plantation. On the surface, this moment is significant because it depicts a cruel irony: an image of an enslaved child unknowingly vocalizing the very principles of American freedom and equality that the country's political regime has denied him. On a deeper level, though, it also alludes to Thomas Jefferson's infamous claim that the African American poet Phillis Wheatley was merely parroting poetic verse, meaning that the "compositions published under her name are below the dignity of criticism."[20] As the narrator puts it: "Michael's ability never amounted to more than a parlor trick, delighting visitors before the discussion turned as it always did to the diminished faculties of niggers."[21] Since readers never witness a scene in which Michael actually performs the Declaration, his recitative ability takes on a ghostly, mythic presence of haunting dehumanization.

Michael's spectral presence is key to Cora's ongoing political awakening throughout the novel. While working as a historical re-enactor at a museum in South Carolina, Cora realizes that the museum's staged set pieces – "Scenes from Darkest Africa," "Life on the Slave Ship," and "Typical Day on the Plantation" – are merely fantasy simulations for its white visitors. Remembering moments when Michael recited the Declaration, his voice "drifting through the village like an angry phantom," Cora experiences an epiphany. "The whites came to this land," Cora realizes, "for a fresh start and to escape the tyranny of their masters, just as the freemen had fled theirs. But the ideals they held up for themselves, they denied others."[22] And even though Michael had not fully understood the Declaration, the "white men who wrote it didn't understand it either, if *all men* did not truly mean all men."[23] Once Cora arrives in North Carolina, she recalls "poor Michael" reciting the Declaration, but this time she doubts not the veracity of its principles, but the veracity of the entity called "America" that the document seemingly signifies. "Cora wasn't sure the document described anything real at all," the narrator informs readers via free indirect speech. "America was a ghost in the darkness, like her."[24]

[20] Thomas Jefferson, *Writings, Autobiography, Notes on the State of Virginia, Public and Private Papers, Addresses, Letters* (New York: Library of America, 1984), 267.
[21] Whitehead, *Underground Railroad*, 32.   [22] Ibid., 119.   [23] Ibid., 119.   [24] Ibid., 184.

Later, when Cora arrives in Indiana, Whitehead again alludes to the Declaration, but in a way that channels Cora's doubts not toward pessimistic despair, but toward a reconceptualization of Black agency. Sitting in an all-Black classroom in the utopian community of Valentine farm, Cora watches the young Black teacher, Georgina, teach the children to recite the Declaration. After class, Georgina explains to Cora that the Declaration is obviously not an accurate representation of American social reality. For Black people especially, it is more "like a map," she says: "You trust that it's right, but you only know by going out and testing it yourself."[25] Georgina's lessons imply that the Declaration can be a tool of liberation if African Americans link a not-yet-existing America with the country's stated ideals. Cora eventually adopts Georgina's perspective after Valentine farm constructs a library that features not only the Declaration but also broad swaths of Black literature and historiography. Reading the Declaration in conjunction with other works about various African empires, Phillis Wheatley, Jupiter Hammon, and Benjamin Banneker, Cora envisions "their stories as her own," grasping finally that they "were the stories of all the colored people she had ever known, the stories of black people yet to be born, the foundation of their triumphs."[26] Regardless of how well the white men who wrote the Declaration understood it, Cora appropriates it as another compelling story about human dignity, one that Black Americans can use as a text of civic attachment to actualize a better America that is still unborn.

In a novel whose fantastical strategy is marked by persistent historical prolepsis, or a calling forward of events that have not yet happened, one of Whitehead's most significant anachronisms is this thematic insistence on the rhetorical authority of the Declaration itself. As historians such as Pauline Maier and Garry Wills have demonstrated, the Declaration was "all but forgotten" upon its signing; it was not until decades later that it "was remade into a sacred text, a statement of basic, enduring truths often described with words borrowed from the vocabulary of religion."[27] The most intense sacralization of the Declaration, Wills argues, occurred only after the Civil War. In his "Gettysburg Address," Lincoln dated the country's founding not to 1787, but to 1776. By substituting the Declaration for the US Constitution as *the* founding document, Lincoln had engaged in a "giant (if benign) swindle," for he "had revolutionized the

---

[25] Ibid., 244.   [26] Ibid., 279.
[27] Pauline Maier, *American Scripture: Making the Declaration of Independence* (New York: Knopf, 1997), xviii.

Revolution, giving people a new past to live with that would change their future indefinitely."[28] Whitehead puts this Lincolnesque penchant for imaginative redescription into the mouth of Elijah Lander, the idealistic founder-hero of Valentine farm. In a speech in which Lander utters the novel's famous phrase – "Sometimes a useful delusion is better than a useless truth" – he boldly claims that America is the greatest political delusion of them all. "This nation shouldn't exist, if there is any justice in this world," he reasons, "for its foundations are murder, theft, and cruelty. Yet here we are ... we are Africans in America. Something new in the history of the world, without models for what we will become."[29] In this climactic moment, Whitehead retains one prominent dimension of twentieth-century Black political thought in relation to the Declaration, but he abandons another. On the one hand, Whitehead retains the emancipatory potential embedded in Martin Luther King, Jr.'s well-known claim that the Declaration, following Lincoln's vision, was always "a promissory note to which every American was to fall heir."[30] On the other hand, Whitehead seems to reject King's teleological religious conviction that "even though the arc of the moral universe is long, it bends toward justice."[31] For Whitehead, the normative ideals espoused by the Declaration may be useful and inspiring for Black people, but their concrete instantiation is not a certainty ordained by God. Black activists who fight to realize the Declaration's principles are just as likely to be killed by white bigots, like the real-life King and the fictional Lander, than live to see positive change.

Ultimately, Whitehead's political vision amounts to a wary optimism – an "impossible hope," as noted above – rooted in a precarious faith in the possibility of progress that brooks no guarantees, metaphysical or otherwise. Indeed, the character who clings hardest to a notion of divine fate is the novel's central antagonist, Arnold Ridgeway, whom Cora eventually humiliates and (most likely) kills. A vile amalgamation of twentieth-century fictional villains such as Toni Morrison's Schoolteacher (*Beloved*), Octavia E. Butler's Rufus Weylin (*Kindred*), and Cormac McCarthy's Judge Holden (*Blood Meridian*), Ridgeway is a slavecatcher

[28] Garry Wills, *Lincoln at Gettysburg: The Words That Remade America* (New York: Simon & Schuster, 1992), 38.

[29] Whitehead, *Underground Railroad*, 291.

[30] Martin Luther King, Jr., *I Have a Dream* (New York: HarperOne, 2022), 13.

[31] Martin Luther King, Jr., "Love, Law, and Civil Disobedience (1961)," in *A Testament of Hope: The Essential Writings and Speeches of Martin Luther King, Jr.*, ed. James M. Washington (New York: HarperCollins, 1991), 52.

of legendary brutality who subscribes to a version of Manifest Destiny stripped of any vestige of benevolent paternalism, which he dubs "the American imperative." According to Ridgeway, if "the white man wasn't destined to take this new world, he wouldn't own it now."[32] Late in the novel, after Cora has been captured by Ridgeway in Tennessee, they engage in their most important conversation. He tells Cora that he is "a notion of order" and that any escaped slave is "a notion, too. Of hope."[33] Crucially, though, this political conversation does not occur in a disembodied theoretical vacuum, but in the intensely embodied, and unmistakably comic, environment of an outhouse, which Cora is using while Ridgeway talks to her through the door. At first, Cora seems to entertain his metaphysical confidence in white supremacy and Black inferiority. "Maybe everything the slave catcher said was true," Cora thinks momentarily, "every justification, and the sons of Ham were cursed and the slave master performed the Lord's will." But in the very next sentence, Whitehead undermines Ridgeway's ideological position by satirizing it, thereby exposing its arbitrary absurdity and catalyzing hope for an American future that eludes any narrative of political inevitability: "And maybe he was just a man talking to an outhouse door, waiting for someone to wipe her ass."[34]

---

[32] Whitehead, *Underground Railroad*, 82.   [33] Ibid., 227.   [34] Ibid., 228.

Further Reading

Amato, Elizabeth. *The Pursuit of Happiness and the American Regime: Political Theory in Literature*. Lanham, MD: Lexington Books, 2018.

Barndt, Susan McWilliams. *The American Road Trip and American Political Thought*. Lanham, MD: Lexington Books, 2018.

Bennett, Joshua. *Being Property Once Myself: Blackness and the End of Man*. Cambridge, MA: Harvard University Press, 2020.

Blotner, Joseph. *The Modern American Political Novel, 1900–1960*. Austin: University of Texas Press, 1966.

Blouin, Michael J. *Stephen King and American Politics*. Cardiff: University of Wales Press, 2021.

Brooks, Ryan M. *Liberalism and American Literature in the Clinton Era*. Cambridge: Cambridge University Press, 2022.

Brühwiler, Claudia Franziska. *Political Initiation in the Novels of Philip Roth*. London and New York: Bloomsbury Academic, 2014.

Brühwiler, Claudia Franziska and Lee Trepanier (eds.). *A Political Companion to Philip Roth*. Lexington: University Press of Kentucky, 2017.

Buell, Lawrence. *The Dream of the Great American Novel*. Cambridge, MA: Harvard University Press, 2016.

Carroll, Jordan S. *Reading the Obscene: Transgressive Editors and the Class Politics of US Literature*. Stanford, CA: Stanford University Press, 2021.

Chang, Juliana. *Inhuman Citizenship: Traumatic Enjoyment and Asian American Literature*. Minneapolis: University of Minnesota Press, 2012.

Chapman, Mary. *Making Noise, Making News: Suffrage Print Culture and US Modernism*. Oxford: Oxford University Press, 2017.

Coffman, Christopher K. *Rewriting Early America: The Prenational Past in Postmodern Literature*. Bethlehem, PA: Lehigh University Press, 2021.

Cohen, Samuel. *After the End of History: American Fiction in the 1990s*. Iowa City: University of Iowa Press, 2009.

Connolly, Andy. *Philip Roth and the American Liberal Tradition*. Lanham, MD: Lexington Books, 2017.

Cronin, Gloria L. and Lee Trepanier (eds.). *A Political Companion to Saul Bellow*. Lexington: University Press of Kentucky, 2014.

Cronin, Thomas E. *Imagining a Great Republic: Political Novels and the Idea of America*. Lanham, MD: Rowman & Littlefield, 2017.

Cullick, Jonathan S. *Robert Penn Warren's All the King's Men: A Reader's Companion*. Lexington: University Press of Kentucky, 2018.

Curtis, Claire P. *Postapocalyptic Fiction and the Social Contract: We'll Not Go Home Again*. Lanham, MD: Lexington Books, 2010.

Davidson, Guy. *Categorically Famous: Literary Celebrity and Sexual Liberation in 1960s America*. Stanford, CA: Stanford University Press, 2019.

Davis, Laurence and Peter Stillman (eds.). *The New Utopian Politics of Ursula K. Le Guin's The Dispossessed*. Lanham, MD: Lexington Books, 2005.

Deneen, Patrick J. and Joseph Romance (eds.). *Democracy's Literature: Politics and Fiction in America*. Lanham, MD: Rowman & Littlefield, 2005.

Dickstein, Morris. *Leopards in the Temple: The Transformation of American Fiction, 1945–1970*. Cambridge, MA: Harvard University Press, 2002.

Douglas, Christopher. *If God Meant to Interfere: American Literature and the Rise of the Christian Right*. Ithaca, NY: Cornell University Press, 2016.

Dubey, Madhu. *Signs and Cities: Black Literary Postmodernism*. Chicago: University of Chicago Press, 2003.

Edwards, Erica R. *Charisma and the Fictions of Black Leadership*. Minneapolis: University of Minnesota Press, 2012.

Field, Douglas. *All Those Strangers: The Art and Lives of James Baldwin*. New York: Oxford University Press, 2015.

Fisher, Laura R. *Reading Reform: The Social Work of Literature in the Progressive Era*. Minneapolis: University of Minnesota Press, 2019.

Foley, Barbara. *Radical Representations: Politics and Form in US Proletarian Fiction, 1929–1941*. Durham, NC: Duke University Press, 1993.

   Wrestling with the Left: The Making of Ralph Ellison's Invisible Man. Durham, NC: Duke University Press, 2010.

Freer, Joanna. *Thomas Pynchon and American Counterculture*. New York: Cambridge University Press, 2014.

Fromer, Yoav. *The Moderate Imagination: The Political Thought of John Updike and the Decline of New Deal Liberalism*. Lawrence: University Press of Kansas, 2020.

Glass, Loren. *Counterculture Colophon: Grove Press, the Evergreen Review, and the Incorporation of the Avant-Garde*. Stanford, CA: Stanford University Press, 2013.

Greif, Mark. *The Age of the Crisis of Man: Thought and Fiction in America, 1933–1973*. Princeton, NJ: Princeton University Press, 2015.

Hardison, Ayesha K. *Writing Through Jane Crow: Race and Gender Politics in African American Literature*. Charlottesville: University of Virginia Press, 2014.

Hassan, Ihab. *Radical Innocence: Studies in the Contemporary Novel*. New York: Harper and Row, 1961.

Hathaway, Heather. *That Damned Fence: The Literature of the Japanese Prison Camps*. New York: Oxford University Press, 2022.

Higgins, David M. *Reverse Colonization: Science Fiction, Imperial Fantasy, and Alt-Victimhood*. Iowa City: University of Iowa Press, 2021.

Hoberek, Andrew. *The Twilight of the Middle Class: Post-World War II American Fiction and White-Collar Work.* Princeton, NJ: Princeton University Press, 2005.

Horsley, Lee. *Political Fiction and the Historical Imagination.* Basingstoke: Palgrave Macmillan, 1990.

Howe, Irving. *Politics and the Novel.* New York: Horizon Press, 1957.

Hurley, Jessica. *Infrastructures of Apocalypse: American Literature and the Nuclear Complex.* Minneapolis: University of Minnesota Press, 2020.

Hutcheon, Linda. *The Politics of Postmodernism.* London: Routledge, 1989.

Hutchinson, George. *Facing the Abyss: American Literature and Culture in the 1940s.* New York: Columbia University Press, 2018.

Hutchison, Anthony. *Writing the Republic: Liberalism and Morality in American Political Fiction.* New York: Columbia University Press, 2007.

Jackson, Lawrence P. *The Indignant Generation: A Narrative History of African American Writers and Critics, 1934–1960.* Princeton, NJ: Princeton University Press, 2010.

Jameson, Frederic. *Archaeologies of the Future: The Desire Called Utopia and Other Science Fictions.* London: Verso, 2005.

The Political Unconscious: Narrative as a Socially Symbolic Act. Ithaca, NY: Cornell University Press, 1981.

Jarrett, Gene Andrew. *Representing the Race: A New Political History of African American Literature.* New York: New York University Press, 2011.

Jay, Gregory S. *White Writers, Race Matters: Fictions of Racial Liberalism from Stowe to Stockett.* New York: Oxford University Press, 2017.

Jillson, Calvin C. *The American Dream: In History, Politics, and Fiction.* Lawrence: University Press of Kansas, 2016.

Jones, Gavin. *American Hungers: The Problem of Poverty in US Literature, 1840–1945.* Princeton, NJ: Princeton University Press, 2007.

Reclaiming John Steinbeck: Writing for the Future of Humanity. New York: Cambridge University Press, 2021.

Kazin, Alfred. *On Native Grounds: An Interpretation of Modern American Prose Literature.* New York: Harcourt Brace, 1942.

Konstantinou, Lee. *Cool Characters: Irony and American Fiction.* Cambridge, MA: Harvard University Press, 2016.

Lawler, Peter Augustine and Brian A. Smith (eds.). *A Political Companion to Walker Percy.* Lexington: University Press of Kentucky, 2014.

LeMenager, Stephanie. *Living Oil: Petroleum Culture in the American Century.* New York: Oxford University Press, 2014.

Lye, Colleen. *America's Asia: Racial Form and American Literature, 1893–1945.* Princeton, NJ: Princeton University Press, 2004.

Mathes, Carter. *Imagine the Sound: Experimental African American Literature after Civil Rights.* Minneapolis: University of Minnesota Press, 2015.

McCann, Sean. *Gumshoe America: Hard-Boiled Crime Fiction and the Rise and Fall of New Deal Liberalism.* Durham, NC: Duke University Press, 2000.

A Pinnacle of Feeling: American Literature and Presidential Government. Princeton, NJ: Princeton University Press, 2008.

McGregor, Jonathan. *Communion of Radicals: The Literary Christian Left in Twentieth-Century America*. Baton Rouge: Louisiana State University Press, 2021.

McKinley, Maggie. *Masculinity and the Paradox of Violence in American Fiction, 1950–75*. London: Bloomsbury Academic, 2016.

McWilliams, Susan J. *A Political Companion to James Baldwin*. Lexington: University Press of Kentucky, 2017.

Melley, Timothy. *The Covert Sphere: Secrecy, Fiction, and the National Security State*. Ithaca, NY: Cornell University Press, 2012.

Empire of Conspiracy: The Culture of Paranoia in Postwar America. Ithaca, NY: Cornell University Press, 1999.

Menrisky, Alexander. *Wild Abandon: American Literature and the Identity Politics of Ecology*. Cambridge: Cambridge University Press, 2020.

Mexal, Stephen J. *The Conservative Aesthetic: Theodore Roosevelt, Popular Darwinism, and the American Literary West*. Lanham, MD: Lexington Books, 2021.

Michaels, Walter Benn. *The Gold Standard and the Logic of Naturalism*. Berkeley: University of California Press, 1987.

Our America: Nativism, Modernism and Pluralism. Durham, NC: Duke University Press, 1995.

The Shape of the Signifier: 1967 to the End of History. Princeton, NJ: Princeton University Press, 2004.

Michels, Steven J. *Sinclair Lewis and American Democracy*. Lanham, MD: Lexington Books, 2018.

Mills, Nathaniel. *Ragged Revolutionaries: The Lumpenproletariat and African American Marxism in Depression-Era Literature*. Amherst: University of Massachusetts Press, 2017.

Milne, Gordon. *The American Political Novel*. Norman: University of Oklahoma Press, 1966.

Nadel, Alan. *Containment Culture: American Narrative, Postmodernism, and the Atomic Age*. Durham, NC: Duke University Press, 1995.

O'Reilly, Andrea. *Toni Morrison and Motherhood: A Politics of the Heart*. New York: State University of New York Press, 2012.

Patterson, Robert J. *Exodus Politics: Civil Rights and Leadership in African American Literature and Culture*. Charlottesville: University of Virginia Press, 2013.

Pepper, Andrew. *Unwilling Executioner: Crime Fiction and the State*. Oxford: Oxford University Press, 2016.

Reed, Thomas Vernon. *Fifteen Jugglers, Five Believers: Literary Politics and the Poetics of American Social Movements*. Berkeley: University of California Press, 1992.

Rideout, Walter. *The Radical Novel in the United States, 1900–1954*. Cambridge, MA: Harvard University Press, 1956.

Rodrigues, Laurie. *The American Novel After Ideology, 1961–2000*. New York: Bloomsbury Academic, 2022.

Rushdy, Ashraf H. A. *Neo-Slave Narratives: Studies in the Social Logic of a Literary Form*. New York: Oxford University Press, 1999.

Santin, Bryan M. *Postwar American Fiction and the Rise of Modern Conservatism: A Literary History, 1945–2008*. Cambridge: Cambridge University Press, 2021.

Schaub, Thomas H. *American Fiction in the Cold War*. Madison: University of Wisconsin Press, 1990.

Schryer, Stephen. *Fantasies of the New Class: Ideologies of Professionalism in Post-World War II American Fiction*. New York: Columbia University Press, 2011.

Maximum Feasible Participation: American Literature and the War on Poverty. Stanford, CA: Stanford University Press, 2018.

Scranton, Roy. *Total Mobilization: World War II and American Literature*. Chicago: University of Chicago Press, 2019.

Shipe, Matthew and Scott Dill (eds.). *Updike and Politics: New Considerations*. Lanham, MD: Lexington Books, 2019.

Sinykin, Dan. *American Literature and the Long Downturn: Neoliberal Apocalypse*. Oxford: Oxford University Press, 2020.

Smit, David. *Power and Class in Political Fiction: Elite Theory and the Post-War Washington Novel*. Cham: Palgrave Macmillan, 2019.

Smith, Brian A. *Walker Percy and the Politics of the Wayfarer*. Lanham, MD: Lexington Books, 2017.

Sollors, Werner. *Ethnic Modernism*. Cambridge, MA: Harvard University Press, 2008.

Neither Black Nor White Yet Both: Thematic Explorations of Interracial Literature. Cambridge, MA: Harvard University Press, 1999.

Spalding, A. Timothy. *Re-forming the Past: History, the Fantastic, and the Postmodern Slave Narrative*. Athens: Ohio State University Press, 2005.

Speare, Morris Edmund. *The Political Novel: Its Development in England and in America*. New York: Oxford University Press, 1924.

Staub, Michael E. *Voices of Persuasion: Politics of Representation in 1930s America*. Cambridge: Cambridge University Press, 1994.

Sundquist, Eric J. *Strangers in the Land: Blacks, Jews, Post-Holocaust America*. Cambridge, MA: Harvard University Press, 2009.

Szalay, Michael. *Hip Figures: A Literary History of the Democratic Party*. Stanford, CA: Stanford University Press, 2012.

New Deal Modernism: American Literature and the Invention of the Welfare State. Durham, NC: Duke University Press, 2000.

Takayoshi, Ichiro. *American Writers and the Approach of World War II, 1935–1941*. New York: Cambridge University Press, 2015.

Thompson, Mark Christian. *Black Fascisms: African American Literature and Culture between the Wars*. Charlottesville: University of Virginia Press, 2007.

Trask, Michael. *Camp Sites: Sex, Politics, and Academic Style in Postwar America.* Stanford, CA: Stanford University Press, 2013.

Trilling, Lionel. *The Liberal Imagination: Essays on Literature and Society.* New York: Viking, 1950.

Trivedi, Harish (ed.). *The American Political Novel: Critical Essays.* New Delhi: Allied, 1984.

Van Wienen, Mark. *American Socialist Triptych: The Literary-Political Work of Charlotte Perkins Gilman, Upton Sinclair, and W. E. B. Du Bois.* Ann Arbor: University of Michigan Press, 2012.

Vials, Chris. *Haunted by Hitler: Liberals, the Left, and the Fight Against Fascism in the United States.* Amherst: University of Massachusetts Press, 2014.

Voelz, Johannes. *The Poetics of Insecurity: American Fiction and the Uses of Threat.* Cambridge: Cambridge University Press, 2017.

Warren, Kenneth W. *So Black and Blue: Ralph Ellison and the Occasion of Criticism.* Chicago: University of Chicago Press, 2003.

What Was African American Literature? Cambridge, MA: Harvard University Press, 2011.

Washington, Mary Helen. *The Other Blacklist: The African American Literary and Cultural Left of the 1950s.* New York: Columbia University Press, 2014.

Whalan, Mark. *World War One, American Literature, and the Federal State.* Cambridge: Cambridge University Press, 2018.

Whalen-Bridge, John. *Political Fiction and the American Self.* Urbana: University of Illinois Press, 1998.

Wilding, Michael. *Political Fictions.* London: Routledge and Kegan Paul, 1980.

Wilkens, Matthew. *Revolution: The Event in Postwar Fiction.* Baltimore: Johns Hopkins University Press, 2016.

Zamalin, Alex. *Black Utopia: The History of an Idea from Black Nationalism to Afrofuturism.* New York: Columbia University Press, 2019.

Zirakzadeh, Cyrus Ernesto and Simon Stow (eds.). *A Political Companion to John Steinbeck.* Lexington: University Press of Kentucky, 2014.

Index

Cambridge Companions To ...

AUTHORS

Edward Albee edited by Stephen J. Bottoms

Margaret Atwood edited by Coral Ann Howells (second edition)

W. H. Auden edited by Stan Smith

Jane Austen edited by Edward Copeland and Juliet McMaster (second edition)

James Baldwin edited by Michele Elam

Balzac edited by Owen Heathcote and Andrew Watts

Beckett edited by John Pilling

Bede edited by Scott DeGregorio

Aphra Behn edited by Derek Hughes and Janet Todd

Saul Bellow edited by Victoria Aarons

Walter Benjamin edited by David S. Ferris

William Blake edited by Morris Eaves

Boccaccio edited by Guyda Armstrong, Rhiannon Daniels, and Stephen J. Milner

Jorge Luis Borges edited by Edwin Williamson

Brecht edited by Peter Thomson and Glendyr Sacks (second edition)

The Brontës edited by Heather Glen

Bunyan edited by Anne Dunan-Page

Frances Burney edited by Peter Sabor

Byron edited by Drummond Bone

Albert Camus edited by Edward J. Hughes

Willa Cather edited by Marilee Lindemann

Catullus edited by Ian Du Quesnay and Tony Woodman

Cervantes edited by Anthony J. Cascardi

Chaucer edited by Piero Boitani and Jill Mann (second edition)

Chekhov edited by Vera Gottlieb and Paul Allain

Kate Chopin edited by Janet Beer

Caryl Churchill edited by Elaine Aston and Elin Diamond

Cicero edited by Catherine Steel

J. M. Coetzee edited by Jarad Zimbler

Coleridge edited by Lucy Newlyn

Coleridge edited by Tim Fulford (new edition)

Wilkie Collins edited by Jenny Bourne Taylor

Joseph Conrad edited by J. H. Stape

H. D. edited by Nephie J. Christodoulides and Polina Mackay

Dante edited by Rachel Jacoff (second edition)

Daniel Defoe edited by John Richetti

Don DeLillo edited by John N. Duvall

Charles Dickens edited by John O. Jordan

Emily Dickinson edited by Wendy Martin

John Donne edited by Achsah Guibbory

Dostoevskii edited by W. J. Leatherbarrow

Theodore Dreiser edited by Leonard Cassuto and Claire Virginia Eby

John Dryden edited by Steven N. Zwicker

W. E. B. Du Bois edited by Shamoon Zamir

George Eliot edited by George Levine and Nancy Henry (second edition)

T. S. Eliot edited by A. David Moody

Ralph Ellison edited by Ross Posnock

Ralph Waldo Emerson edited by Joel Porte and Saundra Morris

William Faulkner edited by Philip M. Weinstein

Henry Fielding edited by Claude Rawson

F. Scott Fitzgerald edited by Ruth Prigozy

F. Scott Fitzgerald edited by Michael Nowlin (second edition)

Flaubert edited by Timothy Unwin

E. M. Forster edited by David Bradshaw

Benjamin Franklin edited by Carla Mulford

Brian Friel edited by Anthony Roche

Robert Frost edited by Robert Faggen

Gabriel García Márquez edited by Philip Swanson

Elizabeth Gaskell edited by Jill L. Matus

Edward Gibbon edited by Karen O'Brien and Brian Young

Goethe edited by Lesley Sharpe

Günter Grass edited by Stuart Taberner

Thomas Hardy edited by Dale Kramer

David Hare edited by Richard Boon

Nathaniel Hawthorne edited by Richard Millington

Seamus Heaney edited by Bernard O'Donoghue

Ernest Hemingway edited by Scott Donaldson

Hildegard of Bingen edited by Jennifer Bain

Homer edited by Robert Fowler

Horace edited by Stephen Harrison

Ted Hughes edited by Terry Gifford

Ibsen edited by James McFarlane

Kazuo Ishiguro edited by Andrew Bennett

Henry James edited by Jonathan Freedman

Samuel Johnson edited by Greg Clingham

Ben Jonson edited by Richard Harp and Stanley Stewart

James Joyce edited by Derek Attridge (second edition)

Kafka edited by Julian Preece

Keats edited by Susan J. Wolfson

Rudyard Kipling edited by Howard J. Booth

Lacan edited by Jean-Michel Rabaté

D. H. Lawrence edited by Anne Fernihough

Primo Levi edited by Robert Gordon

Lucretius edited by Stuart Gillespie and Philip Hardie
Machiavelli edited by John M. Najemy
David Mamet edited by Christopher Bigsby
Thomas Mann edited by Ritchie Robertson
Christopher Marlowe edited by Patrick Cheney
Andrew Marvell edited by Derek Hirst and Steven N. Zwicker
Ian McEwan edited by Dominic Head
Herman Melville edited by Robert S. Levine
Arthur Miller edited by Christopher Bigsby (second edition)
Milton edited by Dennis Danielson (second edition)
Molière edited by David Bradby and Andrew Calder
Toni Morrison edited by Justine Tally
Alice Munro edited by David Staines
Nabokov edited by Julian W. Connolly
Eugene O'Neill edited by Michael Manheim
George Orwell edited by John Rodden
Ovid edited by Philip Hardie
Petrarch edited by Albert Russell Ascoli and Unn Falkeid
Harold Pinter edited by Peter Raby (second edition)
Sylvia Plath edited by Jo Gill
Plutarch edited by Frances B. Titchener and Alexei Zadorojnyi
Edgar Allan Poe edited by Kevin J. Hayes
Alexander Pope edited by Pat Rogers
Ezra Pound edited by Ira B. Nadel
Proust edited by Richard Bales
Pushkin edited by Andrew Kahn
Thomas Pynchon edited by Inger H. Dalsgaard, Luc Herman, and Brian McHale
Rabelais edited by John O'Brien
Rilke edited by Karen Leeder and Robert Vilain
Philip Roth edited by Timothy Parrish
Salman Rushdie edited by Abdulrazak Gurnah
John Ruskin edited by Francis O'Gorman
Sappho edited by P. J. Finglass and Adrian Kelly
Seneca edited by Shadi Bartsch and Alessandro Schiesaro
Shakespeare edited by Margareta de Grazia and Stanley Wells (second edition)

George Bernard Shaw edited by Christopher Innes
Shelley edited by Timothy Morton
Mary Shelley edited by Esther Schor
Sam Shepard edited by Matthew C. Roudané
Spenser edited by Andrew Hadfield
Laurence Sterne edited by Thomas Keymer
Wallace Stevens edited by John N. Serio
Tom Stoppard edited by Katherine E. Kelly
Harriet Beecher Stowe edited by Cindy Weinstein
August Strindberg edited by Michael Robinson
Jonathan Swift edited by Christopher Fox
J. M. Synge edited by P. J. Mathews
Tacitus edited by A. J. Woodman
Henry David Thoreau edited by Joel Myerson
Thucydides edited by Polly Low
Tolstoy edited by Donna Tussing Orwin
Anthony Trollope edited by Carolyn Dever and Lisa Niles
Mark Twain edited by Forrest G. Robinson
John Updike edited by Stacey Olster
Mario Vargas Llosa edited by Efrain Kristal and John King
Virgil edited by Fiachra Mac Góráin and Charles Martindale (second edition)
Voltaire edited by Nicholas Cronk
David Foster Wallace edited by Ralph Clare
Edith Wharton edited by Millicent Bell
Walt Whitman edited by Ezra Greenspan
Oscar Wilde edited by Peter Raby
Tennessee Williams edited by Matthew C. Roudané
William Carlos Williams edited by Christopher MacGowan
August Wilson edited by Christopher Bigsby
Mary Wollstonecraft edited by Claudia L. Johnson
Virginia Woolf edited by Susan Sellers (second edition)
Wordsworth edited by Stephen Gill
Richard Wright edited by Glenda R. Carpio
W. B. Yeats edited by Marjorie Howes and John Kelly
Xenophon edited by Michael A. Flower
Zola edited by Brian Nelson

TOPICS

The Actress edited by Maggie B. Gale and John Stokes
The African American Novel edited by Maryemma Graham
The African American Slave Narrative edited by Audrey A. Fisch

African American Theatre by Harvey Young
Allegory edited by Rita Copeland and Peter Struck
American Crime Fiction edited by Catherine Ross Nickerson
American Gothic edited by Jeffrey Andrew Weinstock